Chinese Awakenings

Chinese Awakenings

Life Stories from the Unofficial China

James & Ann Tyson

Westview Press

Boulder • San Francisco • Oxford

Copyright © 1995 by Westview Press, Inc. Design and composition by Westview Press.

Published in 1995 in the United States of America by Westview Press, Inc., 5500 Central Avenue, Boulder, Colorado 80301-2877, and in the United Kingdom by Westview Press, 12 Hid's Copse Road, Cumnor Hill, Oxford OX2 9JJ

Library of Congress Cataloging-in-Publication Data
Tyson, James L., 1958–
   Chinese awakenings : life stories from the unofficial China /
James L. Tyson Jr. and Ann Scott Tyson.
      p.   cm.
   ISBN 0-8133-2472-6. — ISBN 0-8133-2473-4 (pbk.)
      1. China—Social conditions—1976–   2. Interviews—China.
I. Tyson, Ann Scott, 1959–   . II. Title.
DS779.23.T97   1995
951.05'092'2—dc20
                                                              94-44056
                                                                  CIP

Printed and bound in the United States of America

       The paper used in this publication meets the requirements
(∞)   of the American National Standard for Permanence of Paper
       for Printed Library Materials Z39.48-1984.

10   9   8   7   6   5   4   3   2   1

*To our parents
and grandparents*

Contents

PART FOUR
Chinese Challenge the State
"The Tree Craves Calm but the Wind Rages On"

Preface

The idea of writing *Chinese Awakenings* arose in late 1988 as we interviewed Chinese across the country for a series of fourteen articles for the *Christian Science Monitor*. The articles described how Chinese from many different backgrounds are radically reshaping their lives as China promotes a market economy and eases Maoist social controls. These individuals are seizing opportunities and grappling with new problems from reform as social tensions rise over issues of wealth, ethics, and political power.

To a degree, the series proved prophetic. It identified the volatile mixture of rising expectations and resentment that was to explode in the streets of Beijing and scores of other Chinese cities just a few months later in 1989. The protests showed that as reform weakens the grip of the state over day-to-day life, individual Chinese are taking their future, and the future of their country, into their own hands.

Today, the initiative for change is coming increasingly from the grass roots as millions of Chinese pursuing different dreams propel reform far beyond the Communist Party's original intent. This bottom-up momentum for change is advancing reforms despite resistance from hard-liners within the leadership. We believe the best way to understand this groundswell is by knowing intimately the feelings, aspirations, and workaday lives of ordinary Chinese. Such an understanding is crucial for discerning what lies ahead for China. With this simple but vital idea in mind, we began in 1989 hundreds of hours of face-to-face interviews for this book.

In order to meet the people whose stories we tell in *Chinese Awakenings*, we traveled throughout China, from its money-chasing coastal cities to mud-clogged villages and grassy highlands in the hinterland. In arranging our interviews, we eluded government officials assigned to monitor foreign correspondents. As a result, these Chinese talked with ease despite the repressive political atmosphere. They welcomed us into their homes and offered us their native foods. They provided a place to sleep, whether on a bare board nailed to a rough-hewn wooden frame or on a yak-fur blanket thrown on a tent's dirt floor. They introduced us to their daily labors, their neighborhoods, and their friends and families. Most important, for hours at a time over a span of six years they shared with us their lives and feelings of suffering and joy. (We have used pseudonyms for the leading individuals in Chapters 1, 4, and 9 in order to thwart official reprisal. The name of the migrant's home village in Chapter 1 has also been changed.)

To our knowledge, *Chinese Awakenings* is unique among recent Western books on China for recounting in vivid detail the lives of such a broad spectrum of Chinese. Still, the book in no way does justice to the spellbinding diversity of the 1.2

billion mainland Chinese. Unlike other contemporary surveys on China, our book focuses on just nine individuals. We chose to take deep, representative soundings from the vast sea of Chinese society rather than skim the surface and provide a smattering from dozens of lives.

We hope that by offering a wealth of detail about a few individuals we will minimize the cultural misperceptions that have bedeviled Western reports on China for centuries. Moreover, we hope our grassroots approach conveys some important nuances of life in China that are absent from other books. We believe that a single detail from a person's life can often provide more insight than the grandest analysis or most sophisticated statistic. Most important, we hope to have done justice to the courage and rich personalities of the people we write about.

One of our chief goals is to allow Chinese to speak for themselves. By so doing we hope to provide a firsthand portrait of China by Chinese. Thankfully, our subjects were open in their testimony, and most of them allowed us to use their names. Their confidence and candor are among the most promising signs of progress in China today.

Although Chinese are becoming more outspoken, their country still needs its interpreters. This fact was made unforgettably clear in the streets of Beijing during the blackness of June 3–4, 1989, when Chinese students, workers, and even officials and party members rushed from out of the maelstrom of fire, blood, and steel and shouted: "Tell the whole world what is happening!"

Still, China is slowly outgrowing the period when its people must rely on the sometimes clumsy tongues of foreign journalists to speak for them. As popular pressure compels the regime to ease its grip further on people's lives and open China wider to the world, Chinese individuals will increasingly tell their own stories. Then, from their voices, all the pathos pent up during decades of life under communism will flow. We hope *Chinese Awakenings* rings with some of the first notes from the healing chorus of testimony that is to come.

James L. Tyson Jr.
Ann Scott Tyson

Acknowledgments

Our greatest affection and thanks go to the scores of Chinese, both those named and those who must remain anonymous, who courageously shared their lives with us.

Our colleagues at the *Christian Science Monitor* deserve profound thanks for giving us extraordinary opportunities and steadfast encouragement. Former *Monitor* editor Kay Fanning and former managing editor David Anable posted us to Beijing, making the *Monitor* the first U.S. publication to send a husband and wife team to China. Foreign editors Paul Van Slambrouck and Jane Lampmann and deputy foreign editor Gail Chaddock gave us keen guidance. And Alice Hummer, Sue Leach, and Scott Baldauf offered us tireless editing and pithy advice. In Beijing, the bureau staff was always by our side to help with conundrums big and small.

Many thanks also go to Charles Eisendrath, director of the Michigan Journalism Fellows Program, and his wife, Julia. With warmth, wit, and class, they offered us the precious gift of nine months of free academic inquiry at the University of Michigan. This book would not have been possible without the backing of the program.

Earlier, Professor Ezra Vogel helped us lay the groundwork for an understanding of Asia, both as students at Harvard College and as its alumni. At Northwestern University, Professor Hsu Wen-hsiung offered vital help in reading genealogies in classical Chinese for the chapter on clans. James Watson, Fairbank Professor of Chinese Society at Harvard, kindly answered some technical questions related to the clans chapter. Professor William Parish aided our research by helping us to secure library privileges at the University of Chicago. Gelek Rimpoche and Professor Donald Lopez provided valuable information for the chapter on Tibetan nomads.

Our agent, Malaga Baldi, has given solid support and suggestions. Susan McEachern, our editor at Westview Press, has been invaluable in helping to smooth the style and solidify the substance of the manuscript. Ida May B. Norton, our copy editor, meticulously scrubbed and tightened the prose. Michelle Asakawa skillfully turned a hodgepodge of papers and photos into a book.

Our parents, Joy Scott, Robert Haney Scott, Elizabeth Tyson, and James Tyson Sr., have given us many wise suggestions and boundless encouragement.

We alone are responsible for any faults remaining in the book.

J.L.T. and A.S.T.
Bay Head, N.J.

RUSSIA

KAZAKHSTAN

MONGO

KHIRGHIZSTAN

TADJIKSTAN

PAKISTAN

NEPAL

INDIA

BHUTAN

BANGLADESH

ALTAI MOUNTAINS

DZUNGARIAN BASIN

Urumqi ★

TIAN SHAN

TARIM BASIN

XINJIANG UIGHUR
AUTONOMOUS REGION

TAKLIMAKAN DESERT

INNER MONGOLIA

GANSU

KUNLUN MOUNTAINS

Lake Qinghai

TIBETAN

QINGHAI
A

Xining ★

Lanz

AUTONOMOUS

Jinsha River

M

Xiahe ★ Linxia

TIBETAN PLATEAU

REGION

Lancang River

D

Nu River

O

GANNAN TIBETAN
AUTONOMOUS
PREFECTURE

U - T S A N G

Lhasa ★

K   H   A   M

★ Che

SICHUAN

Chong

Kunming ★

YUNNAN

MYANMAR
(BURMA)

*Bay of
Bengal*

Salween River

Mekong R.

Yuan (Red) R

LAOS

VIETN

THAILAND

0   200   400 mi
0   200   400 km

•••••• Boundaries of regions
        comprising Historic Tibet

━ ━ ━ Boundaries of Tibetan
        Autonomous areas

Internal divisions are provinces
unless labeled otherwise

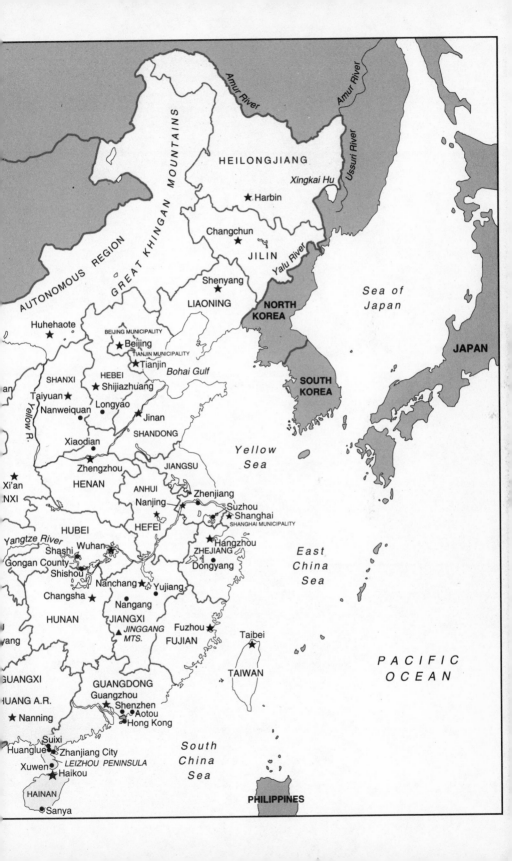

Chinese Awakenings

Introduction

AFTER DECADES OF OPPRESSION, China's 1.2 billion people today are awakening to their inner dreams and aspirations as never before under Communist rule. They are striving for greater wealth, more meaningful lives, and freedom from harsh state controls in a grassroots movement that is shaping China's future and moving the world.

Chinese today are thinking and acting for themselves as individuals, not as the "masses." No longer willing to emulate the steely-eyed workers, peasants, and soldiers of propaganda billboards, Chinese are discovering who they are and who they want to be. They are casting off Marxist dogma and seizing on values and lifestyles as diverse as the kaleidoscopic fashions that flutter from free-market stalls. Deaf to public loudspeakers blaring slogans on "serving the people," Chinese are instead tuned to inner voices that are driving their restless pursuit of riches, status, and success. Amid this rush of self-discovery and ambition, they are unwittingly creating a vibrant new society and the greatest challenge to the Communist Party since it took power in 1949.

Chinese began listening to their inner voices in the late 1970s as they started to come to grips with the collective madness of Mao Zedong's Cultural Revolution (1966–1976). Deeply disillusioned, they asked why they had worshiped Mao as a god. They regretted the murders they had committed as they blindly waged his political witch-hunts. They were fed up with Mao's promises of a workers' utopia, exhausted by malicious political campaigns, and bitter over years of sacrifice for the collective.

China's reformers led by Deng Xiaoping seized on a radically different strategy to recover people's support and rebuild the country after the chaos and penury of the Mao years. Beginning in the early 1980s, Deng offered the people hard incentives: cash bonuses instead of equal wages for workers, family farming instead of communal toil for peasants, and promotions for professionals based on skill instead of Communist fervor. In a break with Maoism, reformist leaders endorsed the idea that Chinese would work harder for themselves than for the sake of the "revolution." But by sanctioning a degree of self-interest, the leadership also began to surrender its totalitarian grip on people's lives.

1

Today, Chinese are pushing to extremes the market-oriented economic reforms gingerly begun by the party. Craving everything from more meat in their diet of rice and wheat to speculative investments and foreign travel, they have grabbed each new chance to make money. In the countryside, peasants have taken control of collective land and property. They have planted cash crops despite official pressure to grow grain. They have pooled their labor and savings to start millions of dynamic rural factories. And from 70 million to 100 million of them have migrated to higher-paying urban jobs, breaking rules that bind them to the village. In cities, residents have rushed to meet a vast, pent-up demand for services and goods. They have launched private enterprises ranging from tiny eateries and bicycle repair shops to international computer firms. Because of their gumption, Chinese individuals, families, and small groups now control the most dynamic parts of the nation's economy. For the first time in decades, ordinary Chinese have gained the wealth and opportunity to stake out a limited realm of dignity and freedom.

As Chinese take charge of their lives, they are together creating a far more complex, competitive, and independent society. This spirited society, with a myriad of new interest groups, is eclipsing the state as the most powerful force for change in China. Chinese are invigorating all sorts of grassroots groups in order to protect their hard-won wealth, celebrate their identity and beliefs, and limit state intrusions into their lives. Peasants are reviving ancient family-centered clans and religious sects. Private entrepreneurs are setting up business and trade associations. Intellectuals are forming unofficial think tanks. And liberal students and workers are running underground unions. Meanwhile, Chinese are co-opting many of the traditional socialist "work units" that were once strands in the vast web of party control. The leadership in state-run factories and schools, women's federations, and regional bureaucracies are shifting their allegiance to their members and away from the central government. Increasingly, they represent constituents below them rather than the authorities above them.

Through these grassroots groups, Chinese are translating their aspirations into political power. Backed by like-minded local officials, neighbors, kin, and colleagues, people can lobby the government more effectively. They can also more easily evade a wide range of unpopular state controls like those on childbearing, religious worship, and free-market business. Local officials in many areas simply lie to thwart interference by Beijing.

"You have policies; we have countermeasures," goes a saying about local authorities who sabotage Beijing's mandates. In the eyes of many Chinese, the central government is weaker than at any time since 1949.

As Chinese clamber helter-skelter toward differing goals in growing defiance of the regime, they have infused society with new energy. But it is an aimless and unguided energy that brings harm as well as progress. In recent years, Chinese driven by greed or ignorance have aggravated problems like corruption, crime, and environmental pollution.

Other problems are arising as China's society grows more varied and unruly. Chinese individuals have more to fight over today than under Mao, when they were all poor together. The losers from market-oriented economic reform have grown more contentious and conspicuous as income gaps widen, wage disputes intensify, and unemployment grows. Peasants infected by the "red-eye disease" of envy poison the livestock of a wealthy neighbor. A blue-collar worker angry over being fired murders his rich boss. In cities across China, beggars have reappeared. They kneel on sidewalks, roam train stations, and scramble at restaurants for scraps of leftovers.

Such problems underscore the urgent need of Chinese for a responsive, rational government that can channel their competing demands toward the common good. The current regime, committed to obsolete Marxist ideals and antiquated political machinery, has failed to keep pace with China's more diverse and complex society. The party is still geared to meeting the needs of "workers," not to balancing the differing demands of a grasping migrant laborer, an idealistic intellectual, a maverick entreprenuer, and other newly assertive Chinese. It lacks the will and vision to strengthen its rule by better representing Chinese citizens. Instead, it clings to the role of dictating to the masses. Afraid of losing control, it shies from advancing risky economic, legal, and political reforms that are vital to solving China's problems. Ironically, the party is undermining its own rule by failing to cope with the consequences of reforms it launched to restore its power.

Angered by the government's ineptitude and abuse, Chinese are more critical than ever before under communism. The citizen in the street is deeply troubled and disillusioned by the government's failure to cope with pervasive corruption, rising crime, widening income gaps, and other problems. City dwellers complain about the growing numbers of swindlers, streetwalkers, gang members, and other signs of social decay. Chinese increasingly bridle at chronic double-digit inflation and mounting layoffs from huge and moribund state industries. They scoff at their leaders as bungling and power-hungry. They are quick to attack the government because their expectations are high. Indeed, popular expectations are far outstripping the achievements of reform. As Chinese grow more prosperous and less constrained by officials, they see clearly how much wealth and freedom they lack.

Chinese have not yet rallied behind a unified force that could replace the Communist Party they so roundly condemn. Lingering, self-imposed restraints to activism are almost as formidable as the party's apparatus of repression. Chinese thinking is still ingrained with a tradition of absolute state dominance thousands of years old. Most Chinese still feel the pull of Confucian ideas that compel them to subordinate themselves to their families, communities, and state. They still have a weak sense of individual rights and no experience with self-rule. And many Chinese, like their leaders, shrink from the prospect of political change for fear of chaos.

Chinese bold enough to take political action tend to express their defiance in sporadic protests instead of organized opposition. Grassroots groups can exert pressure on the regime, but they are too disunified to challenge the party's rule. China still lacks a "civil society," the network of independent, politically active social groups that helped topple Communist regimes in Eastern Europe.

The massive protests in Tiananmen Square in the spring of 1989 revealed the depth of public discontent with China's aged, detached leadership. But the swift, brutal crackdown that followed showed that citizens had failed to sustain a viable alternative to party dictatorship. Unrest among Chinese will probably erupt again as long as the outmoded Marxist state fails to meet the needs of the haphazardly modernizing society.

China's future remains highly uncertain. But a thought from Tolstoy suggests what lies ahead. He wrote that the sum of people's individual wills determines the course of history. By his reasoning, the combined myriad wills of Chinese presage the China to come. Thread by thread, this book weaves profiles of several newly awakened Chinese into a vast tapestry for China's future. The theme of this tapestry, richly woven with the colors of people's struggles and dreams, is the dawning of freedom.

PART ONE

Chinese Society Breaks Free

"Once on the Bow, the Arrow Must Fly"

箭在弦上　不得不發

Jin Xiulin

O N E

"Muddy Legs":
The Peasant Migrant

JIN XIULIN AND HER SON bent behind a rough-hewn wooden handcart and muscled it from the mud. They grimaced as they pushed it and slowly rose from the darkness of their squat, thatched village to the top of a dike where the sunrise blazed the high road to the city. As her husband and son hauled the cart toward a bus stop, Jin faltered behind, rushing abreast of them only when her sewing machine threatened to jostle loose. The sun shone in Jin's eyes, but it was the uncertainty of what lay ahead in the city of Shashi that made her press her sleeve against her face.

Jin looks back on the dawn journey to Shashi in 1986 as an epochal leap for her farming family from penury to prosperity. By migrating to the Hubei Province city for work, she heeded an irresistible call for self-fulfillment. Jin broke deeply rooted traditions that bound her to the hearth in Baihe, her impoverished village fifty miles down the Yangtze River. She also broke the law, violating regulations that forbid peasants to settle in cities and towns.

Working sixteen hours a day as a seamstress in Shashi, Jin pockets an income several times greater than what she earned in her village. She has used her money to build a brick house with a tiled roof back home. She also has put a daughter through medical school and sent another one to Xian to study English. Jin is proudest of how her earnings helped her oldest son parlay a degree in medicine into a scholarship for graduate study in the United States.

By migrating to Shashi, Jin has led her family in a jump in social evolution as profound as the climb from dark primordial mire to sunny terra firma. Within the dikes of the city she has gained refuge from Yangtze River floods that over the years have devastated the meager property of her family back in the village and left it marooned in mud. Now that her family has scrambled to a sure footing, with all but one of her children educated and self-sufficient, they can for the first time realistically reach for comfort and wealth.

Day after day Jin endures grinding drudgery. Early on a typical winter morning, in the darkness before dawn, she slips out from under a cotton quilt, dresses, tiptoes by her sleeping niece, and steals out of her huddled brick dwelling into a cold drizzle. She climbs onto a public bus and wedges herself into the damp, odorous pack of passengers. Rows of apartment houses jostle by, four-story tenements slapped together from concrete slabs into gray cubicles dimly lit by lone lightbulbs. On the edge of the city the bus rises onto the spine of a dike, rides a network of the earthen ramparts, and descends toward a power plant and textile mill built in a wide basin.

Jin steps from the bus in front of a sheet-metal hut. She removes the padlock on the tiny workshop and switches on a fluorescent lamp. As the cold wind rattles the metal around her, she cuts cloth to be sewn into dresses by her employees, her niece and a fellow peasant migrant. Under the cold fluorescent glare, Jin puts in a few hours of work before sunrise heralds the arrival of customers who stop on their way to work in nearby factories. Seven days a week she labors shoulder to shoulder with her seamstresses, bending over scissors or hunching over a foot-powered sewing machine.

Jin is one of from 70 million to 100 million Chinese peasants who are on the road in search of jobs in towns and cities. The migrants are not only coaxed from their villages by the prospect of a better livelihood; they are compelled to leave. Their flight testifies to the poverty, hardship, and unrest in the countryside. They run from corruption, high taxes, and strict state controls on childbirth. They also flee the lack of economic opportunity and the severe slowdown in the rise of living standards in China's villages.

Like many peasants nationwide, one in every five laborers in Jin's village has gone to the city in search of work. Usually, they must accept the dangerous and dirty jobs shunned by city dwellers. The *mangliu* (blind drifters) toil at construction sites on rickety bamboo scaffolding. They haul flatbed carts of garbage and tanks of night soil through the streets. They crouch amid the dust of curbsides, repairing shoes or awaiting work as charwomen or day laborers.

The exodus by Jin and other peasants is a wrenching rite of passage for China as it evolves from an agrarian to an industrial society. In terms of humanity, the stakes are enormous. The "human avalanche," as it is called, is one of the largest peacetime migrations in history. Never have so many people taken to the road at once in search of good fortune beyond the horizon. The migrants are restless forerunners for a vast army of idle laborers among China's 860 million peasants, the world's largest rural population. They began setting out from villages in large numbers in the early 1980s after the Communist Party, in its most far-reaching reform in decades, eased its grip on their lives by dissolving Mao's communes. Family farms revived and dramatically raised productivity. Millions of the peasants left idle by the reform have quit the land in search of prosperity.

By the next century, the number of surplus workers in the countryside will probably increase to 200 million as every year 10 million Chinese born during the 1966–1976 baby boom come of age. Construction on arable land will annually push 4 million farmers from their fields. Rural industry, the most dynamic sector of the economy, has employed tens of millions of peasants. But these firms can absorb only a small part of the vast reservoir of jobless farmers. Many of the redundant workers will seek jobs in cities despite government efforts to stem the exodus.

The migrants are a relentless, volatile force and a major worry for China's leaders. The "muddy legs" loiter in teeming cities across China. Many of the migrants are hungry, tired, poorly educated, and easily abused. They lack urban residence registration and the grain rations, housing, health care, and other benefits that often go with it. They labor with little or no legal protections. Because of the desperation and abundance of the itinerant workers, bosses fire many of them at will, pay them meager wages, and work them in hazardous sweatshops more than fourteen hours a day. Overall, the migration is a symptom of the kind of turmoil and rural discontent that have sparked upheaval and government collapse throughout Chinese history.

Since moving to the city, Jin and millions of migrants have turned their backs on Maoist dogma and embraced modern values that could fuel the widespread unrest feared by the party leadership. By acting on their ambitions, the migrants are shunning the orthodox mores of self-sacrifice, "shared struggle," and equal wealth for all that were advanced by Mao Zedong. They have forsaken the traditional ideal of cooperation and embraced the modern market principle of competition much faster than have peasants back in their native villages.

As her savings and confidence have grown in the city, Jin has become headstrong and fond of fashionable clothes. She has pushed aside the communitarian values of her home village. Jin has also exposed her two daughters and eldest son to a comparatively freewheeling, forward-looking urban lifestyle by sending them to college in the cities of Wuhan and Xian. In the eyes of Jin's husband and other villagers, Jin and her children seem to bristle with individualism and self-assertiveness when they return to the village. As in the households of other migrants, the younger, bolder, or more resourceful members of Jin's family were the first to break the bonds of ancient tradition and Communist edict. Their modern values have split the family, dividing wife from husband, father from son, and sister from brother.

The party has intensified the ethical strains afflicting millions of Chinese families moving from village to city, field to factory, and poverty to plenty. It still tries to control where Chinese live and what they think. Antiquated laws hinder the flow of people and ideas between urban and rural Chinese. The party also bars private ownership of land, a rule that hampers investment between city and countryside and between the flourishing coast and the sleepy hinterland. The restrictions, many left over from the Maoist era, worsen the destabilizing disparity in wealth between urban and rural China and between the coast and the interior. The constraints inhibit a smooth integration of the country and discourage a melding between traditional collectivist mores and modern individualistic values.

In Jin's native Hubei Province and many parts of China's hinterland, the gap in living standards and beliefs between people in the city and countryside remains vast. Nationwide, peasants annually earn less than half the income of city dwellers. The government fails to provide peasants with medical care, schooling, and other services of the same caliber enjoyed by urban Chinese. Rural residents lack the same opportunities for entrepreneurship that enable urbanites to prosper. A party ban on private ownership of land denies peasants the efficiencies and wealth that could come with the freedom of individuals to buy and sell land. So in most of China the transition from city to countryside is abrupt, as one ventures suddenly from paved roads to footpaths, from unruly hawkers in swarming markets to languishing clumps of peasants in torpid village crossroads, from robust hope to blank resignation.

For Jin, the clash in values between city and countryside is as jarring as the move from the comforts of Shashi to the hardship of her native village. In a livelier economy and looser society, Jin and her family could more easily reconcile modern and traditional values. Along the comparatively prosperous and progressive coast, members of the same family who have found work in rural enterprises near their homes can cope with strains in values together. By remaining in their native homes, these families can harmonize conflicting values more easily than can inland migrants. They are attuning urban individualistic values to rural collectivist traditions and turning their coastal villages into suburbs. But both the location and outlook of Jin's native village are too remote for a smooth, rapid transition from old to new ideas. As Jin quickly prospers like many migrants and city dwellers, she increasingly finds her village backward and oppressive.

Jin finds it difficult to return for a visit to her home village. Since moving to Shashi in 1986, she has gone back to Baihe only twice, for the lunar New Year, the holiday Chinese families cherish most. She quickly tires of the crude lifestyle and straitjacket values in the village. Also, she especially feels the sting from inept, corrupt, and intrusive officials; they are closer at hand than in Shashi. Indeed, for Jin a trip back to Baihe affirms the wisdom of her bold migration. It makes her appreciate Shashi and its relative comfort, easier mores, and respite from constant official hectoring.

Returning home, Jin feels a mixture of pride and self-consciousness. Walking alongside a creek past thatched dwellings, she carries pastries, fruits, toys, cassette tapes, and other gifts that many of her fellow villagers will never afford. Her outfit is cleaner, more colorful, and more stylish than the tattered and dirty olive drab and blue clothes they wear. Some of her former neighbors greet her from their yards; others turn away from her into the darkness of their dwellings. Jin again sees the poor, cramped life of those who submit to official restraints on residency and to strict customs that tie women to the home.

As Jin approaches the green double doors of her small dwelling, she must hold inside a storm of conflicting emotions. She can count on a warm, happy welcome from her daughter-in-law and two grandsons who live there. But the heavy doorway symbolizes her subservience to her husband, Peng Min, according to ancient Confucian tradition. (Jin has retained her maiden name, following Chinese custom.)

Indeed, the return to Baihe for Jin is like a return to the values and lifestyle of preindustrial China. In Shashi Jin has a steady supply of electricity; in Baihe elec-

Peng Min. Photo by James Tyson.

tric light comes only in intermittent bursts. In Shashi she gets water from a tap; in Baihe she must carry two buckets on a yoke across a creek to a well. In the city she rides taxis, buses, and cars; in remote Baihe she must rely on water buffalo, bicycles, and horse-drawn carts.

For Jin and millions of villagers in China, the road to the city is the only avenue away from ox-plod poverty. The moribund economy of Baihe offers few opportunities for seamstresses and other skilled laborers. Before going to Shashi, Jin worked throughout the year but was often paid only at harvest time when her customers were paid by the state for grain. Craftsmen like Jin's youngest son, a carpenter, also watch their talents go to waste. He and his father tried to launch an enterprise making wooden packing crates for factories in the nearby city of Shishou. But they confronted myriad obstacles: uncertain transport and a dearth of management expertise, capital, and raw materials. So the young man left his wife and two young sons behind in the village and took up a job with his uncle's roofing company in Shashi.

The villagers' only sure resources—land and labor—also fall short. Quoting a popular adage, villagers say that the land and profits from tilling are so limited that they could not get by even if they reaped gold. Each person in Baihe may lease no more than a third of an acre. Farmers' incomes have shrunk since 1987 because rising prices of plastic sheeting, pesticides, fertilizer, and other goods for agriculture have far outstripped increases in the state purchase price for grain and cotton. As a result, more than half of the village households are in debt.

Of all the symbols of the backwardness and hardship of rural life for Jin and her family, none is more powerful or inescapable than mud. By moving to Shashi, Jin has found refuge from the fickle and cruel shifts of the Yangtze and its ancient, ever present legacy of mire. She has won a separate peace for her family from the epic contest between man and mud that has preoccupied her village for centuries.

Jin's family and other villagers expend much of their sweat, money, and time trying to keep the water and earth of the Yangtze in safe, fruitful proportion. Their efforts are often in vain. According to a local adage, the Lotus Pond River on the western side of the village changes course and overruns the village every thirty years. The river is a tributary of the Yangtze, which flows by the village's eastern side. A ten-yard-high earthen dike encircling the village occasionally gives way to the swelling and capricious shifts of the rivers. At flood time in July, each of the village's 331 families must send out an able-bodied man to stand on the dike around the clock. If necessary, these men reinforce the embankment with a mixture of mud and straw hauled on yokes and baskets. The rivers routinely flood the only road leading to Baihe, turning the village into an island sunk far below water level behind its earthen bulwark. If the surging rivers are especially menacing, all 1,300 villagers mass on the dike with shovels, yokes, and baskets at hand.

Within the dike the villagers can usually control the balance of water and earth in their fields, even during the rainy season from mid-June to the end of July. Using ramshackle sluices, they regulate the water flow from the river into a creek, through the village, and into fields of jute, tangerines, plums, rice, cotton, and sweet potatoes. When heavy rains bring too much water, they pump out the fields.

Outside their fields, however, the villagers throw up their hands and abandon all but the most critical efforts to keep water at bay. Everything assumes a coat of mud: smeared, caked, swiped, or smudged. It covers children from heel to hair and chickens from feet to comb. It outfits man and beast in drab, impressing everything animate into a uniform army of the humble and vulnerable. It seems to ooze up walls and across thresholds, reinforcing the siding and packed earth floors of the wattle and daub dwellings.

To the villagers, mud symbolizes their penury and backwardness. Not even the party, to say nothing of rural entrepreneurs, will build workshops or small factories on the vulnerable land of Baihe. So as many villages in China rush toward prosperity behind a vanguard of rural enterprises, Baihe remains destitute. The per capita annual income is just $130, 20 percent less than that of the national average for peasants and about one-third the income for city dwellers. The mud holds villagers in poverty more than anything else. Its coming every year reminds them of their helplessness before nature. A flood in 1943 swept away the house of Jin's husband and forced his family to spend a sodden, bitter winter huddled on a dike. A surge of the Yangtze in 1954 that killed 33,000 people wiped out the duck flock that Jin's father tended for a living. It is no wonder, then, that Jin and other villagers measure progress by how far they have risen from the mire. They migrate to the city not just for higher pay but for higher ground, to go from muck to macadam.

Jin ostentatiously proclaims her successful rise from mud. Using her earnings and savings, her family built a new brick and tile house in 1987 for $1,300. The whitewashed structure, the only clean-looking dwelling in the village, gleams from among the surrounding brown mire and earthen homes like a shining, arrogant challenge. She enters the house and embraces her children, her crowning achievement.

Day to day, Jin's family cannot hope to maintain its snow-white home in Baihe as a symbol of transcendence over mud. Observing a friendly peasant custom, the family each morning removes a heavy beam from its front doors and flings them open to the dawn. Dogs, cats, sparrows, roosters, hens, chicks, and bugs enter the three-room dwelling as if they pay rent. Each brings in its own distinctive track of mud. Like the neighbors who drop in, the creatures tend to gather in a large, central front room under a ceiling fretted by rough-hewn rafters twenty feet off the concrete floor. The creatures freely peck, gnaw, cluck, scratch, doze, roost, and defecate. At sunset the sparrows and chicks gradually stop chirping and peeping and stay the night. The sparrows perch on the rafters among hung laundry; the chicks nest in a corner beneath a sawhorse and the butts of two fifteen-foot logs to be hewn by Jin's son. The other uninvited visitors file out unprompted before bedtime.

The house Jin built is an indication that in China's poorer villages even well-off peasants live crudely. The design of the 300-square-foot dwelling is basically the same as in peasant homes across most of China. Leading from one side of the front room are doorways to two bedrooms. Jin's second son and his wife sleep in one of the rooms on a bed canopied with mosquito netting. On a small dresser stand neon-colored plastic chrysanthemums, apples, and peaches, a black-and-white television, and a wardrobe. Their two young sons sleep in the other room. Jin's husband, Peng, eats and sleeps in the medical clinic at the village crossroads, a ten-minute walk away. He is one of the village's two doctors. On the other side of the front room is a dark and narrow kitchen with a sagging tar-paper ceiling and two woks fired with sticks and coal. Behind the kitchen lives a pig in a sty. Adjacent to him is the family privy, a crude open tepee made of jute stems partially shielding a hole in the dirt crossed by two parallel boards. The pig, with his grunts and acrid odor, is an eager, intimate companion to those in the kitchen and the privy.

Jin has decorated the house in a way testifying to how migration mixes a bizarre brew of conflicting values within a family. In the front room, posters and scrolls either made in the village or bought in the city suggest a mélange of traditional, Maoist, and modern mores. "Big fortune upon opening the door; good luck when going out," declare couplets written in black on red paper and pasted on the front doors. Directly across from the doors hangs a colorful five-foot scroll from which the wizened and berobed gods of longevity, prosperity, and official prestige beam as they hug frolicking children on a golden horse-drawn cart. On either side are scrolls. One says, "With the blessings of the three gods, this land of intellect produces people of eminence." On the other side, another scroll says, "With the arrival of the five guarantees, the country is in harmony and the people in peace." (Mao mandated that his "people's communes" guarantee childless and infirm senior citizens five benefits: food, clothing, medical care, housing, and free burial.) Beneath the scrolls, in another tribute to Maoism, glare a female Navy pilot wearing a life vest and helmet, a marine with an AK-47 assault rifle and gunbelt, and a woman in a naval dress uniform. Across the bottom of the large, neon-colored plastic poster are the words "The cream rises together." Among the messages of antiquity and dour militarism are the coy, softly seductive images popular in China under reform. In one poster a dewy-eyed young lady cuddles a kitten against her cheek. In another, a smiling girl clinging to a guitar reclines in a hammock. In a third, a shapely lady in a striped bathing suit dallies by the side of a pool.

The stylish posters are the only reminder to Jin of the big-city vibrance she values in Shashi. At Baihe, her family and other villagers haphazardly drift along like flotsam on the Yangtze. When Jin arrives, her daughter-in-law smiles broadly and immediately strides across the front room to her five-year-old son sleeping on a rattan bed. With a loud cackle she gives him a hard slap on the bottom and says, "Wake up and greet your honorable grandmother!"

The boy bolts upright, eyes agape. He swings his feet to the floor, rubbing his eyes and grinning. His little brother looks on with a smile, gnawing on one of several roasted chicken feet his grandmother has brought from the city. He quietly munches his way from claw to joint, his face shining in a surfeit of brown fat. With no trace of sleepiness, the older boy takes two fistfuls of litchi fruits from a sack brought by Jin. He peels the leathery brown skin quarter-by-quarter with his teeth, spits the bits on the floor, and bites into the giant pearl of sweetmeat.

"T-H-W-A-C-K." The boy jumps as his mother, with a jovial grin, slams a ten-foot-long bamboo pole on the concrete floor beside him, screeching, "Don't eat all the litchis!"

The boy pops a whole fruit into his mouth and a small stream of juice escapes through his grin as he strips it of its meat and spits out the seed. The seed spins across the floor and hits the wall as the boy wipes his chin. Neighbors stroll by and peer in the front door and window at Jin. Some stop in and sit on a bench or on short wooden chairs. During the rainy season they wait out each downpour before returning to their fields. Compared to their compatriots in China's booming coastal cities, the peasants enjoy a wealth of spare time. They seem to relish their perpetual riches: They mill about, gape at the clouds, loll, whittle, loiter, nap, daydream, and chat with Jin and Peng, waiting for the rain to stop.

Some villagers still go about their business despite the deluge. A boy holding a gleaming sickle lilts by astride the steaming and bristled gray back of a water buffalo, the boy's slack arm and the sickle flopping outward with every step of the beast. A farmer shouldering a bamboo yoke strung with buckets filled to the brim with night soil bobs through the mire with rapid mincing steps. Two barefoot schoolgirls appear from out of the mist sharing a white umbrella and wearing clean cotton blouses of pastel yellow and pink. As they pass, they turn away with a giggle and a fling of their long ponytails. Meanwhile, a mutinous army of Pekin ducks patters by, their feet plashing in the mud as they flee a white plastic bag tied to the end of a long bamboo pole wielded by their keeper. The plump white ducks lunge down a bank and into a creek in a raucous, waddling charge. Their keeper joins them up to her waist in water. She quickly flicks from a basket golden plumes of grain, and the ducks encircle her like a giant upraised hoop skirt made of flowing, snowy feathers.

For a few days during her rare visits, Jin enjoys the slow rhythm, neighborly warmth, and mud-between-the-toes feeling of the village. But villagers also give her an earful of complaint about the government. The widespread rancor toward officials, like the crude living standard, makes Jin appreciate her life in Shashi. Indeed, corruption is the biggest popular gripe in the countryside and a leading inducement for migration, according to comments by scores of peasants in dozens of villages in China.

In Baihe, village officials have capriciously raised a slew of levies on the peasants. They have set the price of electricity far above the state-suggested rate and pocketed the difference. Also, officials have more than doubled the tax on land since 1987, plunging many families deeper into debt. They frequently seize the grain of villagers who refuse to pay the tax. Jin's daughter-in-law has a large concrete bin for rice next to the back door but she keeps it empty. Instead she stores rice in a large clay vessel next to her bed behind a wardrobe in a room with a locked door and barred windows.

Officials add insult to injury by brazenly engaging in petty abuses. They spend much of their time "building the Great Wall," a slang term for the gambling game of mah-jongg in which players line up dozens of small tiles in a long row. The officials are also guilty of *chihe* (eat-drink), the use of public funds for wining and dining. The village's only eatery opened primarily to serve officials who regularly regale higher cadres touring Baihe. If the village officials have not exhausted their annual banquet budget at the end of the year, they spend the remainder on themselves, according to Dr. Peng, Jin's husband. Villagers have no surefire way to revoke unjust taxes or to unseat abusive officials.

"Even if someone points his finger at an official's face and says 'You're corrupt,' the official will say, 'Okay, so go to Beijing and sue me,'" Jin's brother-in-law said. "Everyone knows there are bigger problems for the leaders to deal with than corruption in the countryside."

Every three years the villagers "elect" a seven-member village council from among eleven candidates selected by the Communist Party branch in the township. But the ballot serves mostly as an announcement. The first seven candidates listed on the slate always win, Peng said.

Among the controls of the state, family planning is the most intrusive, most infuriating, and potentially most abusive.

"Deal resolute blows against excess birth guerrillas!" says an official slogan scrawled in large characters on a wall outside the village. When Jin's youngest son fathered a second child, in violation of the one-child-per-couple policy, he could not pay the fine. So village officials seized his black-and-white television, bed, table, bureau, and other furniture. The officials auctioned the possessions and compelled the son's wife to undergo sterilization. Often officials pocket part or all of the "excess birth" fine of $280, a figure more than twice the per capita annual income in the village, Peng said. Thousands of migrants have become birthing "guerrillas," leaving their villages to evade local birth control officials. The official press has labeled the more than 1 million children illicitly born on the road as "black children."

Peasant hostility toward officials extends beyond corruption and resentment over birth control to all kinds of contacts. The tension is palpable in Baihe. At daybreak the cuckoo begins to sing as the soft dawn light silhouettes the feathery leaves of a water cedar tree standing beside a still creek. It is Sunday, 5:15 A.M. Suddenly, villagers are jolted awake as loudspeakers throughout the village growl with the sound of the local leader clearing his throat.

"Comrades, in some cotton fields farmers have not dug irrigation ditches. Those who have are diligent; those who haven't are lazy," blares the leader.

"Comrades, all work group leaders will meet this morning; the meeting will start on time regardless of wind and rain," the village leader says before delivering a long lecture on farming. (Households, the basic administrative force in agriculture, are organized into "work groups" in Baihe.)

Later, twenty-five minutes after the scheduled start of the meeting, the village leader no longer speaks in a lordly tone but shouts in a high, cracking voice, "Group leaders come to the meeting right now!"

It is more than the sleepiness of a Sunday sunrise that makes it hard to rouse the villagers of Baihe. Throughout rural China, party cadres have seen their power to marshal farmers erode in recent years. With the exception of taxation and birth control policy, the party has eased most day-to-day restrictions on farmers since the move to market-oriented reform. Baihe villagers and other Chinese are far less dependent on the party than before reform. Jin, Peng, and other rural Chinese see the party as irrelevant—or as an outright impediment—to their struggle for prosperity. The party has never been geared to giving material and moral support to a migrant woman like Jin or to other kinds of newly self-assertive Chinese. It is unequipped to ease the social tensions that flare from their gumption.

The party surrendered some of its authority in the early 1980s by making farming families rather than the commune the basic organizational force for agriculture. The "household-based responsibility system" prompted a surge in incomes and grain production in Baihe and villages across China. But by promoting such sweeping change, the party denied itself many day-to-day controls over the land and those who till it. For instance, it no longer can coerce villagers by withholding renumeration for fieldwork as it did when it kept Chinese strictly regimented in communes. In wealthy villages nearer the coast, many farmers have quit farming and prospered in commerce, services, rural enterprises, and other work outside immediate party control. As a result, the party is no longer the sole boss and benefactor for farmers. It is just the most powerful among society's several emerging interest groups.

Jin's brother, Jin Guosheng, has felt party power slip through his own fingers. Mr. Jin built a reputation for efficiency and rectitude during eleven years as party secretary in a village neighboring Baihe. Eight of those years he spent concurrently as village leader. He launched a small lumber mill and other lucrative collective enterprises, and he organized the funding and construction for a $36,360 water tower and pipe system that provides the luxury of running water.

Although the 2,000 villagers respect Mr. Jin, his authority steadily degenerated. He quit his official posts in 1992 because he felt he was becoming the local villain while coping with what he calls the "five difficulties" of the village cadre: land, birth, death, water, and high officials. Mr. Jin repeatedly had to dun his neighbors for tax payments, the most notable example being an annual levy of $22.50 for every acre of land. He also had to collect $272 from couples who broke family planning regulations, a fee 50 percent higher than the average annual per capita income in the village. When villagers died, Mr. Jin had to compel grieving families to cremate the remains in Shishou rather than hold a traditional burial on scarce land. He was also responsible for rallying reluctant farmers to donate their labor and money to common efforts in ditch digging, dike building, and other water conservancy projects. Finally, like his neighbors, Mr. Jin grew exasperated with officials.

"Township officials don't do solid work; they just give orders and expect village cadres to do all the work," he said, strolling through his lush two-acre field of cotton, sweet potato, tangerines, medicinal herbs, red pepper, plums, green beans, and grapes. "The officials' orders keep us running around all the time and meanwhile the higher officials never come down to the grass roots."

Like many of his neighbors, Mr. Jin has forsaken public service in search of personal gain. He is trying to emulate Peng's brother and make a fortune selling and installing tar paper. To do so, he has followed his sister Jin to the city.

Jin's family and other villagers can largely blame the national leadership for poverty, corruption, and most other official abuses. The harm from craven party leaders is clear at Baihe. On most mornings Peng shoulders a bamboo yoke with two pails and sets off into the dawn mist across a crumbling stone bridge toward the village well. In recent years as Peng crossed the bridge, he has regarded the cracked structure as a symbol for China's faltering effort to bridge the gap between indigence and affluence.

"Everyone uses this bridge and some villagers have plenty of money, but still we let it go to ruin," Peng says, pointing at the mossy span and shaking his head. "During the years of reform, we've only worked for ourselves, not for each other," he says as he sweeps a finger toward the mud-and-thatch dwellings around him.

Peng's disgust underlines the failure of the government to carry out full economic reform in the villages of China. Overall, market-oriented change has helped many of China's 860 million rural residents to prosper more than ever before. The per capita income of farmers more than tripled in the decade after senior leader Deng Xiaoping disbanded Mao Zedong's communes and condoned family farming. But as self-reliant peasants like Jin cross the bridge to prosperity, many Chinese who are more dependent on the rickety socialist economy remain behind. State investment in agriculture has sharply declined under reform. Meanwhile, in Baihe and most other villages nationwide, the steep rise in incomes has leveled off. Since the late 1980s, the double-digit annual jump in the rate of inflation has far outstripped the meager rise in farmers' incomes. Consequently, village tax revenues are insufficient to pay for the maintenance of crucial public works like the bridge in Peng's village.

The bridge is crumbling in large part because of political cowardice in Beijing. China's leaders are too ideologically divided and afraid of unrest to finish the high-stakes task of reform. They shy from carrying the economy completely from socialism to a market system. Conservative leaders have ruled out allowing Peng and other peasants to own or sell land. They shrink from completely removing controls on the prices of agricultural goods and undertaking other reforms essential to invigorating the economy. The political uncertainty and irresolute leadership have provoked fears among Peng's neighbors and other Chinese peasants about a return to collective tilling. The farmers refuse to invest in the common good, favoring their own short-term interests instead. The cash-strapped government has not filled in the financial gap as it formerly did. Therefore, vital public projects such as roads, irrigation systems, and the bridge in Peng's village have gone to ruin.

The party, like Jin's family, is shaky because it has not fully adjusted to the profound shift in popular values from collectivism to individualism. Chinese today tend to cooperate less and compete more than at any other time under Communist Party rule. Before the party eased its totalitarian grip in the early 1980s, Jin and other Chinese knew they had to pull together in order to survive. Now that economic reform has all but guaranteed at the least subsistence, common citizens like Jin no longer scratch for mere survival while clinging to a credo of cooperation. They increasingly strive for riches while upholding the idea of competition. Still, the party tries to hold citizens to collectivist values even though they are increasingly living and working for themselves. Party leaders want the enriching benefits from individualism, but they do not want to give up the harsh autocratic powers of their Leninist state.

When Jin returns home, she is vexed most not by the penury and abusive government but by the ethical tensions within her family. Jin and her husband Peng quarrel over the merits of working in the city; Greg Peng, Jin's firstborn son, argues with his sister over whether Chinese are obligated to agitate for political reform. But the relationship between Peng and Greg illustrates most powerfully how the change in the prevailing attitude from sharing to contending has caused strains in society. High expectations and guilt so charge the relationship between father and son that Peng has occasionally resorted to the traditional form of control for a Chinese patriarch and struck his son. At first glance, the two men appear merely to be engaged in the universal conflict between the cautious, skeptical father and the bold, idealistic son. But their differences are wider than those in the standard generation gap.

Greg and his father fell out after Greg migrated to the city as his mother had. In Beijing he joined the 1989 prodemocracy demonstrations, insisting that all Chinese are obligated to fight for their freedoms. Peng, like many farmers, condemns all political activity, saying it is inherently corrupt and brings only retribution and pain. He believes Chinese should leave politics to the party and devote themselves solely to "serving the people." The political dispute is just one of several points of friction arising from the vastly different ways father and son view the world.

Peng was born in 1938 during the severe turmoil of China's civil war. He has been hungry and destitute for most of his life. Although his family has prospered for more than a decade, he still thinks above all about ensuring it food, shelter, and clothing. He tries to maintain the same harmony and close consensus with neighbors that over the years were vital to the survival of his family. Greg, in contrast, grew up during the can-do, enriching era of reform. He takes survival for granted. By going to the city, Greg has completely cut his dependency on the village. He thinks independently, often in conflict with the village mind-set that rules his father. Because of their different experiences, father and son approach the world differently. Peng, whose scant formal schooling involved rote learning, taught himself basic medicine through the traditional Confucian discipline of memorization. His son loathes memorization and relies instead on reasoning.

Perhaps unjustifiably, Jin feels responsible for the conflict between her husband and son. Had Jin stayed home, her family would not have so abruptly suffered the ethical and ideological strains from China's headlong rush to modernization. Without her salary, her children would not have studied in the city and brought home a sense of individuality and other modern ideas.

Jin wants to somehow soften the impact of her migration and restore harmony between her husband and son. But the two men are living in incompatible eras:

Peng embraces the traditional values of an impoverished, tightly knit village; Greg espouses the modern mores of prospering, impersonal cities. The radically different backgrounds and beliefs of Peng and Greg illustrate the magnitude of the challenge Jin faces in her effort to reconcile husband and son. The conflict between the two also shows the strains confronted by newly assertive peasants who try to disown old values that sometimes reinforce the grip of poverty and repression.

Peng pieced together his simple creed of conservatism during years of unrelenting misery. He came of age during one of the most tumultuous periods in China's history. In his youth he suffered constant hunger and cold. He lacked sufficient clothing and shelter. The Yangtze repeatedly destroyed his family's dwellings and crops. He endured an invasion by Japan in 1937 and a civil war that intermittently raged for two decades until 1949. He bridled under a ne'er-do-well father who frittered away the wealth of his comparatively well-off farming family. From his bungling father, Peng received a cruel and convincing lesson in the value of caution and practicality.

Peng's father had twelve siblings, but only he and three brothers survived childhood. Each of them inherited five acres of land, or a quarter of their father's twenty-acre property in Beigongzui, Gongan County, Hubei Province. Peng's father strayed from the land and took up myriad jobs. Initially, he worked as a caretaker for the temple of the family clan, tending the temple grounds and ancestral tablets. He then bought a mechanical rice husker and offered his services during harvest time. When the one-man business faltered, he returned to farming but soon tired of it. He bought a horse and cart and offered his services for transporting grain and other agricultural goods, but Japanese troops soon seized the beast and rig. He bought the cart and horse back from the invaders, but because farming in the area was so disrupted, there was virtually no demand for transport, and Peng's father was idle. Before long Japanese forces withdrew from the area, and the Nationalist (Kuomintang) troops of Chiang Kai-shek moved in and took the horse and cart. They never gave it back.

Peng saw in the male line of his mother's side of the family another example of the harm from a will-o'-the-wisp. One of Peng's uncles made a career by accepting cash from wealthy draftees, substituting for them in the Kuomintang army, and deserting at the first opportunity. The "soldier hoodlum," as such swindlers were called at the time, repeatedly pulled off the scam in different parts of the region. One day, however, a platoon leader recognized Peng's uncle and ordered that he be buried alive. He was covered up to his chin in earth when the company commander happened by and ordered his release. Peng's uncle managed to talk his way out of custody and returned to his family to tell the tale. Despite his relatives' entreaties, he soon set off on another adventure and was never heard from again.

Throughout Peng's life, men have proved as capricious and malevolent as the Yangtze. According to one of Peng's earliest memories, Japanese forces blew up a major dike protecting Gongan County in 1943, when he was five. The flood forced his family to flee to high ground. The Pengs managed to cross the Lotus Pond

River but found themselves huddled unsheltered on a dike with thousands of other refugees. Most of the refugees' rice had been submerged. The scant grain they managed to salvage soon rotted. The Pengs spent the winter in the open with only the putrid, moldy rice to eat. Peng's older sister, whom his father had bought from another peasant family for eventual marriage to his oldest son, fell ill with cholera during an epidemic that claimed hundreds of lives. She eventually recovered.

When the water receded, the family settled precariously between the dike and the river in a makeshift, leaky tepee of sticks. After squandering his resources in failed businesses, Peng's father had to sell all but half an acre of his five acres of inherited property. So during the next summer, the family reaped a meager rice harvest and had only wormy peppers and wild mushrooms and herbs to add to their small portions of rice. The following spring, when Peng was six, his mother gave birth to a fifth son. But Peng's father, believing the family was too destitute, immediately took the baby to the river and drowned him.

The Pengs moved a short distance downriver in 1945 and rented a small hut with some distant relatives who were also refugees. The rice harvest again was paltry, and Peng's father went into debt to secure grain. The family planted sorghum between the river and the dike but lost the crop in flooding. When the water rose, they were trapped and had to be rescued from their home in a boat.

In the early fall, a teacher in the area offered to tutor for a year any boy whose family could pay 330 pounds of rice as tuition. In his youth, Peng's father had been educated by such a private tutor. Because of his poor judgment, he lacked the money to pay for his sons' education. Still, he scraped together 165 pounds of rice to pay for half a year of schooling for Peng. The seven-year-old boy studied the *Book of One Hundred Surnames,* a standard text for elementary classical Chinese. Also, as part of moral education, he memorized such timeworn ditties from the *Three Word Classic* as "When man is born, his nature is good; although the nature of men is alike, their behavior is different." The traditional teaching method used classical Chinese, a vernacular far different from the spoken language Peng knew. It required several years of memorization of Chinese characters. Exposed just briefly to the method, Peng learned how to memorize but not how to think for himself.

Peng set off for his schooling in a long cotton-padded robe his father bought for him. It was in the traditional Mandarin style with a high collar, broad sleeves, and a belt around the waist. Peng had to flick his hands clear of the heavy sleeves and tuck up the flowing garment or it dragged on the ground. The robe at first was a source of pride for Peng and a symbol of his father's high hopes for his son. But over time it became a symbol of the ineptitude of Peng's father and Peng's resentment. Peng wore the robe for eleven years, throughout his adolescence. As he grew taller, the robe seemed to shrink, until it was no more than a tight-fitting jacket ending at his hips. Peng discarded the robe at the height of his indignation toward his father. He left the family and joined the military, donning the green uniform of the Communist People's Liberation Army.

From 1946 until 1949, Peng faced the greatest hardship of his life over what he calls the "four essentials": food, clothes, shelter, and work. The six Pengs shared a leaky home of just 200 square feet with a family of seven. They slept on sticks laid on the dirt floor. Peng's clothes were threadbare. His father worked him extremely hard. They managed to reap a steady harvest from the half acre of land in Beigongzui, but another half acre they leased was constantly waterlogged so the rice would not grow. Peng was always hungry. His father constantly borrowed rice, but the family had less than two pounds of grain per day.

Every day Peng ventured out with his adopted sister to pick edible wild plants, fungus, and mushrooms. Peng's mother chopped up the pickings, put them at the bottom of the pot, and placed the rice on top. When the rice was cooked, she mixed the two together. Usually their meal was a green and brown slime with only a trace of rice. Peng often stole into the kitchen and his mother would slip him a dollop of rice the size of a silver dollar before she mixed it with the vegetables. Sometimes the hunger was unbearable. One day, Peng and his sister stopped to rest near the kitchen door of a prosperous peasant on their way home from foraging for wild plants. His sister spied a plump turnip on the kitchen chopping block and slipped inside to steal it. But the homemaker discovered her and gave her a severe beating, slapping her face and pulling out clumps of her hair.

Poverty drove peasants throughout the region to crime. There were numerous bandits who hid out in woods across the Lotus Pond River in Gongan County. They often crossed the river to prey on peasants. The Kuomintang militia was too small and ineffective to stop them. Soon after the Pengs moved to Baihe in 1948, a bandit repeatedly robbed farmers in and around the village. He disguised himself, held up farmers with a knife, tied them up, and made off with their grain or money. The militia eventually caught the thief, a native peasant. The troops immediately hustled him to the village crossroads and shot him.

In Baihe, the Pengs leased eight acres of low-lying riverside land. They paid for the land only in the rare times when they managed to bring in a harvest. Most years flooding ruined the crops. Peng's older brother hired himself out as a field hand; when Peng was not struggling to grow rice, he worked as a cowherd, caught fish, or gathered firewood and wild edible plants. He obtained a dictionary and studied it when he was not working. Peng's mother bore another son in 1949. His father let the boy live.

After the party took power in 1949, it categorized all Chinese according to their "class background." Baihe officials gave the Pengs the politically desirable title of "poor peasants." Peng attended a public school for twenty children in the village. But he shirked his studies because his superficial knowledge of classical Chinese put him ahead of the other students. His father pulled him from the school and put him back to work in the fields. Peng worked extremely hard. At about 3 A.M. every day his mother would awaken him to graze the water buffalo. If he tried to sleep longer, his mother would say, "The birds are singing. Why are you still sleeping?" He cut grass for the buffalo, ate a small breakfast, then returned to fieldwork for the rest of the day.

"This was how life was every day and it went on and on and on," Peng said. He grew weak because of the hard work and little food and sleep.

Soon after taking power, the party began a nationwide campaign to expropriate the property of rich landlords. Local cadres rounded up the most prosperous residents of Baihe and demanded that they hand over their land, homes, and many possessions to the people. The cadres bound recalcitrant landholders with rope, hung them from trees, and beat them. The Pengs were given three acres of good land, the wattle-and-daub house they had rented, and a few pieces of furniture. Meanwhile, they gave up the unproductive leased land and the half acre in Gongan County that Peng's father had inherited.

Although the family could increasingly rely on the collective organization set up by the party, it continued to suffer under the inept husbandry of the father. Peng's father never saved newly reaped soybeans or barley for the next harvest, so when planting season came, he had to purchase seed at five times the usual price. Moreover, because he failed to manage their winter store of rice properly, the family always faced a few weeks without food before the harvest of barley in the spring. The Pengs had to borrow rice at extremely high interest rates. At the lean time each year, Peng had to handle the laborious task of making green barley edible for the next day. He worked for three hours each night turning the millstone and preparing the unripened barley grain.

Peng's father was generous and honest. He did not gamble, smoke, drink, or indulge in costly habits. But he was extremely incompetent at overseeing the family's property, Peng said. For Peng, the pain from his father's poor management was most acute when his mother died of tuberculosis in 1954. For many years the family had lacked money to provide her with adequate medical care.

"The death of my mother made a very deep impression on me," Peng said. His resentment flared toward his father. He decided to become a doctor and redoubled his self-study. "Common people badly need doctors, so this is my motivation and this is why I love my profession; I can't help my mother but I can see that other people enjoy long lives."

Peng took texts on traditional Chinese medicine into the fields for study during breaks. He memorized such phrases as "The four gentlemen's tonic will bring the body into balance and benefit the patient." (The "four gentlemen" are ginseng and three other traditional medicines.) The phrase was from the *Tangtou*, a collection of aphorisms guiding the treatment of ailments. He pored over the text during lunchtime, the afternoon rest, and after sundown until going to bed at midnight. Before daybreak he was again engrossed in such books. In 1956 he began to study Chinese medicine under the village doctor.

Peng began to feel a hankering for a wife when he was sixteen, an age when peasant youths tended to marry. Many of his peers easily found brides, but Peng vainly courted several village girls. He lacked presentable clothes and borrowed some. But the only decent garments available were a woman's slacks and shirt. Still, he donned the clothes and called on the homes of many girls one by one. Each time he was turned away. Although his intended sweethearts said nothing directly, Peng knew it was his family's poverty that marred his appeal. When it came to courtship, his sterling political classification apparently did him little good.

The resentment of Peng toward his father burned still higher. Because of his father's delinquence, Peng was denied even the basic schooling his father had received. He had faced more cold, hunger, and general destitution than his peers. His father had deeply hurt his mother by killing her fourth son at birth. The death of his mother because of inadequate medical care had deeply hurt Peng. When Peng tried to manage the family property, his father opposed and criticized him. Peng's failure to attract a wife was the final pain and indignity. He felt a strong yearning to break away and be free to use his brains and sweat to gain some prestige.

As was the case for many peasants, Mao's army offered Peng the only way to ensure subsistence and seize an emblem of dignity. The People's Liberation Army (PLA) gave Peng a chance to learn a skill and see the world beyond the two rivers surrounding his village. It exposed him to formal discipline and ethics and gave him an uplifting sense of fellowship with what was then a highly unified and prestigious organization. In short, it was the best opportunity for Peng and other peasants to gain a sense of self-esteem. Peng cast off his tattered childhood robe, left home, and enlisted at the end of 1957. He was assigned to a regiment guarding the labor camp at Shayang, sixty miles to the north. For six months he worked as a sentry. Officers fired the morale of Peng and other soldiers by contriving a story that Kuomintang troops planned an imminent invasion to free the 40,000 political prisoners and common criminals at the camp.

In the army, Peng saved grain coupons worth up to twenty-two pounds of rice a month and sent them to his family in Baihe. He took full advantage of what Mao called the "University of the PLA." He received his first comprehensive and formal education, taking classes in Chinese and math and raising his education to the level of junior high school. As a result, he put many ideas and concepts in medicine within his reach.

Peng also studied Marxist ethics and found reinforcement for his altruistic aim to work as village doctor. He learned to follow the "three disciplines" and the "eight attentions," two series of maxims that included such phrases as "Don't take a needle or a string of thread from the masses," "If you damage the property of the masses, you must pay them back," and "One benefits from not harming others."

Soon after arriving at the labor camp, Peng asked the regional headquarters for the job of a medic who planned to retire soon. An officer turned him down, saying only soldiers with formal medical training would be eligible. Soon thereafter, however, the director of the health department at the camp happened to pass by Peng during a rest and asked him what he was studying. Peng told him he was reading the *Tangtou*, the book on traditional medicine that he had already memorized.

"Since you've memorized the *Tangtou*, we should make you a medic," the director said. Peng was sent to the regional headquarters for training in medicine in May 1958. He entered a program with two textbooks designed for eight months of study. But the headquarters was swept up in the fervid, quixotic spirit that prevailed during Mao's Great Leap Forward (1958–1960) and it tried to squeeze the course into four months. Peng earned an A in six courses and a B in one, a result as much of willpower as of brainpower. Unlike his better-educated classmates, Peng could not fully comprehend the lectures and texts. He retained the material through memorization instead of reasoning, pounding the instructor's points into his mind word for word. The results were sometimes embarrassing; some of the material he could recite but not grasp. For instance, he memorized the two medical terms for throat, *yan* and *hou*, but he did not know the two referred to the same thing. Laypeople use only *yan* to refer to the throat. Similarly, he knew of only one way to say a person was cured: *bing hao le*. So he was perplexed when he saw on the medical reports of many patients the phrase *quan yu*, the medical way to indicate a cure. It was only after the course, when he returned to his unit and studied two junior high texts with the help of better-educated comrades, that he began to master what he had memorized.

Peng's decision to join the army paid off in another big way: He found a wife. The steady stream of grain coupons from Peng to his family, the news of his training as a medic, and the aura surrounding anyone in PLA uniform gradually raised his prestige in the village. So he wiped the mud from his shoes, buttoned his uniform to his chin, and briefly visited the village in July 1959 to meet Jin, a Baihe native introduced to him by a matchmaker. Jin had been a singer and dancer in the Shishou County Ensemble, a state entertainment troupe, until 1959, when she attended a nursing school at the county seat of Shishou. They were married in early 1960.

The two families did their best to make a happy wedding amid a village atmosphere that was the bleakest since the Communists came to power. Mao had thrust China into the Great Leap Forward, hoping to raise production dramatically by stirring up revolutionary ardor and imposing mass organization throughout the country. He took power over economic decisionmaking and industrial production from Beijing bureaucrats and gave it to low-level cadres. Prompted by Mao, local cadres ordered peasants in Baihe and other villages to build their own backyard steel furnaces. Peasants built some 1 million of the small, crude furnaces nationwide. The party also completed the policy of collectivizing peasants in "people's communes," pooling all child-rearing, cooking, and household arrangements as well as labor. Exaggerated tallies on industrial and agricultural production from low-level officials masked the economic disaster. Officials ordered fields to lie fallow in order to avert a grain surplus that would exceed the storage capacity. In Baihe and elsewhere, peasants were too busy "going all out for industry" to tend the fields. In the resulting famine from 1959 until 1962, more than 20 million people, most of them children, died nationwide.

Baihe officials heeded Mao's call to surpass Britain in steel production in fifteen years and dispatched many peasants to work the jerry-built blast furnaces. They ordered peasants to hand over to be melted down virtually all their metal belongings, including pots, pans, woks, tools, farm implements, scales, weights, and cutlery. Most of the items were made of cheap metal; the backyard furnaces essentially did nothing but turn them into large gobs of junk. In order to provide fuel for the furnaces, the peasants chopped down all the trees in the area.

The village had to hand over what little rice it produced to the government. Peasants ate at a communal mess hall and received a ration of no more than seven ounces of unhusked rice each day. Most of the malnourished villagers suffered from dropsy. They tried to supplement their diets with rice husks, tree bark, and other roughage scavenged from woods and neglected fields. As they grew steadily weaker, their bellies and limbs swelled. Peng worked for a year as a doctor at the commune after his unit demobilized him in July 1961 to reduce the number of mouths it had to feed. He and other local doctors determined the condition of starving patients with simple phrases. "When a man's legs swell as if he is wearing boots," he is in critical condition. "When a woman's head or cheeks swell as if she is wearing a hat," she needs urgent care. Often old villagers became weak and died from simple colds. Many babies and toddlers in the village perished from malnutrition.

The party belatedly realized the calamity it had forced on China and in 1962 began to reverse some of the policies of the Great Leap. Peasants returned to the fields as communal cadres in charge of Baihe and other nearby villages passed down the call from Beijing "to go all out for agriculture." Although people's diet in the village remained meager for several months thereafter, the famine abated. Jin gave birth to Greg in 1963.

The baby boy heralded the happiest time of Peng's life. Peng had fulfilled a fundamental Confucian duty by fathering a son, and he was soon to escape completely the cramping confines of his father's household. He built a small wattle-and-daub house consisting of a room with an attached kitchen. While doing regular farmwork, he became a part-time cadre in the commune in 1963 and received a $5 monthly subsidy for handling minor disputes. Jin gave birth to twin boys in 1964. But Peng improperly placed a quilt over one of the babies soon after birth and it suffocated. Then Jin bore daughters in 1965 and in 1966. She had borne five children in four years.

Peng worked feverishly because of the sudden arrival of offspring and harsh memories from his childhood. Unlike other peasants, he did not rest during breaks in collective farmwork or nap in the afternoon. Following the peasant adage to "insert a needle wherever there is an opening," Peng raised beans and sorghum for his family on ten patches of neglected land around tombs and creek banks totaling one-third of an acre. Every day he fertilized the plots with manure and night soil. He sold sweet potato seedlings and earned more than $50 one spring. He cut so much grass that even after thatching the roof of his dwelling there was much to sell on the side. He rigged a pedal irrigation device that enabled members of his work team to toil in shifts and have more spare time. He planted 150 trees around his home and eventually sold the lumber for $1,000, several times the average annual income in the village. In short, Peng lived by the same principles he had so long yearned to see in his father: hard work and steady husbandry.

Once again, however, foolish and abusive policies by the party leadership imperiled the security and welfare of Peng and his family. In 1966 a rivalry between Mao and other leaders erupted nationwide into a decade of ultraleftist violence and chaos known as the Cultural Revolution. The social upheaval provoked by the call for "continuing revolution" swept into Baihe. Red Guard extremists subjected Peng, Jin, and other villagers to lengthy sessions in indoctrination. The youthful fanatics hustled the party secretaries of the commune and the district before the villagers for humiliating "struggle sessions." They beat the officials and forced them to make self-criticisms before the assembled peasants. The Maoist hotheads ordered Peng and other villagers to smash any vestige of the "four olds," old customs, habits, culture, and thinking. The villagers methodically destroyed tablets, shrines, calendars, and books. Then the self-appointed makers-of-revolution spread their purge inside the village to the "four kinds of elements": former landlords, rich peasants, counterrevolutionaries, and "bad elements." Gradually, rival figures in the village channeled the wave of random and violent attacks into crude factional fighting.

The Red Guards criticized Peng because he worked hard tilling formerly neglected land for his family. They criticized Jin for taking up the "bourgeois" trade of sewing dresses and other clothes. Peng was also denounced because he declined to join the factional struggles. He attended the mandatory criticism and indoctrination sessions but declined to speak or serve as the leader of a faction. The Red Guards seized the neglected land Peng had begun to cultivate. Farming and transport were so disrupted in the early years of the campaign that the grain ration for Peng's family shrank to starvation levels.

Peng and Jin were ultimately protected from outright abuse by their impeccable class status. Both were classified as coming from "poor peasant" stock, the highest political pedigree. Moreover, Peng's skills in medicine were deemed socially useful, so he was sent to the county hospital for six months of training as a "barefoot doctor."

In late 1971 Peng was vindicated in his reluctance to engage in factional fighting. The party leadership informed village party leaders that Lin Biao, the heir apparent to Mao, had betrayed the Great Helmsman and been killed in a plane crash. Villagers had spent much of the previous five years of indoctrination praising the sagacity of the party vice chairman and wishing him a long life. All but the most gullible villagers realized that party leaders had whipped up people's idealistic fervor and cast China into turmoil in an effort to subdue their rivals and advance their personal political interests. Peng felt doubly convinced that politics was dangerous and inherently unethical.

The death of Mao in 1976 and the sordid end of the Cultural Revolution found many villagers disillusioned. The morale of the commune was low; grain output was depressed. Corruption returned with a vengeance. Villagers coined a saying: "If the production team leader wants money he just opens his mouth. If the accountant wants money he just uses his pen. If the cashier wants money he just opens the cash box."

The rise of pragmatist Deng Xiaoping as paramount leader in 1978 brought guarded hope to the village. The party gradually condoned a return to family farming and semiautonomous trades, first by making hints in the official press and then by staging experiments in various parts of the country. The communal organization that had repressed the initiative of people in Baihe for a quarter century was disbanded in 1983. Village cadres leased a portion of land to each household according to its size. Grain production surged. Peng's family leased four-fifths of an acre of land that it could till with comparatively little official interference. In one year soon after the reform, Peng harvested 5,500 pounds of rice, or five times the ration his family had earned each year under the commune. He also grew jute and sesame and continued to work as the village doctor. Jin had many more customers for her hand-sewn clothes because villagers had more money to spend. Overall, the annual income of the family tripled.

The prosperity since the early 1980s has muddied Peng's simple outlook. It has eased his obsessive anxiety over survival and enabled Peng to offer his children the education he was denied. But to Peng, prosperity has also tainted people's ethics. It has encouraged materialism, created tensions within his village and family, and destabilized society. It has undermined his ideal of self-sacrifice.

"People are no longer concerned with serving the people; they only care about getting richer themselves," he said. Peng's altruistic ethic is deeply rooted in Chinese tradition. Mao exploited the ideal and made it a central principle of party propaganda. For Peng, the ideal has been critical to survival. As he grew up, his family would not have gotten by without help from others. The ideal of selflessness has been the chief source of meaning for his life since 1954. That year, as he helplessly watched his mother slowly die from tuberculosis, he resolved to provide for the health of others.

"If I serve the people well throughout my life, I will have no regrets when I die," Peng said.

Peng apparently does not serve himself in any way. He seems a paragon of the Maoist ideal of plain living and hard struggle. He is a shy, restless man. When talking about his values, he shifts in his seat, avoids making eye contact, and smiles nervously. There is no ostentation in his asceticism. He lives at the back of the village clinic, a tall one-room building that was once a storehouse. Much of the whitewash on the walls has flaked off. Cobwebs, grime, and smoke have turned the remaining paint dark gray. The floor is made of bumpy earth packed over the years to a brown sheen. He eats and sleeps behind a tall medicine chest in a cramped corner. A small coal-fired brazier sits next to a bed with rattan matting and a gray veil of mosquito netting. Peng looks out onto a field through the wooden bars of a lone window.

"As long as I have food to eat, clothes to wear, and a place to sleep I am happy. I live plainly so I can better help my children," he said, offering a guest a cup of weak jasmine tea.

The altruism of Peng compels him to persevere at a profession that has never paid very well outside the city. In the past several years it has steadily lost its prestige. It is no longer politically fashionable. The term "barefoot doctor" once conjured up images of millions of self-sacrificial medics fanning out across the re-mote countryside to provide free basic care to the peasant masses. But with the decline in state support for rural medicine, the propaganda term today more aptly describes the penury of the rural healers. Village doctors increasingly rely on patients and local governments to pay their salaries, which are often woefully in-adequate. Many doctors supplement their incomes by prescribing excessive medi-cation, harming many patients as a result. During this period of go-it-alone greed, Peng's calling is viewed as excessively idealistic, shabby, and slightly pa-thetic.

The sacrifice Peng has made by remaining in the village is clear in his clinic. Peng works at a counter under the amber glow of a lone lightbulb hanging fifteen feet from one of many rafters. Behind him are 140 kinds of Chinese medicine stacked in a large chest. A rusty, foot-powered dental drill sits in a corner. Gray gauze covers scalpels, tweezers, probes, and mirrors. The sharp scent of antiseptic cannot overcome the musty smell from the dank earthen floor. The clinic sits at the village crossroads and is a popular haunt for the villagers. Peasants come and go or loiter in the wooden doorway. They smoke, spit on the floor, squat and slurp bowls of noodles from the eatery next door, or crack open sunflower seeds one by one with their teeth, eating the meat as the shells scatter on the floor around them. In a sign of how Peng has bound his life to the village, his uninvited neighbors crowd around his tiny bed and brazier as he speaks to a visitor in the back of the clinic.

Peng treats an average of fifteen patients a day, usually for common colds, re-spiratory diseases such as tuberculosis and pneumonia, and headaches and other minor ailments. Each peasant annually pays the township 55 cents for the clinic, part of which is used to provide for Peng's salary. In addition, Peng charges his pa-tients a standard 13 percent premium on medicine. He provides the villagers with basic medical care for free. His annual income from salary and the sale of medi-cine is $220.

Despite his lifestyle and values, Peng is not a Maoist. His outlook is too compli-cated for the simplistic, rigid dogma of Mao. Peng criticizes Mao for his narcissis-tic, utopian policies. And he objects to Mao's principle of equal wealth for all, or "everyone eating from the same big pot." Holding a traditional bias that Mao tried to eradicate, Peng believes families should remain the basic organizing force for farming. Still, he opposes the idea of private ownership of land because he be-lieves it would create sharp differences in wealth and spark unrest. Peng wants prosperity only if it comes with harmony. Farmers should be able to become rich but not too much richer than their neighbors. Families should run autonomous farms but not to the extent that some farmers dominate their poor, less adept neighbors.

Although Peng strongly holds to his altruistic views, he would never promote them through politics. He vehemently opposes any degree of political activity by his family. To him, politics is dangerous. Those who stand up to authority are doomed to failure and destruction. He also believes politics is inherently corrupt and corrupting. It is demeaning and sleazy and cannot be a noble profession. It should be left exclusively to the Communist Party.

"An official will travel 1,000 miles in order to benefit himself," Peng said, reciting an old peasant saw. For centuries, the passive political outlook of peasants like Peng has helped despots perpetuate their rule.

Peng's aversion to politics most infuriates his son Greg when Peng dismisses the massacre of student protesters in Beijing in 1989. He accepts the leadership's decision to order the army to fire on his son and other unarmed demonstrators. Brutal retribution was inevitable because the upstart youth had humiliated senior leader Deng. The students merely got their comeuppance for becoming involved in politics.

Deng "had no choice. He was irritated by the students so he took revenge," Peng said. He refuses to acknowledge that his principles of altruism and political abstinence could conflict. He would avoid political action even if local officials refused to combat a cholera epidemic, he said. "The farthest I'd go in politics is to offer rational proposals to officials in a very objective way. I followed such an approach and so was never humiliated during the Cultural Revolution."

As Peng firmly holds to the traditional values of the village, the world appears to be quickly passing him by. He frequently walks about the village as an unwitting symbol of the conflict over new and old values that divides him from Jin and Greg. Unaware of the irony, the conservative village doctor wears a navy blue T-shirt that Greg gave him with a yellow silk-screen portrait of John Lennon above the bold-faced word "Imagine."

Peng stands firmly at Baihe as Jin, Greg, and many Chinese disregard the ideals of altruism, plain living, and social harmony and rush to the city seeking wealth and independence. On her rare visits home, Jin continually urges Peng to let go of his ideals, leave Baihe, and open a lucrative streetside medical clinic in Shashi. Angry and impatient, she reminds him of his younger brother who left the village for Shashi and runs a company that makes and installs tar paper, hauling in an annual profit of $7,270. Peng responds with a litany of problems he confronts in the city: insomnia, vertigo, car sickness, noise and air pollution, and high blood pressure because of the frenetic lifestyle. Over the years, because of their running quarrel, husband and wife have drifted apart.

Peng has also clashed bitterly with his four children, especially his son Greg; all left Baihe despite his urgings that they stay. Now he is resigned to their departure yet hopes that beyond the village they live by his altruistic teachings. "As long as I am alive, I will continue to tell my children by word or by letter to work hard and serve the people. Greg will educate his son in this way, who will educate his son, all the way through the coming line of generations."

But Greg, like his mother, has parted from his father's values in day-to-day living. He wants eventually to emulate the selflessness of his father. But he has set his father's values aside as he tries to free himself totally from poverty and official restriction. Like his mother, Greg personifies the new assertiveness of Chinese under reform. He is impatient with his father's antipathy toward politics and satisfaction with mere subsistence.

"My father has three basic principles," Greg said in a rare break from medical studies in the United States. "First, never get involved in a political conflict but always walk the middle way; second, people in power are always right so don't oppose them; third, as long as you have food, clothes, and shelter you should be happy."

Peng is just as contemptuous toward the outlook of his son. "My son's chemistry inclines him toward politics. Some people like to meddle in other people's affairs."

Greg shares the disappointment of his mother over the refusal of his father to seek a higher income in Shashi. He largely measures the achievements of his father in terms of money, not morals. "My father is not energetic enough and he doesn't do anything for the family. All the money comes from my mother; my father should be in charge of the family. My mother is very angry with my father."

Jin nurtured her own restlessness in Greg. She disdains the perpetual slog of village life. She brags that her children never worked in the fields when they were growing up. (Her children say otherwise). She quit working in the fields and took up sewing because she hated farming. And she looks down on the coarseness of Baihe. The villagers at her birthplace outside Nan Xian in Hunan Province routinely perform operas, dragon and lion dances, and other folk arts that are lacking in Baihe, she said.

Raised by a mother with a somewhat haughty attitude, Greg was quick to snub village life. But his detachment stems also from the fact that when he was growing up he was a misfit. He did not play with other children much. He was passive and easily manipulated by his peers. Although bright, he rarely studied at elementary school and so earned the nickname Stupid Peng. No teachers paid attention to him. Jin and Peng compounded his estrangement. When Greg's schoolmates were big enough to graze the water buffalo of their families, he asked his parents to buy one too. But they refused, saying they wanted to spend the money on his education. Greg would often play hooky, build a hut out of grass and sticks in a field, crawl into it, and hide. His teachers and classmates noticed him only when he began to show unusual skill in mathematics. Greg grew up to be just the sort of idiosyncratic, brilliant, and independent-minded youth the party finds most threatening.

At the end of primary school Greg leaped from the bottom of the class to the top and sailed into junior high. It was the first high point in a roller-coaster ride in resolve and fortune that would last until his arrival in the United States. Greg earned a widely sought opening at the township high school in 1975 but, after a year, was sent back to the junior high school because he slighted his studies and received poor grades. After another year of studying, Greg returned to the high school and began to work hard. He rose to number three out of forty students in his class. He did well because, unlike his classmates, he tended to reason rather than memorize. Greg excelled at math, physics, and chemistry but faltered in Chinese and party history.

Still, Greg failed the college entrance exams in 1978. He became a teacher at his elementary school but found it so dull he quit after two months. Greg resolved to return to the township high school and take the exams a second time. His father objected, saying he had had his chance and should go to a trade school if he returned to school at all. Greg defied his father and took up his books once again. He knew he had to go to college in order to break away from the village and become a city resident. As Greg studied, he recalled the admonition of his teacher: "Now we'll find out whether throughout your life you'll wear straw sandals or leather shoes."

Every day Greg awakened early in the morning and prepared breakfast for the family before walking two miles to school. After dinner he studied. So as not to keep his family awake, he went into a cotton field with an oil lamp and, amid the mosquitoes, toiled until after midnight on his books.

Greg took the exam a second time and was accepted at the Wuhan Medical College downriver in the provincial capital of Wuhan. "If I had followed my father's advice, I would still be in the village. Since then, I have made my own decisions and never followed my father's advice," he said.

Greg hated medical school and performed miserably. His mind strayed because of his indifference and the rote learning methods imposed by his teachers. He failed anatomy, biology, English, and, once again, party history. As he had in primary school, Greg seemed headed for failure. But in his last year, as the final exam to certify him as a doctor approached, Greg was suddenly overwhelmed by guilt. Because of the hard work of his parents and wealth from market-oriented change, he was able to work less and study more than any of his ancestors in memory. Each semester during his four years in college his mother had sent him $50, a big chunk of her earnings as a seamstress. But by not studying, he had squandered her money and scorned her sacrifice. The prodigal son began to study with all the dogged tenacity his mother applied to cloth.

After five months of study, Greg took a dry-run test for the medical certification examination and scored among the top ten in his class. School officials were ecstatic. Soon thereafter he took the national medical exam and easily passed. The officials fell all over themselves in adulation. Greg, like the peasants of Chinese folklore, had risen above his humble beginnings and limited vision to excellence. He had lived out the ancient myth about the hero who prevailed in the terrifically demanding imperial civil service examinations. In these tales peasants, through brilliance and willpower, passed the three imperial examinations and ascended into the Forbidden City and the host of the Dragon Emperor.

Greg's success also rang with the tinny din of Communist folklore. College administrators gleefully amplified it. Here was the ideal peasant hero, a young man who through self-criticism reformed himself and triumphed against the greatest odds. School officials made Greg an inspirational propaganda figure for the students. They rewarded him with the best job offered to anyone in his class, a position at the People's Health Publishing House in Beijing.

With a warm farewell from his family, Greg headed for Beijing in the summer of 1984. He worked as an editor of medical books at the publishing house. Most significant, he gained official permission to move his residence to Beijing, which Chinese rank as the country's most desirable city. Greg's pride was enormous. His accomplishment had surpassed his parents' wildest fantasies. He was fully vindicated before his father. He edited for three years and began additional graduate study at the Capital Institute of Medicine affiliated with Chaoyang Hospital.

While living in China's most politically charged city, Greg began to express his independent ideas in liberal activism. Like many young, well-educated Chinese nurtured on the unprecedented wealth of the 1980s, Greg was increasingly impatient with the autocratic leadership. He bridled under a government that denied the political freedoms people needed to protect their newfound wealth and advance their diverse interests. He and his friends were especially resentful over the leadership's failure to combat corruption, the most conspicuous and galling sign of the people's political impotence.

Greg and his friends readily joined the democracy protests during the Beijing Spring of 1989. When students staged a hunger strike in Tiananmen Square, Greg helped organize about 100 of his colleagues at Chaoyang Hospital in a march to the plaza. Later, the hospital set up a field tent in the midst of the students. They gave the young protesters water and rushed the weakest ones to the hospital.

On June 3, alarmed by the sight of helicopters flying over Beijing, Greg and his colleagues rushed to the square with surgical masks, rags, and other provisions they thought would be useful against tear gas. Greg remained at the hospital's field tent throughout the day. Late in the evening, rumors that soldiers had shot several protesters flashed about the plaza. Shortly thereafter, Greg and other medical workers began to treat wounded demonstrators fleeing from the river of troop trucks, tanks, and armored personnel carriers advancing from the west down the Avenue of Eternal Peace.

At first the doctors at the tent hurried to staunch the bleeding of wounded protesters carried in on the flatbeds of three-wheeled pedicabs or in the arms of friends. But as the casualties piled up, the doctors had to direct many of the wounded to hospitals east of the square. Greg and his peers treated several soldiers, including a few who were pulled from an armored personnel carrier and severely beaten. When a crowd berated the doctors for bandaging the troops, Greg picked up a megaphone and described the doctor's obligation to save human life. He organized a student picket to form a protective ring around the tent.

Soldiers began to enter the north end of the plaza at 1 A.M. on June 4. A few hours later the troops forced Greg south to the Monument to the People's Heroes along with some thirty-five other doctors and nurses from Chaoyang and other hospitals. After protest leaders negotiated with the military, many students withdrew from the monument. Greg and another Chaoyang doctor strode north into the plaza in an effort to return to their field tent.

"Move another step and you'll be shot!" an officer shouted at them. The doctors were hustled to the east side of the square before the Museum of Revolutionary History. Gunfire sounded sporadically. Greg watched helplessly as armored personnel carriers rolled into the square from the north, flattening dozens of tents that had sheltered the protesters. The soldiers did not look inside the tents before running over them. Again, Greg and a doctor grabbed a stretcher and began to run into the plaza, but soldiers aimed their guns at them and ordered them to halt. When two nurses next to Greg began to cry, a nearby soldier jeered at them.

"Stop that!" Greg yelled.

"Keep talking and I'll shoot you," the soldier said, aiming his AK-47 rifle at Greg.

"Go ahead! Go ahead! Shoot me right here, right now, right in front of everybody!" Greg shouted, opening his blood-stained jacket and shirt to the navel and leaping atop a cement road divider just six feet away from the soldier. The soldier hesitated before his flamboyant target. A few doctors and nurses quickly pulled Greg away. Meanwhile, at the monument, soldiers fell upon students who had remained behind, forcing them to withdraw by beating them with staves and iron bars.

At about 5 A.M. the military piled the debris from the protests in the center of the square and set it on fire. Greg, the other medical staff, and several wounded students withdrew from the plaza. They walked a gauntlet of soldiers south past the Mao mausoleum toward Qianmen Street and into the arms of Beijing residents who hugged and thanked them. As the blood-smeared group of medical workers walked south on Qianmen, they stirred up an impromptu procession.

"Down with Deng Xiaoping. Down with (Premier) Li Peng," some in the crowd yelled as others sang the national anthem. The doctors and nurses stopped and rested at Beijing Hospital. At about 2 P.M. Greg and his colleagues were taken to Chaoyang Hospital. Later Greg stole through the barricaded streets, past soldiers firing randomly into enraged crowds, to the central railway station. At 6 P.M. he took a train to Wuhan, using a ticket he had purchased several days before. He immediately went to the dormitory of his sister Ling at the Wuhan Medical College. He told her about the massacre and his plan to describe the debacle to students. Ling wept and blocked the door. She begged Greg not to spread word of the massacre, echoing their father's injunction against political activism. (Since then, Greg has grown increasingly estranged from his sister, a doctor at Tuanshan Hospital in Wuhan. Like her father, she remains firmly devoted to political passivity. "My sister has a good mind but she never uses it in the right way. She doesn't face up to challenges and always writes to me only about the flowers and sunshine.")

Greg moved Ling aside and gave scores of students outside a dormitory a fifteen-minute eyewitness account of the massacre. He repeated his testimony later to several students in a dormitory. The next day more than 100 students demonstrated against the Beijing crackdown. College officials were furious. After five years in Beijing, their model peasant graduate had returned as a traitorous firebrand. They attempted to ruin his career and prevent him from accepting an offer he had received in the spring for a full scholarship for graduate study at a university in the United States. A city official accused Greg of counterrevolutionary incitement and propaganda, a charge that would lead to lengthy jail terms for several Beijing activists. College and city officials staged a full investigation of "the incident." They submitted a report detailing Greg's seditious actions to the medical publishing house in Beijing, Greg's employer. Officials at the publishing house ordered Greg back to the capital. He could not refuse; the officials controlled his housing, grain ration, medical care, passport, and other vital facets of his life. The officials demanded that he hand over his passport and forget the coveted stateside scholarship or they would turn his case over to the Public Security Bureau for criminal investigation. They also forced Greg to give up his apartment and quit graduate school in Beijing. Finally, they fired him from his part-time work in the hospital.

Like many fugitive activists, Greg made his way to Guangdong Province in the hope of finding a way to slip abroad. He contemplated attempting to flee China via Guangzhou and Shenzhen with the help of Dutch and French tourists. But border security was too tight, so he returned to Beijing, rented a room with another Hubei native, and hustled tours at the Chaoyang Hotel to pay expenses. He approached foreigners and set up guided excursions to the Great Wall or purchased tickets to acrobatic shows and performances of Peking opera. To his surprise, his one-man operation netted him a salary ten times greater than what he had earned at the hospital. Greg wheedled his passport from the publishing house in late 1990, secured a U.S. visa with the help of a foreign friend, and jetted off to the United States for a full scholarship at a midwestern university.

The massacre of unarmed protesters eliminated all doubt in Greg's mind about the legitimacy of the yearning by Chinese for freedom. The confused democracy movement and its rapid rout also affirmed his belief that the traditional passivity of Chinese was ultimately self-destructive.

"I knew that the democracy movement would probably fail and the government would not compromise but would crack down very hard, but I felt it was wrong just to stand by and not take part," Greg said in the United States. "I told my friends that making a democratic government is like creating a big ocean and everyone must contribute their drop in order to realize it; if everyone doesn't give their drop of water to the ocean then it will never be."

Although Greg was fully converted to liberalism and the necessity for political action after June 4, 1989, he was also convinced that for the foreseeable future he would better serve China by studying abroad. Flight overseas was the only step forward open to him. Moreover, Greg felt compelled to go abroad if only to prove his father wrong. Peng strongly disapproved of his decision to study in the United States. Once again, Greg sought vindication in a bold step that defied his father and expressed his determination to be independent.

After completing graduate study and gaining accreditation as an M.D., Greg began an internship in internal medicine at a hospital outside New York in 1994. Now that he has pulled off the ultimate migration and achieved stateside comfort, Greg can easily forget his wounds and look homeward to his father. Although he still bitterly criticizes his father, Greg feels a yearning to fulfill his traditional filial duties. He wants to heed an obligation to pay his parents back for their sacrifice. Such feelings might eventually help Greg and his father find common ground.

"I'll support my father and build a nice house for him, my mother, and myself. My mother works very hard, and that is why I want to be very successful very soon so that she can return to the village and live in a new house," Greg said. He also plans to offer Baihe money for education. The funds, to be managed by his parents, would go toward scholarships, the training of teachers, and the payment for books, paper, and school fees for poor villagers.

Peng cannot ignore the success of his son. He initially opposed the move abroad with great vehemence. He said it was risky and Greg should be satisfied working as a doctor in China. Yet in one generation, Greg has followed his own inner voice and led the family from dirt-scrabble poverty to the promise of riches as a medical doctor in the United States. Peng now strongly supports Greg's plan abroad.

Perhaps Greg, by thrusting forward while heeding what lies behind, shows Chinese migrants one way to ease the strains between village and town and between tradition and change in their rapidly modernizing society. The compulsion to move ahead while minding the past could help ensure that old values evolve in step with the new needs of Chinese.

For Jin, life as a migrant in far away Shashi is nearly over. She is only working now to pay the tuition for her youngest daughter who studies English at the Foreign Language Institute in Xian. She annually sends her daughter $910, an astronomical sum for a peasant family. With all her children nearly educated, Jin thinks less of the future and more about the present. She is considering ending her solitary work in Shashi and returning to the village and her husband.

But going home to Peng will be difficult for Jin. Her differences with Peng are more troubling than those between Peng and Greg. The relationship between a father and son is frequently freighted with guilt and high expectation. But the two men can handle the load knowing they are acting out the often factious patriarchal ritual of passing the torch of family honor and authority to a new generation. They both recognize now that the migration by Greg is a step forward for the family.

Jin and Peng cannot view the tension between them as part of an unavoidable sacrifice they must make for the sake of a brighter time ahead. As husband and wife, they know their needs and expectations for one another are largely geared to the present, not to the future as for Peng and Greg. Like many aging couples, they view the present as increasingly more important than the comparatively short span of time that lies ahead for them. Yet the present offers Jin and Peng only pain from continued separation and bitter disagreement over whether city riches or village ethics are best for the family.

At the end of one of Jin's rare visits home, the Pengs and their kin followed an old Chinese custom and saw her off on her journey back to Shashi. The family trudged the two miles on the road to the bus stop in the nearest town. Jin occasionally glanced at Peng as they silently walked far apart. She climbed onto the bus and sat down. As the engine started up, she quickly turned back to look at Peng. He had already turned away, heading back to the village. The engine roared and he disappeared behind a cloud of dust. As the bus jounced away, Jin tightly shut her eyes and pressed her forehead against the window.

Whereas Jin Xiulin left her peasant home to seek prosperity in a distant city, many Chinese have remained in their native villages and relied only on their wits to make a fortune. The erstwhile tillers of rice and wheat have started millions of small factories in the back rooms, toolsheds, or pigsties of their mud-and-thatched dwellings.

As the rural entrepreneurs pursue their dreams for riches and prestige, they are leading the fastest growing, most dynamic sector of China's economy. They are bringing the prosperity and unruly individualism of a free-market economy to the countryside, long the foundation of Communist Party rule. Through their new assertiveness and wealth, thriving businessmen like Zhang Guoxi are toppling the pillars of traditional party orthodoxy and power.

Zhang Guoxi   *Photo by James Tyson*

T W O

"Turning Iron to Gold": The Entrepreneur

WHEN ZHANG GUOXI LAUGHS, it is as if he tossed up a fistful of gold coins with a smile and let the bullion shower him in bright, ringing abandon. One of the wealthiest men in China, Zhang has much to laugh about: in fact, more than $50 million. But even Zhang speaks softly when describing how he tends a fortune from wood-carving factories under the eyes of Communist Party officials. The farm-born plutocrat has learned that riches cannot buy freedom from his fickle political overlords. He knows the clatter that bursts from his factories as chisels meet wood is a loud enough affront to the party's Communist creed.

The location of Zhang's factories suggests that his road to riches was no easy street. His eleven-story company headquarters sticks up from an impoverished plain in Jiangxi Province like an arrogant capitalist weed in the hothouse of China's Communist revolution. Sixty miles to the northwest in the provincial capital of Nanchang, Zhou Enlai and other army leaders staged a rebellion on August 1, 1927. The Nanchang uprising is celebrated as the founding of China's Red Army. Some 200 miles to the southwest rises Jinggang Mountain, a jagged peak that is one of the most sacred shrines to Maoism. Six weeks after the Nanchang revolt, Mao retreated with some 1,000 rebels into the heavily wooded bandit refuge. From a mountaintop fortress Mao made some of his earliest peasant converts to communism and built his first soviet, the basic framework for China's revolutionary state. And in 1934, some 200 miles to the south, thousands of Communist rebels fleeing from Chiang Kai-shek's armies set out from southern Jiangxi on the 6,000-mile Long March. The epic, headlong retreat across ice-capped mountains, roiling cataracts, and vast grasslands steeled the Communists for eventual victory.

The deep red complexion of the soil and people in Jiangxi is a symbolic testimony to the blood-and-fire zeal of the region's early Communist recruits. It is as if the hardship that the Red Army exploited here is stained into the infertile soil and impoverished people. Jiangxi peasants laboring in the sun assume a rust-red visage that affirms their slavish dependence on the earth. Unless they lavish the earth with water and toil, it yields only a dense scrub of pine.

Gazing at the red earth of his native land from the penthouse balcony of his headquarters, Zhang doesn't seem inspired by the heroics of Mao and other Communist insurgents. Instead, the short, bald, and bubbly millionaire raises a snifter of cognac toward the fiery sun as it sets between Nanchang and Jinggang Mountain and toasts a different sort of idol. "In the future I will face a lot of political and financial difficulties, but if I bravely face these challenges then I will be a real man—like Lee Iacocca," Zhang said.

By his own measure, however, Zhang has already proved his manhood several times over. Since launching his wood-carving empire from a sagging woodworking shop in 1973, the junior high school dropout has overcome adversities that would unnerve some of capitalism's most steely industrialists. But the paddy-to-penthouse climb of Zhang Guoxi is more than a classic tribute to grit and business acumen. His story epitomizes the grim ordeal and touch-and-go return of Chinese capitalists under communism.

As the youngest of seven children from a poor farming family, Zhang shows how China's speedy development is driven by the obsessive desire of Chinese to escape centuries of penury and frequent famine. Zhang's story is woven with political satire worthy of Gogol: He has mastered the absurd task of justifying his riches in a totalitarian state that was founded on the ideal of equal wealth for all. And while flouting the bedrock value of one of the world's most repressive regimes, Zhang must also oppose a political culture that for millennia has barred Chinese merchants from carving out power independent of the state. His story shows that although entrepreneurs must ultimately yield to officials, they have steadily pushed back the bounds of direct government control and enlarged their own limited realms of freedom.

Zhang is one of thousands of go-getters who have amassed millions since senior leader Deng Xiaoping checked the powers of bureaucrats and allowed the market to animate the economy. But few people in China are as rich as Zhang. And no one else had the audacity to father a personal fortune in the cradle of China's Communist revolution during the decade of Maoist fanaticism and virulent anticapitalism known as the Cultural Revolution (1966–1976).

At the start of those ten years of turmoil, Zhang, like most Chinese, was more intent on making a living than on making revolution. He and sixty-nine other workers were languishing in a workshop for wooden farm implements when Red Guards—the young extremists ordered by Mao to "create chaos and make a tremendous mess, the bigger the better"—stormed through Yujiang on pilgrimage to Jinggang Mountain and Nanchang. The swarms of revolutionaries ate the rice rations of Zhang and the other woodworkers. Eventually, strife between rival factions of Maoists disrupted work and drove the enterprise heavily into debt. The woodworkers had no money with which to buy wood or to pay their own wages.

Rejecting Mao's assurance that Chinese could make a living on revolutionary ardor alone, Zhang on May 3, 1972, boarded the overnight train for Shanghai, 260 miles to the northeast. For several decades Jiangxi natives like Zhang who were dismayed at the province's ox-plod poverty had found the wealth of Shanghai tantalizingly close but always beyond reach. No other impoverished, landlocked province near Shanghai was so lacking in the wherewithal to match the coast's prosperity. But Zhang was not thinking of abandoning his native village for the comparative wealth of Shanghai as he rattled toward the East China Sea. Rather, the ambitious nineteen-year-old workshop foreman envisioned Shanghai as a conduit to even greater riches overseas. Zhang was an iconoclast for tradition at a time when radical, destructive leftism was the orthodoxy. He planned to revive the ancient artisanry behind the intricate wooden carvings that Red Guards were smashing as "reactionary relics" in temples and shrines across China. Then he would sell the creations abroad for yen, dollars, deutsche marks, and other hard currency. Such ambitions were dangerous for a young man whose Red Guard peers had recently trashed and murdered their way across China for the love of Mao. At the time, Shanghai was the base for one of the notorious Gang of Four, ultraleftists largely responsible for pushing the Cultural Revolution to radical extremes. The port was a maelstrom of internecine strife waged under the label of "class struggle." Anyone with a glint of the profit motive or personal gain was pilloried as a "running dog of capitalism."

In Shanghai, officials at the Administration of Handicrafts introduced the eager rural woodcraftsman to a factory they said shaped wood into vital household implements. Zhang strode into the factory, turned on his heel, and strode out; the enterprise made chamber pots. Declaring that his workshop would be a vessel for artistry rather than make vessels for night soil, Zhang persuaded the handicraft officials to introduce him to the Number 1 Carving Factory of Shanghai. There he tried to learn how to make carved camphor-wood trunks that sold for ten times the price of the plain trunks his shop made. After a week, though, he found he lacked the talent to learn the skill quickly. So he chose a faster way to acquire the expertise: theft. Zhang plucked several designs from a factory wastebasket and pocketed a few "tiger claws," the intricately carved feet for the trunks. He rushed back to Jiangxi where he and a few cohorts set to work for several weeks making their first trunk. Zhang's euphoria over the completion of the chest was short-lived. People could not tell whether his carvings were birds or flowers.

Zhang took the trunk to Nanchang to present it to the Shanghai Artwork Import and Export Corporation. The company was considering handicrafts for display at the Guangzhou Trade Fair, one of the few venues for trade promotion allowed by the self-isolated country. The Shanghai traders initially spurned the trunk because of its inadvertently surreal carvings. But Zhang's enthusiasm eventually won their sympathy, and he left for Yujiang with a contract to produce twenty sets of camphor trunks.

Back home, however, Zhang confronted a workshop that refused to work. Managers and many woodworkers said during a lengthy factory meeting that they could never master the skills for fine craftsmanship. After failing to rally the factory behind him, Zhang jumped to his feet in what he now calls the seminal moment for his multimillion-dollar enterprise. "I am determined to begin a carving enterprise; all those who are willing to follow me stand up!" he declared. The woodworkers glanced at one another and froze. Twenty-one of the sixty-nine workers slowly rose to their feet. Before the aspiring carvers were to sit down, they faced the first incident of what became years of official hostility. Factory leaders said that before the upstarts launched their own enterprise they had to pay off their share of the factory debt.

Zhang initially managed to sustain his enterprise with his savings and the salary of his wife, who earned 30 yuan a month working in the pharmacy of a hospital in Yujiang. He sought loans from the local credit agency, but even China's most favored form of bribery—an elaborate banquet—failed to soften the doubt of creditors that his workshop would survive. So Zhang eventually sold the home of his adoptive father (his uncle) for $380. Ironically, Mao's policy of redistributing wealth had provided Zhang with seed money for his supremely successful capitalist venture. The Communist government had given his adoptive father a deposed landlord's dwelling when it redistributed land in the early 1950s. Zhang used the money from the sale to build a workshop and on September 16, 1973, registered his company under the politically palatable title of "collective enterprise."

Zhang's workers were carvers in name only. Their most sophisticated accomplishment in shaping wood had been to whittle the prongs on pitchforks. So Zhang journeyed to Dongyang, Zhejiang Province, a center of fine carving in China for more than 1,500 years. There he found a master carver almost as destitute and idle as the woodworkers in Yujiang. Zhang persuaded the craftsman, Ye Shiwen, to return to Yujiang to train carvers.

After a month, the Public Security Bureau of Dongyang wrote demanding the return of Ye. But Ye had been won over by Zhang's enthusiasm and ignored the order. When Dongyang police arrived to take Ye back home, he hid in a worker's dwelling, carving and instructing from there. Only when the police threatened to sue the ragtag band of carvers did Zhang yield up Ye.

Without the tutelage of a master craftsman, the apprentice carvers did more harm than good to wood. So Zhang halted their chiseling and returned to Dongyang, where he recruited another expert carver, Zhao Shigao, and seven assistants. This time, Zhang secured the approval of the carvers' production team and local officials. After dispatching Zhao to Yujiang, Zhang remained in Dongyang with half of his own workers and mastered the carving craft.

Once trained in the basics of carving, Zhang's workers labored for six months and in March 1974 sent twenty camphor chests to the Shanghai trading company. Their profit was meager, but the Guangzhou Trade Fair prominently displayed their trunks, which bore the classic design of nine dragons flitting among clouds. Traders from Southeast Asia placed orders for the trunks with the government, providing the first trickle of a thin but steady stream of orders. Zhang's biggest challenges were yet to come.

While Zhang was pioneering entrepreneurship in one of China's poorest provinces, the father of the country's future economic reforms, Deng Xiaoping, was also in Jiangxi Province working at a tractor repair shop in political disgrace. Zhang was six years ahead of the radical invigoration of China's command economy launched by Deng in 1978. Zhang pioneered his own version of the "factory director responsibility system" that in a decade would be the party line across China. Under the scheme, party cadres were to surrender power to a trained factory manager, who would assume the risks of decisionmaking and earn a high salary and bonus for such leadership. Zhang also introduced his workers to a truly revolutionary concept in Maoist China: If their performance was poor, he fired them. Workers were paid according to a piece-rate wage system tied to the extent and quality of their labor. Hiring and promotion were based on a worker's capabilities, regardless of his class background. Zhang, the fledgling capitalist, epitomized the moxie and management savvy that by the mid-1980s would help lift China to unprecedented prosperity under the command of Deng.

In his rural backwater, Zhang constantly had to face down petty officials and Maoist fanatics. Officials hindered Zhang's supply of wood. They routinely shut off his electricity. They denied him financing. They withheld rail transport to Shanghai. And these were actions only by upper-level bureaucrats. In April 1974 a leading party official of Yujiang County criticized Zhang before 1,000 Maoist devotees as "a new-born, bourgeois thing" and "a capitalist wearing a red hat." He accused Zhang of using the ways of a capitalist "to control, restrict, and exert pressure on workers."

Weeks later the county party committee sent a four-man work team to occupy the factory around the clock and gather information about Zhang's alleged abuses. The team barred Zhang from leaving the factory on business and ordered him to criticize himself regularly in writing. The Maoist zealots hustled Zhang repeatedly before assembled mobs and chastised him. The work team criticized his work and obstructed plans that did not jibe with its extremism. It determined that 90 percent of the staff above the rank of foreman belonged to the "five black classes": former landlords, rich peasants, counterrevolutionaries, rightists, and "bad elements" such as criminals. The team charged Zhang with tax evasion and accused him of corruption for building a new house in his home village with materials from the factory. It also denounced him for his unorthodox methods of hiring, promotion, and determining wages.

Zhang cooperated with the work team but ordered his carvers to concentrate on production and stay clear of the fighting among local party factions, particularly at the Yujiang Administration of Handicrafts where strife was especially intense. Faction leaders criticized the factory for its reluctance to take a political stand. They accused Zhang of attempting to establish "an independent kingdom." In turn, the work team subjected Zhang's workers to lengthy interrogations. To a man, the workers replied only with vague answers and mute smiles.

"The stronger the pressure from the work team, the more determined I became to succeed," Zhang said. After six months in the factory the work team withdrew. Although the party investigators had failed to ferret out enough evidence to jail Zhang, they ruled that he should never be commended as a manager. They deployed informants to watch him constantly, and continued to harass Zhang for five more years.

Zhang acknowledged that his hustling was unusual at the time. But he denied he was the rapacious capitalist so common in China's Communist folklore. In fact, he said his aims would have endeared him to Marx. "My chief desire was to fill the bellies of my workers," he said, noting that during the period of tumult and widespread want, he and his apprentice carvers had no fixed salary and often no income at all.

Zhang ultimately defended himself by pointing to his party membership and impeccable class pedigree. He had joined the party just before his sortie to Shanghai in May 1972, aided by his adoptive mother, a neighborhood party official in Yujiang. Also, he could claim a revolutionary bloodline redder and purer than that of Mao. For centuries, Zhang's impoverished ancestors had grown rice knee-deep in the mud paddies of Mao Jia village five miles outside of Yujiang. His suffering rivaled that of many of his ancestors. Zhang's mother gave birth to her first child at the beginning of China's civil war in 1927. Twenty-five years later, on July 26, 1952, she bore Zhang. He was the youngest of seven children and was so small they nicknamed him Guoli (Tiny Rice Dumpling). Zhang's father, a jack-of-all-trades, worked as a farmer, butcher, barber, ceramics dealer, and tofu maker. He and Zhang's mother worked hard but could not earn enough money to feed the family. Eventually, Zhang's mother worked herself to death. She died of an ulcer while still nursing one-year-old Zhang. The baby was adopted by his mother's sister and raised in a small red sandstone dwelling at the end of a blind alley in Yujiang. Since childhood, Zhang has been dogged by the notion that his mother died while struggling to feed him. Driven by a sense of guilt, Zhang obsessively seeks to earn a fortune and ensure his family will never again face hunger and misery.

By 1976, despite constant political harassment, Zhang had achieved the goal of filling the rice bowls of his workers. The number of export orders had steadily risen and so had the carvers' salaries. Zhang was confronting a growing shortage of skilled hands and asked the Yujiang County Labor Department to approve the hiring of more workers. The officials refused. In one of several bold and shrewd management moves, Zhang sidestepped the official obstacle. In May 1976 he once again traveled to Dongyang, this time bringing jobs rather than seeking expertise. He recruited master carvers as subcontractors for work in their native town and labeled their salaries as "processing fees." Over the next several years, he set up twenty factories outside Yujiang that carved parts for his camphor trunks.

In a similar move later in 1976, Zhang covertly launched a joint venture with the Hoshan Furniture Factory in Shanghai in an effort to reduce his complete dependence on exports. The enterprise would enable Zhang to shift his resources swiftly to making furniture for Chinese consumers should he lose his overseas markets in a diplomatic crisis. Through the initiative, Zhang defied regulations against outside enterprises setting up in Shanghai and risked retribution from the ultraleftists who still controlled China's largest city. As with many of his major decisions, Zhang speaks of his illicit move into Shanghai in military terms. This decision, he said, was a masterstroke. "An enterprise is like an army; a force fighting on one front might face heavy losses and can even be wiped out when attacked by a strong enemy," Zhang said, motioning his hands as if deploying his carvers in a military campaign. "But if the army fights on a secondary front too, the chances of avoiding total defeat and eventually achieving victory are far greater," he said.

Zhang faced a counterattack in 1978 from his long-standing leftist enemies. A deputy commissioner of Shangrou Prefecture, the administrative level above Yujiang County, ordered the county party committee to investigate Zhang's "serious political problems." The assault flopped, however, with the transfer of the county party secretary and the appointment of a new secretary, Gui Changgui, who was sympathetic to Zhang. Without the protection of Gui, Zhang said he would have been jailed.

Zhang and his maverick ways were vindicated in late 1978. Deng staged the third comeback of his political career at the third plenum of the party's eleventh congress. He made prosperity rather than Maoist purity China's cynosure. Deng did not suddenly emerge from the closet as a capitalist. His goal was to use so-called exploiters like Zhang to the party's advantage rather than to nurture them. Chinese were impoverished and embittered toward the party after the disastrous Cultural Revolution, and Deng condoned a measure of market freedom and a get-rich-quick credo primarily to save the party. Deng would jump-start the entrepreneurial motor to power China's development; he could throttle it when it had fulfilled its task. His domineering, manipulative attitude toward merchants was identical to that held by China's rulers for thousands of years. He saw the free-wheeling drive of capitalists like Zhang as a force for building socialism, not as an end in itself. For a time his scheme worked. By 1985 his reforms had energized the economy, raised the living standards of most Chinese, and partially salvaged party legitimacy.

With the blessing of Beijing, Zhang suddenly found officials eager to provide electricity, wood, financing, rail transport, and other help. Inspired by the unprecedented government backing, Zhang traveled to Shanghai again in August 1979 with the ambition of breaking into Japan's highly lucrative market for intricate Buddhist shrines. Zhang strode into the Handicrafts Import and Export Corporation of Shanghai and declared his plan to profit from Japanese piety.

"You must be joking!" snorted a company official. "Many factories in Shanghai and Zhejiang have failed to meet the Japanese standards; you're just dreaming," he said. But Zhang persuaded the corporation to let him try and rushed back to Yujiang. After working on a sample of a part of the shrine for ten days, Zhang returned to Shanghai, impressed a Japanese shrine-maker with the sample, and signed a contract. Zhang had struck what would prove to be his mother lode of riches.

In 1982, after investigating the market and manufacturers for Buddhist shrines in Tokyo and Osaka, Zhang realized he had enough highly skilled carvers to challenge his competitors from Taiwan and South Korea. He had already launched more than thirty carving workshops in Yujiang and Dongyang and upgraded the quality of his craftsmanship. His lower labor costs enabled him to underprice his rivals. Moreover, through wily negotiating he engineered an arrangement by which he became the sole supplier to three Japanese shrine manufacturers. Zhang guaranteed he would provide the parts for the shrines at the same price to the three manufacturers as long as they agreed to divide Japan into three geographical markets and restrict their business to their own territories. Through the cartel,

Zhang eliminated the competition and locked in a profit. Later, he invested 12 million yen in a joint venture with an Osaka firm to produce detailed black and gold lacquerware shrines that sell in Japan for more than $10,000 each.

Commanding a large chunk of the Japanese market and the political support of Beijing, Zhang's company took off. From 1982 until 1988, the profits of the Yinghai Wooden Products Trade Company annually rocketed an average of 143 percent. Still, local leftists continued to badger him. The Jiangxi Province party secretary accused him of profiteering and other alleged illegalities in June 1985. Officials with "near-sighted left eyes" (leftists) and Yujiang natives with the "red-eye disease" of envy spread rumors that Zhang illegally traded in gold. An investigation, however, turned up no evidence.

Zhang's ventures have not always yielded riches. In 1984, flushed with the success of his Japan trade, he began to fling his money into a galaxy of businesses in and outside Jiangxi: metal carving, pesticides, electric fans, garments, plastics, food processing, filmmaking, real estate, and a department store. Most of the initiatives failed within a few years. But when Zhang has focused on the production of wood carvings in his native area, his success has been limited only by the size of the market.

"In terms of expertise and investment, I have carried carving to its ultimate stage," said Zhang from his office balcony overlooking the red sandstone workshops filled with carvers. "No one can compete with me in carving in China and maybe in all the world," he said, speaking over the whine of saws spewing the sawdust and pungent scent from camphor wood.

Today, Zhang runs a conglomerate with 3,000 employees and offices in Hong Kong, West Germany, Japan, and Canada. The Jiangxi Guoxi Industrial Conglomerate Group thrives largely on wood and copper carving, but it is expanding into equally lucrative ventures in real estate, securities, and trade. About 60 percent of Zhang's revenue is in hard currency, which makes his empire a fountain of precious foreign scrip for his poor and restless province. Each year he brings in more than $4 million in profits from exports.

Zhang learned to keep wood carving as the core of his business after the failure of his pell-mell expansion in the mid-1980s. In what he calls the second stage of his business strategy, he started stepping outside the factory to invest in money-making ventures overseas. His Hamburg office designs interior wooden decorations for Chinese restaurants and coordinates orders and deliveries with the carving workshops in Yujiang. Zhang set up a joint venture in 1991 in Toronto with a Chinese-Canadian company to market his wood carvings and furniture. His joint venture in Japan holds more than half of the market in Buddhist shrines and has expanded into black lacquer furniture. In Hong Kong, Mrs. Zhang oversees a trading company, securities investments, and speculation in the dizzying real estate market.

In Shenzhen, across the border from Hong Kong, Zhang has built a carving factory and staffed it with 100 workers from Yujiang. The carvers eat, play, and sleep in the fenced high-rise factory. The Jiangxi dialect hums throughout the compound, an enclave of subdued and callow inlanders amid a booming sprawl peopled largely by brash and worldly wise Cantonese workers. Zhang maintains an office for high-stakes investment on Hainan, a large island in the South China Sea that Beijing has long hoped to transform into an economy as vibrant and prosperous as that of Taiwan. He has invested in three apartment buildings and a hotel in Sanya, a small scenic port on the southern tip of the island. Zhang's Shanghai office runs a small furniture factory and manages exports to Japan.

The heart of the Guoxi Group remains in Yujiang County. Zhang enjoys unrivaled financial and political leverage in the county seat because he has advanced it from oxcarts to trucks and from dirt roads to macadam. Along with his headquarters and a carving school, Zhang runs four factories in Yujiang with 1,300 employees making wood carvings, camphor trunks, copper carvings, and lacquer furniture. He has hired scores of handicapped carvers and pocketed a significant tax break. Teaming up with a labor import company in Tokyo, Zhang initiated a highly profitable scheme in June 1992 that offers Japanese companies the cheap labor of cooks, chemists, entertainers, geologists, and other skilled workers from Jiangxi for six-month spans. He declined to reveal full details of this money-spinning "exchange-of-talents" project. The crowning venture of his Yujiang arm is a new factory complex he opened on seven acres of land in September 1992 that doubled his production capacity.

Making a typically grandiloquent comparison, Zhang said he runs his company as he would run China. "An enterprise should be like a good country, operated by laws rather than by the will of one man; that way, all workers will seriously and happily concentrate on their work." Zhang said he demonstrated his overriding commitment to factory rules when he punished a cousin in 1987 for getting drunk while at the workshop. Despite appeals from an aunt and uncle, Zhang demoted his cousin from the position of vice foreman to a job tending the factory's tangerine orchard.

Still, in running his factory day-to-day, Zhang owes much of his success to his impulsive and frenetic management style. During several interviews in his office over a five-year period beginning in 1988, he often leaped up from his desk, strode onto the balcony, and barked out reprimands to erring sawyers in the lumberyard, loafing drivers in the factory parking lot, or other staff he deemed awry.

On paper and in practice, Zhang is a strict and fatherly taskmaster. He penalizes all his staff, from front-line carvers to vice presidents, up to a half day's wage if they arrive for work after the ring of the factory bell. The fine ensures that the rural carvers forsake the languid rhythms of growing rice. All his employees work seven days a week with four days off each month. Zhang encourages his carvers to bunch their four holidays together so they have enough time to reunite with their families in their remote native villages. In the same paternalistic spirit, he trains his workers in carving and offers his long-term workers subsidized housing, day care, haircuts, baths, medical benefits, a movie twice a week, and a daily cookie. In return, they call him Lao Ban (Boss). The term has such strong overtones of subservience that it was taboo for decades under Communist rule.

Zhang offers a comparatively generous pay scale linked to quality and productivity. The Yujiang carvers work two four-hour shifts a day and earn on average

$58 per month. Highly skilled carvers typically earn $96 per month. Compared to labor costs abroad, these rates are low enough that Zhang can beat out competitors in most other countries and reap a fat profit each year. "Yujiang is the hen that lays the golden eggs; it lays 365 golden eggs a year," Zhang said with a smile.

The strategy of Zhang for coming years illustrates the irrepressibility of his ambition. He plans to put some $6 million in idle funds into stocks and real estate in Hong Kong, Shenzhen, and Hainan. He hopes to expand his exchange-of-talents scheme and send at least 2,000 Jiangxi workers each year to Japan for short-term jobs. And he plans to cooperate with a Taipei-based company in mining and other forms of resource development. Flaunting the grandeur of his mining schemes, Zhang pulled a visitor onto his office balcony and pointed to a large hill on the horizon bristling with pine trees. "I'll move that black marble thing to Taiwan," he said.

For many years, the promise of riches from the distant U.S. market has bedazzled Zhang. But, as in China, he wants big fortune on his own terms: with the low taxes, convenience, and security found only in buddy-buddy relationships with politicians. In August 1989 Zhang visited Pierre, South Dakota, and signed a memorandum with Governor George S. Mickelson for a joint venture in carving. The scheme demonstrated Zhang's shrewdness. He would invest $1 million and South Dakota would put up $800,000 to train and eventually employ Native Americans and the handicapped as carvers of wooden mantelpieces, picture frames, and other items with traditional American designs.

Zhang pieced together the South Dakota deal with loopholes and dodges worthy of the craftiest American entrepreneur. The venture would put the final touches on imports of semifinished wood products and so be a way for Zhang to skirt the high import tax on finished goods. Zhang would exploit the absence of South Dakota state taxes by locating his U.S. headquarters there. When possible, he would funnel revenues to the state from branch offices in Los Angeles, New York, and San Francisco. Finally, Zhang would also seize upon incentives offered to hire Native Americans and the handicapped.

As if to show Zhang that he cannot escape socialist bureaucrats overseas, the Chinese Embassy in Washington nixed the deal in May 1991. Despite the promising partnership with the South Dakota government, the embassy feared that if the venture failed, it would damage China's image. It also was concerned that the hiring of Native Americans and the handicapped would appear exploitative, Zhang said.

Still, Zhang has built other avenues into the huge U.S. market. In August 1989 he launched a joint venture with the Olivier Investment Company of New York to market prefabricated homes made in Yujiang. He set up a similar enterprise with the High Quality Rosewood Furniture Company in June 1991 in which the San Francisco–based company would market furniture imported from China. Closer to home, Zhang agreed to rescue a failing real estate venture in Thailand launched by Jiangxi Province. He intends to use the state-approved office in Bangkok as a beachhead for the marketing of Buddhist carvings in the rapidly developing country.

Today, Zhang is entering what he calls the third stage of his company's development. In the first stage, he sought merely to feed his workers and his family. In the second, he stepped outside the factory and used his wealth to invest in projects that made more money. "In the third and current stage, I'm using my money to recruit talented managers; they will earn money for me," he said.

Since Zhang set out in business, his aims have broadly foreshadowed those of many common Chinese. After launching his workshop in 1973, Zhang sought to eradicate the unspoken credo of collective suffering that characterized Mao's ruinous brand of communism. Wielding capitalist-style management techniques, he swept away party-induced torpor and electrified his enterprise. Then, soon after the comeback of Deng in 1978, Zhang became an early example of the raw, mefirst greed that has prevailed during the era of reform.

As he withdraws from the factory floor, Zhang toys with the idea of retiring in his early forties. But there is nothing in Zhang's lifestyle in Yujiang to suggest that retirement is more than a fancy. He works eighteen hours a day, seven days a week. Beginning at 8 A.M., he spends much of the day and evening entertaining and guiding officials and other guests around his factory. Late at night, until about 2 A.M., he phones his branch offices. Also, Zhang's home, the refurbished dwelling of his adoptive parents, does not suggest that days of leisure are imminent. It is splendorous by Yujiang standards but far beneath his multimillion-dollar means.

"Now I will show you my *pinminku* (slum)," Zhang said, palming the wheel of his Toyota Crown sedan and descending from a dimly lit Yujiang street into a dark blind alley pinched by rough sandstone walls and battered wooden doors. He sped to the end of the alley to the doorway of a two-story house with a narrow balcony. In front of the dwelling stood two stone lions at either end of three-foot-long hedges. Vice President Wu Kunming and lesser employees met Zhang on the steps, opened the door to a vestibule paneled in rosewood, and trailed him in a bent and sibilant pack up a broad staircase. Zhang shoved open a door delicately carved with the imperial seal of China, strode into a sitting room, and cast himself onto a black leather cushion alongside a black lacquer coffee table. He motioned his guests toward a broad and voluptuous sofa in black Italian leather with two matching chairs. Copper lamps jutted from the dark red paneling.

Zhang lunged to his feet and walked to the master bedroom on a wide path of oriental rugs in fluorescent hues of red, gold, and blue. The shouts and racy music from a kung fu movie suddenly burst from the bedroom. A still and neglected grandfather clock stood mutely in a corner, its brass face glaring. Zhang returned carrying a large plastic bag of candy and wearing a white long underwear shirt and long underwear pants ending just below the knee. He ripped open the bag and dumped the candy on the table in a clattering heap.

The chief domestic attendant to Zhang padded into the room and placed on the table a tray with glasses and a tall bottle of Remy Martin cognac. He serves simultaneously as a valet, bartender, doorman, waiter, and all-around servant. But his main function is as a bodyguard. He wore the olive-green pants with red and gold trim that distinguish the dress uniform of the People's Liberation Army. His shirt of military khaki set off a red tie and gold tie clip. On his hip he carried a pistol in a leather holster, doubly secured with a string running from the stock to the belt. Zhang also maintains a police station nearby manned by twelve officers, some of them provided by the Public Security Bureau but most hired by Zhang. The force handles occasional threats from envious citizens and what he called other "security problems."

Zhang uncorked the bottle and poured the cognac to the brim of the beer glasses. Smiling, lifting his shirt, and slapping his belly, Zhang raised his other hand in a toast and offered a tour of his home. In his bedroom, which echoed with the yells of kung fu masters and the cries of their foes, Zhang pointed above his bed to a photo in which he is standing next to a florid carving of China's god of wealth. On one side of his bed stood a bookcase filled with dozens of popular novels about fictional masters in the martial arts, one of Zhang's favorite pastimes as a youth. On the other side, in a corner just a leap away, leaned a rifle and double-barreled shotgun, fully loaded.

Today, most of the enmity the young tycoon faces arises from envy. Provincial officials, determined to protect one of Jiangxi's few impressive resources, have assigned Zhang three bodyguards skilled in martial arts. One of them is a kung fu champion of the People's Armed Police. "I know kung fu," Zhang said, parrying his fists. "But I've got to keep some extra power close at hand anyway," he said with a loud laugh.

Back in the sitting room, Zhang topped off the beer glasses with cognac, going at the alcohol with all the vigor and diligence of a bodybuilder pressing weights. As host, Zhang follows a strategy in drinking that is as calculating as his business methods. If he knows he is drinking with people with a capacity higher than his, he will not only overindulge but also deliberately drive them beyond their limit. That way he saves face by ensuring that everyone loses with him.

The young bodyguard entered carrying a lacquer tray with steaming soup bowls brimming with mushrooms, white fungus, and poached eggs in a sugary broth. He bent over and walked in short, rapid steps in an apparent effort to show fuss and diligence. Zhang leaned over his bowl, slurping the syrupy broth with Wu and his visitors. He suddenly flicked his two eggs into Wu's bowl. "Eat, Little Wu," he said, leaning back from the table, smiling broadly, lifting his shirt, and again slapping his belly with a laugh. Wu, four years Zhang's senior, quickly slurped the sweet soup with his head bowed.

Later, as Zhang slept, Wu said, "We all know that the boss is strict, but he is only thinking of our own good and so we welcome his guidance." He has worked under Zhang since 1970. Zhang considers Wu a good manager and worthy substitute for himself. He plans to grant Wu control over the day-to-day operations at Yujiang.

By the standards of traditional Chinese propriety, Wu is the model subordinate. When facing Zhang, he stands with arms hanging limply at his sides, fingers pointed backward, head slightly bent, and eyes focused on the boss's lapel. He speaks only when spoken to and always maintains a pained smile. Only occasionally does he raise his eyes to meet his boss's face. "I was born in the year of the tiger," Wu boasted, making the grimace that he apparently hopes will look like a confident smile.

Zhang has always surrounded himself with yes men, if only to have relief from officials who always say no. During our visits with Zhang over four years, he frequently subjected his factotums to mild hazing, making them down cognac on command, for instance. Yet gradually, there seemed to be less spontaneity and light-hearted camaraderie between Zhang and his managers. He seemed to indulge in hazing for its own sake. The promotion of subordinates like Wu and the demotion of chief secretary Shen Liushu illustrate the change in tone at the upper level of Zhang's "corporate culture."

Before the 1990s Shen seemed to serve as a fatherly protector for Zhang's peace of mind. Like many graying Shanghainese, the former Kuomintang officer has a ken for capitalism and firsthand experience in deflecting the ham-handed assaults of Maoists. When Chiang Kai-shek and other Nationalists fled from Communist forces to Taiwan in 1949, Shen stayed behind in Shanghai, the world's deepest sump for decadent imperialism and unchecked capitalism. He was immediately arrested. After seven years in jail he was released but soon was seized again as a counterrevolutionary and dispatched to hard labor in a coal mine for another seven years. Shen graduated in 1939 from the Whampoa Military Academy, the elite school founded by Sun Yat-sen and run by Chiang. He has the urbane, cosmopolitan airs that bumpkin Zhang cannot buy for himself.

For many years, Shen was the paternal figure Zhang lacked while being reared by an aunt and reticent uncle. He stood by as the tall, reserved opposite to the short, ebullient multimillionaire. Shen gently savored each cigarette while Zhang sucked down five packs a day. He sipped Remy Martin cognac while Zhang gulped it. He whispered advice while Zhang jovially ordered his squad of foremen, clerks, drivers, and femmes de chambre. Shen was also Zhang's man Friday, fetching and drinking cognac on command, entertaining guests at billiards, and leading his youthful boss to bed and summoning a doctor after too much drink. As Zhang reached his late thirties and felt more confident and assured in his political standing, he apparently decided that he no longer needed an alter ego and father figure. He demoted Shen to a post at the Shanghai branch.

The change in Zhang's treatment of his managers arises naturally from his new, comparatively aloof style of management during the third stage of development. In 1988, before investing in Hong Kong stocks and real estate, Zhang hustled about his complex, throwing himself into the spray of wood chips and the shoulder-to-shoulder bustle on the factory floor. Wearing nothing more ostentatious than a T-shirt, he regularly supervised his workers and frequently drove himself from building to building.

By staying close to his workers, Zhang cracked the whip of factory discipline himself. He directed his employees to follow an eight-character motto: "Pioneer, work hard, seek the truth, show devotion." Back then, Zhang had the simple aims of providing for his workers and becoming the world's premier maker of wood carvings. "As a Chinese saying goes, 'The water flows to the low ground and man moves to high ground'—I plan to be the world's king of carving," Zhang said in

June 1988 above the rapid tapping of scores of carvers turning rough blocks of wood into Buddhas, pagodas, bearded sages, and soaring phoenixes. Zhang claimed his fatherly concern for the carvers justified his vast fortune and lent his capitalistic ways a Communist aura. "I'm different from a capitalist because a capitalist puts profits in his own pockets. My factory principle is to bring success that will raise the welfare of my workers."

That was Zhang in 1988. In subsequent interviews, his attitude toward the initiatives of his "conglomerate with carving at its core" changed from bubbly enthusiasm to flick-of-the-hand dismissal. In the 1990s, Zhang spends less than sixty days a year in Yujiang. Under his new style of management, he leaves most issues in factory administration, including workers' welfare, up to hirelings. He no longer speaks about being the king of carving.

Through his new approach, Zhang betrays his shame over his modest background and his frustration that in China, as in many countries, money can buy only so much face. Like other tycoons, Zhang confronts public scorn because of the deep bias against wealthy businessmen instilled by both Confucius and Mao.

The dissatisfaction and pretentiousness of Zhang are typical of the nouveaux riches. There are more than 5,000 other millionaires throughout China, according to the official *Jiangsu Legal Newspaper* in Nanjing. Some 70 percent of these upstart vulgarians are illiterate or semiliterate, according to official figures. These *da kuan* (big bucks) flaunt their cash with a crude and comical ostentation.

Since Zhang first struck his fortune, his lifestyle has always had a plutocratic glint. He hunts for wild boar and pheasant in nearby hills and plays billiards in his penthouse. He sent his oldest child to Shanghai for schooling and owns eight cars. He asked the province for permission to purchase a helicopter and at one time owned several homes in cities throughout China decked out with the newest electronic hardware. He also planned to lay out his own golf course and acquire a jet. At first he indulged in his little excesses with a wide-eyed, gee-whiz innocence and endearing self-deprecation. But now he increasingly goes about such pastimes with a jaded air.

Zhang reveals his new haughtiness in subtle ways. Before Zhang quit smoking on May 1, 1992, he switched from Marlboros to 555s, an upscale British brand. He has put risers in his shoes. He has grown long nails on his little fingers that preclude carving and other manual labor; the nails have traditionally been a badge in China of affluence and leisure. He has started to collect antiques. And he has begun to slight people less traveled and wealthy than he. He expresses impatience with local officials from "a low cultural level" who walk through his factory gates uninvited for a visit and dinner.

The words of disgust from Zhang are just a trickle from his vast reservoir of resentment against officials. No matter how wealthy he becomes, he cannot get by without pleasing them. Zhang showed his enmity toward the arrogance characteristic of Chinese officials by swiftly punishing one of his key political backers, Ni Xiance. Ni was toppled as governor of Jiangxi Province in October 1986 on charges of corruption stemming from allegations of womanizing and graft. When Ni completed his two-year prison term, he stayed with Zhang in Yujiang for six months and then accepted a job at Zhang's office in Haikou, Hainan. Later, Zhang invested 8 million yuan in a trading company to be managed by Ni in Haikou. But Ni apparently felt he had lost face by accepting aid from someone who once came to him for support. In May 1992, Ni told the staff of Zhang's Hainan office that "if there were no Ni Xiance, there would be no Zhang Guoxi." A few days later, when Zhang learned of the slight, he quickly announced to his branch offices in a telephone conference May 21 the immediate dismissal of the former governor.

Zhang's painful dependence on officialdom is the first fact of his life to impress a visitor. At 6:00 every morning, the factory complex in Yujiang awakens to several loudspeakers blaring Beijing radio broadcasts of the national anthem and propaganda. Zhang built a large radio tower atop one of his buildings to reassure officials that his renegade capitalistic enterprise was firmly snared in the party's nationwide web of power and propaganda. Although it symbolizes Zhang's subservience to the party, the radio message also illustrates the glaring contradiction between the party's twisted ideology and Zhang's straightforward capitalist ways. The shrill broadcasts strike the many buildings of the thriving enterprise and bounce off. The echoing official words scramble into an incomprehensible cacophony. The daily din inadvertently proclaims the irrelevance, inanity, and antagonism in Beijing's message of one-party "market socialism" for dynamic entrepreneurs like Zhang.

Enterprising individuals such as Zhang have faced hostile officials ever since the creation of China's massive bureaucratic apparatus under the Han dynasty in 206 B.C. Private entrepreneurs have always been easy, defenseless whipping boys. They confront a bias written into the Confucian *Analects*, the basis for traditional education. According to this prejudice, Zhang and other millionaires are parasitic, leeching off of China's peasant-based society by not producing any goods themselves; they are uppity and acquisitive and flout the preferred values of hierarchy and conformity.

Moreover, China's rulers have always viewed entrepreneurs like Zhang as rivals for public resources and social dominance. In traditional times, China's gentry and local officials kept merchants under tight control, milking their ingenuity and income much as officials do to Zhang. Early regimes barred merchants from taking the exam in the Confucian classics required for entrance into officialdom. Merchants could enter the gentry through marriage or by purchasing land, and so they tended to be absorbed by the ruling gentry as landlords rather than to break away as independent commercial capitalists. In contrast, burghers in medieval Europe skirted the hold of the landed gentry by gathering in towns, and they derived power from ties to a new authority, the kings of national states.

When discussing Zhang, local cadres occasionally bristle with the ancient arrogance of mandarin officialdom. They are eager to show how he relies on their patronage. Jiangxi Province cadre Hua Tong said the state holds a share in Zhang's company based on a 1981 loan for 100,000 yuan. Zhang vehemently denied in 1988 that the loan entitled the state to any degree of ownership. He said he completely paid back the loan. Several years later he denied ever borrowing money from the state.

Because the party and state are supreme, many capitalists like Zhang have sprung from party and state ranks rather than from a throwback class of prerevolutionary capitalists. The tycoons have derived political power from business skill and riches instead of revolutionary ardor only; they have joined traditional party members who are distinguished by class background, ideological conviction, or contacts rather than wealth.

These emerging merchants and capitalists are as dependent on officialdom as their predecessors were in prerevolutionary China. Like those earlier magnates, they have not been able to build industrial and financial power free of government control and consequently must continually toady to their Communist patrons. "Entrepreneurs in China must be politicians; if they don't know how to be politic, they fail," said Zhang. The bob-and-weave with cadres is the biggest challenge in his business. He spends one out of every three working hours maintaining "a solid political foundation for the company," he said.

Many entrepreneurs stumble in China because of political ineptitude. An example is Bu Xinsheng, a much renowned shirt manufacturer whose clumsy handling of officials was fatal to his enterprise. In the early 1980s, Bu was hailed in the party newspaper *People's Daily* as a model entrepreneur. Because of his deft management of the Haiyan Shirt Factory in Zhejiang Province, Bu won more official adulation than any other entrepreneur under communism. But the praise went to Bu's head; he became aloof and refused to kowtow to officials. When he overreached himself by importing expensive foreign machinery, his enterprise faltered and officials at the local and provincial levels unseated him. Since then, Bu has vainly tried to recapture his former glory. He briefly managed a factory in Shanghai but quit after a dispute with his partners. He became the director of a shirt factory in Panjin, Liaoning Province, in June 1991.

Zhang believes Bu is paying a price for leaving his native area and shifting his political base. Zhang would never move his headquarters from Yujiang. "Jiangxi is my mountain stronghold," Zhang said. "In China the government runs business, but if an entrepreneur can play politics and stay in his native area, he can run the government." Again he draws a military analogy. "'A general who knows his enemy and himself will always be victorious,'" Zhang said, quoting Sun Tzu, the ancient military strategist.

For a while in the late 1980s it appeared that leaders of embattled private businesses would no longer have to engage in a rearguard struggle against officialdom. By the start of the prodemocracy movement in spring 1989, entrepreneurs had ridden the tide of official praise to a seemingly secure political footing. Many members of the vanguard of self-made tycoons fawned and scraped their way from Horatio Alger beginnings to the fringe of political distinction.

In Beijing a teenage, unemployed motorcycle rambler named Liu Xiang founded a motorcycle helmet workshop with some friends in the back room of a peasant's home in 1983. Within three years Liu had launched one of China's earliest joint ventures between a private enterprise and a foreign firm, and his Soar

Helmet Company captured 10 percent of the country's market for motorcycle helmets. Until the liberal struggle in 1989, he basked in the klieg lights of official adulation, winning a post in the Communist Youth League.

So, too, goes the story of Wan Runnan. In 1984 Wan emerged from a workshop in the back of a vegetable store with a design for a computer printer that quickly made him China's high-tech darling. Wan and his Stone Group Company joined with a Japanese firm to produce and market the printers in China. Profits soared, and amid much official fanfare Stone became the model of entrepreneurship and innovation for the country's fledgling high-tech industry.

At the height of reform the party considered opening its doors to millionaires who had not joined in their poor days as Zhang had. Members of China's upstart business class realized that they must work within the system if they wanted to work at all. Many applied to join the party but failed. For example, Li Xigui, a peasant millionaire who was once so poor that he had to sell his blood to a local hospital to get by, almost made party membership. He made solemn statements about Maoism and liberally sprinkled some of his $1.3 million fortune from a fleet of trucks used in various philanthropic projects. Still, his application was rejected. In the end only one tycoon came close to parlaying his fortune into party membership, according to official accounts. Xu Jizhu, the director of a metal factory with a $2.1 million fortune, was accepted on a probationary basis.

After the Beijing massacre the party turned a cold shoulder toward its wealthy suitors, calling them exploiters and criminals. The leadership demonstrated its inveterate disdain for individual gumption and the judicious hand of the free market by shutting down 800,000 private and collective enterprises that it deemed wasteful, redundant, incompetent, or merely unnecessary. The official press railed against private enterprises for evading taxes, engaging in illicit activities like selling pornography, and creating vast disparities in income. Party leader Jiang Zemin said in the party journal *Seeking Truth* that private businessmen had become too wealthy. They had stirred up unrest and were "ruining the atmosphere of society," he wrote soon after the massacre.

Tycoons like Zhang had to choose between condoning the carnage or fleeing overseas with as much of their riches as they could carry. Liu, the former motorcyclist, supported the gunning down of unarmed activists, although some of the victims were from the Flying Tigers, the Wild Goose Gang, and other bands of leather-clad Paul Reveres. Also, Liu began making helmets for the People's Armed Police. (During a fishing excursion several months after the massacre, Liu died when his fishing pole touched a high-tension wire.)

Along with many of his millionaire peers, Zhang chose to stand behind the party's old guard. "China is too poor and overpopulated; it needs stability before democracy," he said. As did many Chinese who publicly supported the massacre, Zhang hid his criticism of the crackdown in order to be left alone by the party.

In contrast, Wan, the high-tech entrepreneurial paragon, rallied to the cry for freedom and quickly fell from grace. Beijing labeled Stone Computer Company a "fighting fortress" for liberal dissent, condemning it for providing student leaders with tactical advice, money from abroad, and equipment ranging from portable telephones to trucks. Beijing accused Wan of seeking to overthrow the party, foster a capitalist system, and establish a "bourgeois, parliamentary democracy." Wan escaped into exile in Paris where he led the Federation for Democracy in China. Stone's profits plunged 31 percent in 1989, but in an unusually good sign for entrepreneurship and economic reform, they rebounded in subsequent years.

Zhang's willingness to endorse the official line helped him to survive the temporary comeback by hard-line Communists after the massacre. Still, his social and political standing declined because of the return of leftists dedicated to equal wealth for all, strict state control of the economy, class struggle, and other tattered banners of Maoism. The leftists sit mostly at the provincial level and above and rarely interfere directly in Zhang's business. But after the Beijing massacre they stirred up a campaign that compelled lower-level officials to treat Zhang's entrepreneurial initiatives like schemes in high treason. The low-level officials put many of Zhang's projects on ice for several months. "After the 1989 incident I felt like retiring, and if something like that happens again I'll go elsewhere," Zhang said.

By early 1992 Deng had succeeded in pushing market reforms ahead, and Zhang's entrepreneurship again won political sanction. Today, Zhang faces hostility mainly from officials who obstruct him in order to protect their powers. They recognize their growing dispensability in a vibrant, freewheeling market economy driven by individuals such as Zhang. These officials are active at the provincial level and below but are most numerous locally, he said. Overall, Zhang estimates that 70 percent of officials he faces are friendly. Most of the remaining cadres are aged and will not be in power much longer, but until then, Zhang will keep his wagons tightly circled.

Although Zhang owns every mallet and wood chip at the factory, he keeps a socialist "red cap" securely on his enterprise. He continues to register his company under the safe title of "collective" rather than apply the sticky label of "private enterprise." In order to preempt any official claim to his carving empire, Zhang denies he ever borrowed a cent from the state. Also, he has kept his son out of public view for fear some officials would use the breach of family planning regulations against him. Zhang, who also has three daughters, has long taken a firm stand in public for the strict one-child-per-family birth control policy. Moreover, for many years he refused to tell grasping Jiangxi tax officials the percentage of his revenues that come from abroad. Finally, if the going gets tough, he can always play his party membership card.

Although a junior high school dropout, Zhang could write the manual for capitalists determined to make enterprises free in a Communist country. He keeps officials off balance and pliant with tactics including flattery, feasting, subterfuge, philanthropy, appeasement, and intimidation.

As part of his cold war against party cadres, Zhang uses a soft kind of espionage. It is one of his most subtle but effective weapons. For several years he has supported a five-man network of lobbyists and intelligence gatherers in Shanghai and Nanchang, the provincial capital of Jiangxi. The part-time "agents" include the editor in chief of *Jiangxi Daily*. They inform Zhang of any change in official policy or attitude and, when necessary, try to sweeten the views of cadres toward him. Zhang also relies on many other sources for information. Without fail, his first question to a visitor from Beijing is about political trends in the capital.

While quietly gathering intelligence, Zhang loudly flaunts the lavish menus that win the minds of officials by subduing their stomachs. Banquets are as vital to the Guoxi Group as chisels and wood. With loud belly laughs, Zhang appears to enjoy the ludicrous task of reconciling his burgeoning personal riches with the Communist ideal of eliminating private property. Most days he regales officials at a large round table in the dining hall of his headquarters. Waving chopsticks above stacks of steaming platters, Zhang softens up his guests with a steady stream of jokes and rollicking self-mockery while ladling out stewed green snapping turtle, gray sea slug, stewed eel, and other prized and costly delicacies. When his guests are ruddy and glutted, Zhang finishes disarming them with offhand comments about the reach of his self-made, multinational conglomerate. Or he describes how he has laid low a former governor of Jiangxi and other top cadres. He tops off the feasts with enough premium cigarettes and French cognac to raise a beatific grin on the face of even the flintiest official.

As with food, Zhang doles out money in an effort to curb envy over his wealth and hostility toward his enterprising ways. He has given Yujiang County $2 million for a junior high school, an elementary school, an educational science center, roads, a broadcast tower, a bridge, and other oblations to "the people." In one much-heralded gesture, Zhang gave color televisions to fourteen retirement homes and a new set of clothes to every widow and widower in the county.

The Zhang Guoxi Bridge symbolizes Zhang's tacit principle that what is good for the people is good for him. For generations the city of Yujiang had ended at the banks of the White Pagoda River; only a few farming families lived on the other side. The farmers had crossed the swift, narrow river from their low-lying paddies to the city on a small pontoon bridge. After the completion of his bridge in July 1992, Zhang began building the twenty-five-acre Guoxi village on the far side of the river for 400 families employed by the Guoxi Group. The bridge has dramatically cut the travel time to Yingtan, the railway depot used by the carving company.

Officials as well as the public have clearly gained from the state-approved union of Midas with Marx. Zhang has brought running water to the 30,000 people in the Yujiang County seat. He has donated more than $400,000 for the construction of schools for training carvers throughout the area. And he has eliminated one of the biggest headaches of rural officials in China: "The problem of unemployment in Yujiang County is no more, thanks to Mr. Zhang," said deputy county leader Yang Dewang.

Content with Zhang's feasts and flattery, officials have cleared the path for him to fortune. Their support follows the slogan "To get rich is glorious," a 1980s ditty that is China's counterpart to "Greed is good." The officials have made Zhang's Yujiang operations a de facto "special economic zone," the name applied to the robust and comparatively unhindered enclaves on the coast. They have raised Zhang's quota on cars to eight, given him an extra allotment of electricity, leased land to him for factory construction at cheap rates, and exempted him from normal restrictions on foreign travel. In October 1991 the government granted Zhang freedom to recruit workers, a task once handled by the labor bureau. Zhang recruited five college graduates in 1992, expanding the core of managers who he says will make money for him during his company's third stage of development. Officials have also offered Zhang "great moral support," said county official Yang. They have summoned him more than twenty times before applauding councils to receive honorary titles like County Model Worker, Provincial Model Worker, and May Fourth Model Worker. The approbation reached cosmic heights in 1993 when the International Astronomy Union approved an application by the provincial government to name after Zhang an asteroid discovered by the China Zijinshan Observatory in Nanjing. The heavenly body is known simply as Zhang Guoxi Asteroid.

"My springtime of opportunity has come," Zhang said, fondly quoting an often repeated comment made to him by the governor of Jiangxi, Wu Guanzheng. "I'm no longer just Zhang Guoxi—I'm a symbol of reform. So it would be very difficult today for officials to remove and eliminate me; in fact, many of the officials who once publicly scorned my business now want to quit their official positions and work for me," he said with a grin.

The words of Governor Wu best illustrate that Zhang's riches are rivaled only by his political fortune. "Zhang is a Communist Party member with lofty ideals: He loves the party, loves the motherland, loves the people, and loves his native town; I hope officials at all levels learn from Zhang."

Despite his alacrity and skill in the sleight of hand of politics, Zhang has ruled out leaving his business for government. He positioned himself in 1988 to win a five-year term as a delegate to the National People's Congress, China's rubber-stamp parliament. But the post is merely a gilded fig-leaf for his naked capitalism. It commits him to no more than three weeks a year of perfunctory meetings in Beijing that ceremoniously approve the decisions of the party leadership. He won a second term in 1993.

At times, Zhang has felt tempted to seize a more substantial official post. After all, China's highly centralized government since ancient times has rewarded bureaucrats with wealth and leisure while tightly controlling entrepreneurs. The constant effort by bureaucrats to secure perquisites, rather than the search by entrepreneurs for business opportunities, has traditionally been the driving force for the economy. But Zhang believes the government's grip on business will ease completely in his lifetime. So when the party secretary in the nearby city of Yingtan offered him the full-time position of vice mayor in 1985, Zhang declined, saying his talent and best opportunity lay with business.

Zhang is quite content with being boss within his factory gates. After the Tiananmen massacre, party secretaries in many enterprises stepped up indoctrination and reasserted control over day-to-day factory affairs. The comeback of the factory ideologues was the latest episode in their long-standing, shifting rivalry with factory managers, who are concerned more with the bottom line than with dogma. But there is no such strife in Zhang's factory. Bursting into laughter, Zhang said, "Yes, we have a Communist Party secretary here: me!"

Zhang hopes that his successful entrepreneurship will ultimately free him from elaborate political maneuvering and the need constantly to flatter officials. He expects that Maoism and its rabid champions will gradually fade just as the hunger of peasant carvers in his native Yujiang County has eased. Each day he sees how private businesses like his own are steadily dismantling the economic foundation of orthodox communism. By the year 2000, private enterprises will produce goods with a total value equal to the output of state-owned businesses, according to the State Information Center, an official think tank. As Zhang and other entrepreneurs bring China unprecedented prosperity, the utopian ideal of communism is becoming increasingly irrelevant and passé.

But until Chinese completely slough off communism, Zhang will probably have more opportunities to emulate his vision of Iacocca and live up to his own motto, "Strive to be a real man." Indeed, Zhang suggests that perhaps Iacocca should adulate Zhang. "You know, when Iacocca was in trouble, the United States government bailed him out," he said, walking away from a deep gash in a pine wasteland where workers are building him an addition to his Yujiang complex. He wiped red soil from his hands. "But when I was in trouble, the government gave me more trouble."

The success of individuals like Zhang raises a thorny question for his country: Are such paddy-born tycoons satisfied? The answer might foreshadow the level of contentment and social stability awaiting the millions of Chinese mainlanders who are growing wealthier by the day.

Zhang and other business managers on the mainland have become more politically secure in their wheeling and dealing than ever before under communism. They have amassed wealth and realized many of their most fantastic dreams. But like their counterparts in rich countries, they have begun to learn that affluence and happiness do not always go hand in hand. So where will Zhang and his peers find happiness now?

Zhang is trying to answer the question on Shenzhen Bay, where he has built an $800,000 "holiday home." The three-story Spanish-style house overlooks a beach of dirty sand and a bay that at low tide turns into a vast mud flat dug by barefoot clammers from a nearby village. Far in the distance glare the lights and beacons from the scores of steel and glass skyscrapers of Hong Kong. The red glow on the horizon shimmers like the prosperity now within the grasp of millions of mainlanders in southern China. Zhang has moved his wife and four children from Yujiang to Hong Kong so that they can enjoy the opulence of the robust capitalist enclave. For him, the distant lights, like those shining from his broad veranda, symbolize the riches firmly in his hand.

Zhang shows off the Shenzhen house with his typical swashbuckler bearing. It is decorated in a hybrid of Italian baroque and Cantonese kitsch. Parquet woodwork in rich brown hues spreads across the floors to every corner. Chandeliers dangle like large globs of glass firing a rainbow, carnival dazzle. Heavy pleated fabric of plush red surrounds the windows in a buxom display. Gigantic specimens of finely detailed woodwork—phoenixes, dragons, and demure fleeing maidens—lunge and leap across tabletops and up the walls. As at Zhang's home in Yujiang, a television the size of a refrigerator performs a never-ending shout.

Outside, a patio overlooks a fountain, a row of manicured hedges, and lush, close-clipped grass. Off to the side, across a white marble wall, a marble dragon's head gapes from a marble bas-relief of two dragons bearing a pearl. The head of the mythical beast spews water into a swimming pool.

As Zhang rides a rising spiral of earning and buying, he seems to have grown more restless. Trips to rich countries and encounters with societies that promote self-absorption and self-gratification have shown him the narrowness and modesty of his rural beginnings. He betrays his shame over his mud-between-the-toes origins through the hazing of his Yujiang staff and the recent signs of pretension: antique collecting, long fingernails, the cutting remarks toward his less sophisticated neighbors in Yujiang. His disdain for Yujiang is clearest in the way he handles his money. In the 1970s he was inspired primarily by the goal of feeding his employees and improving their livelihood. Until the mid-1980s, he invested all his money in the Yujiang factory. Now, Zhang does not mention his workers when discussing his aims. He invests the majority of his profits overseas and unabashedly seeks to multiply his own wealth. Like many Chinese, Zhang is no longer engaged in a shared, collective struggle for subsistence. Rather, he is devoted to a selfish, adversarial grasp for riches.

Despite his turnabout in outlook, Zhang still defines happiness in terms of the performance of his company. "For about ten years, I've been very happy. My business has developed stably; every year I break new ground and so every year I'm happy."

Zhang admits that by centering his life around his business, he has been very lonely. He rarely spends time with his three daughters, son, and businesswoman wife. "I have been so busy I don't know how my three daughters have grown up. My wife is also busy at the enterprise and we can only meet several times a year; this I regret very deeply. Late at night, when I'm alone, what else can I think about but the enterprise? For many years, my enterprise has been my only companion in my dreams."

But Zhang's pursuit of wealth is not as shallow as it appears. By making a fortune, Zhang and millions of Chinese meet the vital Confucian obligations of educating and supporting offspring and bringing honor to one's ancestors. Zhang has sent his daughters to blue-ribbon schools in Hong Kong, and he plans to send his oldest daughter to a university in the United States. He pays whatever sum necessary for his children's education, clothes, and food. Moreover, he is teaching them the value of money. One daughter works in her spare time in a garment factory sewing belts on pants. Another works garnishing hamburgers at a McDonald's restaurant.

Money enables Zhang to meet a deeper and older family obligation. Since his youth Zhang has worked feverishly in an effort to make a fortune that would atone for the death of his mother. "My greatest regret is that my mother died early and I'm unable to fulfill my filial duty to care for her in her old age."

Every day Zhang feels a strong pull from his ancestors and traditional beliefs. When he thinks of his mother, he recalls the exemplary ways that children in Chinese fables fulfill their Confucian obligations. In one story a son lies naked on a pond in order to melt the ice and catch carp, his mother's favorite food. In another story, a man lies on his parents' bed before they sleep so that mosquitoes will glut themselves on his blood and not annoy his parents. The story that rings with the highest piety tells of an impoverished man who resolves to bury his three-year-old son alive in order to ensure enough food for his mother. As he digs the grave, however, heaven intervenes and he unearths a pot of gold.

Zhang could not make sacrifices for his parents in this life. But according to traditional beliefs, Zhang has made the spirits of his father and mother happy by amassing a fortune and guaranteeing the future security of his family. His maniacal work habits and hefty riches will ensure that members of his family never again go hungry and work themselves to death. "My wealth will be enough for ten generations!" Zhang declared, spreading his arms on the veranda of his holiday home as if to hold time itself.

Just outside his ancestral village of Mao Jia, Zhang in 1988 built four ornate tombs for his parents and adoptive parents. Constructed entirely of marble, the tranquil burial ground is worthy of the most pious Confucian son. The pure white edifices gleam against the dark red soil of an adjoining hill. A road from the village ends before a stone dwelling Zhang built for the graveyard attendant. Beyond that is a bridge crossing over a brook. It is flanked by a pond on one side and a large marble pavilion on the other side. The bridge leads to a tall *pailou*, an intricately carved gate with upswinging eaves. Beyond the gate stands a large tablet with carvings recording brief biographies of his mother, father, and adoptive father. On the far side of the tablet, built into the hill and shaded by a circle of trees, are the marble vaults for his deceased parents and one prepared for his adoptive mother. Zhang visits the tombs at least three times a year.

"I feel regret because my mother and father were unable to enjoy or share my success; to make up for it I have built them a resting place," Zhang said. In 1990 Zhang demonstrated the fullest measure of filial piety by fathering a son. According to Confucian principles, Zhang's heir is the crucial link between the family's venerated ancestors and its auspicious future.

Entering his home on Shenzhen Bay, Zhang immediately strides over to a broad sofa identical to the one in his Yujiang home. Stretched out on the soft Italian leather, grinning and chewing on the nipple of a bottle filled with milk, lies his son. Zhang bounces him once and displays him with twinkling eyes and a broad smile. Zhang said he will train the boy as his "successor."

❊

Zhang has found a measure of meaning and happiness by serving his family: his offspring in Hong Kong and elders in Yujiang. But he still anxiously looks elsewhere for greener paddies. As his power and wealth grow, so do people's envy toward him and his dispiriting awareness that he only has more to lose to a capricious government.

"The government should enact a law that somehow encourages people to say, 'I have lots of money, I am very rich,'" Zhang said, filling snifters to the brim with another round of Remy Martin. "A lot of people still don't dare to expose their wealth. The state allows them to get rich, but it has no laws to protect them so that they can openly say they're rich."

More than most of his compatriots, Zhang knows firsthand about the risks for a rich mainland capitalist investing in China and Hong Kong. Back in Yujiang during one of his soft-bribe banquets, in which he has flung open his larder and stood by as officials bolt his substance like cormorants, Zhang pulls a foreign visitor aside and whispers, "Could someone live comfortably in Los Angeles on $20 million?"

Although Zhang Guoxi sits atop a mountain of wealth that is exceptional in Communist China today, many Chinese scaled the same gilded peak before the Communists seized power in 1949. The early Chinese barons of industry, trade, and finance made their fortunes by dealing with foreign merchants in vibrant ports along the coast.

The Communist Party wrested the riches away from the cosmopolitan capitalists. It rounded up millions of wealthy Chinese, banishing them to destitute villages, sentencing them to hard labor in remote prison camps, or executing them by the truckload.

Emboldened by economic reform, Chinese in Shanghai, Tianjin, and other coastal cities are striving today to revive the luxury of the open and dynamic way of life in former colonial ports. As they pursue excitement and affluence, cosmopolites like Xu Cunyao are challenging the party's autocratic traditions and bureaucratic restraints on an outward-looking, free society.

Xu Cunyao   *Photo by James Tyson*

THREE

"Bad Element":
The Shanghai Cosmopolite

XU CUNYAO SAYS A LOT about himself by his smile. It proclaims his approach just as the broad and flashy chrome grilles heralded the 1930s Packards that bounded through the Shanghai of his childhood. It is a lust-for-life smile, an emblem for the jazzy culture, fiery ideas, strike-it-rich hustle, and caviar decadence of pre-Communist, cosmopolitan Shanghai. It is also ironic: Although the smile is real, the teeth are false. Xu lost many of his teeth, and nearly his life, during twenty-two years of imprisonment and official persecution. His smile is a sign of triumph for the worldly curiosity and independence of mind that Communist Party cadres tried to crush in him and other Chinese.

Today, "Harold," as he is known to his foreign friends, has much to smile about. Since the beginning of economic reform in 1978, he has parlayed fluency in a Western language, Shanghai individualism, and fascination with things foreign—all attributes the party once condemned—into lucrative work as a freelance interpreter. With his earnings, Harold has sent his daughter to the United States for graduate study. He has also begun to revive for his family the deluxe Shanghai lifestyle he was forced to give up some three decades ago.

Harold's smile and the verve and suffering behind it, tell the story of the economic boom, political bust, and recent revival of cosmopolitan Chinese under communism. Cosmopolites like Harold have suffered more than any other group for their openness to ideas and lifestyles from abroad. They embody the Communist Party's two bêtes noires: the bourgeoisie and anything foreign. They have long been leading targets for a virulently xenophobic party leadership. Yet during the period of economic reform begun in 1978, these mercantile-minded Chinese have clambered to a tentative footing in political acceptance. Now they show their compatriots the prosperity and excitement awaiting them down the twisting road from sleepy village footpaths to raucous city boulevards.

The story of Harold and his peers typifies the pain in China's struggle to modernize. Throughout his life, Harold has been whipped about by the conflicting crosscurrents of traditional and modern China. Only recently has he learned to finesse the cultural turbulence. From their years of hardship, Harold and other cosmopolites are discovering their own solution to one of China's most profound quandaries: how to preserve their ancient identity as Chinese in a modern industrial society. Confident of their identity and open to foreign influence, Harold and his peers are the vanguard in China's advance toward a cohesive, modern society.

Ironically, Harold was born into a family bound to the imperial traditions that have long hindered the rise of a modern China. His mother's side of the family claims to trace its lineage back to the eleventh son of a noble in the Zhou dynasty (1122–221 B.C.). Harold's paternal grandfather was a Qing dynasty (1644–1911) magistrate in Shandong Province. Like other imperial magistrates, he was the most powerful grassroots authority for the intrusive bureaucratic state. He controlled economic, political, and judicial activity at the local level. He gathered taxes in the towns and countryside and handled day-to-day administration. After the 1911 revolution, Harold's grandfather returned to his native Deqing County in Zhejiang Province. Although the imperial system was eradicated, its bureaucratic traditions remain deeply rooted and influential even today under Communist rule.

Harold's father, Xu Zhuru, stepped gingerly away from the imperial tradition. But he was yanked back by his uncle, his guardian and the president of what is known today as Zhejiang University. Xu was born the family heir in 1900, the first son of the first wife of the magistrate. He graduated from the university run by his uncle and entered a work-study program in electrical engineering with Siemens Corporation in Germany. There he fell in love with a German woman and asked his uncle to approve their engagement. His uncle forbade the relationship and Harold's father returned home alone.

Back in China, Harold's father fully yielded to tradition and married a well-connected woman. His bride, Shen Zaixiao, was related to the Chen family, one of the four leading families in the ruling Kuomintang Party. Her older brother was married to a sister of Chen Guofu, the governor of Jiangsu, and Chen Lifu, also a high-ranking official in the Kuomintang government. After the wedding, Harold's father was made an engineer for the long-distance telephone exchange of the comparatively rich coastal province of Jiangsu. Later, he became the director of Jiangsu's telephone exchange based in Zhenjiang, a city at the juncture of the Grand Canal and Chang River in Jiangsu.

Harold was born in Zhenjiang in 1936 as the turmoil in China from civil war and imperialism was swelling toward a painful climax. He was the first and only child of his parents. Soon after his birth, several years of Japanese aggression flared into full-scale war in July 1937 when Japanese troops seized the Marco Polo railway bridge near Beijing. Within a year Japan took control of Beijing, Tianjin, and all of eastern China, denying the Kuomintang the region's fertile farmland and industry. The Chen clan and the Kuomintang government withdrew far inland up the Yangtze River from Nanjing to safety in Chongqing. In a significant symbolic move, Harold's father took his family in the opposite direction, from Zhenjiang down the Yangtze toward the sea. Harold's father rejected the traditional rural China of peasants and mandarins for the modern urban China of factory workers, financiers, and traders. Acting on lingering cosmopolitan hankerings, he moved his family into a small apartment in the French Concession, one of two foreign enclaves in Shanghai. He no longer clung to the stability and comfort of officialdom deep in China's agricultural-based hinterland. Instead, he chose the risks and potential riches of entrepreneurship in the uproarious international metropolis of Shanghai.

For nearly a century, enterprising and educated Chinese migrants like Xu had found freedom from traditionalism in the foreign-run concessions of Shanghai. They escaped the repressive laws and mores of the bureaucratic Confucian establishment that had dominated the country for millennia. Firebrand students, rebellious writers, merchants, and other groups held in check by traditional China thrived in Shanghai. During its heyday, from 1919 until 1927, the new class of urban, nationalistic Chinese—businessmen, workers, and intellectuals—transformed the commercial port into a dynamic industrial city.

Shanghai became the most intellectually and culturally vibrant city in Asia with a lively movie industry, iconoclastic literature, and cutting-edge political groups, including some of the intellectual elite of the Chinese Communist Party. Shanghainese pitted new against old and Chinese against foreign more explosively than people anywhere else. They made Shanghai a city of grotesque superlatives: "the Paris of the Orient" and "the whore of the East"; "the city that never sleeps" and "a sink of iniquity." The cosmopolitan culture of Shanghai was open to a wide range of ideas and lifestyles that were inimical to the educated Confucian elite of traditional China. Shanghai cosmopolitanism swelled as a powerful force for modern China as the hidebound central government descended into disarray and civil war.

By the time the Xus arrived in 1937, Shanghai was both a robust entrepôt and a place of wild abandon. Although most of the hundreds of thousands of Chinese who poured into Shanghai before 1949 sought work, many also wanted a taste of the West and freedom from stiff Confucian mores. They flaunted their cultural rebelliousness by stepping out in daring fashions and strutting before the cafes, dress shops, nightclubs, and stylish department stores along Nanking Road, Joffre Road, and other bustling avenues. Young men like Harold's father, eager to break the purview of overbearing patriarchs in their well-to-do families, shed traditional robes buttoned to the Adam's apple in favor of trim double-breasted suits for business, trade, and speculation. Young women slipped out of the heavy courtyard gates of their homes and declared their intellectual, professional, and sexual freedom from straitjacket propriety by donning the cheongsam. The frock is tight around the neck like the traditional tunic for women, but in every other way it is a brash, come-hither siren. From the mandarin collar the dress does not give way to a loose bodice but clings to the body down to the hips, where it relents in slits baring the leg from thigh to toe.

Shanghai throve as the rest of China grew weak from internal chaos and foreign invasion. Foreign capitalists and Chinese go-getters gathered fortunes never before seen in China, often through raw exploitation. Foreigners enjoyed extraordinary privileges in Shanghai, where their unrestrained enclaves were immune to Chinese law. In Harold's time, the foreign community was made up of expatriates from some thirty countries. It was an unruly hodgepodge of desperadoes, opportunists, and refugees: White Russians fleeing Bolsheviks, Jews fleeing Nazis, liberal Japanese fleeing repressive militarists.

Foreigners in Shanghai built a grand facade of Western propriety to hide their incessant grasping. Their monumental pretense for colonial rectitude still stretches for several miles along the Bund, an avenue beside the Huangpu River. The buildings rise majestically in a neoclassic, gray granite paean to progress, constancy, and noblesse oblige. Beginning with the British consulate at one end, the former offices for the minions of the British Empire stand in stolid, columned glory: Jardine, Matheson, and Company, Butterfield and Swire, the Chartered Bank, and the Hong Kong and Shanghai Banking Corporation. Above all thrusts the pyramid top of the Cathay Hotel (now the Peace Hotel) built by Sir Victor Sassoon.

The Xus found that behind the facade of the Bund, foreign traders, financiers, and bureaucrats exploited the locals economically and carnally with far greater ease than they could their compatriots back home. As foreign vulgarians in the clubs along the Bund tongued caviar and sucked champagne, starving Chinese crawled right up to the pediments of the avenue's grand temples. Beggars from the famished and war-churned countryside, seeking their only hope of survival in the city, rearranged their rags in between pleas for a pittance from financiers stepping out after sipping pink gins at the 100-foot bar of the august Shanghai Club. The hirelings of the foreign-run municipality whisked away the most obnoxious eyesores. At sunrise each morning they patrolled the streets in trucks and collected the remains of paupers who had died of cold or hunger. In 1938, the year after Harold's family moved to Shanghai, the trucks hauled away 101,047 "exposed corpses," according to municipal statistics.

Foreigners did not always disregard the cheap lives of the natives; some found them especially gratifying. They made Shanghai a livelier priapic playground than any other city of the time. Like customers perusing the many delights in an ice cream shop, expatriates and well-to-do Chinese lingered in their selection at one of the port's factory-size brothels and paid on credit. Or they strolled Nanking Road and eyed the courtesans displayed on gliding rickshaws below auras of delicately strung colored lights.

Foreign and Chinese plutocrats also squeezed the pleasure of high profit from Shanghai's millions of needy. Foreign-owned textile mills and silk filatures voraciously consumed the superabundance of docile workers who flowed into Shanghai from the countryside. The laborers worked up to sixteen hours a day, seven days a week in earsplitting mills. The 200,000 workers, China's first sizable urban proletariat, could find no other work in the overpopulated and impoverished areas outside Shanghai. Their wage was often too meager to pay for even a dollop of rice, a bed in the city's teeming shacks or dovecote tenements, and clothing against the bitter winter fog that blows in from the East China Sea.

By the time Harold's family arrived in Shanghai, the "anything goes" credo that had energized Shanghai had become a social temblor jarring its foundations. Political conflict and lawlessness were shaking Shanghai apart. In 1937, one year before the Xus moved to the French Concession, Japanese troops seized all of Shanghai but its foreign-run areas. In an effort to compel the West into restraining Japan, Kuomintang warplanes returning from a bungled attack on Japanese warships dropped several bombs onto the Bund and other areas of the city. Hundreds of Westerners and Chinese were killed. The Western powers did nothing. The atrocity affirmed the shaky political authority of the city leadership and the flimsy commitment of the imperial powers to Shanghai. It emboldened the underworld, encouraging it to tamper more with the ramshackle machinery of political power.

Even before the bombing, "societies" of the Chinese underworld such as the Razor Clique and the Green Gang had become as blustery and brazen as the Casanova, Del Monte, and the other nightclubs they ran. Du Yuesheng, head of the Green Gang, rose to prominence in Shanghai society after Kuomintang leader Chiang Kai-shek mustered his mob for the execution of 12,000 alleged Communists in April 1927. Du personified the union of criminality and respectability in Shanghai. Under the tutelage of the notorious gangster Pockmarked Huang (Huang Jinrong), Du had orchestrated a cartel among opium dealers and bought off the foreign judiciary and the officials and police in the French Concession. Du and his henchmen, including the colorfully named Fiery Old Crow and Flowery Flag, thrived on the business of vice, running extortion, prostitution, gambling, smuggling, and gunrunning operations. After staging the mass execution of Communists in the "white terror" of 1927, Chiang (also a Green Gang member) decorated Du with the Order of the Brilliant Jade. He also made him chief of the Bureau of Opium Suppression.

While growing up, Harold was largely unaware of the beggars, streetwalkers, thugs, and other shadows of Shanghai. He was snugly insulated in the affluence of the mock-Tudor town houses and sycamore-lined streets in the French Concession. His concerns were personal; his first cosmopolitan encounter was a disaster. He entered an international kindergarten but the foreign students teased him and his parents withdrew him after just a few days. Later he attended the McTyeire School, an elementary school run by Methodist missionaries, and after that entered a spartan Catholic high school and college called St. Francis Xavier's run by Jesuit priests. There, disciplinarians wielding stinging rattan switches enforced a punctilious code of conduct that Harold still lives by today.

Harold acquired a taste for European refinement and modern comfort while growing up under his German-trained father in the walled, well-kept courtyards of the concession. His father always wore custom-tailored suits. He decorated his house with two sets of furniture and two grandfather clocks, all made in Germany. He acquired a General Electric refrigerator and listened to an RCA radio and phonograph. After World War II, Xu bought a brown leather bomber jacket for Harold, who wore the rakish symbol of foreign gallantry until he outgrew it in the early 1950s.

Harold and his family lived in a three-story house purchased by his father. Harold's great-uncle, the guardian to Harold's father, lived next door. When Harold was in grade school, his great-uncle gave him a copy of *Ivanhoe*, which in the Chinese translation was entitled *Heroes Surviving the Saxon Invasion*. The old man apparently hoped the book would inspire Harold to help cast out the Japanese invaders and rebuild China. He inscribed the book with the words "It is my hope that you will become an Ivanhoe of China."

As a schoolboy, Harold especially prized the precision and elegance of a Waterman fountain pen given to him by his father. It symbolized his father's erudition and taste, qualities he hoped to emulate. When the pen was stolen by a classmate, Harold feared telling his father. He felt he had dishonored his father's expectation of good taste and learning. So Harold borrowed money from the family amah and had the family rickshaw boy pull him downtown to a stationery store where he bought an identical model. The incident was symbolic. Harold for much of his life has tried to lead a cultivated life like his father and fulfill his filial obligations.

Although Harold's family aspired in many ways to be continental and modern, it still bowed to the traditional values of rural China. Xu frequently hung up his custom-made suits and donned long, traditional mandarin robes. From 1944 until 1947, Harold's great-uncle, a Buddhist, tutored Harold for six hours each week after school in the Confucian *Analects*, Tang dynasty (618–907) poetry, and other traditional literature. After Harold entered junior high school, Xu took him back to Deqing County to "sweep the grave" of Harold's grandfather during Qingming, the annual springtime festival of homage to ancestors. The Xus also regularly worshiped their forebears at home. Every year they observed an ancient Confucian ritual on Qingming and the birthdays of Harold's deceased grandparents. They arranged six chairs around three sides of a square table facing south in their parlor. On the table they burned joss sticks in a bronze pot surrounded by two burning candles and six wine glasses. Harold's father poured wine in the glasses, and the family kowtowed before the table. In a final symbolic offering to their ancestors, they burned paper money shaped like silver ingots on the patio.

By sending Harold to elite foreign schools and educating him in traditional values at home, Harold's parents sought to shield their son from the volatile economy and wanton ways of Shanghai. Although he was safe from the city behind the high gate of their house, Harold ultimately endured an ample share of misery.

Harold's father was bitterly resentful toward his wife because she wed him without informing him she had been married before. She grew up in a well-to-do family in Huzhou, Zhejiang Province, and graduated from a nearby teachers' college. When she came of age her parents arranged her marriage to a member of another prominent family in the area who was dying of tuberculosis. His parents clung to the old peasant belief that if he were married, he would be happier and luckier in his remaining days and the afterlife. Three months after the wedding, the young man died.

Harold's maternal grandparents did not disclose the earlier marriage when they arranged the betrothal of their daughter to Harold's father. In traditional China it was considered dishonorable for a woman to marry a second time. Such a woman had brought bad luck to her first husband and would do the same to her second husband. The matchmaker did not inform Xu's guardian of the earlier marriage until after the wedding of Harold's parents. The social sin poisoned the relationship between them with guilt and resentment.

Harold regularly escaped from his hard study, Confucian catechism, and the quarrels at home by slipping away to the Roxy, a large gilded and baroque cinema less than two blocks from his home. There, and at the Grand, the Majestic, and other movie theaters, he floated far away with the thrills and romance of Clark Gable, Rita Hayworth, Ingrid Bergman, and Vivien Leigh. He enjoyed Westerns and Tarzan films. But he most admired the hard-boiled persona of Humphrey Bogart; he was especially thrilled by *Casablanca*.

Xu's escape from home was his work. Argumentative and hot tempered around Mrs. Xu, he threw himself into speculation in securities, currencies, and gold. He was a lively, shrewd man, well suited to wheeling and dealing. Still, he had his share of bad setbacks. Harold once saw him slumped in a sofa at home, head in hands, weeping over a big loss as Mrs. Xu tried to comfort him. She apparently reinforced her sympathy with cold cash. Shen Baixian, her older brother who married into the powerful Chen clan, once came to the aid of Xu during a lean spell and enabled him to use public money for his business. Xu eventually played the markets cleverly enough to open an office above a tobacco shop in the International Settlement. On Saturdays, he took Harold to the office, which was outfitted with four large crank phones linked to the city securities exchange. He regaled Harold at a German restaurant for lunch and then returned to work.

Xu did not shrink from risks involving the highest stakes. As World War II neared a close, he mortgaged all his property and put everything he owned in comparatively worthless Hong Kong dollars issued by Japan during its occupation of the British colony. The Japanese currency was steadily losing value against Hong Kong dollars issued by Britain before the war. Flouting conventional wisdom, Xu reckoned that Britain would put social stability above all else and honor the Japanese scrip when it resumed control over Hong Kong and reissued its own Hong Kong dollars. He thrust the promise of penury or wealth on his family, making a classic "penthouse or pavement" gamble typical of pre-Communist, cosmopolitan Shanghai.

Xu calculated correctly and rode skyward on a tide of new riches. He bought a large four-story house in central Shanghai in the International Settlement. He built ten three-story rental houses on a lane across the Suzhou Creek on Tiantongan Road in Zhabei, a district administered by the Chinese. In late 1947, he moved his family into another three-story house he bought in the French Concession, one of four spacious homes with patios in a large walled compound. In a neighboring house lived the chief engineer of the British power plant in Shanghai. Next door lived the mistress of a wealthy Chinese. Harold slept and studied in an upper room of his home. He was fond of looking down from his window across the top of a broad shimmering swath of streetside greenery planted by the French and known as parasol trees. Before his father's financial gamble, Harold went to school in a rickshaw. Now he rode in a dark blue Studebaker sedan.

Xu discovered that his new fortune made possible old-fashioned vice. He had used his moderate riches to insulate Harold at home from blustery Shanghai, but greater wealth gave him the wherewithal for excesses that eventually ruined Harold's family life. When Harold was in the fourth grade, Mrs. Xu hired his schoolteacher as a live-in tutor in English, math, and other subjects. The young lady had attended but not finished studies at a missionary college in Shanghai. She was from Suzhou, a cultured city on the Grand Canal to the west of Shanghai known for the rockeries and limpid ponds in its many gardens. Suzhou was most famous for its ladies, said to be the most beautiful in China. Like men of means in traditional China who acquired concubines as a matter of course, Xu took the tutor as his mistress.

Tipped off to the affair by the maid, Harold's maternal grandparents made veiled, sarcastic remarks to the tutor. She moved out of the house in 1946 and into a lodging provided by Xu, who regularly left home on lengthy "business trips." The mistress eventually bore him four sons. Still, Xu was seemingly indecisive in his commitment to his second family. As victory by the Communists appeared certain, he remitted most of his savings to Hong Kong in early 1949. His mistress had persuaded him to move her and their sons to the British colony. Yet within a year he inexplicably dropped the plan and brought all his money back to Shanghai.

In an effort to mask his appearance as a rich landlord to the Communists, Xu sold his house in the French Concession in early 1949. He moved Harold and Mrs. Xu into the fourth floor of the large house in the International Settlement. Friends or family occupied the lower floors. Xu also stopped speculating.

The fall of Shanghai was so peaceful, however, that Xu's precautions seemed unnecessary. A few days before the Communists entered the city, Harold heard the rumble of artillery from the western outskirts of Shanghai but little else. When he awoke on May 25, 1949, he saw soldiers in the baggy, tattered uniforms of the People's Liberation Army sleeping on the sidewalks. They were strewn along the street as if a strong night wind had blown them from the countryside into the city before dawn. The still troops looked like weather-worn, pea-green bundles bound only with leather belts at the waist and puttees wrapped from the knee to the ankle. On the concrete next to each soldier lay a large, round, flat peasant hat made of woven wicker. The only touch of color was a small red star on their rumpled caps.

One afternoon, a few months after the Communists took over, Xu sat Mrs. Xu and Harold in the parlor of their fourth-floor apartment. "There is something I have to tell you; I have another woman outside," he said. Mrs. Xu had long known it, but the brazen declaration devastated her. Xu was tacitly assigning the care of his wife to Harold, who was then thirteen.

"I felt very, very deep resentment toward my father," Harold said.

After his father's announcement, Harold faced the constant quarreling of his parents at home and rising political tension in the streets. The peaceful "liberation" of Shanghai had misled many people about the Communists' ultimate repressive aims. Communist cadres, many of them from traditional peasant backgrounds, were beginning what would be several years of brutal campaigns against well-to-do cosmopolitans like the Xus. The antiforeign, anticapitalist diatribes especially hit "bourgeois" citizens who had taken up foreign ways or foreign friends. The cadres made Shanghai the main battleground for their political struggles, slapping the glittery face of the city in totalitarian gray. They executed black marketeers. In each neighborhood they formed "street committees," the party's grassroots network of surveillance. They unleashed fanatical students as sidewalk propagandists. Party "reeducation teams" fanned out to stage mandatory political indoctrination throughout the city. The cadres gathered material for the personal political file of each citizen. They turned the racetrack into a barracks and an exercise ground for the Communist Youth League. Buried in the dreary blizzard of Communist orthodoxy, bookstores discarded popular novels and featured the works of Mao and Lenin. Nightclubs and dance halls closed down. Shanghainese shelved their blithe, colorful fashions and donned the androgynous, olive-green uniform of Mao's proletariat.

Political tension in Shanghai intensified after North Korea invaded South Korea in June 1950. Beijing depicted the Korean conflict as an invasion of the north by the United States and its allies. It sent an army into North Korea that eventually exceeded 700,000 men. At home, Communist authorities launched the campaign to Resist America and Aid Korea, one of their first great efforts in mass mobilization after taking power. They lashed out against foreigners and Chinese having virtually any ties to the outside world. They ordered police to investigate and round up alleged spies. They seized objects like firearms and radio receivers and interrogated members of associations that had maintained contact with foreigners. They swept up all of society in the dragnet, including people involved in health care, culture, business, and religion. In Shanghai, the campaign drove a wedge between Chinese and their foreign associates. Communist cadres compelled Chinese employees at foreign-owned factories and businesses to denounce their bosses in mass rallies. They forced foreign businesses to sell out at ridiculously low prices and in December 1950 froze all remaining foreign assets. They imprisoned many leading foreign executives and, through physical and psychological abuse, induced them into confessions of espionage.

Foreigners were a safe and easy target for the new Communist government, even in worldly Shanghai. Chinese bristled from more than a century of abuse by foreign capitalists and militarists. For millennia they had considered themselves citizens of the Middle Kingdom, the cultural heart of the universe, and scorned other peoples as envious, barbaric outsiders. Communist propagandists sought to whip up political support in the 1950s, much as they do today, by tapping a deep well of popular xenophobia and resentment over a long litany of foreign crimes.

Beijing still regularly recalls the 1839–1842 Opium War, in which Britain forcibly broke China's opposition to the highly lucrative trade in opium that had enervated much of Chinese society. From the war Britain gained possession of Hong Kong and secured trading rights in five coastal cities, including Shanghai. Other foreign powers quickly joined Britain in carving up large chunks of maritime China. Beijing especially dwells on the brutality of its enemy in the 1937–1945 Sino-Japanese War. It regularly recalls for the public and Japanese diplomats the "rape of Nanking," an orgy of destruction and terror beginning in December 1937. Japanese troops marched into the city and over a seven-week period raped an estimated 20,000 women and killed more than 40,000 civilians and fugitive soldiers. Foreigners today continue their attempts to abuse and subjugate Chinese, according to the party leadership. Since ordering the massacre of unarmed prodemocracy protesters in Beijing in June 1989, the party has warned of a U.S.-led foreign conspiracy to induce the "peaceful evolution" of China toward capitalism and democracy.

By late 1950, the effort by party officials in Shanghai to whip up hatred toward foreigners was at a peak. Communist authorities had labeled the port as the prime beachhead for foreign abuse and exploitation in China. Tension of a different sort was also roiling the Xu household. Harold could no longer tolerate the constant bickering of his parents. He was delighted when an offer from the Foreign Ministry gave him an excuse to flee Shanghai. He leaped at the chance to study English at the ministry's Foreign Languages School in Beijing. Graduates from the school were working in North Korea as interpreters, and the government was desperately seeking to train more English speakers for the war effort. Harold enlisted his great-uncle in a successful effort to persuade his parents to let him go to Beijing. He left Shanghai for Beijing in December 1950 at the age of fourteen. Although he had been educated only through tenth grade, the government considered Harold a graduate of St. Xavier's. Also, because of hard study and the good tutoring by his father's mistress, he skipped a grade in the three-year English program in Beijing. He was graduated in December 1952.

Soon after Harold went to Beijing, his father left his mother. Xu moved with his mistress into a former dance hall in the French Concession, hoping to sustain the chic opulence of pre-Communist Shanghai. The large hall at the Piccadilly Apartments featured a richly polished parquet floor, broad windows, and a wide balcony in front. No longer allowed to speculate in stocks, currencies, and gold, Xu secured a position teaching electrical engineering at Tongji University through a recommendation by his brother. He was eventually made a full professor.

Xu learned in January 1952 that attempts to hold on to the high style of cosmopolitan Shanghai would be foolish, if not fatal. With most foreigners expelled from China and the conflict in Korea at an impasse, the Communist leadership turned its powers of propaganda and mass mobilization against bourgeois capitalists. Shanghai symbolized everything hateful to the peasant Communists. Although Communist leaders led by peasant-born Mao Zedong talked revolution, they showed the same hankering for intrusive bureaucracy and autocracy as their predecessors in the Kuomintang government and the Qing dynasty. Once in power, they too tried to repress the new force for modernism that had blossomed in Shanghai.

The Communists cleaned up Shanghai in many ways, wiping out prostitution, narcotics trafficking, and organized crime. They closed hundreds of sweatshops and removed beggars from the streets. But they did so using iron-fisted methods driven by an extreme ideological fervor. To them, Shanghai was a sump for sinful, plutocratic decadence with no sense of social justice and egalitarian decency. "Shanghai is a nonproductive city. It is a parasitic city. It is a criminal city. It is a refugee city. It is the paradise of adventurers," the party-run Shanghai newspaper *Economic Weekly* declared in August 1949.

Rao Shushi, head of the Shanghai Municipal Committee and one of China's most powerful leaders, pronounced that month that Shanghai had been "completely dependent on the imperialist economy for its existence and development." Rao embodied the traditional mind-set of inward-looking China that clashed with the modern, cosmopolitan spirit of the Xus and other Shanghai families. The veteran cadre proposed moving Shanghai residents into the hinterland, along with the city's factories and schools. As part of an effort to reinforce peasant values and the old rural-based, heavily bureaucratic economy, he sought to curtail severely the foreign economic relations of Shanghai, strengthen its transport links with the interior, and shift its production to goods only for internal use. The leadership considered coastal Shanghai peripheral to their scheme to emphasize trade with the Soviet Union and expand industry inland. The leaders disregarded the strengths of Shanghai: up-to-date industry, innovation, entrepreneurial vigor, enriching trade, openness to foreign ideas, individuality, creativity, and skepticism toward tradition. They saw in the modernism of Shanghai only the drawbacks of imperialism, exploitation, grotesque inequality, corruption, racism, and weak government.

Enmity toward Shanghai and all that it stood for reached to the pinnacle of party power. Mao flaunted his hostility toward families with a long tradition of refinement and erudition like the Xus. He noted that many emperors were illiterate and gloated that some of his most skillful generals were peasants who had never set foot in school. The party leadership for decades wore Shanghai down. It tapped Shanghai for capital and know-how to build industry. The party moved more than 1 million university graduates, technicians, and skilled laborers to factories and scientific projects in other parts of the country. It also seized Shanghai's coffers, making the port the prime source for central government revenues for more than thirty years.

The party was ironically emulating previous regimes by both chiding and leeching off of cosmopolitan Shanghai. Imperial officials and the Kuomintang leadership had also followed a two-pronged policy of condemning and squeezing independent merchants, bankers, and businessmen like those in Shanghai. Most notably, Chiang Kai-shek used $10 million offered by Shanghai bankers and industrialists in April 1927 to fund the slaughter of 12,000 alleged Communists and tighten his grip on Shanghai and the Kuomintang. Within a matter of weeks, however, Chiang broke the alliance and terrorized his wealthy supporters in order to obtain $30 million to pay his troops and fund his Northern Expedition (1926–1928), a military campaign to unify China under the Kuomintang. Chiang unleashed the Green Gang and extorted money from the "national bourgeoisie" by ordering the kidnap or arrest of wealthy Shanghainese and their children. The abuse by Chiang of the most vigorous force in the economy marked a return to the imperial tradition of "bureaucratic capitalism" and the end of what Shanghai capitalists considered their golden years. Officials and capitalists closely aligned with the government began to dominate industry, trade, and finance. In short, the coup by Chiang was a triumph of traditional autocratic China over the callow force for modern cosmopolitan China epitomized by Shanghai.

The Communists went far beyond imperial and Nationalist officials in cracking down on business and cosmopolitan culture. In 1952 the party launched the Five-Anti Campaign, a mass movement to wipe out "bribery, tax evasion, theft of state property, cheating on government contracts, and stealing of state economic information." Behind the guise of law enforcement, the party waged a bitter class war against businessmen, industrialists, and anyone who represented the capitalist class. It used many of the same techniques of castigation employed in its rout of foreigners the previous year. It thrust businessmen before large crowds where they were forced to criticize themselves and admit to illegalities. Meetings between workers and their bosses thereafter became routine. The party also induced capitalists to denounce one another. It forced them to sell out their businesses at absurdly low prices, pay tremendously high back taxes and fines, or simply hand over their property. Cadres examined and criticized some 70,000 businessmen and sent thousands to labor camps. Many of the humiliated and terrorized capitalists took their own lives. The granite buildings on the Bund, once symbols for the confidence and promise of free trade and industry, became the preferred jumping point for suicidal capitalists. For weeks wary pedestrians left the sidewalks on the Bund to the depressed rich and walked in the gutter instead. The party had made it clear it would no longer tolerate capitalism, the cause of great inequality but also of robust economic growth.

As the party enforced the puritanical values of traditional China and smashed foreigners and capitalists, its government enlisted Harold, a paragon for the forward-looking, moneyed class of "modern China." Although natty in appearance and breezy in spirit, Harold flourished in the foreign service in Beijing, the ancient center for the stodgy values and administration of traditional China. The government tolerated Harold because it needed his expertise. The Foreign Ministry assigned him in December 1952 to the section in the protocol department that handled capitalist countries.

Soon after Harold joined the ministry, Han Xu, chief of the protocol department's section handling the Soviet Union and East European countries, took him to observe a routine photo session for Mao and a new ambassador. (Han later served as ambassador to the United States from 1985 until 1989.) Harold and Han watched from the corridor as Mao accepted the emissary's credentials.

"How fortunate you are. You are just seventeen and yet you've seen Chairman Mao at close quarters," Han said to Harold after the brief ceremony. Wide-eyed and excited, Harold agreed. The party had not yet built the personality cult around Mao. Still, to most Chinese, the chairman was without blemish, a leader considered peerless for his campaign against Japan and revolutionary victory on the mainland.

Harold worked at a feverish pace as he made arrangements for diplomats from capitalist embassies. He would set up meetings between incoming ambassadors and the foreign minister and Mao. He arranged the courtesy calls for new ambassadors, helped out in interpretation, planned official dinners, and set up visits of other foreign dignitaries. Harold was selected in 1954 as one of Mao's interpreters when the chairman met with English-speaking ambassadors. He interpreted for

Mao when ambassadors from Burma, Denmark, Finland, India, Indonesia, Nepal, Sweden, and Switzerland presented their credentials. In one of Harold's proudest moments at the ministry, Mao addressed him after he had interpreted for a women's delegation from India. The Great Helmsman shook the hands of the Indian visitors, took Harold's hand, looked him in the eye, and said in his heavy Hunan accent, *"Ye xie-xie ni le."* ("And thank you, too.")

Harold was assigned to interpret for Mao at a small dinner party given by the Indian ambassador in 1956. It was the first time Mao had accepted such an invitation by an embassy from a capitalist country, and the Indians decked out their mission to entertain their guest. After dinner and a movie, Harold walked downstairs at Mao's side toward the front door. Mao suddenly stopped in the middle of the vestibule and turned completely around in his characteristically slow and shambling way. Harold, the Indian ambassador, and his wife looked on perplexed. Mao's aide-de-camp whispered something to the Great Helmsman. Then the face of the ambassador's wife lit up and she told Harold to ask Mao a question. *"Zhuxi zhao cesuo?"* Harold said. ("Is the chairman looking for a toilet?") Mao quietly grunted.

Not long after the dinner with Mao, Harold was summoned to interpret for Premier Zhou Enlai in a meeting with the Burmese ambassador at the offices of the State Council. Zhou arrived well before the ambassador, sat down, and chatted with Harold for about eight minutes. Focusing immediately on matters of the heart, he asked Harold where his mother lived, what hobbies she liked, and similar questions. When Zhou learned she lived alone, he said the Foreign Ministry should help Harold find her a place to live in Beijing. The brief encounter made a deep impression on Harold.

Mao's awkwardness and Zhou's warm, cheerful poise were particularly striking to Harold. The incident with Mao typified the bumbling, rough manner of the country's peasant leaders. The charismatic, politically skilled chairman seemed to embody the earthy traditionalism that repressed the modernism of Shanghai. In contrast, Harold found Zhou—the urbane, sophisticated, and subtle premier—the direct opposite to Mao. Mao grew up in a peasant family in landlocked Hunan Province and flaunted his ribaldry and humble background. Zhou was born to a comparatively prosperous family in coastal Jiangsu Province and showed a refinement rare among the party leadership. He was the most modern of party leaders: comparatively tolerant of different viewpoints, comfortable and open toward foreigers and their ideas, and adept at reconciling Chinese traditions with foreign and city ways.

Harold speaks fondly of Zhou today. The late premier and foreign minister is the only member of the party's old guard who is unblemished by folly and brutality, although some criticize his alleged subservience to Mao. He is widely venerated for his gentle manner and efforts to moderate Mao's most violent excesses during the Cultural Revolution. A compassionate comment by Zhou later helped Harold return to Beijing and end several years of banishment in the countryside.

Encouraged by Zhou's refined ways, Harold displayed his Shanghai panache despite the nationwide campaign against bourgeois capitalists. He boasts of several sartorial firsts in China's postrevolutionary diplomacy. He was one of the first protocol officers to hang up the Mao jacket and wear Western suits. He said he was the first diplomat to wear oxford shoes from Shanghai ("everyone else wore wing tips") and a sport coat (a bold plaid jacket, "not at work but at parties or informal meetings with foreign diplomats"). Harold had old suits of his father and even the standard cotton-padded winter jacket altered to a dapper fit. He carefully coordinated the color of his shoes and tie.

"You are so well tailored!" the counselor at the Indian Embassy once exclaimed to Harold, much to his delight. Eventually, however, a dangerous mix of fondness for fashion and youthful indiscretion got the better of him.

During a trip by Zhou and Marshal He Long to India, Burma, and Pakistan from November 28 until December 30, 1956, Harold was assigned to handle the delegation's funds. When instructed by Han Xu, his supervisor, Harold tipped the Indian staff at the presidential palace. But the combination of a fat purse and New Delhi's bourgeois delights was too overpowering for a twenty-two-year-old Shanghainese just sprung from years in rigid Beijing. There was no way for Harold or other members of the delegation to convert yuan into rupees. So during time off, without telling his colleagues, Harold used the "people's money" to go to a theater and see a Sherlock Holmes movie, *Twenty-three Paces Back to Baker Street*. He bought two sets of Camel brand playing cards for poker. For his girlfriend in the ministry, he climaxed his spree with the purchase of lipsticks and pairs of stockings. Han discovered Harold's indiscretion when a palace official thanked him by letter and noted the amount of the tips. Some 500 rupees were missing. Han did not question Harold for fear he would defect.

"How about a game of bridge? I have cards," Harold innocently said to his colleagues when they stopped over for a night in Kunming on their way back to Beijing following a second mission by Zhou to India in late January. Harold brought out his new cards. He intended to reimburse the purse after returning to Beijing. But the cards confirmed to Han that Harold had misused public funds.

Harold was called before the desk chief of the protocol department on February 16, two days after their return to Beijing. He immediately confessed and made assurances that he intended to repay the money. Still, they questioned him for two weeks, first about the trip and then about his relations with foreigners. The desk chief made an example of Harold. He was interrogated, forced to make self-criticism, and "struggled against" at three sessions mandatory for every protocol officer. His friends turned away from him. His girlfriend broke off their relationship.

In addition to the charge of misappropriation of public funds, the interrogators accused Harold of "abnormal relationships with foreigners." They noted that the Norwegian chargé d'affaires had routinely sent Harold newspaper clippings about bridge. They recounted that at a diplomatic gathering the wife of the Indian ambassador once called Harold her "adopted son"; he replied that she was his "adopted mother." They recalled that during a party at the Beijing Hotel in 1956 hosted by Premier Zhou for Prince Norodom Sihanouk of Cambodia, Harold had asked Princess Sihanouk to dance and gaily whisked her across the dance floor. They asked him details about his acquaintance with the Indonesian ambassador.

In New Delhi during a state visit by Premier Zhou Enlai in December 1956. In the foreground, from left: Marshal He Long; Han Xu, then assistant director of the Foreign Ministry's protocol department and later ambassador to the United States from 1985 until 1989; and Harold Xu. Zhou is seated at the table in the rear at extreme right, Jawaharlal Nehru is clad in white, Indira Gandhi is seated at the extreme left.

The ambassador had asked Harold to the embassy for a private dinner in 1955, but his superiors in the ministry ordered Harold to decline the invitation. When it was renewed, Harold was granted permission, and the ambassador over dinner passed along important details about Indonesia's stand on the issue of dual nationality. The ambassador had been reluctant to raise the subject directly with the deputy foreign minister.

Such affability with foreign capitalists was bold, if not impudent, at a time when the party was lashing out at both foreigners and capitalists. In retrospect, Harold acknowledges today that there were other facets of his lifestyle that smacked of a bourgeois attachment to the capitalist ways of old Shanghai. He smoked the upscale, imported cigarette 555 from a tin. Although most of his colleagues did their own washing in the spirit of Maoist self-reliance, Harold sent his clothes and handkerchiefs out to a laundry so that they were spotless and crisp.

Harold's interrogators became loud and rabid. Harold answered all the questions in the naive belief that complete openness would bring him lenience. He disclosed details of his contacts with foreigners that raised a far more serious charge than the one that had prompted the grillings. He told his questioners that before leaving on the recent trip to the Asian subcontinent, he had divulged

Premier Zhou Enlai, the Chinese delegation, and their Pakistani hosts leave a mosque in Lahore, Pakistan, in December 1956 during a state visit by Zhou. Zhou is in the foreground to the extreme left. Marshall He Long is third from right, clad in a black suit. Harold Xu, second from right, is the only member of the Chinese delegation wearing a western suit and tie.

Zhou's full itinerary to a Pakistani diplomat, the Indian ambassador, and the British chargé d'affaires. He admitted that he had once told the second secretary of the Pakistani Embassy about a coming visit by a Laotian leader before it had been officially disclosed. He had also described to the Pakistani the administrative structure of the Foreign Ministry.

The questioners were most interested in his confession that in 1956 he had disregarded the decision of a deputy foreign minister. As the date of Zhou's trip approached, the wife of the Indian ambassador asked Harold about Premier Zhou's living habits and preference in food, colors, and other petty matters. Harold asked his superiors if he should reveal such details. The deputy foreign minister told him not to. Yet Harold felt the facts were trifling, and he did not want to lose face before the ambassador's wife. So he told her all: Zhou's favorite color was crimson; his favorite food was the large "lion's head" meatballs of his native Jiangsu Province; he worked until 2 A.M. and rose at 10 A.M.; he used a Chinese calligraphy brush and pencils and spurned fountain pens and ballpoint pens. He also told her the color and size of Zhou's desk and how it was arranged. Harold's interrogators labeled such details "state secrets."

The interrogations ended after about two weeks. Harold was required to write a detailed confession. He awaited punishment for nearly a month, still receiving his sizable monthly salary of 70 yuan and living in the ministry's dormitory. Then on April 27 Harold was summoned to the office of the deputy chief of protocol at 10 A.M. and told that the ministry had handed his case over to the People's Procuratorate, or the state prosecutor. "I want to emphasize that the aim of the Foreign Ministry is still to reeducate you," the deputy foreign minister said. "We will 'cure the sickness in order to save the patient,'" he added, reciting an old saw.

"Fine, I will remain in the ministry and when the court summons me, I will obey the summons," Harold said stoically. But before Harold finished speaking, a man and a woman from the People's Procuratorate entered the office. They immediately asked him his name, age, and place of birth. They did not raise details of the case but handed him a warrant for his arrest. "Xu is likely to try to escape; he will be taken into custody," the warrant read.

Harold signed the document. As the prosecutors handcuffed him, he asked that they not inform his mother, but they did not reply. They hustled him out the main entrance of the ministry in a parade planned by the chief of protocol. It was close to noon, and many diplomats on their way to lunch stopped to watch Harold as he was led away. Harold hung his head and vainly tried to hide the handcuffs within his sleeves as he was bundled into the backseat of a green military jeep flying a red flag.

Harold was put in a temporary house of detention. Guards took away his belt, shoelaces, and spectacles and gave him a wooden tag on a necklace with the number 577. He was told he should forget his surname and refer to himself only as 577. He was put in a large cell with some twenty thieves and other common criminals and briefly interrogated twice during the ten weeks in detention.

In June Harold received a letter from his father informing him that his mother had killed herself. In the years since Xu had moved in with his mistress, Harold's mother had increasingly put her hopes for security and affection in her son. She had cherished a photograph of Harold interpreting for Mao in a meeting with the Indian ambassador. She had frequently said Harold had brought great honor to the family. "I was her only hope," Harold said.

When Beijing officials informed her of the arrest, she became insane with grief. Her sister took her in and cared for her. One day when Xu visited Harold's aunt to discuss how to handle the arrest, Mrs. Xu leaped from a third-floor window of the town house.

Harold was devastated by the news and silently wept in the cell. He felt responsible for her suicide. Superstitious family acquaintances in Shanghai, expressing an old prejudice against widows who marry a second time, said that Harold was the reincarnation of his mother's first husband who had returned to avenge her decision to marry again. Harold still feels guilty for not fulfilling his filial duties and caring for his mother in Shanghai. He had visited her only once between 1952 and 1957 during a trip to Shanghai for the ministry. He had been offered only three days off a year. He feels he neglected her and failed to ensure that she was comfortable and happy. "She sacrificed her whole life for me, but I only crushed her fond dreams."

Not long after receiving the letter, Harold was moved to the Beijing Number 1 Prison, which today is China's showcase penitentiary. The prison was more comfortable than the detention house. He shared a cell with ten inmates. It was cleaner and he could watch movies or operas and musical performances staged by the prisoners. He spent most of his time in the cell studying Marxism and Maoism or making matchboxes. Shortly after his arrival at the jail, a prosecutor picked him up and drove him to his office for a talk. "Your *danwei* [place of work] still has hope for you and wants you to remember English. We hope you will repent," the prosecutor told Harold. "You'll most likely be sentenced to two years. After your sentencing you'll receive English books for study."

Soon after the meeting, however, Harold for the first time fell victim to a political campaign. At the end of June, Mao abruptly halted a brief period of openness called the Hundred Flowers movement, in which he had called for the "blooming of a hundred flowers and the contending of a hundred schools of thought." He swiftly cracked down on intellectuals and officials who had criticized the party in what was called an "antirightist campaign." By the end of the year the party had branded some 300,000 intellectuals as rightists. It sent many of them to jail or labor camps. Those deemed less threatening were banished to the countryside. Many gifted youths never regained their urban residence and saw their talents go to waste.

Harold learned of the campaign from editorials in the party newspaper *People's Daily* and from whispers among the inmates that "prices were quickly rising," a slang phrase for a stiffening of sentences. The attack on rightists triggered harsher treatment of all people the party considered criminal. When Harold met a pickpocket who was given a five-year term instead of the usual two-year sentence, he prepared himself for harsh punishment.

Harold went to trial in October at the Intermediate People's Court in Beijing on charges of misappropriation of public funds and revealing state secrets. He faced the judge, a secretary, and two "people's assessors." He was denied a lawyer for his defense, and no one from the ministry attended. The trial lasted less than two hours because Harold had fully confessed in writing.

"The party and government have trained and educated you and you did not live up to their expectations. Do you feel guilty?" an assessor asked.

"I do feel guilty; the party and government educated me and put high hopes in me," Harold replied. He was bundled back to prison.

The following month Harold was taken back to the court for sentencing. At the end of the fifteen-minute hearing the judge read a statement that ended with a sentence of ten years. Harold cocked his head and thought, "Oh, ten years in prison?" He was not disturbed; he was prepared for worse. "By the time I get out I'll still be young; I'll just be thirty-two," Harold thought. He was much younger than his erstwhile colleagues at the ministry, and he had always considered youth to be one of his best advantages. He naively believed he would emerge from jail and still have much to look forward to in his career and life.

The next month, as the cutting winter wind from the Gobi Desert began to lash Beijing, Harold was suddenly overwhelmed by a realization of coming misery.

Late one night public security police handcuffed Harold and herded him with hundreds of prisoners from the Beijing Number 1 Prison and other jails into open trucks. Standing packed together against the frigid wind, they were driven in a convoy through the dark and empty streets to the Beijing railway station. There they were told their permits to live in Beijing were canceled and they were being taken far northeast to Promoting Victory Lake (Xingkai Hu) labor camp in Manchuria on the Soviet border. Harold realized that, like all but a small minority of convicts, he was likely to remain within the vast system of labor camps for the rest of his life. When his term expired, he would be retained as a *jiuyerenyuan* (prison employee) and be considered a second-class citizen. He could live outside the prison walls, but he would have to remain in the desolate areas surrounding the labor camps and continue in backbreaking toil. "Everyone knew that we would probably never see Beijing again or even leave the labor camp; we were all very, very depressed," Harold said.

Harold and the other prisoners shuffled onto a train reserved for them. As the metal brakes of the carriages released with a crash and the train slowly chuffed out of the station, Harold recalled a Tang dynasty (618–907) poem that his great-uncle had him memorize as a youth in Shanghai. "Seeing Yuan the Second Off on a Mission to Anxi" is a farewell written by poet Wang Wei to a friend leaving China proper for Central Asia and areas considered barbaric.

> *A morning shower in Weicheng has settled the light dust;*
> *The willows by the hostel are fresh and green;*
> *Come, drink one more cup of wine,*
> *West of the pass you will meet no more old friends.*

Huddled in the dark, cold carriage, Harold yearned for a warm farewell from friends and the implicit promise of eventual return and reunion. Yet he had never really belonged in tradition-bound Beijing. The Communist capital was not ready for modern cosmopolites from a place like Shanghai, a tumultuous port open to change, foreigners, and the sea.

Even today Beijing is largely a somber city of ancient walls erected to resist change, protect the past, and keep out foreigners and their ideas. Indeed, Beijing was a wall before it was a city, a rampart defending the Yellow River civilization from invaders storming down from the steppes. Throughout history, the city barriers often hid ossification within before they fell to Mongol, Manchu, European, and Japanese conquerers. The walls are a reminder of China's long history of highly centralized rule and so help explain why the Communist leadership governs with an iron fist. They symbolize the authoritarian political traditions that, like the hard casing of a bomb, intensified the explosive cry for democratic reform in the Beijing Spring of 1989. The walls even today frame the core of China's stodgy ruling elite. These hidebound Communist reactionaries loathe the skepticism, individualism, liberalism, openness, and sheer joie de vivre of Harold and other cosmopolitans from the coast. They still uphold facets of traditionalism over the force of modernism personified by Harold.

Harold was one of countless intellectuals whom central authorities have punished over the centuries for upholding challenging, unorthodox views. Through banishment to a remote and desolate region, Harold suffered what has traditionally been one of the milder punishments for political outcasts. His fellow convicts were a motley group of people the party considered criminal: counterrevolutionaries and rightists as well as murderers, rapists, burglars, embezzlers, and arsonists.

After a journey to the northeast of more than 900 miles, Harold and his fellow convicts stepped onto a frigid landscape of stark black and white. A dense shroud of clouds blended into the snow. The only break in the limitless white was the faint gray outline ahead of distant Promoting Victory Lake and, behind, the black railway tracks that had led Harold away from civilization. Harold and the other convicts wore the standard outfit then for workers in labor camps run by the Beijing Public Security Bureau: a black cotton-padded jacket and pants, black boots with rubber soles and rubber and canvas uppers, and a hat with earflaps made of dog fur. Soon after the inmates arrived, guards gave each of them a thick vest of goat skin with fur at least three inches long.

Harold was assigned to Branch Number 2, one of at least six subdivisions at the camp. The branch was divided into seven teams. Each team was sheltered in four or five crude barracks holding about fifty prisoners each. A tall barbwire fence interspersed with guard towers surrounded the barracks, a cookhouse, a medical clinic, a small store, and offices for the camp officials. To construct the barracks, inmates had earlier driven wooden stakes into the ground, woven grass between the stakes, applied mud to the grass, and laid a thatched roof. The central doorway on the barracks led to a room on either side. A narrow aisle ran the length of the room between long sleeping platforms (*kang*). The inmates slept on grass mats jammed together shoulder-to-shoulder on the *kang*, which were heated from below in the winter. They used grass as a vital source of warmth: an insulator and absorber of moisture for their boots and fuel for stoves and the *kang*.

Harold and the other inmates ate in the barracks. At the start of mealtime they sat with legs crossed on the *kang* where they slept, facing the aisle and holding bowls no wider than tea saucers before them with both hands. An inmate entered the barracks, walked down the aisle with a bucket of corn porridge, and slopped it into the bowls with a ladle. Another inmate handed out *wotou* (steamed buns made of corn flour). A third inmate doled out a small portion of vegetables. When Harold first arrived at the camp, inmates could eat corn porridge and corn buns until they were full. Every fifteen days they were given a ladleful of pork, vegetables, and noodles made from the starch of either beans or sweet potatoes. On National Day, Spring Festival, and other holidays, they ate a meal of pork with rice, pork dumplings, and *mantou* (steamed wheat buns).

"Initially, eating was the big event; our only comfort was food," Harold said, smiling even today over the sheer pleasure of a full stomach. Food offered a brief respite from the pains of a desolate, brutal labor camp. "During some Spring Festivals we ate pork dumplings. It was a great luxury, and the joy would last for more than a week."

After breakfast, just as the sky was brightening, Harold and the other inmates lined up to sound off their numbers in roll call. Then they shouldered pickaxes and shovels and set out under guard in the snow. Each team was directed by a Public Security officer with two to four deputies and a "technician," a former convict retained as an employee. After a long march into the grasslands they began digging irrigation ditches in the frozen black earth. They worked ten hours each day. In the evening the camp officers mustered them again to upbraid recalcitrant inmates, lecture about discipline, and review the plans for ditch digging and agricultural production. The hard routine wore on without a day for rest. In May, when the frost gave way, inmates considered trustworthy by the wardens began sowing grain. They lived in makeshift shelters in the fields, raising primarily rice but also wheat, corn, and soybeans. Harold and most of the other inmates continued to dig and maintain the irrigation ditches.

Harold was one of about 10 million inmates in an archipelago of prisons and labor camps sweeping across China. The number of convicts did not begin to decline until the death of Mao in 1976 and the easing of social regimentation in the late 1970s. It stood at an estimated 3 million to 5 million convicts in the early 1990s. During the period of economic reform, prison officials have continued to systematically exploit this vast pool of cheap laborers by developing lucrative export industries in the labor camps and jails.

In late winter of 1958, just a few months after Harold arrived, officials at the labor camp informed the inmates that they no longer could eat their fill of steamed corn buns but would have to ration food among themselves. Harold and his fellow prisoners met and each estimated the amount of staple food he would need in a month. Unlike inmates who had worked in fields or factories, Harold had no idea how much grain he needed. Since his affluent childhood he had always lived well beyond subsistence and had never had to count the grains in his rice bowl. He figured his ration should be on the low side because he was short and slight. So he arbitrarily estimated he needed thirty-five pounds of grain a month. The other inmates did not correct Harold; a small ration for him meant a larger ration for them. Many of them signed on for sixty-six pounds a month, nearly twice the allotment for Harold.

On the day rationing began, the camp officers told the inmates they would march two miles into the grasslands to dig irrigation channels. They would not return to the camp until after sunset, so each of them wrapped up his lunch in a small bag. All the convicts but Harold received a slice of salted turnip and three corn buns. He was given no turnip and just two buns. It was especially cold that day, and the convicts began hacking away at the frozen earth with shovels and pickaxes soon after sunrise. Harold felt extremely hungry well before the noon lunch break. After what seemed like a full day's work, the foreman blew the lunch whistle and marched them to a hall at the nearby farm headquarters. All that awaited them as a supplement to lunch was *bai cha* (white tea), a euphemism for hot water. The cold had shrunk Harold's corn buns into two small stony lumps. He dipped them in the hot water to thaw them out before eating them. His stomach felt empty as he trudged back into the cold to work. He had no hope of increasing his ration. He was the weakest convict, and he would reduce the share of his workmates if he secured a larger portion for himself. "I had miscalculated and I felt very, very depressed," Harold said.

In early summer of 1958, camp officers moved Harold and his team to Branch Number 1 on a stem of the Ussuri River originating from Promoting Victory Lake. The river traces a long section of the northeastern Sino-Russian border before flowing into the Amur River. From their barracks the inmates could look across the Ussuri and see Soviet territory. As they dug irrigation channels for wheat and corn fields, the convicts often watched Soviet sailors pass by on patrol boats. Harold grew increasingly weak because of his meager ration. Compared to the peasants and factory workers in his squad, he was clumsy and inept at handling a shovel, so camp officers assigned him to do light tasks. But the officers still expected his squad to complete the same amount of work as other squads. As the squad lagged behind, its members blamed Harold and gave him the withering nickname Glasses. Harold had no hope of raising his ration because of his poor performance. He grew increasingly despondent.

In desperation, Harold decided to strike up once again what his superiors at the Foreign Ministry would have called an "abnormal relationship" with a foreigner. He wrote a letter to a friend, a third secretary at the Indian Embassy in Beijing, asking that he meet with the ambassador and consider ways to help Harold win release from the camp. Harold figured the ministry would satisfy the ambassador because China was diplomatically isolated and depended on the support of India in world politics. But Harold had no way to post the letter from the camp. He was allowed to write only one letter a month to his family, and camp guards routinely read the letters before mailing them. Harold persuaded an inmate about to be released to post the letter outside the camp. In return he gave the inmate a coat lined in fox fur. Harold's mother had made the coat, and he had worn it in the protocol department.

Before he gave the letter to the departing inmate, Harold one morning put it with his deluxe Parker fountain pen in a satchel that he left in the barracks before setting off into the fields. When he returned in the evening, the letter and pen were gone. Harold knew the letter was likely to bring him harsh punishment. But he regretted the loss of the Parker pen almost as much; it was the only reminder of his former privileged life. His Western suits had been sent back to his father in Shanghai after his arrest. He had to return to the ministry the suits it had provided for his trips with Zhou to the Asian subcontinent. The pen symbolized the Shanghai refinement Harold cherished and reminded him of the Waterman pen given to him by his father and later stolen. Amid the dreary labor camp, the Parker pen had bolstered Harold's hope that he would again have an opportunity to emulate the scholarship and cultivation of his father.

Harold figured that either a guard or an inmate took what was in the satchel. Guards routinely rifled through convicts' belongings for razor blades, knives, nails, sickles, and other potential weapons. In the middle of the night, after Harold discovered the pen and letter were missing, two guards entered the barracks, shone their flashlights in Harold's face, told him to dress, and hustled him to the branch headquarters. There, a camp officer told Harold he was to be returned to Branch Number 2 and put in confinement. The guards handcuffed Harold, put shackles on his ankles, and ordered him to climb into the back of a horse cart. Accompanied by two guards, Harold bumped along in the cart throughout the night. Despite the springtime warmth, the cold light of the moon seemed to freeze the two-wheel track leading to the farm and the endless sea of unripe corn sweeping in all directions. Bound by the heavy fetters, Harold could not drive off a cloud of mosquitoes. Throughout the night he agonized over the likelihood that camp officers would lengthen his ten-year sentence. The officers routinely sentenced convicts guilty of minor crimes to an additional five years at the camp.

Harold arrived at Branch Number 2 around noon and was immediately thrust into a dark, filthy cell with three other convicts. The cell was seven feet square with one small barred window. Soon thereafter a fifth prisoner was locked in the cell. Everything was difficult in the small room, even sleeping. At night, if Harold wanted to roll over, he had to tell his cellmates and they had to move together. In one corner of the packed dirt floor was a bucket used as a privy. It was emptied only once a day, in the morning after the convicts had moved their bowels in turn. Some of Harold's cellmates had a short wire running from their handcuffs to their ankle shackles so they could only move around the cell bent over double. One convict was bound in a straitjacket. Harold and the other cellmates had to help him get up and lie down.

The convicts were each given less than a pound of porridge a day divided into three portions. At mealtime, a guard opened a small window on the door and ladled the porridge into the convicts' bowls. Harold could manipulate his bowl and spoon despite his handcuffs. He helped his cellmates who were immobilized by their shackles. He held their bowls at the window under the ladle and put them on the floor. The fettered convicts then lay on the floor, put their faces in the bowls, and slurped up the porridge with their tongues.

After four months in the cell, Harold was ordered to write a confession. He was removed from confinement and returned to his old barracks in November 1958. His sentence was not lengthened. He was fortunate. One of his cellmates had slipped away from Branch Number 1 and swum across the narrowest part of the Ussuri River to Soviet territory. Soviet soldiers captured him, blindfolded him, and returned him to the camp. His sentence was raised to life. But Harold emerged weaker and hungrier than ever before; his ration in the cell had been 25 percent less than before his confinement.

The diet for all convicts began to shrink in December 1958. The farm at the labor camp began sending an increasing percentage of its grain to the cities and keeping less for itself. Camp officials became stricter in enforcing the ration. They were responding to government efforts to cope with the beginning of a nationwide famine caused by Mao. The Great Helmsman had triggered a drastic slump in grain output in 1958 by launching a three-year effort to advance industry in the Great Leap Forward. Mao shifted control over industry from central government bureaucrats to local party cadres. He hoped that the campaign to raise industrial production would help subdue his rivals in the party. At his bidding, Mao's grassroots cadres organized peasants into huge people's communes. They herded millions of peasants to work in tiny, jerry-built blast furnaces and allowed fields to go untended. The low-level officials then issued false, glowing accounts that masked the extent of the economic disaster and famine. Eventually, more than 20 million people died from hunger.

Harold believes he would have starved in late 1958 had he remained a common camp laborer. But one morning in December, the public security officer in charge of Harold's team, Ye Changqing, summoned him to the branch office. In a decision worthy of the absurd irony in a Joseph Heller novel, he made Harold a camp accountant, although Harold had been imprisoned for misappropriating funds. The convict responsible for the tasks had just been released after a two-and-a-half-year sentence. He was a former guard at the Peking Hotel who had been imprisoned for fatally shooting someone by mistake. The guard "was a cadre before he came to the camp and you were an official. You both committed crimes, but we still trust you," the officer told Harold.

Harold accounted for the cash inmates handed over when they entered the camp and the money they received by mail from their families. He also deducted money from the inmates' accounts when they bought soap, cigarettes, or toothpaste from the camp store. He checked in and checked out the shovels, pickaxes, and other implements from the toolshed. Best of all, he kept tabs on the rations for the team. Each week he handed the cookhouse a squad-by-squad list of rations for breakfast, lunch, and dinner for the next seven days. When the convicts were too far from camp to return for lunch, he put the steamed buns and other food in a wheelbarrow and pushed it to the fields. Because some buns were stuck together or broken in half, the cooks always gave more than the ration required. Although Harold and other convicts in charge of rations were required to return leftovers to the cookhouse, they always ate them instead. He no longer ate in the barracks with the inmates; he ate in the cookhouse among pots, pans, and woks filled with food.

The convicts in 1959 steadily saw more signs of the famine sweeping the rest of China. Although the harvests at the camp were plentiful, camp officers began to mix scholar tree leaves into the steamed corn buns. Later, the prisoners noticed the buns included wheat chaff and wild herbs. They felt increasingly weak as the nutritional value of the buns declined. In the fall, several hundred famished and sick convicts from the giant Qinghe labor camp in Hebei Province were moved the more than 1,000 miles northeast to the Xingkai camp. Some 200 of the Qinghe prisoners were housed at Branch Number 2. Many of them suffered from dropsy. They apparently were moved to Xingkai to die. The camp medics gave many of the emaciated newcomers a malnutrition rating of "1++++" denoting the most critical cases. The Qinghe convicts slept in the same barracks as those from Xingkai, did no work, and received the minimum ration of 0.9 pound a day. About a month after their arrival, they began to perish one by one. After a death the Xingkai convicts rolled up the corpse in a straw mat and removed it from the barracks for burial. The Xingkai convicts increasingly began to develop dropsy too and felt the deaths foreshadowed their own. Almost all the Qinghe prisoners died within three months; several Xingkai inmates died too.

By the end of 1959, camp officers deemed the Xingkai convicts so weak and sickened that they worked them just two hours a day and had them otherwise rest. The prisoners were too feeble to flail all the harvested rice. So through the fall and into the winter of 1960, piles of grain went unthreshed. The officers ordered the inmates during the long breaks to remove their shoes, sit on the *kang*, and meditate in the lotus position with "five hearts up": face, palms, and soles of the feet facing upward. They began to give convicts with a malnourishment rating of 1+++ or worse a small ration of soy flour, which they said could cure dropsy. Prisoners rated 1++ were told not to eat anything with salt because such food worsens the accumulation of fluids and swelling that is a symptom of dropsy. Inmates rated 1++++ were considered beyond help. The camp guards and officers also began to ration their own food. They, too, started to look drawn and sallow. "If I hadn't been made the team accountant, I would have died," Harold said.

Despite the famine and death, camp officers still saw that prisoners enjoyed routine "recreation." One evening every two weeks, guards herded convicts who could walk out of the barracks and sat them in rows on wooden stools. Bundled up in their fur hats and heavy coats against subzero temperatures, the prisoners dutifully watched feature films in the gelid night. Camp officers were suspicious of convicts who said they were weak or sick and remained in the barracks.

Imprisonment and famine exacted an ethical toll. Prisoners fought and quarreled over every crumb of corn bun. Camp officers worsened the tension by sprinkling informers among the barracks and work squads. "Because of the informers, I learned not to trust any Chinese and not to open my heart or tell my true thoughts to anyone unless they're close friends or family. I still observe this today," Harold said. "The people around you are your most dangerous enemies," he added.

Although he held a privileged job, Harold was still watched and betrayed by the informers. He was often accompanied in his tasks by one of four prisoners who kept an eye on the inmates in the barracks during the night and slept for much of the day. One of the prisoners would go with Harold into the fields when he delivered the ration of corn buns.

One day the team officer ordered Harold to his office. "I understand you are against the ration policy. You think the *wotou* are too small," he said, glowering. The previous day, Harold had casually said while dispensing the ration, "Oh, the corn buns today are very small."

Another day, when Harold was rationing the small helping of pork and rice the prisoners received every two weeks, he said in exasperation, "There's too little pork. How can I split it up evenly to all the squads?" The team officer immediately called him in and railed at him, quoting the comment word for word.

Harold frequently faced such reprimands from the team officer, all based on offhand comments he had made. "The officers at the labor camp said they would transform the 'bad elements' in society into 'good elements,' but actually the inmates learned worse habits: to inform on others and to fight for every little bit of food," Harold said.

In early 1962, several inmates from branches of the labor camp along the Ussuri River were moved into Branch Number 2. Harold learned from one of the incoming prisoners, a former employee of the Western Europe section of the Foreign Ministry, that the camp leaders had closed Branch Number 1 because of a sudden chill in Sino-Soviet relations. The prisoner said the camp had begun to return to Beijing convicts who had once handled classified information for fear they would be captured in any hostilities. The close relationship between Beijing and Moscow had steadily deteriorated since the mid-1950s over fundamental differences in ideology and foreign policy. China's Communist leaders considered Moscow guilty of revisionism and found the rift especially vexing. Since taking power in 1949, they had depended on Moscow for guidance and aid in handling the economy, education, science, and the arts and in developing power supplies, communications, and other basic services. Moscow suddenly withdrew 1,390 experts from China in September 1960 and canceled hundreds of vital contracts and technical projects. Thereafter, it steadily built up its military forces along the border with China's western region of Xinjiang and along the Ussuri. The two countries clashed along the border in 1969.

Harold felt hopeful that he would again benefit from his privileged background and be returned to Beijing. Although not adjacent to the frontier, Branch Number 2 could be quickly overrun by Soviet troops. One day in April, the officer in charge of the team ordered Harold to update fully the prisoners' accounts. When Harold handed over the account book the following day, the officer ordered him to apply his fingerprint to the record. Toward evening another officer took the keys to the toolshed from Harold and told him he would be moved out of the labor camp. The next morning Harold and thirteen other prisoners were escorted to camp headquarters by a lone guard and put on a train bound for Beijing. Harold felt elated as the train headed south. He still wore the fur hat and black padded jacket of a labor camp convict, but he was packed together in the carriage with civilians. And not only were the accompanying guards unarmed; they allowed him to use the train toilet unsupervised. He was freer than at any time since his arrest four years before.

As he jounced toward Beijing, Harold felt a guarded satisfaction over the simple fact that he had endured the labor camp. He reckoned the worst part of his ten-year sentence was over. He remembered a line from *Gadfly*, a novel about a martyred Italian revolutionary published in 1900 by the British author Ethel Lilian Voynich. Just prior to his execution, the gallant hero in the party-sanctioned novel courageously concludes a farewell letter to his lover by recalling a rhyme:

> *Then am I*
> *A happy fly,*
> *If I live*
> *Or if I die.*

"Like the fly I learned that I didn't have any control over my future, so the best way for me to live was not to think about the future but just to deal with reality," Harold said.

Compared to other prisoners, Harold flourished in the labor camp after he was made accountant. He weighed 132 pounds when he arrived in Beijing, 11 pounds more than his weight today. "I had no way to get out of the camp, so I figured why not be in good spirits, take the challenge, deal with reality, and try my best to survive," he said.

Once back in Beijing, Harold and the other Xingkai inmates were moved to an uncompleted elevator factory in Lianxiang, a township outside the capital. The large building was one of hundreds of projects the Soviets had dropped before they hastily pulled out of China eight months before. The Beijing Public Security Bureau had turned the crude three-story hulk into a makeshift hospital for prisoners. Convicts with tuberculosis were on the first floor, those with other major diseases were on the second, and those with minor ailments were kept on the third. Harold was put in a large room with about twenty other prisoners on the third floor. They slept on hay strewn on the concrete floor of the whitewashed room.

For Harold the move from a labor camp to a prison hospital was poetically fitting. He committed his "crimes" not because of an inherent felonious nature but because he approached the world far differently from most Chinese of his time. The state should have dealt with him not as a criminal diplomat but as a modern Shanghainese whose cosmopolitan point of view clashed with that of the tradition-bound Communists who ruled China. His crimes were more in thought than in deed; his was a case for a Maoist psychiatrist (had one existed), not for an iron-fisted commandant of a Communist labor camp.

In the hospital Harold quickly found a like-minded companion. The doctor in charge of the third floor came to examine Harold the day after his arrival from Manchuria. "Are you from the Foreign Ministry?" the doctor asked after reading Harold's name. The doctor had served as the third secretary of the embassy in Pakistan before being sentenced to a two-year jail term for alleged embezzlement. The ministry had sent his wife to work on its farm in Manchuria near Daqing, a vast oil field. After his term expired, the Public Security Bureau retained him as an employee. The bureau has usually not let highly trained former convicts such as doctors return to private life.

Beijing prison officials had assumed that Harold and his fellow Xingkai convicts were weak and sick after years of hacking away at the permafrost wasteland in Manchuria. But Harold, twenty-six, was in fine health. Still, he exploited the bureau's rare gesture of concern by parlaying it into a sinecure. He wore the gown and robe of a hospital invalid and finagled a comfortable position with a farcical cleverness worthy of R. P. McMurphy in Ken Kesey's *One Flew Over the Cuckoo's Nest.*

The doctor in charge of the third floor assigned Harold to work as a nurse, translate the names of medicines from Latin to Chinese, and write prescriptions. Harold was also made responsible for maintaining medical records on the prisoners and rationing food. Every morning, dressed in the slippers and loose clothes of a patient, he attended to others in the ward. He helped the doctors by taking prisoners' temperatures and blood pressure. Meanwhile, another inmate sat in the corridor loudly reading propaganda from official newspapers. After his early tasks, Harold and another "sick" convict shouldered a pole attached to a heavy waist-high bucket filled with rice gruel, hauled it up to the third floor, and doled out breakfast to the patients. Then he collected the bowls and returned the cutlery to the kitchen. For the remainder of the day, Harold usually loitered in the doctor's clinic. He was subject to the ration, but the doctor frequently brought him rice cakes and cigarettes from the city. "We had a good time together," Harold said.

Unlike other shut-ins, Harold could move about the building with some freedom. He could leave the building if he offered a legitimate reason, such as to find out for a patient the price of an item at the hospital store. When he wanted to get some fresh air, he could work in the vegetable garden and soybean field run by the hospital.

In the first of several lucrative translations over the course of his career, Harold worked in the clinic or the ward compiling a medical reference book with the doctor. He included the Chinese and Western name for ailments and the symptoms and treatment. He had no need to hustle for cash. Since his arrest, Harold had received 10 yuan each month from his father. There were few things to spend the money on, so he built up a comfortable savings.

The spare time and comparative comfort in the hospital intensified the longing by Harold for the refined life he had lost. One day as he was weeding the field of soybeans, he heard an employee whistling a piece from *Carmen*. Harold leaned on his hoe. The crisp, bright tune was spellbinding. It was the first time he had heard music other than an anthem or march since his arrest. He had not heard a bar of Western music for more than four years. He was flooded by nostalgia for his life as a protocol officer.

Harold wrote a letter to Han Xu, one of his erstwhile superiors in the protocol department. One Sunday, during the visitation period offered inmates twice a month, Harold was summoned to a meeting room. Across the table sat Han, and they chatted for about fifteen minutes. "I heard that when you were in the northeast you failed to straighten out the problems in your mind," Han told Harold, referring to the vain effort to contact the Indian diplomat. "I hope you completely reform yourself."

Despite his overbearing tone, Han showed by the visit a measure of courage and compassion. A few years later, at the height of the Cultural Revolution, Mao's fanatical Red Guards attacked Han for failing to ask the permission of the ministry before visiting Harold. They also rebuked him for "failing to draw a distinct line between himself and a criminal."

One day early in 1965, the officer in charge of the third floor ordered Harold to hand over his tasks to another inmate, gather his things together, and move into a large room at the end of the main corridor. That afternoon a dozen inmates arrived from various reform-through-labor prisons and moved into the room with

Harold. A prisoner from the Tuanhe labor camp was made leader of the group, and Harold was made his deputy with responsibilities for the rations. The officer sternly told the new group not to say a word to other prisoners on the floor. He told Harold not to talk to other prisoners even when he routinely went to the kitchen for the group's food. Whenever a prisoner from the group went to the toilet, he had to take another group member with him. Among themselves, the members of the group were ordered not to whisper or to discuss their cases.

Despite the restrictions, the members of the group quickly came to know each other and their reasons for imprisonment. One convict formerly was with the Public Security Ministry. He had written an unauthorized letter to the Yugoslav Embassy and during his interrogation had commandeered a jeep. When the jeep ran out of fuel, he had to surrender to the police. Another prisoner in the group claimed to be the former chauffeur of Marshal He Long, an uneducated peasant from Hunan who became one of the party's leading military heroes during World War II and the final years of the civil war. Still another inmate was attached to the Ministry for State Security, the spy organ handling both internal and external threats. Most members of the group were charged with crimes of counterrevolution.

A week after the group was formed, prisoners in military uniforms stripped of epaulets were moved into a room across the corridor. Members of the two groups were not allowed to communicate with one another. But Harold handled their food rations and gradually learned that the disgraced soldiers had worked for the Number 7 Machinery Ministry. The highly secretive ministry handled the design and production of weapons and missiles. The prisoners had worked for Qian Xuesen, the U.S.-trained mastermind of China's nuclear missile program. Harold and his comrades concluded that because tensions with Moscow were still acute, the government wanted to keep the soldiers together and secluded. In the event of war, it wanted to prevent Moscow from tapping their knowledge of highly classified information.

Harold and the other prisoners in his group were required each day to sit in their room and listen to an inmate read the daily newspapers. Afterward, they often had to discuss the articles. Because some group members were well educated, the discussions at times were heated. One prisoner had graduated with degrees in Marxism and Leninism and philosophy from People's University. The sparring over Communist ideology and dialectical materialism inspired Harold to check out related books from the hospital library. He diligently wrote notes on several books on world history from a Marxist perspective.

The surge of ultraradical activism that became the Cultural Revolution prompted prison officials in fall 1966 suddenly to move Harold and most of the other prisoners out of the makeshift hospital. In confinement, Harold got only a hint of the turmoil as Red Guards, Mao's young minions of revolution, stormed into factories and government offices and criticized, tortured, and killed those they deemed rightists or counterrevolutionaries. Mao had reviewed massive parades of Red Guards in August 1966 from atop Tiananmen Gate, the entrance to the Forbidden City in Beijing, and unleashed them in an orgy of violence and destruction. He hoped through the campaign to subdue his rivals in the party leadership. The Red Guards attacked any figure in authority, from parents to party leaders. They destroyed temples, old buildings, books, and artwork throughout the country. The nationwide campaign quickly descended into chaos as the radical groups, unrestrained by central controls, fought with party leaders and among themselves.

Prison officials moved many inmates back to hometown jails as part of a policy to purge Beijing of undesirable elements. Natives of Tianjin, Shanghai, and other especially tumultuous places were held in Beijing because the inmates were likely to be attacked back home. Harold and the two groups of specially treated prisoners on the third floor were moved to a brick factory run by the reform-through-labor administration at Yanqing, thirty miles northwest of Beijing. They were locked up in a small, exclusive compound that had been recently built to hold high-level cadres accused of being "capitalist roaders." The rooms were built for one prisoner and were luxurious compared to the other prison accommodations Harold had endured. They were eighteen feet square with a cement desk and stool, a toilet in the corner, radiators, and a small patio. Harold and his fellow inmates slept in bunks, six to eight of them to a room. They occasionally worked in the vegetable plots of the prison but spent most of the time locked in the room studying the newspapers and official documents.

As the cold and dusty northwest winds gave way to the cool rain and energizing sun of spring in 1967, Harold became increasingly preoccupied with thoughts of the end of his ten-year sentence and imminent release. He found it difficult to sleep, and when he did he dreamed of a return to past grandeur. In one dream Han Xu arrived in a car and whisked Harold back to his old job at the Foreign Ministry.

One evening, exactly ten years after his arrest, a prison guard told Harold to collect his belongings and leave the cell. But once outside the warden's office, Harold found no yawning prison gate, no wide-open green-and-golden springtime vista. Instead, a guard marched Harold about forty yards into another compound in the factory and locked another heavy door behind him. To his dismay, Harold had received a new label but retained pretty much the same life. He had become a *jiuyerenyuan.*

Harold lived with several other prison workers in a large abandoned kiln. The vaulted, quarter-sphere structure had two large windows at the back and several *kang,* across the floor. Harold was allowed to walk freely in some areas of the compound but could not leave the factory without permission. On Sundays, if granted permission, he could go to Yanqing. Prison workers with family in Beijing could visit the capital every two weeks.

Eventually, as turmoil continued outside the prison, Harold and the other workers considered the walls more a rampart than a pen. Red Guards delighted in ferreting out and assaulting so-called bad elements like Harold: former convicts, counterrevolutionaries, rich peasants, and former landlords. Prison guards warned the workers that Maoist fanatics would assault them if they went to Beijing. On a sultry summer day, hundreds of Red Guards from Yanqing surrounded the prison. They demanded that the warden open the gates and allow them to "struggle against" the enemies of Mao. The warden persuaded them to withdraw. But soon thereafter, a female prison worker went to Yanqing one Sunday. She neglected to hide her ponytail, a gross sign of bourgeois decadence. Red Guards fell upon her as she walked through the town. They pushed her into a barbershop, cut off her ponytail, and shaved off the hair on half of her head.

Along with sanctuary from political madness, the prison factory gave Harold a monthly allowance of 12 yuan but withheld 10.5 yuan for food. He ate a spare diet but was usually given steamed buns made of wheat flour, which Chinese generally prefer over corn flour. Harold had savings of more than 200 yuan that his father had sent him over a decade. After Harold's sentence expired, Xu said he would send him 15 yuan a month until he found a job.

In July, however, Xu sent a letter saying he had recently been branded a "reactionary bourgeois academic authority" and his salary at Tongji University had been reduced from 186 yuan to 40 yuan a month. He could no longer send money. Harold applied to make a brief family visit to Shanghai, but prison officials denied the request, saying that Shanghai was chaotic and too dangerous for a former convict.

Although Harold did not know it at the time, his life as a prisoner was in all but name far preferable to the life of his father in Shanghai. Red Guards had raided Xu's luxurious apartment twice, forcibly seizing all his valuables, including a piano. His savings of more than 10,000 yuan were frozen. Maoists at the university required him regularly to attend struggle sessions, perform manual labor, and study the works of Mao. They repeatedly hung a placard from his neck that read "Xu Zhuru: reactionary bourgeois academic authority and degenerate" and paraded him around campus. At one point the young extremists herded Xu and other undesirable elements to a place on campus labeled "the zoo of reactionary bourgeois academic authorities" for a lengthy session in self-criticism.

One day during a struggle session on a building's upper floor, Red Guards opened a window and ordered Xu to jump. Desperate and depressed, Xu began to obey. But as he lifted his second leg over the windowsill he realized that if he jumped, his tormentors would characterize him in his epitaph as "an unrepentant bourgeois element who committed suicide to escape punishment." Xu pulled himself back inside the room where he was badly beaten.

Late in the fall of 1967, Xu's mistress informed Harold by letter that Red Guards had hit Xu hard on the head during a struggle session, causing a severe concussion. Hospital authorities refused to treat an undesirable element like Xu. Thereafter, Xu's memory was poor, his handwriting almost illegible. After Xu had recovered sufficiently to move around, he was ordered back to campus to perform manual labor. He arose every morning before dawn and never returned home from his campus labors until after dark. For a timepiece he wrapped a cumbersome alarm clock in a sheet of cotton and nestled it in his handbag. Red Guards had long before seized his stylish Movado wristwatch.

Despite the widespread cruelty by the Red Guards, Harold continued trying to renew contacts beyond the high walls of the brickyard. He tried to get in touch with Han Xu and asked a fellow worker who planned to visit Beijing to telephone the diplomat.

"I'm calling on behalf of Xu Cunyao [Harold]," the worker said to Han on the telephone one Sunday. Han said nothing for more than a minute.

"Xu should rely on his current *danwei* to solve his problems," Han said before abruptly hanging up. In a struggle session with him the previous day, Red Guards had forced Han to write a lengthy essay in self-criticism.

The factory had stopped producing bricks, and Harold and his peers spent most of their time reading newspapers and official documents. The prison officials ordered them to study the quotations and selected works of Mao. But the former convicts only skimmed the windy, grandiose speeches and instead pored over classified documents published and widely circulated by rival factions of Red Guards. Competing groups of Maoist extremists raided government offices for the secret papers and published them as proof that they were the true defenders of Chairman Mao's revolutionary line. Rather than reveal to Harold the supposedly glorious wisdom and benevolence of Mao, the documents disclosed the Great Helmsman's vanity and brutality. One speech, "On the Correct Handling of Contradictions Among the People," differed markedly from the published version. In it, after noting that the first emperor of China had burned books and buried 360 scholars alive, Mao bragged that he had executed 360,000 counterrevolutionaries during his campaign to suppress them (1950–1951).

The gloating by Mao over his tyrannical policies substantiated reports of atrocities Harold had heard while at the labor camp on Promoting Victory Lake. During the campaign against counterrevolutionaries, camp officials routinely roused prisoners from their barracks late at night for roll call, hauled several of the bleary-eyed inmates away in trucks to a distant barren field, and mowed them down with machine guns. Now and then the hardworking executioners would mistakenly shoot a convict with the same surname as the intended victim.

"I was really shocked because the more I read, the more I realized that Mao was a dictator and tyrant like Hitler," Harold said. "The unpublished speeches disclosed to me the real features of Mao, and I started to question the Great Helmsman."

Harold began again to study Marx and Engels in an effort to discover the flaw in Mao's thought. He repeatedly read the writings of Engels on dialectics. A former convict who also lived in the kiln reported Harold's fascination with Engels to a prison official, who sternly told Harold to focus on Mao. But Harold continued to study to uncover his own political epiphany. He learned that whereas Hegel and Engels asserted that opposite forces in society could sometimes unify and achieve harmony, Mao claimed that opposites would continually struggle. Harold realized that because Mao believed in the inevitability of perpetual conflict in society, he would always seek out an enemy. If no adversary existed, he would create one. As a result, Mao would repeatedly provoke strife, turmoil, and suffering on a grand scale.

Not long after discerning the ruinous flaw in Mao's thought, Harold fell victim to one of Mao's favorite lessons. Lin Biao, the vice chairman of the party and Mao's chosen successor, ordered all bad elements such as Harold out of Beijing in the fall of 1969 in an effort to make the capital "ever red." The party also sent hundreds of thousands of cadres, intellectuals, and students to the countryside for re-education through toil with peasants. The former city dwellers were restricted to May Seventh Cadre Schools, prisonlike encampments named after a directive by Mao on that date earlier in the Cultural Revolution. When not compelled to labor in the fields, they criticized themselves, studied Mao's works, and endured other forms of indoctrination. Most of the exiles had hope of returning to the cities, although many of them remain in rural areas today. But Harold and other former prisoners were sent as a punishment and would remain there indefinitely. As Harold left Beijing, his hopes faded of returning to the capital and reviving a glimmer of his past life.

Harold and other former convicts were moved south to Longyao in Hebei Province. Officials detained them there for six months while they decided whether to dispatch the cheap laborers to lowland villages for farmwork or to remote mountainous areas to build factories for idle and poor peasants. After six months, in spring 1970, Harold was assigned to work with the Gucheng brigade of the Gucheng commune in Longyao County. The Public Security Bureau gave commune officials 150 yuan for each of the former convicts to help them settle into their brigades. Harold lived in a village of 3,000 peasants administered by the commune. One of the seventeen production teams in the brigade accepted Harold and another former convict because it desperately needed to pay for spring plowing with the 300-yuan settlement subsidy that came with them. The team immediately put the newcomers to work planting cottonseed.

Harold initially lived with the other former convict in two rooms at the mud-brick headquarters of the team. The team gave them a new wok and promised to provide them with all other necessities. Ultimately, though, it gave them only old tools, and they had to acquire a kitchen bellows and many other essentials.

At 5 A.M. in the summer, brigade commanders rang the bell suspended over a large central yard, calling Harold and the peasants to assemble for fieldwork. Harold tilled cotton, wheat, corn, millet, or sorghum until a brief respite for breakfast at 8 A.M. He hurriedly made his own meal and wolfed it down. Before he could wash his bowl the brigade bell again summoned him to the yard. He worked until 12:30 P.M., when he would cook his lunch and take refuge from the heat until the commanders beat the bell again at 4 P.M. Harold assembled with the other peasants and worked the fields until dinner at 8 P.M. In the spring and fall, when the period of daylight was shorter, the afternoon rest was also shorter and the workday ended earlier.

Most peasants every workday were credited ten work points: two points for the early morning, four for the late morning, and four for the afternoon. When they irrigated the fields, they received twelve points per day. Harold was as clumsy with a shovel and hoe as when he was in the wilds of Manchuria. The city slicker from Shanghai hacked and poked at the earth, fighting gravity and wasting his energy. The peasants stroked the implements into the soil, using gravity, resting their muscles, and husbanding their energy after each graceful movement. During 1971 Harold was demoted and credited only nine and a half points per day. He felt ashamed and so he sharpened his skills, worked hard, and rose again to ten-point status in 1972.

Peasants resented having to share their grain ration with Harold and the other newcomers. But otherwise, farmers and brigade commanders alike were tolerant and warmhearted toward their new workmates. They were largely oblivious to ideology, and so, unlike most officials and city dwellers, they did not share the prejudice of the party leadership toward the so-called bad elements.

Harold was only openly discriminated against in 1976 when brigade officials barred the former prisoners from taking part in a memorial service for Zhou Enlai. "All through the years in the countryside, only this ban reminded me that I was a second-class member of the commune, so I was very impressed with the peasants," Harold said. (He felt so devoted toward the late premier that he used a large chunk of his meager savings to buy a transistor radio so that he could listen to a broadcast of the memorial service from Beijing.)

Not long after arriving at the commune, Harold and the other former convict moved into a dwelling made from bricks of mud and straw, the standard construction materials in the village. The small shack was attached to a stable sheltering a horse and three oxen tended by Harold's housemate. Harold slept on a straw mat spread on a *kang* behind the horse. His comrade could afford every winter to visit his family in Beijing, and Harold cared for the livestock while he was away. He gathered fodder and water for the beasts from midnight until peasants came for them at 4 A.M. The peasants would inspect the bellies of the animals to make sure Harold had tended them well. Harold then slept.

Harold and his comrade every year raised a pig, a prime source and symbol of prosperity for peasants. Of any moneymaking endeavor in the countryside, a pig at that time yielded perhaps the best return for the smallest investment of time and money. They fed it scraps of food and wild grasses and then sold its manure to the commune. At the end of a year they sold the pig at market for a good sum.

While tending the pig, Harold decided that Mao had sent educated city dwellers to the countryside not just to attune them to the hardships endured by most Chinese but to demean them as well. Among the features of the countryside, the pig was the vilest agent for Mao in his effort to ensure the triumph of traditional China over the cosmopolitan culture that had nurtured Harold. In gastronomic matters, a pig has no discretion. When a villager approached the outhouse, Harold's pig squealed long and loud, trotted beneath the privy, peered up the hole, and, with a crescendo of snuffles and grunts, poked its hairy pink snout up toward the descending treat. Harold compared the routine spectacle to his erstwhile elegance in Shanghai and Beijing and judged the debasement Mao had prescribed was complete.

In the winter of 1970, after gaining approval for his first trip back to Shanghai since 1955, Harold discovered just how total was his fall from cosmopolitan grandeur. When he stepped off the train at the Shanghai railway station, he recalled the madcap adventures of the excursionists in Mark Twain's *The Innocents Abroad*:

> We made Rome howl. We could have made any place howl when we had all our clothes on. ... At Constantinople, how we turned out! Turbans, scimetars, fezzes, horse-pistols, tunics, sashes, baggy trowsers, yellow slippers—Oh, we were gorgeous! The illustrious dogs of Constantinople barked their under jaws off, and even then failed to do us justice. They are all dead by this time. They could not go through such a run of business as we gave them and survive.

Despite the ultraleftist political tone, Shanghai residents still wore trim clothes and walked at a brisk, haughty pace. Harold resembled a walking parcel in his heavy peasant clothes. He wore the best outfit he owned: black cotton-padded canvas shoes, a black cotton-padded jacket, and a blue Mao cap. He shouldered two lumpy canvas bags, one dark brown, the other light brown. "My jacket and hat didn't even match," Harold said, shaking his head. "Everyone who saw me must have thought that I was a country bumpkin."

By donning a cap, Harold had knowingly identified himself as a rustic. Most Shanghainese spurn hats even during the rawest winter chill. But Harold had no choice. In the countryside, he routinely shaved his head to promote hygiene and avoid having to wash his hair. If his head became dirty he merely splashed water over it. He had allowed his hair to grow a few weeks before his trip to Shanghai. But it had sprouted in short, prickly bristles, making him resemble a large bur that had clung a ride into the city.

During his six-week visit with his family, Harold felt the alienation encountered by peasants from the China of rice paddies and Confucian rectitude when they first come to sparkling Shanghai. He was overwhelmed by a feeling that he did not belong. They knew what was happening in China and the rest of the world; he did not. They spoke the latest Shanghai dialect and slang; his speech was fifteen years behind the times. They were clean, trim, and fair skinned; he was dirty, frumpy, and ruddy.

Harold's family subjected him to small humiliations. Xu and his mistress did not put Harold up in their large apartment but offered him a bed in the corridor. After Harold arrived, Xu's mistress remarked that his towel was filthy and, turning her head away, threw a clean towel at him. "Overall, my family treated me well, but I felt like I belonged in another world, as if everyone in the street was looking at me and saying, 'Ha! Look at this guy, he's just walked out of the fields!'"

Harold's aunt gave him 10 yuan as pocket money, which he accepted despite the shame of a thirty-four-year-old taking money from an old relative. In order to save money he walked and did not ride the trolley. He coveted the Shanghai watches of the pedestrians. (The Swiss-made watch his father had bought for him in Hong Kong in 1950 was broken when the prison returned it at the end of his sentence.) He made his way down Nanjing Road, the closest thing to Fifth Avenue in China during the Cultural Revolution, and stepped into the Number 1 Department Store. He fingered what were considered the best clothes in China: Shanghai-made shirts, socks, and silk padded jackets in the traditional style. He lingered outside restaurants and pastry shops, eyeing the delicately prepared dishes and inhaling the rich aromas from cakes, pies, succulent meats, and *xiaolong baozi,* the petite, juicy pork dumplings that are a regional specialty.

Harold visited Shanghai three other times during the 1970s and was often at odds with his father, who had grown curmudgeonly since suffering the concussion at the hands of Red Guards. "My father became a bad-tempered, stubborn old man," Harold said. One day, during one of his father's unjustified ravings, Harold lost all Confucian self-restraint. "I will leave home right now and never come back!" Harold yelled. Xu's mistress persuaded him to remain another night. Late that night, as Harold lay in bed angry and sleepless, his father walked into the room and stood by his bedside in the dark for a time. Harold decided not to leave the next day.

The feeling of alienation after his first visit to Shanghai made his return to the village easier, but it did not ease the wrenching hardship of meeting basic needs like food. In the spring of 1972, Harold realized that he would soon be hungry and penniless. His savings from the decade as a convict was eroding, as was his grain supply. His grain ration and wage were too meager to get by on. He figured he would run out of food and money well before the autumn. Harold asked his father for money but received a letter back that said he had none to spare. Then he wrote his two aunts in Shanghai. They remitted him 50 yuan, which he used to buy enough sorghum to carry him through the summer.

To boost his meager earnings, Harold joined a county work crew in spring 1973 that was constructing a reservoir in Hebei. Every spring and fall thereafter, he dug and hauled earth with the crew and logged twelve work points per day. With such a whopping tally, Harold became a seller rather than a buyer of grain at the village market.

Although Harold's livelihood improved, he still remained down and out in political terms. His status did not change even after the death of Mao in 1976 and the arrest of the Gang of Four, the extremists officially blamed for creating and directing the Cultural Revolution. Beijing avoided the sticky issue of repatriating the rural exiles to the city and rehabilitating the bad elements. By chance in the spring of 1978, Harold was reading an old issue of the monthly magazine *People's Literature* at the reservoir when he came across the name of a former superior at the protocol department, Bi Shuowang. Bi had taken part in a literary discussion. Harold wrote to him in care of the magazine. Shortly afterward he received a reply. "All these years my colleagues and I at the Foreign Ministry have been thinking of you," Bi said in the letter. He invited Harold to visit him in Beijing, meet his "old friends" in the ministry, and try to ferret out a job.

Harold was ecstatic. He immediately returned to the village, gathered up some belongings, and took a train to Shanghai. Once back home he told his family of the coming trip and bought two white polyester shirts and some slacks. He also spent 125 yuan for a Shanghai watch. "I saw my trip to Shanghai as an investment to ensure the success of my expedition to Beijing," Harold said.

Bi wrote to say that because he could not find other lodgings for Harold in Beijing, he would stay with the Bis, seven people in four rooms: Bi, his wife, two daughters, a son, a granddaughter, and a nanny. Harold slept on a cot and during the weeklong visit met with his former superiors and peers at the ministry. "Now it is time for us to help out our young brother," Bi said at the start of every meeting.

During one session Harold's old section chief at the protocol department asked Harold to translate a chapter from a book by Franklin D. Roosevelt. He was very impressed with Harold's language skills, particularly how Harold pronounced "Pakistan" and other words in the most genteel English. "I will do my best to get you a job," the former section chief said.

Harold was deliriously happy. Bi carried his bag to the front gate of his compound and bade him farewell. Harold boarded a bus for the railway station and the train back to Longyao. "The street lights were very dim with just a faint, brown light, but all of Beijing seemed ablaze," Harold said.

Harold did not join the work crew at the reservoir site that fall but stayed in Longyao awaiting word from Beijing. Toward the end of 1978 he was called away from hoeing irrigation channels and taken before two officials who asked him to teach at a junior high school elsewhere in Longyao County. "Do you know my background?" Harold asked them.

"Of course we know your background, but it isn't important," one of the officials said. The offhand comment seemed to break the official spell that had kept Harold down for more than twenty-one years. Harold quickly accepted the offer. Late that afternoon, he was called away from his hoeing again by the principal of the commune's Number 8 Junior High School. "You belong to this commune. This is where you live and work, and this is where you shall teach," the principal said.

Harold sat silently for a moment. "Not only have I been removed from the official blacklist, but officials are competing for me!" he thought to himself.

"Tomorrow we'll send someone to move your belongings to the school; don't worry about your commitment to the county school," the principal said.

Harold rushed back to his dwelling and packed. The next day a worker arrived with a cart and hauled Harold's belongings to the commune school. Harold was given a room to himself. For the first time in twenty-one years, he slept in a bed in a warm room with a coal-burning stove. The joy over the unexpected privacy and comfort after years of sleeping in cold, crowded rooms on hard floors muddled his judgment. Beguiled by the prospect of recapturing the comparative luxury of Shanghai, he did not open the flue enough. Sometime after midnight he awoke feeling dizzy. He felt a piercing pain in his head. Realizing the room was filled with gas from the stove, he got out of bed and tried to feel his way to the door. Because of his dizziness, he pitched forward and slammed his mouth on the brick floor. He crawled to the door and opened it. His lips had been badly cut and his front teeth knocked out. He rested for ten days and then was fitted for false teeth by a local dentist.

Harold worked hard at the school as an English teacher. He often taught into the evening without pay, instructing by candlelight when the electricity was shut off. English soon became one of the key subjects at the middle school. Still, Harold was paid just 32 yuan a month. Because he had to pay 12 yuan a month for board and 15 yuan each month to his production team for his grain ration, cotton, and other essentials, he saved very little money. Moreover, county officials were unable to transfer his residence registration from the village to the township. Because of Harold's touchy political status, the school could not even officially employ him.

After wavering for three years, the political wind in China shifted decisively in favor of Harold and other pragmatic, open-minded Chinese in December 1978. At a party plenum that month, Deng Xiaoping subdued his orthodox Maoist rivals after years of bitter political sparring. He formally reoriented China away from a fanatical adherence to Marxist purity and toward an emphasis on building a strong economy. He set down an overarching goal called Four Modernizations: development of agriculture, industry, national defense, and science and technology. Deng's bold initiative legitimized the enriching, market-oriented economic reforms of the 1980s. The complete turnabout in theory also allowed cosmopolitan Chinese like Harold to slough off a heavy mantle of political disgrace and gradually rehabilitate themselves.

Four months after the plenum, Bi wrote Harold asking if he would help edit an album for the People's Publishing House in memory of Norman Bethune, an American physician who spent much of his life treating Chinese. Bi said that the house could not offer a salary and would pay Harold only after the album was published. "This is a stepping-stone for you into Beijing," Bi wrote.

Harold quit his job at the middle school and traveled to Beijing on April 28, 1979. Bi had arranged for Harold to share a room with a worker at the International Book Store. Harold met editors from the publishing house and the Chinese Writers' Association and began working at a desk in his room. "I felt that I had reentered civilized society," Harold said.

After finishing the translation, Harold was prepared to return to Longyao and resume his job as a teacher. But Bi recommended him to teach one of the English classes organized by the Foreign Languages Press under the Culture Ministry. Mrs. Bi, in an effort to clear Harold's name, persuaded the director of the political department at the Foreign Ministry to state officially that Harold's punishment had been too severe. She found an ally in Zhou Enlai. After Harold's arrest in 1957, Zhou had asked the chief of protocol about Harold's whereabouts at a dinner given by the Swiss ambassador. "How could you deal with him so severely?" Zhou asked, after being told of the case.

The former chief of protocol wrote the Foreign Ministry in 1979 confirming Zhou's comments. Still, the ministry declined to take the risky step of fully rehabilitating Harold. Meanwhile, Mrs. Bi lobbied the director of the Foreign Languages Press, who declined to accept Harold as a full-time worker. She told the director that he could hire Harold as a temporary teacher without political risk, much as businesses hired temporary laborers. The director agreed and Harold became a teacher in September 1979 at a salary of 60 yuan per month, 10 yuan less than he had received at the Foreign Ministry twenty-two years before. He was allowed to eat at the school canteen. At night he slept on a bed in the corner of the teacher's common room.

Harold lacked confidence during his first semester as a teacher. He badly lost face when he was unable to explain adequately the use of "as" in the book *Study As Lenin Studied.* He nearly resigned. But his students liked his instruction and began to help him piece his life back together. In the middle of the first semester, they persuaded the director of the press to try to move Harold's residence registration from the village in Longyao County to Beijing. In February 1980 the director successfully petitioned the Ministry of Civil Affairs for a transfer of the registration. Harold was given a small room with a bed, desk, and bookshelf.

Having started Harold's career and reputation on the mend, the students went to work restoring his wardrobe and spirits. In the winter they took Harold to Xidan, one of the finest shopping areas in Beijing, and helped him select a traditional, silk padded jacket and three-quarter-length trench coat. "My taste for good clothes revived," Harold said.

One day Harold opened the top drawer of his desk and found a "thousand-year-old egg" glistening on a small dish. The pickled egg, a delicacy betokening the affection of some mysterious admirer, shone in a marbled jelly of cigar-butt black and swamp green.

Harold was surprised. He felt he was ugly in many ways. Although he had been charged with tenuous crimes, he was still officially a former convict. He had no more than 200 yuan to his name. He was a political outcast. At best, he could hope that Communist cadres would spare him as a bad element and commit him to perpetual limbo. His clothes were few and baggy. He wore fluorescent-white dentures that jutted and snapped like a trap for some small mammal. Gradually, however, he realized that despite his drawbacks, he had gained the sympathy of Liu Jinfeng, a divorcee, translator in Turkish, and one of his students. She invited him to her family's apartment for festivals like National Day or Chinese New Year. Sometimes she sent her daughter Lily to his room bearing plates of fried noodles or chopped sausages and vegetables scrambled with eggs in rich, glistening peanut oil.

In an effort to expunge the most glaring sign of his time in the countryside, Harold bought a new set of dentures in Shanghai in January 1982. ("When Linda [Liu Jinfeng] first saw me with the false teeth she said to herself, 'There's a man from the grave,'" Harold said.) Harold arrived in Shanghai for a visit of vindication wearing a woolen overcoat that symbolized his rise in status. Xu's mistress and her sons offered him a decent bed. They made no more disparaging gestures. Indeed, Harold had become the most accomplished of Xu's sons. Among Harold's four stepbrothers, two had been sent during the Cultural Revolution to the countryside, where one of them committed suicide. The other two brothers were bricklayers. The youngest, Xu's favorite, had lost a leg in an accident.

Despite her education at a missionary university in Shanghai, Xu's mistress "had become a typical Shanghai woman," Harold said. Each night before going to bed she counted all her cash and change and logged it in a small register. If one cent was missing she was uneasy.

Soon after Harold returned to Beijing from a three-week visit to Shanghai, his aunt called to say that his father was severely ill. By the time Harold got back to Shanghai, his father was dead. "My father died in misery. His other sons were not filial, and for many years he was just a lonely old man sitting at his desk in his apartment doing nothing."

Soon after Harold returned from Shanghai, Bi encouraged him to marry Linda. The suggestion was bold. Most Chinese, cautious over matters of romance and family, would have discouraged it. They would have doubted Harold could adapt to family life after so many years of living on his own and would have questioned whether he could win over Linda's two daughters, Lily and Gloria. But Harold had begun to build up some savings by translating articles and novels from English to Chinese. At Bi's urging, he bought a refrigerator, a large color television—whatever Linda's relatives in Beijing owned. After a bit of persuasion, Harold won the support of the school dean and was married in May 1983. In a crowning act of kindness, Bi turned over his apartment to Harold and moved into one provided by the Chinese Writers' Association.

To an extent, Harold and Linda came together because they had both for decades faced the same bitter wind: long-standing hostility of traditional China toward the emerging modern China. She was the oldest daughter of a Chinese businessman who in 1937 moved his family from Tianmen, a poor city in Hubei Province known as the home of overseas Chinese, to Tulungagung, Indonesia. In a fit of patriotism after the revolution, Linda's father dispatched her to China in 1957. She was one of thousands of overseas Chinese who returned in answer to a call by Beijing to help rebuild the country from the desolation of foreign invasion and civil war.

Linda attended the Broadcast Academy in Beijing, where she was required to learn Turkish for a career in international radio programming through which the party aimed to export revolution. Soon after she arrived, however, Mao thrust China into the disastrous Great Leap Forward. The party compelled her to join work teams to dig a reservoir, forge iron in a backyard blast furnace, and perform other hard labor.

At the academy Linda was discriminated against by students and officials because her status as an overseas Chinese rang with heavy overtones of bourgeois decadence. After graduation her attempt to join the People's Liberation Army was rejected. She was assigned with other of her politically outcast peers to work at the Foreign Languages Press. Although in 1966 she married a classmate from the mainland who was an army officer, she still was not insulated from political bias. The Cultural Revolution erupted soon after their wedding, and her husband, a rabid Maoist, used her family ties to Indonesia against her. When his application for membership in the party was delayed, he blamed Linda and informed his superiors that she regularly wrote to her family in Indonesia. She stopped writing home.

The period of ultraleftist turmoil intensified, and Linda suffered severe isolation and abuse. Red Guards stormed through her workplace and grilled her in several struggle sessions. One of her friends committed suicide and the Maoist hotheads blamed her. She was sent to the countryside several times to labor and learn of the revolutionary purity of peasants. Her marriage grew stormier because her husband could not break ties with his peasant past. He wanted their two daughters to be raised in his home village, not in the city. Moreover, in the spirit of a dogged peasant revolutionary, he worked seven days a week and neglected his family. Linda and he were separated when he took up work in Kunming. She eventually divorced him.

Harold considers Linda by far the brightest flower on the forbidding landscape of his past. When he looks back, he otherwise has good cause to have feelings of regret and resentment. Indeed, on plenty of occasions he might consider how he would have advanced at the Foreign Ministry had he not been arrested. He frequently hears about the successes of his former colleagues at the ministry. Zhu Qizhen, ambassador to the United States from 1989 until 1993, was a diplomatic courier when Harold was in the protocol department. A peer of Harold's served as ambassador to Spain. An officer who was junior to Harold is a deputy foreign minister. Still, Harold feels no regrets. "My philosophy is never lament over the past, don't dream of the future, deal with present reality. It's useless to look back."

Harold has also forgiven his accusers. He believes the officials who persecuted him were merely pawns in a flawed political system. Many of them became victims too. The deputy foreign minister who handed Harold's case over to the police was killed by Red Guards during the Cultural Revolution.

Magnanimity comes easier amid comfort. Harold has led his family toward a lifestyle surpassed only by his gilded childhood in Shanghai. Since the mid-1980s, Harold's family has reveled in consumerism. They write with Parker pens. Harold's wife and daughters use Camay and Oil of Olay facial cream, relish foreign chocolates and shop weekly at a department store catering to foreigners and affluent Beijing residents. Harold smokes Salems, Marlboros, and the British cigarette 555. He wears Arrow shirts, tailored blazers, and oxfords made of Italian leather. He is reviving a life of modern bourgeois opulence in the stodgy capital of traditionalist China. "The decadent lifestyle continues; this is the way Shanghai people live!" he said with a loud laugh.

Harold won official sanction for the high life. The State Council, China's cabinet, commended him in 1992 as "an expert who has made remarkable contributions to the cause of higher education." He was given a monthly bonus of 100 yuan and a four-bedroom apartment usually provided to government officials at the departmental level. He aims to make his family still more comfortable. He worked relentlessly to enable his stepdaughter, Gloria, to study in the United States. She earned a degree in accounting and gained the status of a permanent U.S. resident in 1993. Now she is the chief accountant for a Dallas company. Harold took early retirement from the school in 1995 and works as a reporter for the New York–based *Bloomberg Business News.* At home and at work he lives the distinctive Shanghai way: particular and precise in matters of appearance, time, taste, and money.

Since ushering in the era of reform in 1978, the party has exploited the gumption of cosmopolitans like Harold in its effort to build up the economy. The policy has given Harold and his peers more leeway to engage in entrepreneurship and live the high life than at any other time under communism. Millions of intellectuals and officials have prospered by *xiahai* (plunging into the sea), a slang term for going into business. Although common Chinese still revile plutocratic arrogance, the rich flaunt their foreign sedans, fashions, jewelry, and electronic gadgetry.

As with Harold, the party has treated Shanghainese more sympathetically in recent years. Breaking with several decades of unremitting abuse, it has encouraged the 14 million residents of Shanghai to revive their entrepreneurial spirit and promoted efforts by the port to resurrect itself as a regional hub of trade and finance. Since the late 1980s, Beijing has extended several preferential policies. Most notably, it has curbed its long-standing, voracious appetite for tax revenues from Shanghai and allowed the port to retain funds for solving its problems in housing, sanitation, and transportation.

With the blessings of Beijing, Shanghai has launched a nationwide foreign exchange center, ten commodities exchanges, and the country's largest stock market. Also, Beijing is loudly inviting foreign firms to return to Shanghai to develop the Pudong area, a large swath of ramshackle buildings and rice paddies on the Huangpu River opposite the city center. Since the beginning of the 1990s, the central government has annually invested an average of $575 million in Pudong, including bank loans and direct investment. In a move that symbolizes the revivifying confidence and autonomy of Shanghai, the government has allowed foreign companies to bid for the neo-Gothic edifices built by capitalist powers on the Bund early in the twentieth century. Central government officials describe Shanghai as the head of a robust awakening dragon, the crucial nerve center for a growing, vital economy that will stretch across China's midriff, from the Shanghai docks up the Yangtze River to cities deep in the hinterland.

The party has reaped handsome rewards by easing its leash on urban residents like Harold. The incomes of city dwellers have more than doubled since the late 1970s. Trade by China grew more than 12 percent a year from 1980 well into the 1990s, a pace twice that of global trade. Exports by China have swelled more than five times over the 1980 figure.

Internationally minded Chinese like Harold and Linda are responsible for much of the surge in foreign commerce and investment. Like Linda's family in Indonesia, many of the 40 million overseas Chinese across the globe have seized on their family, cultural, and ethnic connections in China to get rich. Harold hopes to arrange some trade deals on the mainland for his overseas in-laws. While enabling Harold and millions of other Chinese to prosper, the policy of releasing market forces has helped the party sustain the minimum level of popular support it needs to hold on to power.

❋

With a suave bearing, snappy wardrobe, and entrepreneurial gusto, Harold has recaptured a dash of the stylish life he looked forward to as a young man in Shanghai. Still, Harold has held true to his upbringing in Confucianism, the ancient system of ethics that emphasizes harmony within families and between ruler and ruled. Throughout his life he has seen firsthand that Confucian ethics are vital to lasting happiness and social cohesion. The immorality of his father, the suicide of his mother, and the treachery among labor camp prisoners made him appreciate the moral code he learned as a child. Beneath his jauntiness, he remains deeply devoted to family harmony and personal loyalty. "I learned how important it is for a couple to stay close, and for a man to be a caring son, caring husband, and caring father," Harold said. Indeed, he works hard today for his wife and stepdaughters because of the guilt he feels for neglecting his mother from 1952 until her suicide in 1957, he said.

Harold believes Confucian ethics can serve as a crucial bonding force for Chinese society as it endures the extreme stresses from rapid growth and change. In his view, Chinese in Hong Kong, Taiwan, and other fast-growing East Asian societies have shown that with Confucianism they can tread solid ethical ground as they leave the land to seek a more prosperous, sophisticated life in the city. Without the ethical cohesion offered by Confucianism, the explosive self-assertiveness that has surged among Chinese during reform could lead to chaos rather than prosperity.

Today, Harold embodies a hybrid of modern Shanghai verve and traditional Confucian rectitude. He is fond of quoting Confucian maxims. One of his favorites is "A promise is worth 100 taels of gold." As a streetwise pragmatist, however, Harold knows that Confucian beliefs must evolve along with the rapid changes in China. So he advocates a neo-Confucianism. For example, at home Harold is not a classic Confucian patriarch, cool and haughty toward his wife and always mindful of his supreme status. Instead, he cooks breakfast, dusts the furniture, runs errands, does the laundry, and helps out with other housework. He puts the happiness of his wife above all else. "Making Linda happy is my top priority. She chose to marry me when I was a nonperson, when my sole asset was the head on my shoulders—I'm happy when Linda is relaxing and enjoying life," he said. Unlike many Chinese, Harold is not bound by traditional ideas. Rather, the ideas help him to live a life of confidence and direct purpose.

Harold has most markedly updated Confucian teachings by refusing to subordinate all his individual interests to the demands of the state. He has realized that because of his submissiveness the government found him an easy target for abuse. Had he been bold and resolute toward authority, the government might not have sent him to the labor camp. He might not have suffered twenty-two years of imprisonment and exile in the countryside.

"I was silent for many, many years, and now I'm determined to defend my interests and the interests of my family," he said. He calls his new approach "assertiveness with Confucian characteristics": He lashes out when wronged but tries to make peace if the wrongdoer admits a mistake. Harold gained notoriety at the school for threatening to resign over a 10-cent shortfall in his hourly pay. The dean apologized and corrected the error.

Harold shows how the pluck of Chinese has risen since the party eased restrictions on their lives and allowed them to pursue riches. After decades enduring party dictatorship, many Chinese like Harold are standing up against official folly and abuse. As if updating Confucius's *Analects* with a new truism, Harold said, "When it's stepped on, even a beetle makes a crackling sound."

PART TWO

The Revival of Old Ways

"Dying Embers Flare Again"

死灰復燃

As Xu Cunyao endured a Communist labor camp, Tibetan nomad Sonam and millions of ethnic minorities struggled against the regime's efforts to destroy their way of life. High on the Tibetan steppe, Sonam helplessly watched Communist invaders massacre his fellow nomads and force survivors into communes. But the brutal campaign to eradicate Tibetan culture failed to shake the belief of Sonam, his daughter Lhamo, and their tribe in Buddhism and nomadic customs.

Lhamo

Photo by Ann Scott Tyson

F O U R

"People of the Black Tents": The Tibetan Nomads

MOONLIGHT STREAMS OVER the grassland as Lhamo lifts the flap of her family's tent and steps into the frosty morning air. Ignoring the whine of a scraggly Tibetan mastiff curled up at the tent door, the young nomad woman rouses a herd of yaks tethered nearby. She squats beside one yak, finding refuge from the cold as her cheek brushes against its shaggy black hair. With a smooth tug she sends warm milk jetting into a wooden bucket held between her knees.

As she works, Lhamo gazes over the broad pasture bathed in silver light. In the middle of the grassy expanse, an icy stream glistens as it gambols down its narrow, rocky bed. About a mile beyond the stream, Lhamo can see the cream-colored summer tents of her family's nearest neighbors pitched against the slopes of the shallow mountain valley. She longs for the conversation of other nomad women who, like she, spend hours each day milking yak and sheep, churning butter, and making cheese. For Lhamo, the hush is broken only by the tripping stream and quiet thud of yak hooves on soft, springy earth.

A pale light stretches across the rugged horizon. As the sun rises, it warms summer pastures thick with sweet-smelling grass. Dew sparkles on the purple clover, buttercups, and sprays of lacy white wildflowers. Lhamo stands, straightens her ankle-length skirt and turquoise apron, and loosens the bright pink scarf holding back her long, ebony braids. Her bucket brims with frothy milk. From inside the yak-hair tent, she hears her two younger brothers giggling as they and their father stir from snug sheepskin beddings.

Lhamo's father, Sonam, also starts the day with a ritual. To him, it is just as vital as the daily milking. As Lhamo stokes the breakfast fire with yak dung, Sonam rises and wraps a wool blanket around his ragged cotton shirt and pants. He reaches up and unties a kerchief hanging from a rope. Unfolding it, he carefully lifts out a stack of Tibetan Buddhist scriptures, tattered from use. Lhamo scoops some hot coals from the stove with a metal plate. Over the coals she spoons *tsampa* (roast barley flour) and sets the offering on a small mud altar in front of the tent door. As the *tsampa* smolders, Sonam belts out a deep "Ohhhhhm" and begins chanting. He sits cross-legged on a sheepskin on the tamped earth floor, snapping his fingers and clapping his hands to punctuate the scriptures.

Like most Tibetan nomads, Sonam is a devout Buddhist. The faith permeates his life, anchoring his values and ideas about the world as it has for Tibetans for centuries. Over and over each day, Sonam recites prayers that he believes will bring spiritual enlightenment and escape from the "wheel of life," a meaningless cycle of death and rebirth in which humans are reincarnated as gods or hell-beings, animals or "hungry ghosts." Sonam also chants to nurture compassion and alleviate the suffering of others. Again and again he murmurs *om mani padme hum,* a mantra chanted constantly by Tibetans to invoke the popular bodhisattva of compassion, Avalokitesvara.

But Sonam's prayers for compassion are often disrupted by images of brutality against Tibetans by Chinese occupation forces. He offers *tsampa* each morning not only for Buddhist deities but also as sustenance for his murdered father. When Sonam was seven years old in 1949, Communist Chinese troops occupied his homeland in eastern Tibet and set out to eradicate the nomads' ancient, devout way of life. On a crisp spring day in 1958, Chinese troops gunned down his father during a bloody Tibetan uprising against Communist rule. Sonam's father was one of tens of thousands of Tibetans killed as they struggled to expel Chinese lowland invaders from their Himalayan kingdom.

The cries of Tibetan fighters like Sonam's father were easily silenced on the desolate highlands of the Land of Snows. For much of the previous 150 years, the exotic Buddhist kingdom had withdrawn into secrecy as deep and dark as the mazelike corridors of its vast monasteries. Tibetan leaders shunned diplomatic ties and banned foreigners. Hidden from world view, the people of Tibet suffered some of the worst atrocities committed by Mao Zedong's Communist regime. Indeed, the story of the subjugation of Tibet is one of the least-reported, large-scale programs of oppression by one ethnic group against another in the twentieth century. After the Chinese People's Liberation Army (PLA) crushed the 1950s uprisings, Maoist cadres forced Sonam's family and other nomads into communes, where people and livestock perished in great numbers. They jailed or executed the Tibetan political elite of high lamas, landholders, and wealthy nomads. In an attempt to wipe out Tibetan culture, they looted and demolished hundreds of monasteries and sent thousands of monks to farms or labor camps. In some areas the Tibetan population declined, and an influx of Chinese settlers threatened to make Tibetans a minority in their own land.

More than four decades of Chinese brutality have scarred Sonam and most Tibetans. Nevertheless, Sonam has not lost hope for his people and culture. Taking advantage of China's eased repression since 1980, Sonam is again openly practicing his unquestioning faith in Buddhism. He and his family are reviving nomadic ways they once feared were gone forever. With renewed confidence and pride in being Tibetan, Sonam has grown bolder than ever before in resisting China's ongoing controls. Far from being resigned to Beijing's military-backed rule, Sonam and other Tibetans are increasingly outspoken in their demands for independence.

As he watches *tsampa* slowly burning over the coals, Sonam feels himself consumed by the desire to avenge his father's killing, push out the Han Chinese, and reclaim freedom for Tibet. "We Tibetans hate the Chinese," says Sonam, his eyes flashing. "We don't want to be part of China. We want our own country."

From Sonam's lonely, yak-hair tent high on the windswept grassland of northeastern Tibet, China seems a world apart. Sonam's encampment lies near the eastern frontier of ethnic Tibet, less than 100 miles from China proper. But the geographic and cultural divide between the two regions is immense.

Sonam and his fellow nomads drive their herds at about 12,000 feet above sea level on the eastern edge of the Tibetan plateau. This rugged, sparsely populated steppe country falls within the former Tibetan province of Amdo, a land prized as the finest herding territory in Tibet. Amdo was one of three major regions of Tibet, bordered by Kham to the south and U-Tsang, or central Tibet, to the west. After the Chinese Communist takeover, however, Amdo was carved up and incorporated as China's provinces of Qinghai and Gansu. Sonam lives in southern Gansu Province, or Gannan, an area the size of West Virginia. The climate is one of the most extreme in the world. The weather changes violently, and blizzards and hailstorms strike with little warning. Winters are long, and the average annual temperature is just above freezing. The high elevation and thin stony soil make the region unsuitable for farming. For thousands of years, Tibetan nomads have subsisted in the harsh terrain much as Sonam does today. Sonam's life is linked inseparably to herds of yak, sheep, and goats that graze on the wild grasses of the steppe. He relies on the animals for food, clothing, shelter, and transport. Survival depends on his ability constantly to outsmart the elements because natural disasters can wipe out whole herds overnight.

From Sonam's camp, the mountains fall away steeply. The icy stream from which Lhamo draws water flows into the Daxia River as it begins a dramatic descent between two cultures, from nomad territory to China proper. The Daxia cascades down narrow green gorges, then levels as pastures begin to blend with farms. Here, Tibetans live in square adobe houses with prayer flags fluttering from poles planted in the corners of flat roofs. They graze herds but also cultivate barley, the Tibetan staple, and other crops. A few remaining monasteries dot the rolling countryside, including the once-powerful spiritual center of Labrang. The Daxia tumbles noisily past the gilded temples of Labrang at about 9,000 feet and rushes on for another thirty miles before gushing through the Earthen Gate Pass.

The pass marks the boundary of the mountainous region of ethnic Tibet. Beyond it to the east lie the flat, dusty settlements and domed mosques of China's tenacious Muslim minority, the Hui. Descendants of ancient Arab mercenaries, the Hui are famed as formidable fighters and skilled traders. For centuries, they have profited as middlemen between Tibetans and Chinese, exchanging the nomads' livestock, pelts, and wool for Chinese teas, grain, cloth, and metal pots. The Hui are also aggressive traffickers in illicit goods. Earlier this century, they ran a lucrative gunrunning business, smuggling firearms of every class and vintage to eager Tibetan buyers. They sold to Chinese vast quantities of locally grown opium. Today, they deal in heroin from southwest China. In towns such as Linxia along the Silk Road caravan route linking China with Central Asia, Hui men in white or black skullcaps and tunics drive wooden donkey carts through crowded marketplaces. Rug merchants hang out wares of crimson and gold. Eateries exude a pungent smell of roast mutton spiced with hot peppers and Chinese prickly ash.

Just as quickly as they appear, the Hui market towns give way to the clustered mud-brick farming villages that mark the fringes of China proper. Beyond Linxia, the Daxia empties into the muddy Yellow River. Here, Chinese peasants scratch out a living from the powder-fine ocher loess of the Yellow River valley, the cradle of China's sedentary agricultural civilization. For centuries, life in the closely huddled communities of ethnic Chinese, or Hans, has been a never-ending cycle of sowing and reaping wheat, cotton, and other crops. Men and women in plain shirts and pants shoulder hoes as they walk or bicycle to ancestral fields. The villages are often dominated by one clan and are tightly knit by Confucian values of stability and self-sacrifice for the group.

The farther the Yellow River meanders east, away from Sonam's solitary camp and into the cheek-by-jowl hubbub of Chinese villages, the more striking becomes the contrast between the nomadic civilization of the Tibetan highlands and the staid lowland farming culture—between the otherworldliness of Tibetan Buddhism and the Confucian preoccupation with temporal order. The sharp cultural differences have pitted Tibetans and Chinese against each other for centuries, especially in the borderlands where Sonam lives.

In the eyes of a Han Chinese peasant in Gansu Province who painstakingly works the tiny plot of land tilled by generations of his ancestors, Sonam's independent, transient way of life is not only abhorrent but also barbaric. Indeed, the Hans have long considered themselves morally and culturally superior to Tibetans, whom they depict as wild, filthy, and lawless. In Gannan's Xiahe County, where Sonam lives, Hans labeled Tibetan nomads "raw barbarians," "cooked barbarians," or "semibarbarians" depending on whether the Tibetans spoke Chinese and engaged in farming, a Chinese historian observed in 1935. Common Chinese, officials, and scholars still widely refer to Tibetans as a "backward" minority group with a population of "low quality" and a "low cultural level." The proud Tibetans resent these attitudes as much as they disdain the Hans' conservative, farm-bound existence.

For centuries, Chinese have used claims to cultural superiority to justify efforts to dominate Tibetans like Sonam and other peoples living on their periphery. The Chinese call their country Zhongguo (Middle Kingdom), the center of the universe. Their emperors reigned with the title Son of Heaven and a divine mandate to govern the world. From the fourteenth century on, China demanded that Tibet, Nepal, and other border kingdoms accept the emperor's supremacy as a precondition for relations. "Barbarian" envoys were required to kowtow and present a tribute of local products to symbolize their subservience. Underlying the delicate court rituals were hard-headed Chinese territorial ambitions. China's chief aim was to annex Tibet and thereby to safeguard its western frontier and gain control over the militarily strategic Central Asian highlands.

For most of the history of relations from the seventh century until the Communist invasion, however, Tibet succeeded in resisting subjugation by China. The Himalayan kingdom enjoyed full independence from China for spans of several hundred years at a time. Tibetan rulers rejected the role of imperial vassals and bowed to the authority of Chinese emperors in name only. They saw the tributary ritual as a formality for trade and diplomatic ties with China, not as a stamp of their subservience. They viewed their relationship with Chinese emperors as a personal one between priest and patron: Tibet's Buddhist leader provided spiritual guidance to the Chinese emperor, who in turn worshiped and protected him. This relationship was established in the thirteenth century and served on and off through the end of China's last dynasty, the Qing, in the early 1900s.

Tibet enjoyed one more brief period of independence after the fall of imperial China in 1911. But in September 1951, Mao's battle-hardened troops, fresh from their revolutionary victory in 1949, marched into the Tibetan capital of Lhasa and completed their military occupation of Tibet. The Communists had achieved China's long-standing goal of annexing Tibet. But they miscalculated in believing they could readily subdue Tibetans like Sonam and uproot a civilization that in many ways rivaled their own.

❈

The sun has chased all but a few shadows from the wide-open grassland by the time Lhamo starts to make breakfast. She crumbles coarse leaves from a brick of tea into a kettle and ladles fresh yak milk over them. She sets the kettle on the single-burner stove in the middle of the tent, where it will offer steaming nourishment throughout the day.

Sonam and his sons, Chamba and Dorje, sit around the stove warming their hands. Lhamo spoons yak butter into bowls for each of them and then drowns the yellow butter with the hot, milky tea. "Our way of life, our food, our herding, has not changed much for hundreds of years," says Sonam. "It is just the same as before," he says, taking a sip of yak-butter tea from his brimming bowl.

The creamy brew symbolizes the nomadic culture that is central to Sonam's identity. Sonam dips his fingertips into the pool of melting yak-butter and rubs it between his palms and over his creased face. The liquid helps protect his skin against the burning sunlight, biting cold, and whipping winds of the grasslands.

After the boys eagerly sip some of their tea, Lhamo opens a wooden box and scoops out several spoonfuls of *tsampa* for each bowl. She then sprinkles hard bits of dried cheese on top. The boys mix the buttery tea, cheese bits, and flour into a doughlike ball, using one hand to stir and the other to rotate the bowls in a gentle, tossing motion. A Tibetan staple, the extremely rich dough, called *ba,* fortifies the nomads against the cold.

Chamba, the elder son, slurps down a second bowl of tea and begins pulling on a pair of leather boots. He will need the extra energy. Chamba is responsible for taking the family's thirty yaks out to graze every day. After leaving camp at midmorning, the teenage boy usually has no hot food or drink until his return at dusk. Often he comes back wet from the rainshowers and hailstorms that drum the pastures in summer months. In winter, he must drive the herd despite the risk of deadly blizzards.

Nomads consider herding a routine task, and where Chamba lives children as young as seven tend whole flocks. But the herder must always be vigilant to prevent livestock from wandering off and falling prey to the wolves that roam the grasslands. As an amulet to ward off misfortune, Chamba wears around his neck a frayed sea-green strip of cloth given to him by a local monk. He also carries a large metal stave tied at the end to a seven-foot-long leather thong. By holding the thong and whirling the stave around his body, Chamba can hold off the vicious Tibetan mastiffs kept as guard dogs by other nomads.

Chamba puts on a weather-beaten, broad-brimmed felt hat. He tilts it at a jaunty angle and goes out to untie the yaks. As the herd begins ambling up the valley, Chamba guides them by hurling small rocks with a snap of his slingshot made of wool and leather. Striding into the expanse, he drives the yaks over a hill and out of sight.

After saying goodbye to her brother, Lhamo continues her chores. She leaves the tent and returns a few minutes later with stream water in a huge container strapped to her back. Lowering the water gently to the ground, she sprinkles a little on the dirt floor and uses a bunch of twigs to sweep out the tent. Stacked around the edges of the tent are the family's main posessions: blankets, boots, a saddle, a large sword, and a pile of wooden yokes. The yaks wear the yokes for transporting the camp to fresh pastures several times each summer.

With the tent tidy, Lhamo goes out to gather yak dung. She scoops up a pile of fresh droppings with two hands and slaps it down on top of another. After piling up three or four of the black mounds, she spreads them on the ground to dry in the sun. The dried dung is the family's most important source of fuel, burned to boil water, cook meals, and heat the tent. The only other visible fuel is a small amount of oil in a glass jar that hangs from a tent post and serves as a crude lamp by means of a rope wick. The long tapering flame provides the tent's only light after sunset.

Lhamo rinses her hands, slides on elasticized cotton bands to cover her sleeves up past the elbows, and begins churning butter. She works quickly, filling the tent with the sound of sloshing milk and the dull rhythmic pounding of wood on wood. Summertime, when the milk of yaks and goats is abundant, is the peak season for making dairy foods. Nomad women must store as much butter and cheese as possible for the lean winter months. After several minutes, Lhamo stops and removes the paste of *tsampa* that seals the churn. She takes out chunks of butter, squeezes them to force out the liquid, and molds them into a shiny yellow bar for storage.

A moist black nose pokes through the tent flap, sniffing. Lhamo smiles and gives the family dog a bowl of whey left over from her earlier cheese-making. The dog and yaks often nose into the tent looking for whey and scraps of food. The night before, a yak lapped up the whey as it seeped from a sack of curds left out-

Sonam and his son Dorje at their summer camp. Photo by Ann Scott Tyson.

doors to drain. Now, Lhamo takes crumbly white cheese from the sack and spreads it out in the sun. It will dry in a few days into pebblelike bits.

Like most Tibetan women, Lhamo is busy from before daybreak until nightfall handling most of the work in camp while the men and boys are herding. This summer Lhamo must labor alone. The eldest child, she is taking the place of her mother, who is tending the family's winter home a few miles down the valley. Despite the lack of female company, Lhamo seems comfortable with her role in the household. She knows her labor is indispensable and earns her a voice in family affairs. She works steadily, often passing time by singing the atonal Tibetan folk songs that wail like the wind over the high steppe. "Women work hard, harder than men," says Sonam, leaning back in a favorite position of repose with his elbow on a rolled-up sheepskin. "But that is how things should be."

At fifty-three, Sonam is enjoying the traditional Tibetan role of the elder male household head. With Chamba and a family friend responsible for the daily herding, Sonam can afford to spend more time relaxing in the tent and visiting other nomads. But this is not retirement. As the family's chief strategist, Sonam makes all the critical decisions on where to herd, when to break camp, and which animals to slaughter for food each year. His experienced judgment is vital to the family's well-being. A single mistake in predicting the weather, for example, could prove devastating for his family's key source of wealth, its herds of thirty yak and 200 sheep.

Chamba leaving for a day of herding. Photo by Ann Scott Tyson.

At midday, Sonam leaves the tent on foot for a neighboring camp on the far side of the wide, sloping plain. Shadows of clouds race over the sunny valley, whisked along by the constant wind. A furry tan Himalayan marmot scurries up a hillside of shrubs and disappears into its burrow. High overhead, the native white-collar bird dips and soars on the gusts. The only sounds are the wind and Sonam's footsteps. As his tent fades in the distance, Sonam is alone in the vast expanse of sky and land. But he strides on, at ease with boundless nature.

Like generations of Tibetan nomads before him, Sonam is proud of how skillfully he and his family make their livelihood in a terrain intolerable to most Han Chinese and members of other ethnic groups. He loves the adventure of life in the saddle and enjoys his far-off but friendly relations with other nomads, who often come no nearer than shouting distance for weeks at a time. He would feel crushed by the eavesdropping intimacy of Chinese villages, where mud-brick dwellings cluster around shoulder-width dirt paths. He treasures his far-roaming herds and would not dream of trading them for the heavy plows and postage-stamp plots of Chinese settlers. He savors his meat, butter, and cheese and shuns the Chinese diet of grains and vegetables. Nomad life is harsh and relatively crude, but Sonam does not feel deprived. For him, subsisting on the grasslands is not primitive or backward. It is proof that he can make the best of what nature offers.

❋

Sonam was born on the grasslands in 1942, the first son of a moderately wealthy nomad couple. His mother bore him alone, perhaps because of a Tibetan animist belief that childbirth is a polluting act that offends household gods. Like most Tibetans, the baby boy had only one name but one with religious meaning. A local Buddhist lama named him Sonam, or "merit" in Tibetan.

As a baby, Sonam was carried naked inside his mother's robes, even in midwinter. Periodically, his mother prompted him to relieve himself and held him out over the snow, his tanned body dangling in the subzero cold. Nomads still expose infants almost from birth to the frigid climate to temper them for life on the highlands. At a neighboring camp, a two-year-old nomad girl plays naked among a herd of yaks, oblivious to a nipping wind. To strengthen and fatten her baby, Sonam's mother fed him yak butter, a common practice among Tibetan mothers today. Sonam remembers his childhood with images evoking comfort and safety. "When I was a little child, I loved to drink milk and eat mutton. That made me the happiest." He would often sidle up to a gentle female yak, yank at her teats, and open his mouth to catch the spurts of warm milk. Sonam's youngest son, Dorje, snacks in the same way today.

Sonam's parents were well-off by the standards of Tibet, where prosperity is measured in terms of livestock and the word for "wealth" also means "yaks." Sonam's family owned a respectable herd of 60 of the sturdy beasts. They also raised 200 sheep and 50 horses. The horses were a luxury that only prosperous households like Sonam's could afford. Used exclusively for transport, horses did not provide·the food and clothing other animals did. They cost more to raise because of fodder and gear like saddles and blankets. The ownership of a horse is still prestigious in Tibet. When Sonam visited the camp of a wealthy male friend, the friend insisted on rounding up his horse and mounting before being photographed. "When I was growing up, my family was like *this*," Sonam said, holding up his first finger in a Tibetan gesture meaning "almost the best," or "well-to-do."

That wealth meant Sonam's family faced a constant demand for herders. Sonam began tending livestock as soon as he was strong enough to endure the long days and bitter weather. Wearing yak-leather boots and a fur-lined jacket made of sheepskin, he would trudge off into the pastures, proudly aware of the approaching manhood that the job symbolized.

"Here, young children can take care of a herd of 200 sheep," Sonam boasts. On his way home from the neighbor's tent, he points to a seven-year-old girl sprinting barefoot after a large flock of sheep. The girl's braids fly wildly in the wind as she grips a slingshot and runs after an errant ewe. "That little girl knows every sheep. If one is missing, she can tell you," Sonam says.

Like most Tibetans, Sonam's parents hoped to follow the tradition of volunteering at least one son to enter a monastery, virtually the only place where common Tibetan children could receive formal education. But they needed Sonam as a herder, and by custom the firstborn son should stay home to help them. So they planned to send Sonam's baby brother instead. They made the decision gladly, viewing it as a good deed that would bring them honor while benefiting their faith. Most families sent their sons to monasteries at the age of eight or ten and afterward continued providing them with food and clothing. The devotion of nomads to the monasteries was so strong that up until 1958 monks represented 20 percent to 30 percent of the male population in Gannan.

The powerful lamas at the Labrang monastery dominated religious, military, and economic life on the grasslands. Founded in 1710, Labrang (literally, "the lama's residence") was one of the two most influential monasteries in northeastern Tibet, a center of learning for the dominant Yellow Hat (Gelug) sect of Tibetan Buddhism. With 108 smaller monasteries under it, Labrang controlled a wide territory, including the pastures of Sonam's tribe and most of Gannan.

Sonam made frequent pilgrimages to Labrang with his family when he was growing up in the 1940s and 1950s. After descending along the Daxia River valley for several hours, he would spy the gilded eaves of Labrang sweeping skyward against the backdrop of steep hills thickly forested with spruce, juniper, and poplar. As he drew nearer to the towering edifice, he could make out the gaping golden dragons that stood guard on temple roofs. Above the temple windows, pleated white awnings flapped in the breeze. Labrang's inward-tapering walls and broad base recalled the majestic Potala, the seat of Tibet's theocracy in the capital, Lhasa. Clustered below its ornate halls and pagodas were scores of squat, earthen courtyard dwellings that housed the monastery's 3,000 to 4,000 monks.

To enter Labrang, Sonam and his parents had to pick their way around hundreds of nomads camped outside the monastery walls. Many of the nomads had walked for days, prostrating every three steps, on their pilgrimage to Labrang. Once inside, the family would follow the narrow pathways that ran between the monastery's tall stone walls, chanting mantras, spinning long rows of wooden prayer wheels, and circumambulating temples clockwise for good luck. They offered gifts before statues of Buddhist deities on altars aglow with small brass bowls of burning yak-butter oil. Sonam's parents often contributed surplus grain and yak butter to Labrang or brought supplies of food for a coming religious festival. Labrang, like other Tibetan monasteries, depended on the offerings of nomads. Sonam's family gave the food readily, as did most nomads, according to historical accounts. In return, Labrang's lamas recited prayers for the nomads, exorcised spirits believed to cause their sicknesses, and gave them protective amulets. Monks also gave nomads advice on secular matters. They predicted the best place to ambush criminals and the best time to raid a rival tribe and acted as scribes in business transactions. "Our religious life was very free," Sonam recalled. "We often went to festivals and asked the lamas to read scriptures for us. So, naturally, I learned about my religion."

When Sonam was a boy, all important religious decisions fell to Labrang's spiritual leader. The lama was the fifth in a line of incarnations named Jamyangshaypa, after the monastery's eighteenth-century founder. Jamyangshaypa's elder brother, Omangtshang, dominated local military affairs as the security chief of Labrang. Omangtshang commanded a Tibetan cavalry equipped with a primitive arsenal of rifles and swords. In wartime, Omangtshang called on tribal chiefs to recruit soldiers and weapons. Every nomad tent had to provide at least one fighter. If that was impossible, the nomads supplied weapons or horses. Labrang's hierarchs often appointed the tribal chieftains, who each ruled over several nomadic encampments like Sonam's. Individual tribes were fiercely jealous of their territory and independence, and feuds among them were common. Within each tribe, the chiefs broadly regulated the use of pastureland, judged crimes, and ordered punishments. But they also granted the far-flung nomad camps the autonomy a herding life demanded. As a result, their authority was largely accepted by Tibetans like Sonam and his family.

"The tribal chiefs were not chosen by us, but they were always people we could accept. They were wise, strong, and had popular trust," said Sonam.

Labrang's leaders and the tribal chiefs below them wielded tremendous power. Still, they did not go unchallenged. The Tibetan rulers had to defend their autonomy against outside encroachments by two self-confident ethnic opponents: the Muslim Hui and the Han Chinese.

Unlike more isolated regions of Tibet farther west, Gannan was a borderland prone to the explosive conflicts and bloody feuds of an ethnic frontier. Labrang and its adjoining marketplace, where Sonam and his family often stopped to buy goods, bristled with the tensions of a rough border town. Tibetan men and women toted long swords and daggers, many of which were ornately inlaid with turquoise and coral. Some carried crude hunting guns. Minor disputes easily sparked fighting between Tibetan pilgrims and the Hui merchants who controlled the bazaar half a mile from Labrang. The Hui made up more than a third of the population of Labrang's market town, and Muslim middlemen dominated the trade of Chinese and Tibetan goods. Another fifth of the town's residents were Han Chinese.

When Sonam's parents were young, the monastery and its marketplace witnessed some of the region's most gruesome ethnic violence. In 1918 fighting broke out over a minor incident between Tibetans and Hui at Labrang. The Tibetans were overcome by troops of the imposing Muslim warlord Ma Qi, who stationed a garrison at the market town. For the next eight years, Ma's troops and tax collectors controlled the town and milked its lucrative border trade. But in 1925 tens of thousands of Tibetans rose up against the Hui and drove them from the town. Ma dispatched 3,000 heavily armed troops. They retook Labrang and mowed down fleeing monks with machine guns. The war plunged the entire region into a maelstrom of ethnic strife. Thousands of Tibetans and Muslims died.

Han Chinese authorities, meanwhile, fueled the conflict through their old tactic of pitting one group of "barbarians" against another. After the 1925 war, they stepped in and took the spoils. Labrang and surrounding areas, which had fallen under Muslim-dominated Qinghai Province, were carved off and incorporated into Chinese-governed Gansu Province as Xiahe County in 1928. At the same time, the Kuomintang (KMT) government under Chiang Kai-shek attempted to co-opt Jamyangshaypa and Omangtshang by giving them official titles. Nationalist influence in Xiahe remained superficial, however, and was limited mainly to token tax collection. Day to day, Tibetans settled their own conflicts, supported tribal militia, engaged in herding or farming, and held religious festivals with little interference from the Chinese administration. Sonam's family and other nomads paid no taxes to China. In their camps Chinese law was completely ineffective, and the arm of Chinese Nationalist rule in the 1940s seemed weak indeed.

In 1949 Communist forces routed the Nationalists and occupied Xiahe. Tibetans offered little resistance, apparently because many of them believed Mao's Communists would become just another aloof Chinese administration and essentially leave them alone. On September 20, 1949, Chinese commanders entered the county seat with one battalion of PLA troops and announced the "peaceful liberation" of Xiahe. In their propaganda, the Communists promised to maintain the traditional Tibetan social, economic, and political system. Initially, Sonam's father and other Tibetans believed these pledges might be true. "In 1949 the Communist Party announced that we were 'liberated,' but there was no big change here then," Sonam recalled.

During the first years of Communist rule in the early 1950s, Sonam's simple life of herding went on much as before. There was no redivision of property. The tribal chieftains remained in power. Sonam freely worshiped a wide pantheon of Buddhist and local animistic gods. Every summer on an auspicious day, Sonam and his father mounted their best horses decorated with colorful bridles and saddle rugs and left the encampment at dawn. They galloped away with a crowd of other Tibetan horsemen, shouting and whooping above the rumble of hooves. Gripping sacrificial wooden arrows several feet long, they bolted to the summit of a sacred mountain. There, amid deep chanting and the musty fragrance of smoldering juniper branches, they stuck the arrows into the quiver shrine that crowned the peak and made offerings of *tsampa* and yak butter to the local mountain spirit (*dralha*). In a ceremony combining primitive folk culture, Buddhism, and the animistic Tibetan faith Bon, Sonam and his father asked the mountain spirit to protect their tribe against sickness, famine, livestock diseases, and in war.

At Labrang, as well, the Communist presence at first was mild. The lamas held Buddhist festivals and rites as before. They inducted new monks, studied Buddhist doctrines, held oral examinations, and provided rigorous training in Tibetan opera, dance, and music. Norbu, a boy just a year younger than Sonam, arrived at the monastery from Sonam's tent community at the age of seven in 1950. Norbu's parents had decided long before that it would be a great privilege for him to become a monk. It took a little longer, however, for the idea to dawn on Norbu.

"When I left my family, I was a little bit homesick," the elderly, maroon-robed monk recalls from his quiet sunlit dwelling at the monastery. "But after two or three years I understood some written Tibetan, and I knew I could learn about culture here," says Norbu, whose name means "jewel."

The illusion that life would go on with little change was perhaps the main reason Sonam's father did not resist the Chinese Communist takeover early on. But Tibetans were deluded for other reasons as well. Some were swayed by a naive idealism and faith in Marxist propaganda. This was true for the families of Tupden, one of Sonam's relatives, and Tupden's friend, Ngawang. Ngawang's father had joined the Communist underground in Gannan before 1949. His job was to maintain secret contacts between the Communists and their sympathizers in the Tibetan community. In 1949 he worked as an interpreter for the first regiment of the

First Field Army under General Wang Zhen, the hard-liner who directed the "liberation" of Xiahe County from a headquarters in the nearby Hui town of Linxia.

Other Tibetans simply chose to collaborate. For example, the KMT-appointed military commander at Labrang, Omangtshang, fled Xiahe on the eve of the Chinese takeover. But he apparently changed his mind only a few days later when he showed up at the propaganda rally staged to welcome the PLA troops. According to Communist histories, Omangtshang, who took the Chinese name Huang Zhengqing, attended a rally of some 10,000 people at Labrang on September 21, 1949. The crowd supposedly shouted "Long live the Communist Party!" amid dancing and firecrackers. Omangtshang may have realized the futility of resisting the well-trained PLA with his loosely organized, tribal-based Tibetan calvary. In any case, he was rewarded with a string of high offices. On October 1, 1953, he was appointed chairman of the new Gannan Tibetan Autonomous District.

Another important collaborator was Labrang's new spiritual leader. The fifth Jamyangshaypa had died suddenly in 1947, and according to Tibetan Buddhist tradition a search team was formed at Labrang to find his reincarnation. Scouting in nearby Qinghai Province, the search team discovered a Tibetan boy who would become the sixth Jamyangshaypa. Conveniently for the Communists, he was only seventeen months old when the PLA marched into Xiahe in 1949. The Communist regime used the boy in an attempt to win over the Tibetan faithful. To bolster its image, it dispatched a delegation of high-ranking PLA and party officials to Labrang in 1952 bearing the customary Tibetan gift of long silk scarves. The scarves were presented to the child reincarnation at his installation ceremony. In 1957 officials named the nine-year-old Jamyangshaypa head of the state-controlled Buddhist Association of Gansu Province. It was the first of a series of highly visible yet powerless positions the Communists gave him in an effort to legitimize their rule.

Jamyangshaypa, Omangtshang, Ngawang's father, and others like them were among the Tibetans first recruited to a new privileged class of minority cadres and figureheads groomed by the Chinese Communists. Whether out of naïveté or by design, they played a crucial role in speeding China's subjugation of Tibet.

For almost thirty years since its founding in 1921, the Chinese Communist Party had sought to "liberate" Tibet. Now, fresh from defeating the Nationalists, the Communists had the toughened, well-equipped army to achieve that goal. The Communists wanted to move quickly to occupy the strategic Tibetan highlands and secure China's borders with India and Central Asia. In September 1949, as Chinese troops swept into Sonam's homeland in eastern Amdo, Beijing was already announcing plans to annex the entire Himalayan kingdom, by force if necessary. "Tibet is Chinese territory and no foreign aggression is allowed. The Tibetan people are an indivisible part of the Chinese people," Radio Beijing warned in a broadcast in September.

The next summer, the PLA invaded the southeastern Tibetan province of Kham and captured its capital, Chamdo, in early October 1950. Fielding a force of about 40,000 troops, the PLA quickly decimated the Tibetan army of 8,000 soldiers and officers. Half were killed and the rest forced to surrender. From there, the Chinese army advanced toward central Tibet. On September 9, 1951, some 3,000 PLA troops entered the capital of Lhasa. Within three months the occupation force had grown to 20,000 men. With troops garrisoned in all major cities, Chinese military control of the Buddhist kingdom was virtually complete.

Initially, China pledged to grant Tibet a limited degree of autonomy. Beijing said it would maintain Tibet's political system and religious freedoms while taking charge of its foreign affairs and defense. Any "reforms" in Tibet would be carried out only after consultation with "leading Tibetan personnel," it said. Beijing formalized these pledges in a seventeen-point agreement it imposed on central Tibet in 1951.

Although Beijing made similiar promises of autonomy for the eastern Tibetan regions of Amdo and Kham, it excluded these regions from the accord. From the beginning of their invasion, the Communists marked Amdo and Kham for much closer integration with China. Using a classic divide-and-conquer strategy, the Communists worked to exploit the historical tensions between the Tibetan government in Lhasa and the semiindependent tribes of eastern Tibet. They effectively partitioned the country by limiting the accord to central Tibet. Beijing then moved to speed the integration of Amdo and Kham with Chinese border provinces.

In the mid-1950s, the Communist regime abandoned any self-imposed restraints in eastern Tibet and launched a series of policies flagrantly aimed at remolding life there. Swept up by Mao's radicalism, Chinese authorities in Amdo and Kham set out to end family-based herding, force nomads into collectives, and remake Tibetan society in line with the "socialist transformation" under way in the Chinese lowlands.

In March 1956, Maoist officials in Gannan's Xiahe County, where Sonam lives, met to discuss "the question of pastoral areas going the socialist road." Over the past two months, higher-ups in Gansu Province and Gannan had called for collectivizing the nomad economy, and Xiahe's cadres gushed with enthusiasm for the idea. They scrambled to organize "mutual aid cooperatives" in herding areas. That year alone, Xiahe and nearby Zhuoni County set up a total of 170 such groups. In 1957, Xiahe officials were spurred on to new heights of leftist zealotry by Mao's nationwide attack on his rightist critics. Again, Xiahe accelerated the drive to collectivize, and by February 1958 the county was on the brink of banning family-based herding and imposing full-fledged people's communes.

Once it became clear that the Communist Party intended to eradicate their way of life, nomads in eastern Tibet rose up. Nomads like Sonam's father were alarmed by the push to collectivize. They resented official intrusions on their age-old customs, such as attempts to confiscate the ornate swords and guns they wore so proudly. After long years of suspicion and sporadic hostilities, the deep-seated animosity between the border nomads and Han Chinese erupted into open conflict.

All along Tibet's eastern frontier with China, nomads formed guerrilla bands and began attacking the Communist occupation forces in dozens of bloody sorties. In the spring of 1958, Sonam's father took up arms with his fellow tribesmen in a major uprising against Chinese rule in Gannan.

Sonam recalls that the night after the insurrection began, his father burst into the family tent, his eyes aflame. He spoke to Sonam's mother in a hushed voice as he sat drinking tea and eating *tsampa*. Then, saying nothing, he began cleaning his hunting rifle and making bullets by hand. Sonam, then sixteen, watched from his sheepskin bed as his father worked by the light of an oil lamp late into the cold night. Sonam drifted into sleep. When he awoke at dawn, his father was gone.

Chinese retaliation against the revolt came swiftly and brutally. A detachment of about 100 PLA troops attacked Sonam's tribe the next day, but the nomads managed to defeat them. "They were Hans and we killed them all," Sonam said.

But soon a second phalanx of Chinese soldiers armed with machine guns and backed by artillery and shells assaulted the mountain encampment. This time the nomads, equipped only with swords, knives, and a few hunting rifles, were hopelessly outgunned. "Although our people are very brave, we could not fight the Hans off," Sonam said.

Sonam's father never came home. He was killed by Chinese troops along with hundreds of other members of the tribe, Sonam said. Sonam had no time to mourn his father's death. As the oldest son, he had to take charge of his family amid the chaos unleashed by the massacre. "So many adults were killed or arrested at that time. Nowadays, you don't see many old people around here," he recalled years later.

Party authorities in Gannan labeled the uprising an "armed rebellion" led by "an extremely small number of reactionary elements who tricked the masses." They accused Tibetan "rebels" of laying siege to government offices, "murdering grassroots cadres," and destroying roads, telephone lines, and other "state property." Chinese troops "suppressed the rebellion within a very short time," although "not a few comrades" lost their lives, according to biased official histories of the event.

As the PLA decimated Sonam's tribe, Chinese authorities dispatched more than 150,000 troops to put down the unrest flaring all across eastern Tibet. The troops were aided by Tibetan quislings who served as guides, translators, and "dog beaters" as the PLA moved in to nomad camps. Many Tibetan guerrillas escaped by fleeing from Amdo and Kham to central Tibet. There, they were active in huge protests in Lhasa in March 1959. According to Chinese military sources, more than 80,000 Tibetans were killed outright as the PLA crushed the uprisings of the 1950s. Western Tibetologists say most of the killings occurred not in central Tibet but in communities like Sonam's in the border regions of Amdo and Kham.

China's use of force in Tibet in the mid-1950s destroyed all pretensions that its rule would be benign. Thereafter, superior military strength was the mainstay for China's highly unpopular rule. The uprising in Lhasa in 1959 and the flight of Tibet's god-king, the fourteenth Dalai Lama, to exile in India gave Beijing the opportunity to launch long-planned socialist "reforms" throughout Tibet. Chinese authorities swiftly silenced any opposition to the repressive policies.

After the PLA crushed the uprising by Sonam's tribe, troops seized the Tibetans' prized weapons. One day about three months later, Sonam watched as a Chinese "work team" made up of some forty soldiers and cadres entered his encampment. Similar teams were stationed at every nomadic and farming settlement in Gannan that summer. "No one could oppose them. It was their 'land under heaven,' their dominion. If you resisted at all, you would be shot immediately," Sonam said. He had never felt so humiliated and defenseless.

The work team led a sweeping witch-hunt for any Tibetans suspected of having joined or sympathized with the resistance. It is impossible to state with certainty how many Tibetans in Gannan were executed or sent to labor camps for "reeducation." But Tibetan cadres today say more than 20,000 Tibetans in the region, or one out of seven, were severely persecuted in 1958 alone. Even Chinese authorities admit to using excessive force in "suppressing the rebellion" in Gannan. They made "grave mistakes" and inflicted "great injustices" on Tibetans, according to recent official histories.

After eradicating potential resistance, Gannan authorities launched their most aggressive campaign yet to impose communism on the grasslands. They called the fanatical movement an "antifeudal struggle"; through it, they aimed to obliterate all Tibetan political, economic, and religious institutions deemed exploitative by the Communists. In Sonam's encampment, cadres categorized all nomad families along Marxist class lines. Then they formed "antifeudal struggle work teams," which recruited the poorest nomads to "expose the crimes" of tribal chiefs and wealthier nomads. These headmen, who Sonam says enjoyed the genuine respect of the nomads, were publicly beaten, jailed, or sometimes killed by Communist activists. Sonam's maternal uncle was arrested. He owned large herds of sheep, yak, and horses and was one of the richest nomads in the tribe. For his alleged crimes of exploitation he spent the next twenty years in a prison near Lanzhou, Gansu's capital. In 1962, Sonam made his farthest trip ever from home to take food to his jailed uncle. It was Sonam's first—and last—venture into China's vast lowlands to the east.

"All the people like *this* went to jail," Sonam said, sticking up his thumb in a Tibetan gesture that means "number one." "All the people like *this* became cadres," he said, flicking up his little finger to signify people of low social status or character.

The purging of tribal headmen and wealthy nomads cleared the way for a drastic reorganization of the nomadic economy in Sonam's encampment and the rest of Gannan. In the summer of 1958, spurred by the party's quixotic vision of the Great Leap Forward in economic production, Gannan authorities redoubled their drive to set up communes. The herds of Sonam's family and those of all other nomads were corralled by authorities and put under communal ownership. Each family was assigned to labor on a production brigade, a subdivision of a commune. By September 1958, Gannan had forty-seven hastily organized communes. It was the first region in Gansu Province to invest all grassroots political and economic power in the commune leadership.

As Gannan's cadres bragged that they had "reached heaven in a single bound," Sonam and his family languished under the earthly disaster caused by Mao's policies. The communes abolished the delicately balanced system of family-based herding that was vital to the survival of the livestock. Nomads lacked the means and incentive to ensure that the large, unwieldy communal herds were amply grazed, skillfully bred, and promptly treated for disease. As a result, the sheep and yaks began to die in large numbers. The total number of livestock in Gannan plummeted by 35 percent between 1957 and 1962, from 1.7 million head to only 1.1 million head, official Chinese figures revealed later.

Additional thousands of livestock died when one-track economic policies destroyed the animals' winter grazing lands. In line with Mao's dictum to "take grain as the key link," officials forced nomads in Gannan to break out some 200,000 acres of pastureland for cultivation. The effort to make the region self-sufficient in grain was exhausting and futile; the grasslands are ill-suited for farming because of their high altitude and thin stony soil. Despite the increased acreage, by 1962 grain output in Gannan had fallen 42 percent from the 1957 level. The production of oil-bearing crops plunged 86 percent, according to recent official statistics.

The economic mismanagement gave rise to a devastating famine in Gannan and across China from 1959 through 1961. Sonam and other nomads, whose survival depended almost exclusively on their herds, were hit especially hard by the disaster. "After the animals died, the people started dying," Sonam said.

Sonam and other nomads were forced to live on a Chinese-style diet of grain. At the communal canteen, Sonam received one small bowl of barley flour a day. The hardy youth hungered for the yak butter, dried cheese, and meat essential to the nomads' diet. In the early months of the commune, cadres sometimes secretly drank yak milk. But the supply dried up quickly as sickness and famine ravaged the livestock. Soon, even grain fell short. "I was so hungry," Sonam recalled. "A lot of people were starving to death."

Sonam felt his strength being slowly sapped away. One day, he could no longer bear the emptiness in his stomach. He sneaked away from the production brigade and struggled out of view over a hill. He fell to his knees and began digging in the earth. He pulled up several wild plants, devouring them on the spot. Soon afterward, Sonam fell violently ill when his gut was invaded by some toxin or infection from the unwashed plants. He was sick for a year.

Sonam was fortunate. His body fought off the ailment and slowly recovered. Many thousands of other Tibetans lost their lives during the man-made famine and political purges in the first decade of Chinese rule. In an indication of the immense human toll, the Tibetan population of Gansu Province, most of which lives in Gannan, dropped 31 percent between 1957 and 1961, according to official Chinese statistics. Moreover, far fewer Tibetans were born and survived between 1958 and 1962 than in previous years.

Chinese rule also exacted a huge toll on the spiritual life of Sonam and other nomads. The Communists compelled the nomads to abandon their Buddhist worship for the atheistic rituals of Marxism. In Sonam's camp, authorities banned all religious practices, including the chanting of Buddhist mantras, the reciting of scriptures, and the conducting of rites such as the arrow-planting festival. "Religion was completely forbidden. We could not worship at all," said Sonam, "but we held onto our faith."

One night, Sonam stole away from his production brigade into the nearby hills, dug a hole, and buried his family's Buddhist scriptures, portraits of incarnate lamas, and other religious objects to save them from destruction. Later, he moved the treasures to one of the remote mountain dugouts where herders took shelter from blizzards.

The nomads were not the only target. Communist authorities also assaulted the monastic system that formed the institutional bedrock of Tibetan Buddhism. They purged thousands of monks and demolished Labrang's powerful network of monasteries. The PLA staged a ruthless campaign at Labrang in 1958, plundering the monastery and setting up a headquarters there. All other monasteries in Gannan were either shut down or razed, their religious treasures looted and shipped to China proper or melted down as scrap metal. Of the 16,000 monks in Gannan, Communist cadres killed some, sent others to labor camps, and forced the rest to return to a secular life of herding or farming. The cadres compelled many of the clergy to disgrace themselves by marrying, drinking liquor, or smoking in violation of strict monastic discipline, say Labrang monks.

"I was not beaten. I was too young. But I could not practice my religion," recalled Norbu, the monk from Sonam's tribe, who was fifteen years old in 1958. Norbu was forced to leave Labrang and return to the grassland, where he would spend the next fourteen years as a herdsman on a commune.

Young Tibetans like Sonam and Norbu felt enraged but powerless as Communist officials turned their lives upside down. Sonam had ample reason to detest the Maoist cadres. They had killed his father, driven his prosperous family to near starvation, and abolished a way of life embraced by his ancestors for centuries. But Sonam would have further cause for anger. The Communists were not satisfied with laying waste to traditional Tibet. They wanted to destroy the identity of Tibetans and remold them as ethnic Chinese.

After the 1958 uprising by his tribesmen, Sonam watched Chinese authorities work systematically to assimilate Tibetans. In creating the Gannan Tibetan Autonomous District in 1953, authorities drew the boundaries to include a predominantly Chinese county, thereby diluting the district's Tibetan population to just over 50 percent. Now, the government promoted a massive resettlement of Han Chinese to nomadic areas. Sonam estimates that 6,000 Chinese from the central and eastern provinces of Henan and Hebei moved to the vicinity of his tribe. The Han settlers brought with them their sedentary farming culture. But their attempts to transplant such practices in the grasslands proved catastrophic. The settlers harvested only scant crops of millet and wheat. Soon they too began to perish. "Many of the Hans starved. Women had to abandon their babies because they couldn't feed them. People from Henan did that," Sonam said with a grimace. Still, Han Chinese soldiers, officials, workers, and peasants continued to move into Gannan in large numbers.

In another effort to impose Chinese ways and tighten controls over the no-mads, authorities forced them to quit their tents in 1958 and move into a new village of permanent adobe dwellings. The nomads feared that digging aroused the wrath of the earth spirits and abhorred building the houses. Even more, these herding families—known locally as "the people of the black tents"—felt their very identity destroyed by the confining boxlike dwellings. Sonam had grown up feeling the sunlight, wind, and rain swirl around the family's tent; he felt trapped by thick walls that shut life out.

The Communists also set up schools to indoctrinate nomad children with Marxist philosophy and teach them Chinese language, history, and culture. Sonam attended a primary school for six months at the age of sixteen before he fell ill from malnourishment and eating wild plants.

To strengthen its policies of assimilation and control after 1958, the Communist Party stepped up its drive to recruit and train Tibetan cadres. As Sonam labored on the commune, the party groomed his young relative Tupden and Tupden's friend, Ngawang, to become officials. Ngawang, the son of the Tibetan PLA interpreter, was sent to kindergarten in the Chinese city of Lanzhou in 1956 at the age of four. "I was educated entirely by the Communist Party," said Ngawang, now a government official, in fluent Mandarin. Ngawang spent twenty years in schools in China proper.

Tupden, the bright son of nomad parents from Sonam's tribe, went to school in Xiahe County. In 1977, he was enrolled for eight years at the Central Institute for Nationalities in Beijing, an exclusive college for training minority cadres. He was trained as a translator of Chinese and Tibetan. In all, more than 4,200 young Tibetans like Tupden were recruited in Gannan alone in the thirty years after the Chinese takeover as part of the party's effort to "energetically nurture minority cadres with Communist consciousness."

Ultimately, however, China's efforts at remolding Tibet backfired. The closer the contact between the lowland occupiers and the highland nomads, the more their cultures clashed. Mutual contempt between the two groups deepened.

Communist policies in Tibet were founded on an assumption of Chinese superiority that propaganda could hardly disguise. Occupation forces swaggered with the chauvinistic Chinese view of Tibetans as barbarians. Typical are the impressions of a Sichuanese soldier who spent eleven years as a PLA driver in Tibet in the 1960s and 1970s.

"Tibetans are primitive. They aren't clean. They have water, clear water, but they don't wash," said Qi Bangquan, now a taxi driver in the city of Chengdu. "In the winter, to prevent frostbite, Tibetans will kill a sheep and wipe the blood all over their faces. They don't wash it off, they just keep wiping on more blood. It's frightful. They look like ghosts with their red faces." Many Han Chinese are so convinced of Tibetan savagery that they unthinkingly tell such tales. The driver likely confused for blood the red makeup commonly used by nomads.

For their part, Tibetans chafed at the paternalistic attitude of Chinese, whose culture and ideology were anathema to them. Sonam and other nomads scorned Chinese agrarian life as impractical and unsustainable on the grasslands. As a

Buddhist, Sonam was repulsed by the Chinese practice of infanticide. Monks like Norbu recoiled at the atheism of the Communists. And Tibetan cadres like Tupden emerged from years of indoctrination as some of the most vehement critics of the regime they were groomed to serve.

Indeed, China's draconian policies in Tibet only strengthened the nationalism and ethnic consciousness of Tibetans. Lacking arms and strong organization, Tibetans had no conceivable chance of overthrowing Chinese rule. But silent opposition intensified, especially as Tibetans were lashed by a new storm of Maoist fanaticism during the Cultural Revolution (1966–1976).

Sonam was quickly assaulted by Maoist zealots. His family's past wealth and father's role in the "rebellion" made him an obvious target for "struggle." Sonam hated most the mass rallies staged by Red Guards. At the rallies, the Red Guards forced nomads with lower or "revolutionary" class backgrounds to chant abuses at the "class enemies" among their kinsmen. The Red Guards often dragged Sonam before such a crowd, shrilly denounced him, and beat him viciously with a thick leather cord. "They said my 'thinking' was bad," Sonam recalled with a scornful smile.

Red Guards also compelled the nomads to "draw a line" between themselves and former monks like Norbu. They ordered the nomads to denounce the revered holy men as "monsters and demons." Meanwhile, the young radicals destroyed any vestiges of Tibetan Buddhism they could find, smashing and burning relics as part of Mao's campaign to eliminate "old customs, old habits, old culture, and old thinking." In a further sign of the rabid extremism of the Cultural Revolution, authorities in Gannan banned Tibetan New Year celebrations and forced nomads to undergo military training instead "to prevent class enemies from waging destructive activities."

The decade-long campaign further impoverished Sonam and his family. In the face of widespread famine in 1961, moderate leaders in Gannan had briefly seized control of the economy and scaled back the communes. Surviving herds, though sparse, were redivided among families in Sonam's tribe and elsewhere on the grasslands. Living conditions improved slightly. But during the Cultural Revolution this moderate line was attacked as "revisionist" and its advocates were purged. Communes returned in full force.

Maoist authorities urged Sonam and other nomads to sacrifice all to "herd for the revolution." Propagandists created political martyrs for the nomads to emulate. They glorified one poor nomad in Gannan who supposedly demanded to go on tending the commune's herds despite his advanced liver cancer. He herded until he dropped. With his dying breath, he allegedly assured his mother that with Mao at the helm she could "put her heart at ease."

Sonam swallowed his rage as local leaders, slaves to Mao's whims, launched one disastrous economic policy after another. Many of the policies marked an attempt by local authorities to match the largely fictional successes boasted by Dazhai, Mao's model commune in Shanxi Province. In the early 1970s, Gannan authorities were determined to prove that they, too, could "transform heaven and earth." Their call for a rapid increase in the region's livestock provoked a sudden spurt in the size of the herds. This upset the natural balance between animals and land by seriously damaging the pastures. Soon, large numbers of livestock starved.

Blindly following mandates from above, cadres forced the nomads to dig costly wells despite Gannan's plentiful rainfall. The authorities also led several exhausting drives to exterminate the pika, a short-legged, round-eared mammal similar to a rabbit and native to the grasslands. The Chinese called pikas "rats." "Exterminating the rats is not only a battle against nature. First, it is a revolution in thought, a rupturing with the feudal superstition and customs of the old era," states a 1973 propaganda booklet on Gannan. "Rats are the enemies of the grassland. To eliminate one more rat is to eliminate one more enemy," the booklet declares in the militant language of the time.

The campaign to poison the pikas sapped the nomads' energy and violated the Tibetan religious taboo on killing animals unnecessarily. It may also have damaged the pastures. The pikas, considered harmless by Tibetans, actually promote grass growth because their burrows aerate the ground, according to Western scientists. In some nomadic areas, the Chinese even killed off the Tibetan dogs, perhaps to protect themselves from attack. Consequently, wolves and other predators devoured many head of livestock.

For Sonam, the decade of beatings, humiliation, and freakish political events was the worst time of his life. As he looks back over the ten gloomy years, his only bright memories are of his marriage in 1967 and the birth of his first two children, Lhamo and Chamba.

※

A midafternoon rainstorm rolls down the valley, drums on the tent roof, and rushes away. Sonam reaches up and yanks on a yak-wool tether, opening a flap in the tent roof and letting crisp air and blue sky pour through.

"Yeeeeeeee!" All around the glistening mountain vale, the shrill cries of nomads celebrate the storm's passing. Sonam steps out onto the wet grass and watches a rainbow arching over the encampment. "The grasslands are the most beautiful at this moment, when the sun comes out after a rain," he says.

Since the Cultural Revolution ended in 1976 and China eased its repression in Tibet, Sonam has watched many Tibetan traditions reappear like rainbows after the monotonous, gray storm of Maoism. But Sonam's dream of fully reviving nomadic life under a free Tibet has proved as elusive as the shimmering mist.

Inside the tent, Sonam rakes the coals and settles down on his sheepskin rug. Dorje, his youngest son, pounces on him with a giggle and then hangs around his neck, stroking his sideburns and mussing his hair. Sonam sits patiently, clearly enjoying his frolicking boy. When Dorje is out of earshot, Sonam chides him for being too irresponsible to trust as a herder. Dorje is impish and small. But Sonam may also keep Dorje off the range simply because he likes having him nearby.

A lone visitor arrives at the tent, a stocky young man sporting a broad-brimmed wool hat. Lhamo quickly steps out to greet him. Dorje springs catlike to the flap door behind her and, flashing a grin, cranes his neck to eavesdrop on the conversation. Lhamo and the man chat quietly. She has reached the age when Ti-

Sonam and a young member of his tribe. Photo by Ann Scott Tyson.

betan women can freely entertain suitors. But for Lhamo, marriage poses a dilemma. Sonam has chosen her, his most dependable child, as the one to stay home. Unless she elopes, as some Tibetan nomads do, Lhamo will have to find a man who is willing to "marry in."

As Lhamo and the young man talk, they watch a nomad caravan approaching from the head of the valley. The heavy plodding of yaks laden with wooden tent beams and other gear rumbles like distant thunder. A herd of bleating sheep, some carrying small saddlebags, trots in front. Men on horseback drive the animals. Some women and children ride behind the men; others walk alongside the slow procession. The caravan stops beside the stream, and Lhamo runs to help the newcomers make camp. She joins the other women busily driving in tent stakes with heavy wooden mallets and pulling the tent strings taut. Within minutes, the first tent is standing, its yak-hair and canvas fabric offering ready cover from another rain shower.

Lhamo ducks into the tent, talking and laughing with the other women as she helps them unpack. She is glad to have girlfriends close by. She has heard much about this nomad family by word of mouth. But she rarely has an opportunity to visit with its members. Because the nomads need to spread out to locate ample pastureland for their herds, Lhamo may not see a member of her tribe for months at a time. The long separations make each coming and going especially bittersweet.

Today, an aura of calm has returned to the encampment as Sonam and his family revive their ancient way of life. Like thousands of other Tibetan nomads, the family is taking advantage of social and economic reforms initiated by China's post-Mao leadership. Beijing began loosening Mao's totalitarian controls on the Tibetan highlands in 1978. China's reformist leaders realized that Tibetans and other ethnic groups were deeply alienated by Mao's rule. Non–Han Chinese ethnic groups make up only 7 percent of China's population, but they inhabit 60 percent of its territory, mainly in strategic border regions. An estimated 5 million Tibetans, including more than a million nomads, live in China today. To woo this small but important population, the Communist Party scrapped some of Mao's most radical policies. It rehabilitated political prisoners, dismantled communes, and allowed a limited restoration of Tibetan religion and ethnic customs.

In Gannan, authorities announced in August 1978 that they would begin "redressing false and unjust cases" from the 1958 crackdown. The suppression had gone too far, they said, and led Tibetans to suffer "great political injustices." The authorities agreed to rehabilitate those who were wronged and grant them economic compensation for their hardship and losses. After twenty years, Sonam's uncle was released from prison. He returned to the tribe weak from years of physical abuse and malnourishment. Sonam, vindicated politically after the public beatings of the Cultural Revolution, emerged as a popular and trusted member of his tribe. Since 1983, he has led a nomadic group of 400 people, winning support with his easygoing and down-to-earth style.

By 1981, authorities had disbanded Gannan's communes in all but name and redistributed livestock and other communal property among the nomads. Once again, Sonam's family grazed its own herds. Nomads in many areas who had suffered severely when forced to take up farming under Mao quickly reverted to family-based herding. Gannan authorities pledged to restore herding as the mainstay of the region's economy. Gannan, they said, would become a "modern base for herding and forestry of the first rank."

In the early 1980s, Sonam and fellow nomads watched their income rise rapidly as their herds grew. By 1984, the number of livestock in Gannan reached 2.6 million, nearly double the 1957 figure. Sonam's area was named an "advanced herding zone." For the first time in years, Sonam and his family had enough to eat. In 1983, he was able to afford a metal butter churn. (He still prefers the worn wooden one, though.) Today, Sonam's family remains poor by Chinese standards. But with 30 yaks, 200 sheep, and 3 horses, it can meet its basic needs. A few nomads have become prosperous. The wealthiest man in Sonam's tribe, for example, has 1,400 sheep and 90 yaks. He recently bought a tractor for $1,800.

Just as Sonam has filled his stomach, he has satisfied a spiritual hunger by practicing Tibetan Buddhist rites. Sonam and thousands of other nomads have gained more leeway to worship since the early 1980s, when Gannan authorities ended bans on many popular Buddhist rituals and began reopening Labrang and other monasteries. The authorities also admitted that the 1958 crackdown and its aftermath led to "brutal interference in the legitimate religious beliefs and customs of the masses."

Once again, Sonam is free to mount his horse on a summer morning and ride to a mountain summit for the arrow-planting festival. Recalling his boyhood excursions with his father, Sonam now takes his eldest son Chamba along. Sonam chants scriptures every morning and hangs a large photograph of the Dalai Lama in a wooden frame from his tent beam without fear of harassment. Chamba wears his protective amulet as he leaves camp for a day of herding. And Lhamo makes her 100 daily prostrations before the tent door, praying to ward off sickness and other misfortunes from her family. Tightly grasping her string of multi-colored prayer beads, she kneels down, stretches her body to the ground, stands, touches her forehead with folded hands, and kneels again.

As some of the peaceful rhythms of prayer, churning, and herding return to Sonam's life, his vehement opposition to Chinese rule remains. The rebirth of ancient customs has given Sonam new confidence and pride in being Tibetan, making China's overlordship all the harder to bear. Although he enjoys some renewed freedoms, Sonam realizes that Beijing's reforms have merely softened the guise of its domination over Tibet. He and other Tibetans are frustrated by what they see as China's continued economic exploitation, ethnic discrimination, and political and religious restraints.

Sonam strongly opposes Beijing's heavy-handed intrusion in the nomadic economy. Above all, he resents Beijing's persistent efforts to force Tibetan herders to settle down. In 1991 the government carved up the winter pastures of Sonam's tribe, assigned each family a fixed plot for grazing its herd, and charged an annual fee for the use of the land.

Chinese experts claim that the policy will encourage nomads to take better care of the pastures. However, the program ignores the need for redistributing pastures periodically to account for changes in the size of family herds, say Western Tibetologists. The government has ruled out such readjustments by binding nomads to one plot and banning the ownership or sale of land. If a family's herd expands, for example, it will not have enough grass. Over the long term, the policy minimizes the number of livestock. This runs against the Tibetan strategy of maximizing herds as protection against natural disaster. Nomads like Sonam complain, moreover, that the policy is causing tension within the tribe by disrupting the system of open pastures. "Each household has only a little bit of land, but the yaks need a lot of room," Sonam said, as he stood near a neighbor's tent overlooking the broad mountain valley. "Now, if my yaks cross over and eat your grass, we will fight!"

Although authorities have already parceled up the tribe's winter pastures, Sonam and his kinsmen have resisted pressure to divide their summer grazing land. "The nomads are telling the government 'no,'" he said.

Sonam and other nomads also bitterly resent economic exploitation by China, mainly in the form of heavy taxes. Each year, nomad families in Gannan must pay taxes on every sheep, yak, and horse they own. The government also taxes the production of wool, dairy products, and meat. The levies eat up more than half of Sonam's annual income. "Except for pissing and shitting, the Chinese tax the Tibetans for everything here," said a middle-aged woman from Sonam's tribe. "The

Chinese say that in the old society Tibetans were exploited by landlords, and now they call this voluntary!"

Nomads say the squeeze by China is worse than any financial obligations they had under Tibetan rulers. "Before 1958, we paid no taxes like this. We gave food to the monastery. But we didn't have to give it; we did because we wanted to," Sonam said.

Even Tibetan cadres such as Sonam's relative Tupden, a beneficiary of Chinese rule, harshly criticize what they call China's economic "colonialism" in Tibetan regions like Gannan. Indeed, some of the most sweeping attacks on Chinese rule today come from cadres like Tupden. A thin middle-aged man with a pockmarked face, Tupden has worked for the Xiahe County government for nearly ten years. His intimate familiarity with China's mechanisms of control has intensified his contempt.

"The Communist Party treats us like a colony. We have no economic freedom," said Tupden as he sat cross-legged in a window seat on the upper floor of his Tibetan-style home in Xiahe. "For more than forty years we have walked in lockstep with the Communist Party, but we are still poor. We have forests, grasslands, and water resources. All of these are controlled by the Chinese. They plunder our resources at will. They tear down our forests as they please. No one can oppose them. The government says: 'This belongs to the country, not to you.'"

Since reforms began in the late 1970s, the government has continued to siphon off Gannan's abundant, cheap supplies of leather, wool, and lumber and transfer them to Chinese areas for processing. Partly as a result of such ongoing exploitation, Tibet and other inland ethnic regions have fallen far behind China's prospering coast, a fact that adds to the resentment of cadres like Tupden. Chinese officials and scholars have blamed the poverty of Tibetan areas on the inherent backwardness and "poor quality" of the Tibetan population. This prejudice pervades government policies and limits opportunities for Tibetans, Tupden said.

Ethnic discrimination by Chinese against Tibetans is widespread in Xiahe County. Schools, for example, are dominated by Han Chinese teachers, books, and curricula. This poses a tall hurdle for Tibetan students, who must often learn Chinese in order to study at all. As a result, the attrition rate for Tibetan students is much higher than for Chinese in the area. A large percentage of Tibetan children start school late or stay away altogether, according to official statistics. For nomad children, poverty, long distances, and cultural barriers make schooling especially difficult. Sonam's children have not attended school. Instead, Sonam taught himself rudimentary Tibetan and is now teaching his children the Tibetan alphabet at home.

The bias against Tibetans is also strong in Xiahe's government, Tupden said. Local affairs are dominated by Han Chinese. Most Chinese officials can speak only a few words of Tibetan, and so official business goes on in Mandarin Chinese. Virtually all reports, official documents, and communications are in Chinese. Although there are many Tibetan cadres in Xiahe, Tupden said they lack any real influence or responsibility. Tibetans in high positions are mere figureheads, he said. Real power lies in the hands of Han Communist Party members and their shadow government. "Even if I became county chief, the Chinese would not give me any genuine power. The Hans really don't trust us," he said.

Chinese most flagrantly show their hostility toward Tibetans, Tupden said, in official policies making Tibetans a minority in their own land. Since the Communists came to power in 1949, there has been a massive influx of Han Chinese to Gannan. In Xiahe County during the mid-1930s, Tibetans made up 96 percent of the population. Today, they comprise less than two-thirds of the county's inhabitants. Between 1949 and the early 1980s, Gannan's Tibetan population dropped from 60 percent to 40 percent, and the Han population grew to surpass 50 percent. Hans are largely responsible for a surge of births in Ganna, with a birth rate two and a half times that of Tibetans between 1953 and 1980. Nevertheless, China began imposing birth control on Tibetans and other minorities in the early 1980s. Tibetan couples, like Hans, are limited to one child in towns and other areas where the population is concentrated. One Tibetan woman who works in the city of Lanzhou said that unless she signed an "only-child certificate" promising not to have another baby, she could not gain urban residence for her newborn girl. In herding areas, nomads can have two children or at most three if they live in a very remote area. If they have an extra child, they face a fine of $54, or more than half of their annual income. Women who violate birth quotas risk being forcibly sterilized, Tupden said. He described one case in which a Tibetan woman died from infection after doctors left a surgical implement in her abdomen during the procedure.

"Here, there is a lot of land and few people, so why are they trying to control our population? Their final goal is to eliminate our nationality," Tupden said.

Communist restrictions on Tibetan religion and monasteries, though more subtle and insidious than under Mao, also anger the people of Gannan. Norbu the monk, for example, deeply resents the constant efforts of Communist authorities to watch and manipulate him. Norbu returned to Labrang in 1982 after twenty-four years of forced exile on the grasslands. He joined a group of some 1,000 surviving monks in Gannan, their numbers drastically reduced from the 16,000 Buddhist clergy in 1957.

In 1980, however, as workmen repaired Labrang's ornate stupas, authorities were crafting new internal control mechanisms for the monastery. In October that year, Gannan established an official Buddhist association, and in 1981 a management committee was set up inside Labrang. Both organizations had the aim of promoting "patriotic" religious activities, including "propagating party policy." The management committee of twenty-odd members restricts the number, age, and selection of monks and dominates day-to-day affairs at Labrang. Although boys as young as seven or eight live at the monastery supported by their parents, the committee bars them from formally becoming monks until they pass a test at the age of eighteen.

The party quietly works to indoctrinate young monks through a Buddhist institute set up in 1986 to train teachers for the monasteries. All monks who enter the institute must gain approval from the management committee. The students are required to undergo indoctrination in the party's policy and its Marxist critique of religion. In 1992, for example, the institute circulated an internal document issued by the State Council, China's cabinet, that stressed the inevitable "withering away" of all religion. It characterized Tibetan Buddhism and other faiths as mere tools used by rebels to manipulate people. And it warned of the continuing need to "strike down counterrevolutionary elements wearing religious cloaks."

In a blatant attempt at thought control, the management committee bars all monks except those at the institute from listening to radios or watching television, monks say. Shortwave radio broadcasts by the Voice of America, which has a Tibetan-language service, are popular among Tibetans in Gannan as a source of objective news about their exiled leader, the Dalai Lama. Beijing considers the Dalai Lama a subversive who, along with his "separatist clique," is intent on separating Tibet from the Chinese "motherland." When the Dalai Lama won the Nobel Peace Prize in 1989, authorities attempted to suppress spontaneous celebrations by Tibetans at Labrang and across the country. They also forbid the sale of the Dalai Lama's photograph at Labrang and force monks to prominently display pictures of the late Panchen Lama, a collaborator of the Chinese regime who died in January 1989.

Sitting on a wooden bunk in his quarters at Labrang, Norbu carefully sews a golden lining into his long-sleeved winter overcoat. Sunshine streams in the window, falling across his bare shoulder and maroon robe. Norbu, now in his fifties, stops sewing and wipes a hand over his bald head. His face is placid, but he speaks in hushed tones. "All the monks wear the same robes, but we don't know their inner feelings," Norbu whispers. "There are a lot of police informers in monk's clothing."

Labrang is rife with tension and intrigue, according to Norbu and other monks. Police constantly watch the monks, relying on spies and the monastery's own "security group." Informers are instructed to alert police to any sign of political activism among Labrang's clergy. Police patrol Labrang nightly, jogging in groups along the main street outside. They frequently search the monks' quarters. All monks must be inside Labrang before a 10 P.M. curfew. To escape the repression, scores of monks from Labrang have attempted to flee across the China-Nepal border to Dharmsala, India, the seat of the Dalai Lama's exiled government, Norbu said. "We don't have much freedom." The creases deepen on Norbu's tanned face. "My greatest hope was to go happily through life, but I can't now. I am just sustaining a life of bitterness."

❄

For Norbu, Tupden, Sonam, and many other Tibetans, the bitterness of Chinese rule has but one radical antidote: independence for Tibet and the return of the Dalai Lama. Tibetans have voiced these demands with growing assertiveness in recent years, despite the vast political and military obstacles.

"We all believe it would be better if Tibet were an independent country," Sonam said, to the nods of a nephew and burly fellow nomad sitting around him in the tent. In their native Amdo dialect, the three men held an animated discussion of a protest for independence staged by monks at Labrang. "We want to split with China," Sonam said, shoving a few chips of dried yak dung into the hot coals of the stove.

Although Sonam craves freedom, he knows firsthand the power of China's military. The army's control over the grasslands is as formidable now as on the day in 1958 when the PLA killed his father and other nomad fighters. "Now, Tibetans don't have any weapons. It is even hard to carry a good knife. Tibetans like guns very much. But if we get one, the police will throw us in jail," Sonam said. "We don't dare defy the Communist Party now," he said. "We have to survive."

Sonam, like many nomads, does not see himself as an activist. But he firmly supports the sporadic demonstrations against Chinese rule staged by thousands of urban Tibetans since the late 1980s. Many of those protests, beginning with a huge demonstration in Lhasa in September 1987 in which several Tibetans died, have been led by young Tibetan monks, cadres, and intellectuals who are part of an active underground independence movement. Protests are frequent at Labrang, despite the omnipresence of police. In March 1992, for example, a dozen monks were jailed and badly beaten for distributing proindependence leaflets in Xiahe.

Off a dusty alley in the monks' quarters at Labrang, a young activist monk named Lobsang describes why he risks his safety, and possibly his life, for Tibetan independence. He sees his mission as political as well as spiritual. "I became a Buddhist because Buddhism is for helping people. That is what I want to do," Lobsang said in quarters decorated with a poster of a snowcapped mountain and colorful wallpaper.

Lobsang, the son of Tibetan farmers near Xiahe, entered Labrang at the age of fifteen. He left the monastery temporarily to gain a university education in Lanzhou, then returned. Now, he is in his late twenties. "Some monks don't get involved in politics. But in Tibet religion and politics cannot be separated. They are like your two eyes or two arms."

Many Tibetan cadres like Tupden are also strongly committed to independence. As he smokes cigarette after cigarettte in a late-night conversation at his Xiahe home, Tupden betrays an agonizing guilt for serving a regime he secretly despises. Such feelings make him and other cadres potentially powerful subversives. "I feel very contradictory," Tupden admits, looking out the window over the rooftops of Xiahe. "I do the work of the government; I depend on it to live. But I hate the Communist Party."

Still, Tupden believes that the chances for Tibetan independence are rising with the decline of communism in China and the rest of the world. "As the Hans kill off Tibetans one by one in protests, opposition is growing stronger," says Tupden, who has connections with Tibetan activists as far away as Lhasa. "For Tibetans, independence is an imperative."

Tupden's friend Ngawang, the Xiahe official who was groomed by the party since kindergarten, has also emerged as an ardent nationalist. He admires the fourteenth-century Tibetan leader Changchup Gyentsen, who launched the country on a 300-year golden era of genuine independence and prompted a renaissance of Tibetan Buddhism. With the ebb and flow of history, Ngawang believes, Tibet will one day prevail. "For ninety years, the river flows east. For forty years, it flows west. A Tibetan must fight his entire life for his nationality."

What unites ordinary nomads like Sonam, activists like Lobsang, and disaffected cadres like Tupden is a powerful sense of anticipation as Tibet awaits the right opportunity to reassert its nationhood. But perhaps more than Sonam, Lobsang and Tupden look with growing urgency toward the day that Tibetans will rule themselves. For even as Tibetans struggle to break free from China's political controls and efforts at cultural assimilation, they face the equally daunting challenge of rapid modernization. Tibetans, they believe, must prepare for a growing onslaught of foreign tourists, high technology, and materialism if their culture is to adapt and survive. "If we don't have revolutionary change and change the traditional outlook, one day they will put us in a museum and lock the door," said Lobsang as he sipped a bowl of noodle soup in the garden of his courtyard dwelling.

As dogs barked on a path outside, Lobsang spoke of Tibet's pressing need to absorb new ideas from abroad and integrate them with its age-old culture. One of the first concepts Lobsang wants Tibet to adopt is democracy. Before the 1950s, Tibet was an isolated theocratic state with religious and political power concentrated in the hands of the Dalai Lama and the influential but conservative monasteries. The failure of Tibet's leaders to institute democratic reforms early this century weakened the country and made it easier for the Chinese Communists to take over. China's occupation halted any movement toward political pluralism in Tibet. Lobsang hopes independence will clear the way for democracy. "I think Tibet will certainly become independent, but I also want it to become democratic, so the people can change their leaders if they like. I heard on the radio that the Dalai Lama wants a system with a premier and a president. That is very good," Lobsang said.

Lobsang believes that Tibet also vitally needs its own modern educational system. He and other activists have plans to fund independent schools that pretend to support the government while secretly promoting Tibetan culture and nationalism. "Knowledge is like a weapon for us," he said. "But many Tibetans are without knowledge. They are very poor, and they are blind."

Nomads like Sonam know little about the modern world. Sonam's most sophisticated piece of technology is a Swiss-made Roamer-Breveté watch that is more than forty years old. He was given the stainless steel antique by a senior monk at Labrang, who had worn it for thirty-six years. Except for his journey to Lanzhou in 1962 to take food to his imprisoned uncle, Sonam has spent his entire life on the grasslands. His picture of the world beyond his remote mountain camp is a patchwork of bits of information from outside travelers. "Is it true that night darkens other parts of the world when it is daytime on the grasslands?" Sonam asks a visitor to his tent as he whittles pieces of dried meat off a mutton bone.

The nomadic ways of Sonam and his children will inevitably change as modernity encroaches on the grasslands. Already, in Lhasa and other cities many young Tibetans appear to be as taken by pool and pop music as they are by prayer wheels and mantras. But the footloose herding life runs deep in Sonam's blood, just as Buddhist piety infuses his spirit. Sonam has held to his traditions through decades of persecution by China's Communists. He will not easily abandon them amid the excitement and distraction of a modern age.

The sun is setting over Sonam's encampment. On the horizon, shimmering clouds of smoke waft from the black silhouettes of neighboring tents. As twilight dims the grasslands, an evening chill settles in the mountain valley. Lhamo puts on a black cotton wrap and leaves the tent, humming a song about the Dalai Lama that is always on her lips. She strides quickly up the mountainside to meet her brother as he drives the yaks homeward. Whistling and snapping a slingshot, he sends the yaks running. Like shadows in the dusk, the shaggy creatures gracefully pass over the crest of a hill and descend toward camp, their long black hair waving.

As darkness falls outside, Sonam and his children gather around the glowing stove making supper. Sonam cuts up a strip of fresh mutton, drops the meat into a pot, and adds water and salt to the stew. Lhamo mixes up a flour dough, Chamba kneads it, and together the family members toss pieces of flattened dough strips into the stew, making noodles. After the dinner simmers, Lhamo gives each person a bowl and a twig to eat with. Under the flickering oil lamp, they talk and laugh as they grow warm from the hot meal. During a lull in the conversation, Sonam reflects on his future, his dreams. "Of course I wish that the Dalai Lama would return to his own land. But I'm already over fifty, and I'm afraid that I may be dead before he comes here," Sonam says softly. He uses a stick to rake some hot coals into the pit before the stove.

Like many Tibetans, Sonam yearns to set eyes on the Dalai Lama. Sonam worships the Dalai, who was born in an Amdo village in 1937, as both a god-king and national savior. But with liberation for Tibet still remote, Sonam seeks the simpler, immediate freedom to live out his traditions. "We have been herdsmen for thousands of years. We have no real desire other than to stay here, herd our yaks, and sustain our lives."

After a bowl of tea, it is time for bed. Sonam lays a thick wool mat on the ground and covers his sons with a heavy sheepskin jacket and yak-fur coat. He snuffs out the lamp. As the children settle down, Sonam lies awake in the darkness. Lifting the edge of the tent, he gazes at the moon rising between the hills, its silver light flooding over the backs of grazing horses and glistening in the stream.

As Tibetans and other ethnic nationalists challenge the Communist Party's grip on border regions, clansmen like Wang Bao are undermining party power at its rural base. A former Red Army guerrilla and Communist cadre, Wang has turned his back on the party and embraced the village clan. Like millions of rural Chinese, he spurns Marxism as he rediscovers his ancient bloodline and beliefs.

Wang Bao   *Photo by Ann Scott Tyson*

FIVE

"Descendants of Kings":
The Wang Clan

IT IS MIDDAY. Wang Bao and thousands of his clansmen, some brandishing knives and bamboo staves, gather on a grassy rolling bluff on the outskirts of their ancestral home. On the opposite bluff about a half mile away, Yang Huan and his ragtag army of kinsmen hurl curses at the Wangs. They hoist red flags, signaling they are ready for battle.

Between the bedraggled armies of the clans, a broad, verdant valley glistens in the subtropical sun. A stream runs down the middle of the bright green checkerboard of paddy rice and sugarcane. Not far away, it flows into Zhanjiang Harbor on the South China Sea. More than twenty years before, this remote stretch of land in southwestern Guangdong Province was covered by the sea. But in 1968, Maoist officials mobilized thousands of peasants to fill the inlet in a massive land reclamation drive. Where fishing junks once sailed, farmers wearing straw hats trudge in mud behind water buffalo yoked to plows. With the waters gone, the rival Wang and Yang clans clash face to face on land, their territories divided only by the narrow stream.

Under the burning sun, a dare-to-die corps of two dozen Yang clansmen scrambles down one side of the bluff and into the fields. The men step nimbly along raised dirt paths that crisscross toward the stream boundary. A shouting band of Wang men rushes to counter them. Gunfire bursts from the fields. As it echoes between the bluffs, cries and puffs of smoke rise from the lush valley. Two Wang men, a youth of twenty and a thirty-one-year-old father of three, lie dying in the muddy fields. "This is war!" yells Wang Bao, a clan elder from the Wang settlement of Huanglue.

After dark that night, as Wang families mourn, scores of Wang clansmen storm out of Huanglue bound for the nearby county seat of Suixi. There, they raid the arsenal of the county militia, seizing hundreds of Mauser pistols and machine guns, thousands of bullets and shells, and six antiaircraft guns. At daybreak the next morning, the Wangs begin firing the antiaircraft guns at the Yang village of Wenche. In a weeklong bombardment, they hit dozens of homes with hundreds of shells. Meanwhile, far out of range on a distant hill, local policemen squat on their haunches and watch.

❋

Wu Ai climbs the dirt path rising from Mawen village to a hillside and stops before a pile of shattered stone, the ruins of an ancestral tomb sacred to his kinsmen. "The Wangs demolished it, like all the others!" says the wiry, leather-skinned village chief. He points to a dozen rubble-strewn grave mounds scattered across the misty clearing. "They are savages. But they outnumber us, so we can't do anything about it," Wu spits out each word.

Strife between another branch of the powerful, far-flung Wang clan and the embattled, tightly huddled Wus is rooted in the clans' conflicting claims to the graveyard at Mawen village, twenty-five miles northeast of the scene of the Wang-Yang clash. Groves of shade trees ring the site and fall away into a gentle valley. Local geomancers trained in the Chinese art of divination, *feng shui,* believe the tranquil burial ground is steeped in life-giving forces. Knowing this, both Wangs and Wus seek to bury their ancestors in the auspicious site, tap the flow of beneficial forces, and secure wealth, many offspring, and outstanding success for their kin. For decades, the Wangs have prevailed.

Dominating the hillside is the elaborate black tomb of a founding ancestor of the Wang clan, an imperial official of the Song dynasty (960–1279). Each year during the Chinese Qingming (Pure Brightness) festival honoring ancestors, thousands of Wangs join a pilgrimage to the grave. There, they sacrifice meat and wine and burn paper money for their ancestral spirit in a celebration of clan solidarity. As part of the ritual "grave sweeping," the Wangs pick weeds and repaint the tombstone with bright red characters. They also smash or exhume rogue Wu graves and chop down encroaching trees to stop them from leeching the site of its rich forces.

The feud intensified with a bloody clash in 1990, when some 5,000 Wangs descended on the gravesite on foot and in a convoy of 53 cars and 1,000 bicycles. Now, as Qingming approaches, both sides seek to avenge their fallen blood brothers. Wu Ai rallies his young kinsmen from nearby towns, arming them with knives and wooden clubs to defend their village of 600 people. Meanwhile, Wang elders, vowing to level Mawen, mobilize some 10,000 kin from as far away as neighboring Guangxi Province, more than 100 miles to the west.

❋

Lin Yaheng beams at the crashing of gongs, drums, and firecrackers across the unsown winter fields of his village of Shibu, a few miles down a winding dirt road from Mawen. The jubilant din of the religious rite rings out a personal victory for Lin, who recently bribed his way out of the township jail. Lin spent four months in the squalid jail after township officials labeled him a "spirit scoundrel" for enthusiastically reviving the worship of Shibu's ancient deity, Kang Wang. Now, each resounding drumbeat affirms Lin's certainty that the Communist Party's struggle against his native faith is doomed to fail. "People here don't care about

Marxism. They don't follow any party line. They just pray to the god for sustenance," says Lin, a young entrepreneur who manages the village firecracker factory.

Defying official warnings, Lin and other Shibu residents take a brightly painted, intricately carved wooden statue of Kang Wang out of hiding and place it in the village temple on every important holiday. The statue is worth $1,000, more than the average yearly income of village households. It is the third commissioned by the villagers in as many years, after one was destroyed and another confiscated by police.

Today, on the eleventh day of the lunar New Year, Lin and some 300 villagers gather before the temple. Three men hoist Kang Wang onto an awaiting palanquin. Others grasp a colorful flag. Then, to the loud banging of drums, gongs, and bursting firecrackers, the entourage sets off across the fields in the traditional "touring of the god." The band of celebrants stops at neighboring villages to feast, drink, and watch plays performed for Kang Wang. In turn, villagers in Shibu host touring deities from other hamlets. "Every village around here has a god, and 90 percent of the villagers believe in this," says Lin Bingliang, a long-serving Shibu cadre and Communist Party member. "It has no bad influence. It's harmless. Moreover, it's our tradition, so why oppose it?"

Wang Bao, Wu Ai, and Lin Yaheng fight separate battles in the lush hills of southwestern Guangdong Province, the rough and unruly southernmost corner of China's mainland. But their struggles, all of which unfolded in 1991, dramatize a common story: the revival in rural China of ancient ways long suppressed, but not uprooted, by the Communist state.

Across China's countryside, villagers like Wang, Wu, and Lin are reveling in the strength and profound moral appeal of family-based clans, native religious sects, and other traditional groups that once permeated rural life. Virtually eradicated under Mao Zedong, these groups are reemerging in new forms today to unite millions of rural Chinese in an embrace of blood, money, and ritual.

China's peasants began rediscovering their traditions in the early 1980s with the breakup of communes, return to family farming, and easing of Maoist controls on village life. For the first time since 1949, villagers dared to explore quietly their prerevolutionary past. No longer afraid of Mao's radicals, they unearthed genealogies buried by their kinsmen that revealed forgotten histories of ancestors often dating back more than a millennium. Elderly villagers retold the legends behind local deities and described rituals surrounding birth, marriage, and death, defying the party's effort to quash the so-called feudal superstitions.

Many villagers like Wang, Wu, and Lin had lost confidence in the party and Marxism after suffering repeated economic disasters and radical campaigns in the 1950s, 1960s, and 1970s. For them, the revival of beliefs deeply rooted in Chinese culture filled an ethical and spiritual void. They embraced the worship of ancestors and local gods and with it age-old Chinese explanations of life and death. Official evangelism for a "socialist spiritual civilization" rang hollow; prayers at the village temple and the grave sweeping at Qingming met their need for sustenance. Clans and religious groups emerged as vital sources of moral authority in villages.

Chinese peasants also began looking to clans and other native groups for a more pragmatic reason. They needed organizations to lead, unify, and protect them as market reforms weakened the party's rural apparatus. Villagers naturally turned for leadership to clan chiefs and other figures whose blood ties, charisma, seniority, or natural talent commanded popular trust. For example, Lin Yaheng is influential in Shibu because villagers respect his skill as a factory director and religious organizer. The celebrations of Lin and other Shibu villagers have unified their community, and the "touring of the god" helps them overcome conflicts with neighboring hamlets. In Huanglue, Wang Bao and other clan elders resolve disputes among kinsmen, enforce clan law, and organize the clan's defense against rivals. The clan itself serves as a ready-made support network, smoothing business deals and expanding trade, bailing members out of jail, or paying for their funerals. It often reaches to Chinese overseas.

Today's Chinese clans and religious sects have not regained the full strength of their imperial and Nationalist-era predecessors. They lack the ideological backing of a Confucian state supportive of patriarchal kinship and instead face ongoing hostility from the Communist regime. Enmeshed in petty rivalries and parochial disputes, they are too fragmented to throw off party rule entirely. More conservative than rebellious by nature, they usually avoid direct conflict with the state.

Still, in thousands of Chinese villages, the rising autonomy of kinship and religious groups is speeding the party's slide into irrelevance. Peasants in these same villages backed the Communists in the 1949 revolution and remain vital to the party's long-term survival. Now, however, they often follow their own agenda, laws, rituals, and leadership. Many unofficial peasant groups control their own funds and territory. And, more than ever before, they blatantly ignore party policy and Marxist dogma to ensure their own survival and growth.

As millions of peasants shift their loyalties to kin and cult, they deny the party its lifeblood. Even the most stalwart party members are defecting from its ranks. Clan elder Wang Bao, for example, is a former Communist guerrilla and soldier and a long-serving party cadre. By embracing the clan and its beliefs, Wang and others like him are co-opting the party at the grass roots.

In an era of jarring social change, peasants like Wang are gaining a sense of unity, security, and meaning from traditional groups that the party has long failed to provide. With surprising flexibility, these groups are emerging, village by village, as a decisive force in China's awakening rural society.

The story of Wang Bao traces the history of a Chinese clan from its primacy in dynastic China, through its brutal suppression by Communist activists under Mao, to its reemergence with the decline of the Marxist state in the 1980s and 1990s. Today, as Marxist rituals and controls fade, it is celebrating the revival of ancient rites and spreading its all-embracing paternalistic rule.

On the road to Wang's farming settlement of Huanglue, bright green stalks of sugarcane sprout in the fields. At a roadside stall, a man peddles coconut milk and steamed mounds of glutinous rice wrapped in lotus leaves. Pigtailed girls on bicycles ride by munching on sticks of raw sugarcane. A motorcycle and sidecar buzz past a plodding ox as it hauls a wooden cart toward the cluster of red-brick homes with gray-tiled roofs.

In Huanglue, signs of the clan's resilience are as bountiful as bamboo shoots after a spring rain. Villagers, almost all surnamed Wang, crowd around a lively ancestral temple in the center of town at noon. Inside, they kowtow to the temple gods, guardians of their well-being. Some villagers offer plates of steaming chicken and bowls heaped with rice at the altar before carrying them home in straw baskets.

In the land of Wang, the first question asked a stranger, even a foreign one, is "What's your clan name?"

Down a muddy path from the temple in a spacious two-story farmhouse, Wang Bao and two other elders sit on a wooden bench admiring their most prized possession: an elaborate clan genealogy recorded during the Qing dynasty (1644–1911). To Wang and his kinsmen, the genealogy (*zupu*) is a vital, living symbol of the clan's status, prosperity, and power. It is also the clan's *Who's Who*. Spanning nearly 1,000 years, it is a treasury of famous ancestors, glorious episodes in clan history, and Confucian morals to be inherited by every Wang today. Wang Bao gently opens the tattered red cover. "This is our earliest ancestor," he says proudly, tapping a wrinkled forefinger on a smooth yellowed page. "I belong to the twenty-sixth generation of his descendants."

An entry of bold hand-stroked characters in classical Chinese reveals that the clan's founding father, Wang Yueyan, was a high-ranking official of the Song dynasty. Centuries before Yueyan's birth, the Wang clan originated in the rugged northwestern city of Taiyuan, claiming to be offspring of China's legendary Yellow Emperor. (The Chinese character for "Wang" means "king.") From there, the clan branched out across the country. In the ninth century, Yueyan's ancestors led the Tang dynasty's (618–907) military conquest of Fujian. Yueyan was born in Fujian's Min County in the late tenth century. In 994, he passed the highest imperial examinations for Confucian scholars and entered the prestigious Imperial Academy. But one day in about 1006, after gaining an official rank, Yueyan dared to criticize the government. As punishment, he was banished to a poor backwater of the realm, Xuwen County on the tip of Guangdong's southwestern Leizhou Peninsula.

For Yueyan, the subtropical outpost was like the end of the earth. Lonely promontories overlooking the shark-infested South China Sea bore names like End of the Line. The coast was dotted with the fishing villages of the Li, Miao, and Yao minorities, who were considered barbarians by Yueyan and most Han Chinese. The soil was sandy and parched, which made farming difficult. Across a narrow strait lay Hainan, an island dreaded by Chinese exiles for its dark mists, strange diseases, and alien people.

In 1016, Yueyan moved 100 miles north to better land in Huanglue, Suixi County, where he started a farm, fathered a son, and founded the local Wang clan. "He is our most important ancestor," says Wang Bao, to the nods of the elders sitting beside him. Each year during Qingming, most of Huanglue's 10,000 residents worship at Yueyan's grave. "Everyone has a father and mother. Everyone should worship their ancestors," Wang says matter-of-factly.

In the two centuries following Yueyan's move to Huanglue, the Wangs and other clans gained strength from a large migration of imperial officials to China's southern frontier regions. Many officials sailed south from Fujian to the Leizhou Peninsula to flee invading northern tribes during the southern Song dynasty (1127–1279). On the remote peninsula, the officials had a relatively free hand in building up sophisticated clans, undeterred by the dynastic struggles, political intrigue, and imperial armies of the north. Strong, tightly knit clan organizations helped the Han Chinese migrants push out local ethnic minorities and survive the peninsula's frequent typhoons and droughts.

Wang carefully turns the genealogy's worn pages, past Yueyan's son, his grandsons, and his great-grandsons. The strict rules that dictate the listings underscore the patriarchal nature of Chinese clans and rural society. Only the direct male descendants of the founding father are listed, in order of seniority. Each man's entry briefly describes his marriage, male offspring, birth, and death. Eldest sons are recorded first, and sons of wives outrank those born to concubines. Men without sons are forbidden from secretly "substituting a cow for a horse" by adopting a brother's child, for this would "confuse the line." Daughters are excluded altogether. After marriage, a woman may appear in her husband's genealogy, but she lacks any individuality. She is listed only by her surname to show which clan she came from and only if she bears a son—her supreme obligation. Upon a man's death, the *zupu* records his age, burial place, and often the alignment of his grave, which is thought to affect the flow of good or evil forces to descendants.

As Wang Bao slowly leafs through the genealogy, he stops at the name of a ninth-generation descendant, Wang Taishou. One of the clan's most illustrious ancestors, Taishou gets a lot of ink in the *zupu*. In the early 1400s, he passed exams in the Confucian classics and entered the Imperial College of the Ming dynasty (1368–1644). Beginning in 1424, he served for twenty years in a string of high-ranking imperial posts in Zhejiang, Guangxi, and Fujian provinces. His wife and two concubines bore him six sons. In 1445 he retired in Huanglue, where he died at age ninety-nine.

Taishou's fame and power ushered in a golden era for the Wang clan. Grateful to the clan for giving him a rigorous Confucian education, Taishou used his high office to enrich his kinsmen's fortunes and status. By the time of Taishou's death, the Wangs had overpowered other lineages in the area. They evicted a rival clan and occupied Huanglue's most auspicious burial ground. Taishou was buried there, amid effusive eulogizing, next to the transferred remains of the Wangs' founding ancestor, Yueyan.

The Wangs and other clans benefited handsomely from ties to China's ruling elite. But their success ultimately lay in their appeal to ordinary Chinese. For merchants and landowners, the clans offered an important channel for acquiring status. For common farmers, they organized irrigation, roads, and other public works projects. For the poor, they offered charity, relief, and jobs. And for all clansmen, they resolved disputes without resorting to official courts. In return, Chinese helped their clans amass territory, wealth, and manpower.

Kinship groups like the Wangs also offered Chinese a firm philosophical and emotional grounding. They gave order to people's day-to-day lives by upholding a strict Confucian hierarchy: Fathers should be benevolent, sons dutiful, and wives obedient. Through ancestor worship, they gave meaning to death and the afterlife. A powerful lineage guaranteed loyal clansmen honor, veneration, and a chance of immortality after death—with gifts of food to keep the spirit from melting away as a "hungry ghost."

By the nineteenth century, influential clans like the Wangs as well as smaller lineages permeated Chinese society, especially in the south. The self-regulating kinship groups filled a power vacuum left by the imperial regime at the village level. They commanded local militia, controlled marketplaces, fought for territory, and built up huge ancestral estates, eventually owning as much as 35 percent of the land in south China. In the Wangs' home province of Guangdong, up to half of the peasants lived in villages together with their lineages.

Wang Bao closes the *zupu* and lays it gently into an old wooden box. "We protected this," Wang says, patting the musty tome. "After the revolution [in 1949], clan elders buried it in a wooden box. If they hadn't done that, the *zupu* would have been burned up! We wouldn't know any of this, who our ancestors were, what offices they held, where they lived," he says, raising his voice and slapping his knobby knees.

"A few years ago, Wang Bangzhen dug it out. Bangzhen is cultured. He writes characters very well," Wang says, nodding toward the wizened octogenarian sitting beside him. Wang Bangzhen smiles broadly, raising his thick white eyebrows.

❦

Wang Bao takes a pinch of homegrown tobacco out of its newspaper wrapping. He picks up his yard-long bamboo water pipe, stuffs the tobacco in the bowl, and lights it with a match. The pipe gurgles deeply and he puffs out a cloud of blue-gray smoke that swirls around his gaunt face. Wang is tall and extremely thin. His high cheekbones, sunken cheeks, and hollow eyes are framed by gray-speckled brush-cut hair. As he smokes, Wang slips off his brown plastic sandals and props a foot on the wooden bench. His bent legs look like broken chopsticks. Wang hands the pipe to Bangzhen and then to sixty-seven-year-old Wang Zhenghe. Zhenghe, also a retired cadre like Wang, is a wealthy, influential clan patriarch and the owner of the roomy farmhouse.

Wang Bao rests the water pipe against his leg, settles back on the wooden bench, and mulls over the recent tumultuous history of his family and clan. "In my grandfather's day, the Wangs had great power," he says. "My grandfather was powerful too. He had a lot of land in Huanglue. He was rich. But he loved to gamble."

Wang's paternal grandfather, Wang Tingjie, was born into a well-off Huanglue household in the mid-1800s. As the eldest son, Tingjie was obligated by Confucian moral codes to care for his three siblings and provide for his parents in their old age. He was also expected to be a success and, most vital, to father sons. Tingjie married a young woman surnamed Li from a neighboring hamlet. Fortunately for Tingjie, she bore him three boys. The eldest, born in 1881 when Li was only eighteen, was named Huaigong (Cherish Fairness). The second, Huaiping (Cherish Peace), was born in 1888. The third, Wang Bao's father Huaizheng (Cherish Justice), was born in 1897.

Two years later in 1899, French warships sailed into the harbor of Guangzhou Bay (the old name for Zhanjiang). At the time, China's last dynasty, the Qing, was crumbling from popular uprisings and foreign invasion. A wave of Western aggression had forced the Qing's Manchu rulers to open a dozen treaty ports on China's coasts and inland waterways. France, expanding its colonial empire north from Indochina into Guangdong, wanted the city of Zhanjiang with its fine deepwater port as a place to store and transport coal. When the Qing resisted, French marines occupied Xiashan, the southern district of Zhanjiang. They built camps and forts equipped with cannon and took control of the harbor.

The French met little resistance from the submissive Qing magistrate, named Xiong. But as they stepped up their campaign in Zhangjiang in the summer of 1899, a new magistrate named Li Zhongjue opposed them. Li enlisted the Wang clan chief in Huanglue, a few miles north of the city, to command the defense. The Wang chief mustered a militia of 1,600 men headquartered in Huanglue's main ancestral hall. The clan also collected 40,000 taels of silver to purchase guns, ammunition, swords, and shoes for the recruits. On the eve of the campaign, the clan chief and his troops rallied before the hall. Together they drank pig blood mixed with white spirits and swore to fight the French to the last man.

The Wang-led militia humiliated the French in two skirmishes in October 1899. But the following month, the French attacked Huanglue with a force of several thousand marines. Lacking reinforcements, the Chinese militia was routed on November 16. Nearly forty of Huanglue's fighters were killed and hundreds wounded. Residents also suffered high casualties. Most of the thatched dwellings in Huanglue were set on fire and razed.

Enraged, the Wang chief sought to mobilize a counterattack. But he had no support from the Qing magistrate Li, who upon hearing of the defeat merely buried his face in his hands and sobbed. As Huanglue smoldered, the Qing emperor dispatched an envoy to sign a treaty granting France a ninety-nine-year concession on a 140-square-mile territory including Zhanjiang.

That year, Wang's grandmother died at the age of thirty-six. Wang does not know whether she perished from an illness or at the hands of the French as they killed, looted, and burned their way through Huanglue. Nevertheless, her death was especially hard on Wang's father, Huaizheng, who was only a toddler at the time.

Not long after his wife's death, Wang's grandfather remarried. His second wife, a surly woman named Chen, bore him a fourth son. But within a year of the baby's birth, Wang's grandfather passed away, his fortune destroyed by gambling debts and the pillaging of Huanglue.

Wang's father, Huaizheng, was left as the only survivor of his original family. His parents were gone. His two full brothers had also died, one in 1898 at the age of ten, the other in 1902 at the age of twenty-one. Alone and defenseless, Huaizheng suffered under the care of his stepmother. She was a fierce, jealous woman, who blatantly favored her own son over her stepchild. Soon after her husband died, she took the young Huaizheng to Pingshi village, seven miles away from Huanglue on the sea, and abandoned him to live with his aunt. Later, Chen remarried into the rival Yang clan in Wenche. She grew more irascible with age and beat her son's bride so badly that the young woman ran away to neighboring Guangxi Province.

In Pingshi, the orphaned Huaizheng could not help feeling like an unwanted burden. Although his aunt was kind, the family was poor and had little to feed the boy. When he was six, Huaizheng went to work gathering kindling and tall grass to sell as cattle feed. He also helped the family farm and caught a few fish to sell. But the day he could fend for himself, he left Pingshi and walked back to Huanglue.

Huaizheng arrived in Huanglue with little more than the rags on his scrawny teenage body. He moved back into his father's once comfortable farmhouse, which had survived the 1899 fire but was now decrepit, empty, and overgrown with weeds. Given his family's well-to-do past, Huaizheng was determined to survive on his own. For food, he scavenged in village fields at night, gathering sweet potatoes left to rot as too small to harvest. He sold grass, hired out his labor, and eventually saved enough to start a tiny farm and find a wife. A matchmaker arranged his marriage to a seventeen-year-old peasant girl surnamed Huang from nearby Tianping village. Until their wedding day, as was the custom, neither bride nor groom laid eyes on each other.

After marriage, Huaizheng, as his father's eldest surviving son, felt a strong obligation to sire a boy to carry on the paternal line. But Huang gave birth to a string of six girls, two of whom died young. Finally, Huaizheng was delighted and relieved when Huang bore a son, Wang Najin, in 1925. In March of 1927, the couple had a second son, Wang Bao. A third son, given the odd name Fei, meaning "concubine," or "light pink," died in infancy. The fourth, Wang Qiuyu, survived.

Wang Bao stuffs another pinch of tobacco into his pipe and lights it, flicking away the match. He puffs on the pipe, half closing his eyes as he recalls his childhood.

Wang's earliest memories are overwhelmingly of hardship and hunger. He was born into a turbulent era of warlordism and civil war. The Qing dynasty had collapsed in 1911, and the new Chinese republic was too frail to curb the spreading internal strife. A month after Wang's birth, China drifted closer to civil war when a massacre of leftist unionists in Shanghai ruptured the alliance between the Communist Party and the Nationalists led by Chiang Kai-shek. As fighting spread in the 1920s and 1930s, so did the suffering for China's vast peasant population. Military campaigns pushed taxes higher, and landlords intensified their exploitation. Worst off were the tens of millions of impoverished peasants like Wang and his family, who could not grow enough grain to survive on their tiny plots of land.

Throughout Wang's childhood, his family was bound in a struggle to stave off starvation. Every year, the family sowed sugarcane, sweet potatoes, and a little paddy rice. But the meager harvests never sustained them for long. To supplement their diet, the children picked wild plants. Wang's mother soaked the leaves in salty water to try to mask the bitter flavor, but still they were barely edible. Sharp pangs of hunger tormented Wang for days at a time.

To bring in extra income, the family worked at odd jobs. Wang's mother fetched water for prosperous villagers, balancing two heavy ceramic vessels with a bamboo shoulder pole. At the age of six, Wang began harvesting wild grass just as his father had done. Early in the morning, he set off for the rolling Eight Horn Mountains some ten miles to the west. There, gripping a sickle, he bent over in the tall grass and cut it, handful by handful. It usually took him five or six hours to gather a single *dan* (2.75 bushels) of grass.

When it rained, as it often did in the April to October monsoon season, the load of grass grew so heavy that Wang could hardly carry it. Bent under the weight of the bushy mass, the bedraggled boy staggered along. He was all but hidden by the grass except for his long thin legs, which moved stiffly under the load. His knobby knees poked through tattered pants of coarse black cloth. His shoes, pieces of wood with thick rubber straps, slapped the dirt path as he walked.

At the market town, Wang traded the *dan* of grass for a catty (1.1 pounds) of rice, the reward for his hours of labor. "I had to work all day. I could never play," Wang recalled.

When winter came to Guangdong Province with its piercing chill, Wang put on every shred of clothing he had. Usually, this meant only an extra threadbare pair of pants and a black tunic shirt. At night, he shivered next to his brothers under itchy hemp gunnysacks. The family could not afford even one blanket.

Despite the hardship, Wang's family life was relatively harmonious. His father was even-tempered. He scolded Wang and his siblings harshly for misbehaving. But unlike many traditional Chinese parents, neither Wang's father nor mother beat the children. Still, the constant press of hunger left little room for lightheartedness in the house.

"My father often spoke of his difficulties," said Wang. Born into a well-off household, Huaizheng was consumed by feelings of guilt and humiliation over the family's hand-to-mouth existence.

Sensing his father's anguish, Wang worked all the harder. In 1938, at the age of eleven, he began smuggling oxen and water buffalo from Suixi County into the French concession of Zhanjiang. The animals were slaughtered in Zhanjiang, and the meat was shipped 250 miles northeast for sale in the markets of Hong Kong.

The smuggling was risky. Chinese authorities in Suixi County had banned the sale of oxen and other commodities to the French. If Wang was caught, the government would fine his boss and confiscate the animals. Wang would get no pay.

The Wang clan also publicly frowned on the illicit trade with the French "barbarians," although some clansmen grew rich from the smuggling. Apart from razing Huanglue, the French had horrified clan elders by damaging ancient gravesites when building a road and barracks.

Roving bandits posed another constant threat. But Wang was too desperate for the money to worry much. He made the trips with his older brother, Najin. They set out before dawn, each driving an ox. To escape notice by local officials, they followed less-traveled overgrown paths. When it rained and rushing streams swelled up in their path, Wang and his brother clung to the necks of the oxen as the animals swam across. The two youths were often drenched to the skin in downpours as rain soaked through their makeshift hats of woven bamboo leaves. Sunshine was their only comfort.

The boys carried a small pouch containing a few coins for food given to them by their boss, who deducted the money from their pay. If they made it to Zhanjiang, they would buy some cheap gruel, sleep overnight on the street, and set off for home early the next morning. For the two-day trip, Wang and his brother earned ten pounds of rice each. It was a rich reward for a poor boy but a pittance compared to the profit made by their boss.

Men like Wang's boss, as well as wealthy merchants and landowners, ran the clan during Wang's youth. The blood brotherhood dominated life in Huanglue, and clan chiefs ruled with an iron fist. "The clan leaders controlled their own villages. They had their own rules," Wang said.

The clan upheld a set of ten commandments, or "warnings to the family" (*jiajie*), set down by the revered clansman Taishou in the fifteenth century. The supreme rule required all sons to be dutiful. Any son who rebelled against his elders or abandoned his parents would be formally denounced in front of the ancestral hall.

Children like Wang must be "taught to work hard," another rule instructed. A classical education, a luxury Wang never had, was also emphasized by the clan. Children were not to be spoiled by wealth. "Do not just build up your family with money. If you do, your offspring will become rude and will not exert themselves," warned the clan law set down in the genealogy.

Gambling, the vice that ruined Wang's grandfather, was, in theory, forbidden. "Sons who are addicted to gambling and loitering are always the ones to bankrupt a family," the rules admonished. "Therefore, this clan strictly prohibits gambling. Even on the occasion of feasts, guests are allowed only to chat and play chess. They should not play mah-jongg, for this will only give sons the habit. Offenders will be fined 1,000 coppers." Gambling was so popular, however, that many clansmen chose to pay the fine.

In most cases, the clan disciplined its own members. In fact, it prohibited clansmen from taking disputes directly to the government. "Whenever a dispute arises, do not bring the case to court. This will not only waste money, but will split the clan," it warned. "Instead, clan elders should be summoned to the ancestral hall to mediate. If anyone reports to the officials without prior notice to the clan, he will be vilified, regardless of whether he is in the right."

When Wang was a boy, only the most violent, unrepentant members of the clan, such as murderers or arsonists, were handed over to local officials for punishment. Other miscreants, such as unscrupulous clansmen who failed to "cultivate their moral rectitude" and sullied the Wang name, were scolded in front of the ancestral hall. The harshest penalty meted out by the clan was to expunge a kinsman entirely, which entailed crossing out his name in the genealogy with red ink and barring his remains from the ancestral graveyard.

As a youth, Wang often joined a crowd watching clan elders punish kinsmen who disregarded the communal laws. They would drag the offender in front of the gates of the main ancestral hall, castigate him, and give him a beating—in essence shaming him before both the living and the pantheon of ancestors. "The elders were very powerful. You had to obey them," Wang said.

Yet despite its ethos of coercion and control, the Wang clan also had a paternalistic side. It encouraged kindness and mutual aid among kinsmen. If a boy was orphaned, his uncles were obligated to raise him. If a poor clansman died, his family could ask the ancestral estate to pay for a coffin. "No kinsman should be cast off and his corpse left exposed and deserted like that of a passer-by," the rules instructed.

The Wang clan, the most formidable lineage in the Zhanjiang region, prospered from its strong organization and loyal members. Through regular donations, the clan supported a wealthy and growing ancestral trust. All clan members gained, though not always equally, from the richness of this common fund. The clan used it for everything from festivals and scholarships to weapons and disaster relief.

The affluent clan proudly maintained one main ancestral hall (*citang*) and six smaller halls. With tall doorways and sweeping, upturned roofs, the imposing structures were the center of ancestor worship and community life in Huanglue. On important festival days, Wang, his father, and his brothers gathered with other clansmen at the halls to pray, burn incense, and offer gifts of meat and wine to the ancestors. They also watched operas and plays in the Leizhou dialect that dramatized the stories of famous clansmen. The dramas were meant both to teach young Wangs clan history and to entertain the ancestral spirits, whose memorial tablets were housed in the halls. All these celebrations, down to the offerings of raw or roasted pig meat, were paid for by the ancestral trust. In that way, even poor families like Wang's could take part.

The Wang clan fought fiercely to defend its wealth and territory. When Wang Bao was young, feuds with other clans were common, especially with long-standing rivals like the Yangs of Wenche.

The Yangs arrived in Wenche not long after the Wangs settled in Huanglue. The founder of the Yang clan, Yang Panche, migrated to the Leizhou Peninsula from Fujian during the Song dynasty. Like the Wangs' ancestor Yueyan, Panche had passed the highest imperial examinations. He served as a county magistrate and later a prefecture head on Hainan Island. In retirement, he moved to Suixi County, settling in a place he named Wenxiang. Panche found Wenxiang lacking because it was a land of "rice but no fish"—in other words, it was not on the sea.

(A "land of fish and rice" is to Chinese what a "land of milk and honey" is to Westerners.) He sent his four grown sons off in search of greater bounty. One son, Yang Wenche, came to a bluff overlooking a broad inlet and there founded Wenche village. Yangs boast that the name Wenche, or "cart of culture," implies a place of great learning. A cartful of carved bamboo strips, the paper of ancient China, is an old metaphor for knowledge.

The Yangs were poorer and less numerous than the Wangs but also more feisty and aggressive. As the two clans harvested fish from the ocean inlet that washed between their villages, each sought a territorial advantage on the sea. In 1892, five years before Wang's father was born, a dispute over fishing nets sparked a bloody conflict. The feuding lasted seven years and claimed 100 lives. Finally, the French invasion in 1899 forced the warring clans to ally.

When not feuding outright, the Wangs and Yangs usually refrained from killing each other. Instead, if the Wangs caught a Yang in their territory, they would cut off one of his ears and let him go. For their part, the Yangs would sever a Wang's Achilles' tendon just above the heel. As a boy, Wang thought his clan's punishment the cleverer of the two. "If a Yang tried to cut my tendon, he would have to bend over, and I could grab his ear and ... HAH!" he said, slashing the air with his hand and smiling.

These crude punishments matched the derogatory names traded by the clans. The Wangs called the Yangs "sheep," because the surname Yang sounds the same as the Chinese word for sheep (*yang*). (During Qingming, the Wangs sacrifice sheep, but the Yangs do not.) Similarly, the Yangs called the Wangs "cattle." The name Wang in the Leizhou dialect is pronounced like the first character in the Chinese word for cattle (*huangniu*).

Wang was too busy smuggling cattle to spend much time feuding, however. For five years, for lack of better jobs, Wang and his brother made the hazardous trips to Zhanjiang. Wang watched Zhanjiang grow. In the 1930s and early 1940s, the city gained vitality from an influx of Cantonese, who brought with them their money, shrewd business sense, and loud, brassy dialect. Factories for making textiles, fireworks, and machinery sprang up. Many of the Cantonese were refugees who had fled Guangdong's capital, Guangzhou, to escape the Japanese army. War between Japan and China had erupted in 1937, and within a year the Japanese had occupied much of eastern China. They took Guangzhou in October 1938.

In 1943, when Wang was sixteen, the Japanese took control of Zhanjiang and surrounding areas. As the Japanese approached, some Huanglue residents, especially the wealthy, fled with their property. Other villagers hid behind bolted gates, afraid to till the fields or walk to their factory jobs. Wang could no longer smuggle. But otherwise life went on much the same for Wang and his family. "We poor people weren't afraid. We had no money. We couldn't run anyplace. We had to keep working."

As China was ravaged by war, corruption, and hyperinflation in the 1940s, Wang watched the economic exploitation that had always existed to a degree within the clan worsen. Swayed by Communist propaganda, Wang resented the demands of local landlords for grain from needy households like his own. Increasingly, he believed that despite its strengths the clan mirrored many social ills. Wang's doubts about the clan led him after Japan's defeat in 1945 to join the Communists in China's intensifying civil war.

In October 1945, Wang Mo, a clansman who secretly sympathized with the Communists, recruited Wang and his brother, Najin, to join a band of guerrillas operating in the hills around Huanglue. Since discovery would mean execution by the Nationalists, who controlled Guangdong and south-central China, the two brothers kept their new mission secret from the rest of the family. At night, they stole out to attend clandestine meetings of the Communist-led Peasant Association, where undergound party members instructed clansmen on how to "wage revolution."

Communist operatives organized Wang, Najin, and other recruits to steal weapons from local government arsenals and from boats anchored in Zhanjiang Harbor. They also staged surprise armed raids on landlord households in Huanglue. Working under disguise in groups of two to six people, the young guerrillas demanded money, grain, and other goods from wealthy families, threatening to shoot anyone who alerted the Nationalists. In this way, eighteen-year-old Wang took revenge for what he now saw as the abuse of his family by greedy, unethical clansmen. "My family is poor and hungry, but still they take our grain," Wang thought at the time.

In 1947, Wang had a close scrape when Nationalist troops arrived at Huanglue to press local peasants into military service. Once before, Wang had seen Nationalist soldiers marching a chain of bound peasant conscripts past Huanglue at gunpoint. Knowing his life was at risk, Wang fled into the hills, hiding out with the Communist guerrillas for three days until the Nationalists moved on.

Within a year, Wang decided to leave home to fight full-time with the guerrillas. On April 14, 1948, his guerrilla band became part of the newly created Eighth Regiment of the Guangdong-Guangxi Border Column of the PLA. The Eighth Regiment was founded in Angong village of Suixi County and was composed mainly of Suixi natives like Wang as well as men from the Communist base area of Donghai. As the civil war escalated on the Leizhou Peninsula, Wang and his comrades clashed with Nationalist forces dozens of times.

In heavy fighting, Wang's regiment proved potent on the battlefield. All told, the regiment wiped out nearly 3,000 Nationalist troops, seized more than 1,300 rifles, pistols, and machine guns, and captured 6 large artillery pieces, according to an official account.

Wang and his regiment moved south to the tip of the peninsula. They captured Xuwen, the county seat where Wang's earliest ancestor, Yueyan, had lived in exile. Next, in a string of victories, the regiment took the four other county seats of Huazhou, Lianjiang, Suixi, and Haikang. Their control of the peninsula virtually complete, Wang and his comrades finally joined the Communist army commanded by Lin Biao in a march on the city of Zhanjiang. Lin Biao's troops had faced heavy opposition in their drive into China's southeast. After an arduous battle, the Communists proclaimed Zhanjiang "liberated."

Soon afterward, Wang's regiment joined in Lin Biao's campaign to retake Hainan Island. In April 1950, the island outpost became the last Chinese region to fall to the Communists in the civil war.

After the Hainan campaign, Wang returned to Huanglue for the first time since the Communist victory. But far from the euphoria he expected, he found tensions high. Huanglue was in the first throes of "land reform," a movement vital to the Communists' goal of uprooting China's old social order. The movement, outlined in a June 1950 agrarian reform law, called for a sweeping abolition of the "system of feudal exploitation by the landlord class." But in Huanglue, as in much of Guangdong and China's rural southeast, the drive to redistribute land and overthrow wealthy landholders met strong resistance. Landlords worked strenuously to thwart the confiscation of their property. Clansmen opposed the breakup of the huge ancestral estates. Even poor peasants such as Wang's parents, who stood to gain economically from land reallocation, lacked enthusiasm. Peasants were reluctant to publicly denounce landlords, many of whom were respected clan elders and a source of pride to the lineage. Their loyalty toward fellow clansmen—even those who had abused and might have exploited them—ran deeper than toward Communist outsiders, or *wai xing*.

Lineages were so strong in Guangdong that the province soon lagged far behind in the crackdown on landlords and "counterrevolutionaries." In late 1951, the government had to mobilize PLA militiamen to impose the policy in parts of Guangdong where peasants were not cooperating. Eventually, the campaign reached a brutal climax. Between October 1950 and August 1951, more than 28,000 people were executed and over 100,000 "criminals" and "bandits" were caught or arrested in Guangdong. Nationwide, an estimated 1 million landlords were executed during the land redistribution movement.

In Huanglue, the redivision of property was also violently imposed. All households were classified as "poor peasants," "middle peasants," "rich peasants," or "landlords." Then, a team of poor peasant activists led by the chairman of the Communist-run Peasant Association split up the Wang ancestral estate. They confiscated all the houses, paddy fields, and other property of landlords and took most of the land of rich peasants.

Wang's family was classified as a poor peasant household and therefore qualified to receive small parcels of the confiscated land. The family was given about half an acre of "dry land," which it used to grow sugarcane, and about one-eighth acre of "water land," or paddy field, for cultivating rice. Because of the area's relatively dense population, Wang's family members received slightly less than the national average of one-sixth to one-half acre distributed per person.

In a further effort to decimate the power of the Wang clan, Communist activists publicly beat Huanglue's landlords, sent some to labor reform camps, and executed others. "If a landlord had done bad things in the past, he was killed," Wang said.

Party activists also viciously attacked clan institutions and customs. Huanglue's elaborate main ancestral hall was demolished. Another hall was turned into a school, and the smaller ones were used as cowsheds or for grain storage. Ancestral tablets inscribed with the names of generations of clansmen were destroyed. Temple gods were smashed. All the major clan rituals—feasts, celebrations, plays, ancestor worship—were banned in the drive to "eradicate superstition." Clan elders managed to bury the Qing dynasty genealogy, but many other documents were lost.

Years later, Wang recalled his uneasiness over the party's harsh suppression of the clan. "We all had complaints about it, but we kept them in our hearts. Few dared to voice opposition. If they did, they were struggled against."

At the time, however, Wang was less anguished than older villagers over the assault on clan power, ritual, and wealth. As a young man swept up in the Communist victory, he was prepared to tolerate some social upheaval in his home village. He trusted the party's promise that communism would bring a better life. Above all, as a poor boy from a big family, he welcomed a more equal division of land.

Even before the land redistribution campaign played itself out, Wang decided to leave Huanglue to join the PLA as a professional soldier. The Korean War had erupted in June 1950 when North Korean troops crossed the thirty-eighth parallel in a massive attack on the south. In late October, as victories by U.S.-commanded United Nations forces mounted, China secretly entered the war to aid the North Koreans. That month, Wang enlisted as a member of the PLA's Thirty-eighth Army. "I had been a local fighter long enough. I wanted to go to war."

One day soon after his enlistment, Wang stood in the back of an olive-green PLA truck, jostling against other peasant recruits as the vehicle bounced down the dirt road from Huanglue. As his ancestral home fell from view, Wang felt a pang of sadness. But the further the truck bumped down the road, the more narrow and insignificant seemed the world of his clan. For Wang, as for millions of Chinese peasant youths in the 1950s and 1960s, the army offered one of the few possible escapes from a life of penury, mediocrity, and isolation on the farm. As Huanglue disappeared behind a bamboo grove at a curve in the road and the truck headed toward Guangzhou, the scruffy cowherd-turned-soldier felt his heartbeat quicken.

In Guangzhou, the army issued Wang a baggy olive-green uniform, a cotton-padded coat, leather shoes, and a raincoat. In disbelief, Wang felt the smooth cloth and the thickness of the coat. He removed his worn rags and carefully put on the uniform. He held the shiny leather shoes admiringly before putting them on. At first they felt stiff and awkward. Until then, his only footwear had been sandals of wood or straw. "It was the first time in my life that I had enough to wear."

In Guangzhou, Wang boarded a troop train bound for China's far northeast. As the train slowly traversed the length of China, Wang watched the terrain change dramatically from the densely populated villages and tiny rice plots of Guangdong to the frozen, desolate expanse of Manchuria. From other troops, Wang learned that clans were far weaker in northern China, especially among the scattered settlers of the Manchurian frontier. Because it faced less concerted opposition from clans, the government had announced months earlier in April 1950 that land redistribution was complete in the Communist base areas of Manchuria.

After seven days, the train jerked to a halt near the Chinese border. Wang and his comrades, bearlike in their thick hats and padded overcoats, marched across the frozen Yalu River into the rugged mountains of North Korea.

Wang reached the war zone in November, just as China and North Korea were launching a full-scale offensive against South Korean and U.N. forces. He joined some 300,000 Chinese troops already engaged in the war. Wang took part in the bitter fighting of late November and early December as the Chinese and North Koreans drove south, recovering Pyongyang and several other cities by mid-December.

As the Chinese pushed the allied forces back to the thirty-eighth parallel, Wang's army proved a scrappy vanguard unit. "Our main job was to break through the American line and cut off their retreat," said Wang.

Wang was assigned to an engineering company of the army's Fourth Division. With 120 other troops, he was responsible for building bridges, making and repairing roads, and removing land mines. Unaided by mine detectors, Wang and his companions relied on sharp eyes to spot telltale signs of the planted explosives. When they found one, they moved back and hurled a wooden plank at it. If it didn't explode, they dug it out by hand. The duties left the men highly vulnerable to enemy fire. "We always had to advance first and retreat last," Wang said.

Wang's division pressed south with other Chinese and North Korean units, capturing the gutted city of Seoul on the heels of retreating U.N. forces in January 1951. As he marched through the city's smoldering rubble, Wang felt a mixture of awe at the scale of the destruction and pride at China's success in repelling the Americans. "There wasn't anything left," Wang recalled. "Not a house was standing. People were living in air-raid shelters." Wang stayed in Seoul for only a few days. Before long, the U.N. forces rallied and retook the city.

Wang's division retreated with the main Chinese and North Korean forces into the mountains just north of the thirty-eighth parallel. This hilly zone became the front line of the war. Wang and his comrades scrambled to dig shallow holes in the frozen earth of the mountain face for shelter. At night, they slept upright in the hollows, grasping their rifles by their side. By day, they tunneled deeper into the mountains making dugouts for permanent shelter. Every evening at about 6:00, American squadrons of jet fighters began bombarding the Chinese positions. Confined to their dugouts, Wang and the other troops listened in darkness as the bombs whistled toward the earth and exploded, shaking the ground under their feet. Often, they spent several hours a day inside the caves, venturing out only to take short sunbaths. At night, they slept in their cotton-padded coats on the cave floor. The troops lived on a gruel of sorghum or rice and sometimes bread. But food, medicine, and other supplies often fell short. In the howling winter, hunger and pain from their wounds gnawed at the troops' morale.

Opposite the mountainside where Wang's division was positioned, American-led U.N. units occupied a chain of hills. The two sides fought brutally for strategic advantage along the thirty-eighth parallel. A river ran between the two mountain ridges, and the Chinese and Americans battled for access to the water. But the Chinese were disadvantaged by weaponry far inferior to that of the U.N. forces. In Wang's division, troops mainly used old weapons abandoned in Manchuria by Japan after World War II. The Soviet Union, which had occupied Manchuria's major cities in August 1945, let the weapons fall into Chinese Communist hands. Wang had an antique, single-shot rifle, and his ammunition was severely limited. "We fought one bullet at a time," Wang said. In one battle, a third of Wang's company, a platoon of about forty men, was killed.

Chinese casualties mounted as the war dragged on into its third year. Outgunned by superior artillery and air power, the Chinese suffered by far the heaviest losses of the war. By the time a truce was signed in July 1953, an estimated 700,000 to 900,000 Chinese troops were dead, wounded, or missing—a figure exceeding the combined casualties of the United States and South Korea. Wang estimates that seven out of ten men in the Thirty-eighth Army lost their lives in Korea.

"Army cadres were buried in graves with wooden markers," Wang said. "But ordinary soldiers had nothing. We laid them in the river and put sand over them. That was all. The earth was hardened mud, and we had no time for so much digging," he said, shaking his head. Coming from a strong clan, Wang couldn't help but view the absence of a proper burial as a great dishonor for his comrades.

In the months after the truce, China gradually withdrew its troops from Korea. Wang and the bedraggled remnants of his division made their way north to the border, marching over a bridge on the Yalu River into China.

Despite the misery of the war, Wang didn't regret enlisting. The army had thrust Wang for the first time into the world beyond the parochial confines of his village and clan. As he huddled in dugouts swapping stories with troops from across China, learned to speak Mandarin Chinese, and fought to survive in an alien terrain, Wang cast off many of his provincial prejudices. And although the war was brutal, Wang found meaning for the bloody sacrifice in army propaganda about the evils of American imperialism. Indeed, Wang felt his life take on a far grander design when he became a fighter for world communism rather than a follower of the narrow Confucian obligations of the clan.

In China, returning Korean War veterans like Wang were glorified as soldier-heroes and models of the party's creed of revolutionary struggle. Martyrs like Huang Jiguang, a soldier said to have "given his life on October 20, 1952, by using his chest to block enemy fire," won posthumous first-class citations. Wang's Thirty-eighth Army was among those hailed as courageous military units. Peng Dehuai, the revolutionary commander who directed Chinese forces in Korea, praised the army. Wang's zeal for the Communist-led "new China" reached new heights. "I felt very patriotic, very proud that we fought to a stalemate with America," Wang recalled. Years later, Wang still waves his arms and re-creates the sounds of exploding bombs as he relives the battles, tracing formations on a table with his chopsticks.

Soldiering marked a high point of Wang's life and revolutionary ardor, but his military career ended tragically. Upon his return to China, Wang was posted to a military base in Jilin Province across the border from North Korea. On the base, he was assigned to dig wells and build troop barracks. In a construction accident in early 1954, Wang broke his back. For nearly two years, he was confined to an army hospital. In September 1955, he chose to be discharged rather than go to a military convalescent home. He returned to Huanglue at the age of twenty-eight, an ordinary "third grade, B-level disabled soldier."

Back home, Wang was shocked to see that five years after the revolution, life remained extremely hard for his family and other poor villagers. During his years at war, many crops had been lost to droughts and typhoons. His large family was still hungry, unable to feed itself from its small plots of redistributed land. Wang looked on helplessly as his parents and siblings toiled in the fields. Because of his back injury, he could never again do heavy farm labor, only the lightest tasks. Desperate to help his family, Wang spent all his savings from the army on two oxen and a wooden cart. The family used the beasts in the field and hired them out for extra income. "I had no high expectations. All I wanted to do was to help my kin fill their stomachs."

Wang's hopes were lifted in 1958, however, when the government assigned him an office job in Suixi County. The job made good on the state's pledge to support disabled and demobilized soldiers. It meant a steady salary, grain rations, and highly coveted urban residence. Wang was elated that at last he could help ease his family's poverty. He was assigned to the financial office of a county mining team, which employed 6,000 people. He had no formal education, but he learned enough on the job to handle routine office work.

Wang felt grateful to the party. When an older cadre in his office encouraged him to apply for party membership, he readily agreed. Later that year, his application was accepted.

As a PLA veteran and party member, Wang ranked high in revolutionary prestige. But at age thirty-one he was still a bachelor. Again the elderly cadre stepped in, hinting that it was time for Wang to find a wife. A few days later, the cadre introduced Wang formally to a young colleague named Chen. Chen had been assigned to the office by her commune. As a poor peasant's daughter, she had pristine class credentials. Under the Maoist social etiquette of the day, she was considered a compatible match for Wang. After a courtship of several months, Wang gained the party's required approval to marry Chen in 1959. They registered the betrothal at their *danwei* and received an official red-sealed marriage certificate.

Wang was relieved that the party had resolved the awkward issue of marriage for him. His family could never have afforded the feast and bride price required for a traditional clan wedding, which was now officially discouraged. Still, Wang felt strange being wed by party authorities in a government office instead of kowtowing before his ancestors at the Wang lineage hall. The party, by arranging the match and giving its blessing, was usurping a vital cultural role of the clan. As it tightened its totalitarian grip on rural China, the party would suppress clan rites with growing force while imposing its own political rituals in their place.

The first months of Wang's marriage were a golden time. During the week, he and Chen walked to work together in Suixi. Often on Sunday they returned to Huanglue to visit Wang's parents. The young couple seemed destined for a bright future. With government jobs, urban residence, and state grain rations, Wang and Chen looked ahead to a respectable, economically secure life. But their dreams were built on the teetering edifice of the Great Leap Forward launched in 1958.

The campaign's demand for vast increases in industrial output compelled millions of peasants to leave the land to work in factories and prospect for precious ores. In Suixi, the rapid development of mudstone mines, sugar factories, and other industrial ventures led to a parallel growth in local bureaucracy, to which Wang and Chen both owed their jobs. The movement was also a leap toward communism, as shown by the rush to organize all of China into people's communes. In Huanglue, as in thousands of rural communities, peasants were forced to give up private plots and hand over to the collective their major livestock and farming equipment. Wang's parents reluctantly gave up the two oxen and cart he had bought for them. Yet the campaign quickly exhausted the peasants' enthusiasm and energy, causing the amount of grain per capita in the countryside to plummet.

By 1960, as famine gripped China, grain rations for Wang and other Suixi government workers were cut back severely. In mid-1961, a Suixi County directive abruptly announced that grain supplies had run out. Wang and all but twenty of the 6,000 peasant workers of the county mining team were ordered back to their home villages.

Wang felt deeply betrayed, especially when he thought of Chen, by then pregnant with their first child. But he had no recourse. The loss of his job was part of a nationwide economic retrenchment aimed at hastening China's recovery from the Great Leap. Some 30 million Chinese peasants who had entered towns and cities after 1957 were being sent back to the countryside. Meanwhile, the state stiffened barriers to urban migration, a move that bound peasants to the farm.

Wang left Suixi in late 1961, denied his grain rations, back pay, and urban residence, and moved with Chen to Huanglue. Commune authorities assigned him work as a production brigade leader overseeing the collective farming of 500 households. Because of the rigid controls on migration, Wang was back on the farm for good.

Conditions in Huanglue were far worse than in the county seat. Famine had devastated the village, preying especially on the elderly and the young. Wang's family, no strangers to poverty and hunger, had husbanded a small supply of sweet potato meal. They also reverted to their prerevolutionary supplements of wild plants. But the food could not sustain them for long. Chen, now beginning to fill out, looked especially pale. In early 1962, she gave birth to a daughter but remained weak and anemic long after the delivery.

That spring, Wang watched his father's body begin to swell alarmingly from the effects of malnutrition. The edema slowly spread up from the feet until both legs were grotesquely bloated. The family had no money to pay for a hospital visit, but

Wang managed to obtain some medicinal herbs. The herbal cure failed, though, and Wang's father died soon afterward at the age of sixty-five.

Wang was devastated by guilt for failing to meet his Confucian obligation to care for his father. At the same time, he felt his anger rise over the party's inept policies. Villagers across China shared Wang's anguish as tens of millions of Chinese died in the famine.

After his father's death, Wang decided the family should finally leave his grandfather's crumbling old house. His father had stubbornly remained in the family home, which was his inheritance as the eldest living son. But Wang and his brothers tore down the structure. In its place, they built a thatched cottage of coarse cogon grass and mud, the cheapest, simplest kind of dwelling in the village. "Our clothes were ragged. We ate sweet potato meal. It was as if nothing had changed" since before the revolution, Wang said.

As China slowly recovered from famine in the mid-1960s, conditions improved slightly in Huanglue. Wang's annual income measured in work points was worth a meager 300 pounds of grain. This was far from adequate to nourish his growing family, as Chen had given birth to another daughter in 1963, but was considerably more than the 100 to 200 pounds distributed on average to peasants. Only the brigade's party secretary received more. He was allotted 400 to 500 pounds of grain a year. "We often had to borrow grain. We never had enough to eat and wear under Mao," Wang said.

As a grassroots cadre, Wang grew increasingly disillusioned with Mao's commune system. Wang was in charge of managing farm production by the brigade's 2,000 peasants. He saw firsthand the hunger and deprivation caused by Maoist economic policy. Years later, his voice still shakes when he describes his frustration over his work.

"At that time, we had Mao's communes and the 'big rice pot' [*da guo fan*]. We had to do everything together. All sideline production was banned. The peasants were not allowed to raise ducks or pigs or hens. If we let the peasants have private production, the higher leaders would attack us as capitalists and confiscate the hens, crops, or whatever the peasants grew.

"Most of the peasants opposed the system. They didn't work hard. They just went through the motions. All the brigade cadres knew this system was wrong, too. On that, we saw eye to eye. But our hands were tied. The controls were too tight, and we couldn't change anything. We had no way out.

"The collective was no good!"

Wang's confidence in the party leadership plummeted further in 1966 when Mao launched China's most violent political campaign, the decade-long Cultural Revolution. To Wang, the nationwide turmoil underscored the leadership's insensitivity to the peasants' bedrock interests and deep-seated aversion to *luan* (chaos). Wang had never been a political radical, even in his days as a guerrilla fighter. Like many Chinese peasants, he was practical and down-to-earth. He judged things as he saw them, and he saw clearly that Maoist rule had condemned Huanglue's villagers to a life of poverty.

Fortunately, as in many rural backwaters, the factional violence and persecution of the Cultural Revolution made barely a ripple in Huanglue. Maoist Red Guards staged their mass criticism sessions mostly at the county and commune level. There, several party officials were publicly denounced, thrown out of office, and sent to labor on farms. In Huanglue, the few youths who became Red Guards left the village to attend rallies in larger towns or Beijing. Maoist fanatics overlooked grassroots cadres in the villages like Wang.

Although unscathed, Wang grew increasingly alienated by the Cultural Revolution. The more he doubted the chaotic political order of the day, the more Wang, then in his forties, began pondering Huanglue's prerevolutionary past. Images of clan exploitation embellished by Communist propagandists had long faded. Instead, he revived memories of the elaborate clan celebrations with their rich symbolism of male solidarity and common purpose. In maturity, Wang felt himself drawn to the clan ethos that he had cast off as a young Communist fighter. As factional warfare tore China apart, he found new appeal in the idea of a community bound by blood ties, family-based ethics, and reverence for ancestors. For the first time in years, Wang felt the urge to pay respects to his forefathers during Qingming.

One overcast morning in March 1969, Wang left the village alone and walked to Waterlily Pond Hill where his father, grandfather, and great-great-grandfather were buried. He sat down beside the neglected tombs, which faced east toward the sea. As a cool breeze rustled the tall grasses around the graves, Wang's thoughts drifted to his father's harsh life and pitiful death. He berated himself for waiting so long to tend to his father's lonely soul. After sitting in silence for several minutes, Wang looked around to make sure no one was watching. Then he knelt down and slowly kowtowed three times before the graves.

Wang turned away from the tombs and walked down the windswept hillside toward Huanglue. As he went, his mind wandered to his own eventual death. He felt a powerful longing for a son who could honor his memory. Chen was pregnant for the third time. But when the baby came later that year, Wang was disappointed. It was another daughter. Two years later, in 1971, Wang's fourth daughter was born. She would be his last child.

In 1973, Chen fell ill. The family could not afford to spend much on medicine, and the local "barefoot doctor" lacked the skills to diagnose her condition properly. The sickness slowly sapped all her strength. One day in 1975, after two years of steady decline, Chen could no longer rise from her bed. She remained bedridden for five agonizing years. "When my wife got sick it was the most difficult time for us," Wang said, looking away and falling silent.

The psychological strain of Chen's illness was hardest on Wang, but the physical burden fell on his daughters. Wang's old back injury still made it impossible for him to farm. So the three eldest daughters had to labor in the fields as well as keep house and go to school. Wang's seventy-eight-year-old mother, Huang, helped nurse Chen and care for the youngest daughter, Wang Yueling, until she entered school. As often as she could, Huang cooked meals for the family and washed their clothes with her knobby but quick hands. Dressed in her black tunic and pants, the thin, stooped widow would hobble from task to task, a comforting presence during Wang's darkest days.

In 1980, just as China's initial post-Mao agricultural reforms were beginning to ease the poverty in Huanglue, Chen died. She was forty-five.

❋

Chen's death brought Wang's long-simmering resentment against the party to a boil. As a veteran who had given his all for the revolution, Wang felt deceived and abused by the party. In 1961, the party had dashed his hopes for economic security by forcing him back to the village. By denying Wang a state job and steady salary, the party was at least indirectly to blame for the deaths of his wife and father, both of whom lacked adequate medical care. Worse, the party's radical policies had hamstrung Wang and other village cadres, denying them the chance to take practical steps to lift Huanglue out of poverty. Many villagers in Huanglue shared Wang's anger over the needless suffering imposed by Mao's rule. No longer confident in the Communist Party and its Marxist creed, they sought another anchor for their beliefs.

Just as villagers like Wang were most doubting the Communist system, the party's sweeping rural reforms provided the seeds for a revival of the Wang clan. By the early 1980s, the market-oriented policies of Deng Xiaoping were transforming Huanglue's farm economy. Authorities redistributed collectively held land and other property among peasant households and disbanded the commune. They returned to Wang's family the half acre of dry land and one-eighth acre of paddy field given his parents in the 1950s. Huanglue peasants slogged out of the miserly communal rice paddies for the last time and began reaping a richer harvest from more efficient family farms. "After the reforms, our lives became a little better. We had enough to eat and wear," Wang said.

With the breakup of communes and the return to family farming, the ties of kinship in Huanglue grew stronger. These emotional bonds extended to the clan, which as a close community of relatives had never disappeared. Ironically, the party had unwittingly preserved the social foundation of the clan in Huanglue and elsewhere even as it destroyed the institution. The party's commune system had left intact the natural villages populated by relatives of the same surname that formed the clan's base. Production brigades and teams were often set up along old kinship and village boundaries. Moreover, party policies had made communities like Huanglue more parochial and inward-looking by isolating them with controls on migration and trade.

Once reform opened the way, the Wangs of Huanglue began to recreate the clan as a source of moral authority, social organization, and material support. For Wang, the clan held special appeal. It offered him a new identity as a clan elder, a far more respected and purposeful role than that of party cadre. Wang was able to shift allegiances from the party to the clan as reforms weakened the party's control over villages and gave Wang and millions of other rural cadres greater leeway. As a result, Wang and other cadres increasingly ignored state mandates and started putting fellow clansmen—and themselves—first. In Huanglue, Wang joined other villagers in promoting the strength and prosperity of the clan above all else.

One day in 1981, Wang, the cultured elder Bangzhen, and their wealthy kinsman Zhenghe furtively read the Qing dynasty *zupu* for the first time since the 1950s, poring over biographies of their kin and accounts of clan history. Each traced his own family line back as many generations as possible through the musty pages. "We could see correctly who were the elders, the fathers, the sons. We could know which generation we all belonged to. It was all written clearly in the *zupu*," Wang said.

The unearthing of the *zupu* was a revelation for the entire village. For the elderly, it symbolized the rediscovery of their roots in the clan. For the young, it disclosed a rich heritage long suppressed and distorted by the Communist state. For Wang, it furnished a ballast of meaning and direction for a life unsteadied by loss and frustration. Over the next decade, the villagers' fascination with their past fueled a renaissance of the clan and its rituals. As Huanglue grew more prosperous and autonomous from state controls, the Wang clan flourished.

❧

A tour of Huanglue with Wang today shows villagers living comfortably off their paddy rice and cash crops of sugarcane, peanuts, and vegetables. Young farmers haul fresh produce to the busy markets of Zhanjiang. Other peasants bicycle to work in enterprises that hum with activity. Agriculture is the mainstay of the local economy. Although farmers' incomes in Huanglue are average by national standards, they are high compared with those elsewhere on the Leizhou Peninsula.

Huanglue villagers live at a slow but deliberate pace. Women sitting on wooden stools chat as they scrub bucketfuls of laundry on washboards. Others go about their chores with babies in makeshift cotton knapsacks slung on their backs. Older men idly pass hours in dim gambling dens amid the loud clatter of mahjongg tiles.

"Have you drunk tea yet?" asks a villager in a sleeveless undershirt as he squats whittling a piece of wood. The friendly inquiry is an old-fashioned way of saying "hello" in Huanglue and other parts of southern China.

Signs of the Wang clan's revival are everywhere in the settlement of red-brick farmhouses. Near the center of Huanglue, Wang steps over the high threshold of an imposing, partly renovated ancestral hall. Its traditional hipped roof with graceful upturned eaves attests to its former grandeur. The twelve-foot-high doorway is adorned with two large, onion-shaped white paper lamps. Framing the doorway are bold black characters painted on strips of red declaring "Wang Family Ancestral Hall." Inside, on newly whitewashed walls, hangs a portrait of the founding ancestor, Yueyan. Nearby sits Yueyan's ancestral tablet. Goblets filled with offerings of wine stand on the altar, and violet sticks of incense smolder in a brass pot. The hall, built in 1926, was originally the second largest in Huanglue. For decades after the revolution, it served as a village school. But in 1991, the clansmen donated 10 yuan each to build a new school and reclaimed the impressive structure for their ancestors. Huanglue has six ancestral halls in various stages of repair.

From Huanglue's main road, Wang strides down a muddy path into another neighborhood. He stops before a smaller branch hall of the Wang lineage. "Grandchildren help the grandparents in, sons follow the fathers in," announce characters on either side of the doorway. Inside, on the wall above the altar, a brightly painted Chinese unicorn stands on billowing clouds as a symbol of good fortune. From its mouth comes a stream of vapor on which lies a book depicting the clan's emphasis on learning. The word "book" in Leizhou dialect is also synonymous with the word for "long life." On the altar stand the memorial tablets of ancestors from the twelfth generation.

Wang opens a checkered umbrella to shade himself from the intense subtropical sun. With his pant legs rolled up above the mud, he heads toward the village temple. On the way he passes a corner store with shelves full of candy, paper "spirit money," and strings of firecrackers. A faded image of Mao gazes out at him from an old poster on the shop's wall.

The temple, which was renovated by Wang and his kinsmen, is today a lively meeting place. Inside, candles flicker once again. Villagers flock to pray to the temple gods. Their appeals range from the metaphysical to the mundane. Kowtowing to the deities, one villager asks for protection from evil ghosts, while another seeks a cure for a brood of sick ducklings. Across from the temple, a long stage stretches before a yard of packed earth.

"Here, we put on operas for the ancestors to watch on their birthdays," Wang says grandly, his arm sweeping toward the stage. Wang and his kinsmen built the stage for $10,000 in 1991 with donations from the villagers. Cloth curtains drape across the stage from a recent performance. A peasant opera troupe from Haikang, another Wang settlement in Leizhou, enacted colorful clan legends dating from the tenth century. The Wangs paid the troupe $80 a night, collecting 1 yuan to 10 yuan from each person in the audience.

Just as the Wangs are rebuilding the structures of the lineage, they are reviving kinship rites and ceremonies. Today, high-spirited clan rituals again dominate village life and culture. Every year as the winter solstice casts long shadows across Huanglue's fields, villagers retreat to the ancestral hall for a communal celebration honoring the Wangs' elderly. They slaughter pigs and sheep, place the raw meat on the altar in a symbolic offering to the ancestors, and then divide up the pork and mutton among the oldest kin.

When spring arrives with its first crisp sunny days, clansmen perform the rites of Qingming. Gathering in groups of a dozen or as many as 1,000, worshipers carry baskets laden with steaming pork and chicken, rice, and boiled eggs to the village temple for prayers. They then go in procession into the grassy hills surrounding Huanglue, visiting the tombs of their ancestors. Before each grave, they set off long bunches of red firecrackers, noisily summoning the ephemeral spirits to the world of the living. Old and young kowtow rapidly before the tombstone. They flatter and placate the ancestors with offerings of food and wine. Finally, they scatter wads of spirit money around the grave. Wang and his family visit more than twenty gravesites. "If the weather is good, we can do it in one day. If not, it takes two days," Wang said.

One of Huanglue's biggest clan rites takes place each year in midautumn, when thousands of Wangs from around the region descend on the township in a display of strength and solidarity. Officially, the meeting commemorates the Wangs' 1899 campaign against French invaders. But the gathering also serves as a powwow for chiefs from related branches of the clan. "We drink tea, chat about clan affairs, and compare our *zupu*," Wang says.

The Wang lineage today is weaker and more diffuse than when Wang was a boy. Although the Communist regime has eased controls, it remains far more hostile to clans than was the paternalistic Confucian state of Wang's youth. Partly as a result, the Wangs have not yet forged the powerful overarching organization they had before the 1949 revolution. Most important, they have not reestablished an ancestral estate, the traditional economic foundation for the clan. Other lineages in Suixi County control large tracts of land, but the Wangs of Huanglue still fund their activities with direct contributions from individual members. "Before 1949, the *zugong* [founding ancestor] had land, money, and pigs and he would take them out for ceremonies and worship," Wang says, referring to his forefather as if he were alive. "Now, we pay by ourselves with donations."

The Wang lineage is also different today because the needs and attitudes of its members have changed. As a result of Communist policies, Wang and his kinsmen live in a far less rigidly hierarchical society than in the past. They also place greater value on their independence, having suffered decades of Mao's totalitarian rule. Consequently, although the clan is weaker, it is also more tolerant and egalitarian. Daughters, for example, are listed in family genealogies. Members from poor families, like Wang, play prominent roles along with descendants of landlords.

By adapting and thriving, the Wang clan demonstrates the resilience of lineages as a mainstay of China's changing rural society. Signs of the clan's relevance permeate day-to-day life in Huanglue.

❋

As peeping chicks scurry around his feet, Wang sits at a wooden table in his modest farmhouse showing a visitor his family genealogy, or *jiapu*. Unlike before 1949, today almost every household in Huanglue keeps a *jiapu*, which is smaller than the clan genealogy and traces more narrowly the descent of one family. Wang's *jiapu* was copied down and updated in 1990 by a well-educated kinsman in Zhanjiang for $4. The men in Wang's family and their sons and wives each paid 40 cents to be recorded in the *jiapu*. The daughters, who receive the least mention, paid nothing. "In the past two to three years, every family has started maintaining a *jiapu*," Wang says. "They realize that if they don't have one, the family won't remember their history. If they don't write anything down, their ancestors will be lost, forgotten."

The clan drills the importance of the genealogy into the minds of youngsters at an early age. Wang eagerly explains the genealogy to his closest male descendant,

From left, Wang Bao, Wang Xiulin, Wang Zhenghe, and Wang Bangzhen outside the main ancestral hall in Huanglue. Photo by Ann Scott Tyson.

ten-year-old nephew Wang Weiming, the son of Wang's younger brother. And in village primary schools, students must write a history of their family and Huanglue. "If they don't know what to write, they can look it up in the *jiapu*," says Wang Xiulin, a mother of five who runs a shop near the village temple.

In Huanglue, the clan is respected by young and old. "Everyone has faith in the clan," says twenty-year-old driver Wang Zhonglin, as his motorized cart sputters and jerks down one of the village's dirt roads. When asked why, Zhonglin says, "The clan heads solve our conflicts."

In many parts of China's rural south, the growing influence of clans in the lives of villagers like Wang is undermining the authority of the Communist regime. Today, as historically, clans harbor no aim of overthrowing the state. Nevertheless, they often brazenly defy authorities and laws that threaten their interests. As they emerge as powerful and autonomous grassroots forces, clans like the Wangs are fast eroding the regime's remaining totalitarian controls.

In Huanglue, the interests of clan and state clash in many domains but in none so intensely as birth control. Under China's "one child per couple" family planning regime, most rural couples are only given approval to have one child. In some provinces, two children are allowed under special circumstances. But in Huanglue, the goal of producing male descendants completely overrides national efforts to limit the population.

In his comfortable farmhouse, wealthy clan elder Zhenghe squats on the black-and-white tiled sitting room floor, surrounded by a noisy flock of grandchildren. As Wang and other elders smoke and chat, Zhenghe clucks and talks baby talk to his toddler grandson in Leizhou dialect, a blend of Fujianese and Cantonese. Zhenghe's affection for the boy, the hope of the clan, is obvious. Although he is just over a year old, the boy has already been dutifully recorded in Zhenghe's *jiapu*.

Sitting nearby, the boy's mother, Yang, passes time eating watermelon seeds and chatting with Zhenghe's newly married daughter, Wang Wanhua (Gentle Flower). The women crack the seeds with a small metal mallet on a stool, eat the meats, and brush the shells onto the floor. Beside them, Yang's barefoot daughters play with the shiny black shells and make faces to amuse their younger brothers.

At age thirty-two, Yang has six children. The first four were girls, the last two boys. If Yang had lived in one of many other parts of rural China or in the city, local officials would have compelled her to undergo abortion and possibly sterilization long before her sixth child was born. But in Huanglue, Yang and her husband, Zhenghe's oldest son, have faced no punishment, not even a fine.

"The first four were girls, so they didn't count," says Zhenghe, as he gently steadies his wobbling grandson. In Huanglue, villagers typically have three or four children.

"Cadres here are thinking about the *houdai*, the descendants," explains Wang. "If the babies are girls, the cadres don't seize their mothers or fine them. The women must be allowed to bear sons, or there will be no descendants!"

Male offspring are so vital to the clan that favoritism toward sons pervades the local culture. On the second day of the Chinese New Year, every family graced with sons in the past year sets off firecrackers in celebration. When a woman in Huanglue gives birth to a boy, she is congratulated for having a *wan jin*, literally "10,000 pieces of gold." Girls, in contrast, are valued only as *qian jin*, or "1,000 gold pieces." "Daughters are not important," Wang says plainly. "They are just married off to someone in another village. And they don't pay attention to the *zupu*," he adds.

Clans' marriage practices also pit them against the state. Clans commonly seek to forge closer alliances by marrying off their young women to friendly lineages.

Often as part of this clan diplomacy, women are promised as brides before they reach the legal marriage age of twenty. Sometimes girls as young as eight or nine are engaged. Weddings are sanctioned not by state functionaries but by the ancestors, as bride and groom kowtow in the memorial hall.

As with birth and marriage, the clans' death rituals also clash with Communist policies. The countryside around Huanglue is dotted with large circular, gray stone tombs, many of them recently built. The tombs demonstrate the widespread resurgence of ancestor worship and also serve as status symbols for newly affluent peasants. In building the tombs, Huanglue clansmen have defied government attempts to promote cremation and preserve farmland. Villagers and cadres alike have ignored party criticism of Qingming rites as feudal superstition and a source of economic waste. "These days, all the cadres worship their ancestors," says Wang.

Indeed, as cadres in Huanglue vigorously promote the clan, they illustrate how the party is losing a crucial battle for the hearts and minds of grassroots officials. Despite decades of indoctrination in Marxism, thousands of longtime cadres like Wang have tossed out Mao's "little red book" of quotations and taken up the clan *zupu* instead. In Huanglue, virtually all cadres are influential clansmen who work to further interests of the lineage.

One morning at breakfast, as Zhenghe and his son drink white spirits from bowls, a government official pokes his head in the door. Zhenghe, a retired production brigade cadre like Wang, invites the official in and pours him a bowl of the liquor. Wang joins them for a bowl of soda pop.

The official is a clansman from Huanglue township, an administrative division encompassing some 70,000 people, including the 10,000 residents of Huanglue village. A former PLA man, the official now handles civil affairs for the township. He has come to consult the elders about their strategy for obtaining government funding to rebuild Huanglue's main ancestral hall, the one torn down during the 1950s land redistribution campaign. "Our ancestors built that hall. We, the descendants, must rebuild it and move the ancestral tablets back in," Wang Bao explains.

After a rapid-fire discussion in Leizhou dialect, the elders give the official the go-ahead to apply for a loan of about $100,000 from the Guangdong Province Cultural Relics Preservation Bureau. The application will describe the project as a "memorial to the anti-French resistance," the 1899 campaign endorsed by the party as patriotic. Villagers will also donate money, and their names and contributions will be publicly recorded. The official rises and leaves, munching a stalk of raw sugarcane.

Cadres today "speak the clan's language, handle clan affairs, preside over clan meetings, and protect clan interests," according to a popular saying around Huanglue. Wielding their official seals, local cadres literally give the stamp of approval for clans to delve into a wide range of legal and illegal activities.

Backed by grassroots officials, the Wangs and neighboring clans engage in business and trade as well as in smuggling and gambling operations. The clans focus their entreprenurial energies in nearby Zhanjiang. The port city is now a hub of regional commerce as well as a center for gambling halls, prostitution enclaves that grow rich from their many brothels, and drug-smuggling and gunrunning operations. Tens of thousands of weapons are smuggled from Vietnam through Guangxi Province and Zhanjiang to Hong Kong each year, according to Zhanjiang sources.

The Wangs and their foes, the Yangs of Wenche, have both found a profitable niche collecting gambling debts and bad loans. Zhanjiang's casinos lure customers from as far away as Beijing. In White Sands, a village full of gambling dens near Huanglue, houses permit a customer to bet the equivalent of $10,000 an hour, a huge sum for most Chinese. Zhanjiang's corrupt police skim off the establishments by raiding the dens, fining each gambler a token $100 to $200, and pocketing the fines. The Wangs and Yangs have staked out respective territories in Zhanjiang for their dunning businesses and protect them fiercely.

The further Zhanjiang drifts into frontier lawlessness, the greater the room for clans to maneuver. The Wangs, Yangs, and other clans operating in the area have as their muscle a force of young loyal kinsmen to rally in troubled times. Clan chiefs discipline their own members. They also protect them from police, providing a hideout or springing them from jail, if need be. After violent feuding or confrontations with police, the clans assume all medical expenses and funeral fees.

The escalation of clan feuds around Zhanjiang underscores the party's inability to rein in the powerful blood brotherhoods. In a five-month period in 1991, clan warfare in and around Zhanjiang left 14 residents dead and 270 injured. Some 9,000 clansmen took part in the melees, which caused $200,000 in damages, according to official statistics. With state authority waning, life for the Wangs and other clans boils down to a kind of Darwinian survival of the fittest. Deadly feuds erupt over events as petty as the chess game that triggered the Wang-Yang fracas in 1991.

On May 12, 1991, Wang was at the temple when a group of young clansmen rushed into the village. A crowd quickly gathered around as the men described how an argument over a chess game had turned to blows with some Yangs at Zhanjiang's North Bridge market. In the scuffle, an explosive blew off a hand of one of the Wangs. Police jailed the injured man and some other Wangs but let the Yangs go.

Wang and the other villagers were furious. They knew a gang of about 200 young Yang hoodlums ran loose in Zhanjiang, stealing, drinking, and fighting undeterred by police who had ties to the clan. Vowing revenge, several dozen Wangs rushed to Zhanjiang. There, they managed to free their kinsmen, including the injured man, who went into hiding. The Yangs, too, were up in arms. They claimed the Wangs had wounded one of their men in Zhanjiang and forced him to lick his own blood off the street.

The next day, the rival forces rallied their men on opposite bluffs for what would be the biggest battle between the two clans in decades. Wang watched from the grassy promontory as two of his kinsmen were shot down. Good to its promise, the Wang clan collected about $8,000 from its members to bury the men and make donations to their families. The Wangs' retaliatory bombardment of the Yang village with antiaircraft guns lasted a week, as local police looked on helplessly.

Finally, about nine days into the conflict, the state dispatched a large paramilitary force. About 600 police from Suixi arrived in Huanglue in a convoy of trucks and jeeps and set up camp at the government headquarters. Another paramilitary force from Zhanjiang occupied Wenche.

"They ordered us to give up the guns within three days. Otherwise, they would execute us," Wang said. "We gave them the weapons."

The police sealed off both feuding villages, blocking the roads with stones and trees. No one was allowed to leave. Schools were closed, and the mail service was halted. Meanwhile, all the Wangs and Yangs from outside the villages were summoned home for an investigation. "The authorities were afraid of more chaos," Wang said.

One night after the crackdown, as Wang and his kinsmen slept, police arrived secretly to arrest three villagers. Silently, they hauled them from their beds and hustled them away in the darkness. In Wenche, a dozen Yangs were arrested in the same way. The police were too afraid of the clans to arrest the men in daylight.

But the arrests and military intervention left the Wang clan unscathed. In about two weeks, the paramilitary police pulled out of Huanglue. The "investigation" of tight-lipped clansmen turned up nothing. As for those arrested, the clan raised a few thousand dollars as bribe money and bought their freedom. The Wang whose hand had been blown off was still wanted by the police for his part in the Zhanjiang skirmish. But several months after the conflict, he sat laughing and chatting with friends at Zhenghe's house.

❉

Communist Party leaders in Beijing have grown alarmed as traditional forces like the Wang clan gain control in rural China. "An enormous clan force is taking shape in the countryside," warned China's official *Legal Daily* newspaper in 1992. "This force ... is assaulting the party leadership."

Clans pose a major obstacle to the party's efforts to shore up its rural power base. In 1990, Beijing launched its biggest mass campaign since the 1960s to indoctrinate farmers and strengthen rural party branches. But the "socialist education campaign" fizzled at the grass roots by failing to undermine the popular appeal of clans and other traditional groups. While paying lip service to Beijing, Chinese officials at the provincial level on down tend to tolerate clans. They know only a massive use of force could suppress them.

In Zhanjiang, teams of officials were sent to Huanglue and other villages under the socialist education campaign to halt the rise of clan power. The drive to subdue clans was launched in May 1991 as part of the city government's response to the feud of Wangs and Yangs. By January 1992, Zhanjiang party secretary Wang Ye claimed in an interview with a Chinese newspaper that the campaign had "effectively restrained the spread of clan forces."

But the effort was a farce. Even as Zhanjiang officials publicly attacked the clans, privately they were dealing with clan chiefs to get things done. For example, when the Wang clan threatened to demolish the Wu village of Mawen in early 1991, Zhanjiang authorities appealed to Wang clan chiefs from as far away as Guangxi Province to restrain their men. In the end, it worked. On March 29, the date of the Wang grave-sweeping pilgrimage, police cordoned off Mawen and forced the Wus to remain indoors while the Wangs held their rite peacefully. Still, the incident illustrates how Zhanjiang authorities have been reduced to mollifying clan chiefs and policing their territorial battles. Officials admitted that soliciting help from the Wang clan chiefs was vital. "They have prestige and popular trust," said Zhanjiang party committee information chief Chen Fa.

❋

Wang Bao sits near the open door of his farmhouse on a summer afternoon, his chopstick legs protruding from rolled-up pant legs, his bare feet propped up on a chair. Wang's trousers are held up at the waist, PLA-style, by a belt several inches too long. Knobby shoulders poke out from his sleeveless white-cotton undershirt. His hollow eyes and sunken cheeks betray a life of hardship. But he grows animated and jovial when he talks about the clan.

"We Wangs are the biggest clan in the Zhanjiang area," he boasts, reveling in the clan's newfound power and influence. "There are Wangs in Guangxi, Hainan, and all over Guangdong. Wang is the biggest surname in all China!" (Some experts say Wang is second to Chen as the most common Chinese name.)

Since he retired in 1989 at age sixty-two, Wang's life has been consumed by clan affairs and his desire to strengthen and perpetuate the lineage. After nearly thirty years as a Communist cadre, Wang is now a kind of clan ambassador, traveling as often as he can to other Wang settlements to share family histories and bolster ties.

In 1990, for example, Wang boarded a bus for Xuwen County, the site of Yueyan's exile in 1006. As the bus bounced toward the tip of the Leizhou Peninsula, Wang talked excitedly with five other clansmen, including the elder with fine calligraphy, Bangzhen. Wang led the clan-funded expedition to Xuwen to compare genealogies with Wang people there. To Wang's delight, the *zupus* matched, confirming the lineages were related. "I was very happy when I found the genealogy in the other village," Wang says, his face brightening with a broad display of false teeth. Such achievements as a clan elder are where Wang finds meaning in a life blotted with tragedies and disappointments.

Wang is as devoted to the clan as he is bitter toward the party-led regime. Although the clan offers Wang little financial support, it buoys his soul. In contrast, Wang blames the party for both his family's suffering and major national problems. "I have some big complaints about the government," Wang says, as he lights his bamboo water pipe. "But I'm already old. I have no great demands. If I did, it would be useless. All I want is to keep my stomach from being hungry. I live one day at a time."

Fifty years after he joined Communist guerrillas encamped in the hills around Huanglue, Wang still lives in poverty relative to other villagers. In China, where a farmer's home is the surest measure of his well-being, Wang's simple dwelling is decrepit. Sheets of plastic hang under the ceiling to catch the debris that falls from the thatch-and-tile roof. Day and night, the three-room home is dim because Wang cannot afford electricity. For fuel, he burns dried sugarcane leaves or rice straw. The only brightness in the main room comes from the flame under the wok and several large mirrors, gifts from fellow clansmen, that hang on the wall. Baskets and farming tools also clutter the wall. In one corner, a hen and her brood of chicks nest in an earthen pit lined with straw. A large ceramic pot in a makeshift shed of dried stems and leaves serves as an outhouse.

With the help of relatives, Wang harvests a small crop of rice and sugarcane each year from the family plots. After paying the government grain tax, about 700 pounds of hulled rice remains to feed Wang, his youngest daughter Wang Yueling, and his nearly 100-year-old mother Huang. The amount puts them below the government poverty line for grain consumption. "We eat everything we grow and also buy a little, just to fill our stomachs," Wang says, knocking the end of his bamboo pipe on the floor to shoo the chicks. The family rarely eats meat, killing a hen only to celebrate Chinese New Year or Qingming.

Wang's daughter Yueling is the household breadwinner. She earns $38 a month at her government job distributing the *Zhanjiang Daily* in Huanglue. "I wanted to go to high school, but my father retired and we had no money so I gave up the idea," says Yueling, a cheerful young woman in her early twenties. She puts aside every penny possible to pay for medical expenses in case Wang falls ill.

Yueling has looked after her father ever since her two eldest sisters married into the Xie clan and another left home to live at the Zhanjiang blanket factory where she works. Every day, Yueling rises at 5:30 A.M. She boils the rice and cooks the vegetables Wang buys fresh from the market before she goes to work at 7:30 A.M. Wang sweeps the floors, but otherwise Yueling keeps house. Yueling pushes her own hopes of marriage to the back of her mind. "If I leave home, Dad will be too lonely," she confides.

Wang blames the government's stinginess for forcing him to depend on his daughter. Every month, he collects just $16 in retirement pay and other subsidies from the state. Wang is most offended by the $5 a month he receives for his army disability. "I was a soldier for nothing," he says, taking out his "disabled soldier" certificate. "I am a third-grade disabled serviceman, but I barely have enough to eat and wear." In April 1992, Wang and a group of more than 100 army veterans demonstrated at the Suixi County government to demand more retirement and medical benefits. Later, they sent a five-man delegation to the provincial capital, Guangzhou. But officials disregarded the group.

Wang sees himself not as a lone victim but as one of millions of Chinese suffering from the corruption and crime now rife under the Communist regime. Although Wang trusts the clansmen serving as cadres in Huanglue, he spits out disdain for bureaucrats in higher posts outside the lineage. "Today, all the cadres are corrupt. The county cadres are corrupt, the bank cadres are corrupt, the court

Wang Bao (far right) seated next to his mother and younger brother outside the brother's house in Huanglue. Wang's daughter, Wang Yueling, is standing behind him. Photo by Ann Scott Tyson.

cadres are corrupt, and the state-run store cadres are corrupt," Wang huffs. "There is a saying: 'Big cadre, big corruption. Small cadre, small corruption.' They all take public money. They build houses. They buy nice-looking clothes. They take bribes to give you a job. When I was a cadre things were not like that. My clothes were tattered."

As corrupt cadres milk public funds with one hand, they use the other to squeeze big fees from farmers like Wang. Wang gives readily to the clan, but he resents increasingly onerous taxes for the local militia, cadres' salaries, and other expenses the government has shouldered in the past. "The burden on peasants is very great now," Wang says. "They have to pay for everything themselves."

In Wang's view, the rampant official abuses are signs of mammoth government incompetence. His greatest worry is that such an incapable regime will fail to prevent a general drift toward chaos. "Social order is very chaotic," Wang says, the creases on his brow betraying the visceral Chinese aversion to *luan*.

"Nowadays, we farmers don't fear a change in [reform] policy. We are afraid of being robbed. Now robbers can buy guns. If they see someone has money, they can just come take it. The government can't control them. We have to lock our door at night, or criminals will steal our chicks and cooking pots." He points out the wooden bolt on the door. "If crime and corruption get any worse, our country will fall into civil war!" Wang says.

What China needs, Wang concludes, is a government that will "fine who it should, jail who it should, send to labor reform who it should, and free who it should"—in essence a just, responsible, and effective government. "But in Zhanjiang, Guangzhou, everywhere, it's the same: The government is not in charge."

A neighbor comes to Wang's door with a bowl, asking to borrow some soy sauce. Outside, the smoke from wok fires drifts through the village along paths muddy and rutted with bicycle tracks. As night falls over Huanglue, the croaking of hundreds of frogs fills the air. Wang, his daughter, and his mother sleep on straw mats behind locked windows and doors.

Many Chinese view the comeback of clans as another sign of the declining social order that so alarms Wang. To Wang, the clan represents just the opposite: a refuge in China's tumultuous society, a source of security, solace, and solidarity amid the decay of state power and ideology.

"Now we can worship again," Wang laughs one chilly spring morning during Qingming. "After all, everyone has ancestors!" He pulls on a turtleneck sweater, his old blue Mao suit, and a green felt hat and leaves his home on foot. He walks through tall wet grass toward the ancestral burial ground on the outskirts of Huanglue.

Wang views the prospect from the tomb. The rich green fields seem to melt into the misty horizon. In the fifteenth century, Wang's ancestors chose this spot as their main gravesite because the contours of the land resemble the wings of a goose in flight. According to geomancers, the auspicious alignment would help beneficial forces flow to living descendants, bringing them wealth, power, and sons.

As the distant firecrackers of Qingming echo across the fields, Wang kneels down and kowtows before the tomb of the Song dynasty scholar-official Wang Yueyan. A light rain begins to fall on the tan and rose colored strips of spirit money anchored with stones around the tomb.

PART THREE

The Losers from Reform

"The Bold Feast While the Timid Starve"

撐死膽大的

餓死膽小的

As Wang Bao celebrates clan power, peasant woman Zhao Xinlan must endure the revival of patriarchal traditions that openly favor men. In the central China village of Xiaodian, Zhao and her women neighbors face a resurgence in wife buying and other ancient forms of abuse. They are also exploited economically. As their husbands seek better work in cities, women like Zhao are left to rear children and farm the land back home.

Zhao Xinlan and her eldest son, Ran Fachun

Photo by Ann Scott Tyson

S I X

"The Moon Reflecting the Sunlight": The Village Woman

ZHAO XINLAN RISES EARLY, quaffs a ladleful of cool water, and leaves her farmhouse before the June day grows too hot. She walks a mile down a dirt path to the family plot, passing acre after acre of golden wheat that seems to touch the sky. As she walks, a migrating cuckoo pipes its whimsical song from a nearby poplar. For Zhao, the cuckoo's call is the surest sign that harvest time has come again to her village in China's heartland. "Cuckoo, cuckoo. Sprinkle vinegar on the noodles. First harvest the barley and then the wheat," Zhao hums as she walks, reciting the summer harvest rhyme she learned as a girl.

Zhao's song does little, however, to lighten the backbreaking task that lies ahead. She sets to work, stooping and cutting the bundles of ripened grain with a sickle. Her body is wiry; her hands are rough and tanned dark brown. As in many summers past, Zhao will bring in the harvest alone, laboring to feed her three boys without help from her husband, a coal miner in a distant city. "I do all the work, the man's half as well as the woman's," says Zhao, tucking a loose strand of hair behind her ear. "If I didn't do it, who would?"

For the first time, millions of peasant women like Zhao have been left in charge of what was men's work in China for centuries: the grueling, never-ending production of food. In many villages, such as Zhao's home of Xiaodian in China's central Henan Province, women now shoulder 90 percent of the farming. Nationwide, women handle from 60 percent to 70 percent of farmwork in addition to their traditional household tasks, official figures show.

Zhao's life shows the kind of sweeping change that market-oriented reforms have brought to the lives of China's 430 million rural women since 1980. The reforms have spurred tens of millions of men to quit the land in less developed regions like Henan and migrate to more lucrative jobs in cities and towns. As a result, rural women like Zhao have assumed the vital economic role of farming.

The shift in roles illustrates how reform has brought new responsibility but also greater hardship to many women in the countryside, especially in poor regions. Zhao and others like her have gained pride and self-esteem as they run family farms. However, like Zhao, most peasant women are managing China's farms not by choice but by necessity. Left behind by their husbands, these women find their opportunities to move beyond the toil are almost nil. Just as bound feet kept women close to the hearth in traditional China, rural women today are bound to land and home by the endless chores of farming, sewing, housekeeping, and caring for their children.

In other ways, China's peasant women have faced growing, sometimes vicious discrimination under reform. As Maoist social controls have eased, women in Xiaodian and thousands of other villages have seen a revival of customs such as wife buying, concubinage, the arranged marriage of child brides, and the sale or abandonment of baby girls. Widespread in China's patriarchal society before the 1949 revolution, such practices are again rampant in many parts of rural China.

In addition to old oppression, women face new forms of exploitation in China under reform. As crude, unbridled capitalism spreads outside the state-run economy, many women are maltreated by unethical bosses who profit from a buyer's market for labor. Some rural women, although far fewer than men, migrate to towns and cities seeking jobs. Most of these are unmarried teenage girls, who work as maids, babysitters, or in unskilled, low-paid factory jobs. In the cities, these girls often labor fourteen hours a day in dangerous sweatshops. They sleep crowded in locked dormitories of corrugated tin despite the threat of fires that have killed thousands of others like them. They are easy victims of wage exploitation and sexual abuse. A handful of these girls marry city residents and escape their poor villages for good. But most eventually return to the countryside to wed, bear children, and farm the land.

The plight of rural women shows how social justice and equality lag behind gains in prosperity in China under reform. Many of the harmful offshoots of reform most hurt women, both rural and urban. As a group, peasant women are especially vulnerable because they are among the least educated Chinese. One out of three women in China's countryside is illiterate. In the cities, better-educated women also face new pressures from reform. As employers gain the freedom to hire and fire workers, qualified urban women are increasingly denied jobs because of the widespread bias that men are more competent. Women employees work longer hours for less pay than men and are twice as likely to be laid off by state firms. Women and others who have faced setbacks under reform—the poor, state workers, the elderly—are growing disaffected as the Communist Party gives them no outlet for defending their interests.

Many rural women are traditional in outlook and lack the confidence and resources to fight discrimination. Unlike the millions of Chinese who have grown more assertive under reform, women like Zhao and her neighbors in Xiaodian tend to accept their fate. Deeply influenced by the prejudices of China's ancient patriarchal culture, they still see themselves as naturally subordinate to men, even as they shoulder unprecedented responsibility on the farm. They are "the moon reflecting the sunlight," the shadowy, negative force of yin enlivened only by the masculine brightness of yang. Passively, they often allow their lives to be molded by the needs and demands of others rather than pursue their own aspirations.

One morning in the middle of June, Zhao returns home from the market with a basketful of spring onions. She has finished the difficult summer harvest. Her 4,000 pounds of wheat have been threshed, sun-dried, and stored in gunnysacks. Once again, the busy season has passed, and Zhao has begun the lighter work of hoeing and weeding her newly planted cotton crop. This morning, she can afford to stay home. As often happens, several neighborhood women drop in. They pull up wooden stools and chairs in the main room of Zhao's two-room farmhouse, chatting as they clean the fresh onions. Country women like to talk together as they work, Zhao says, because it makes the chores go more quickly. She joins her circle of friends to trade jokes as well as stories of the bitterness life has dished up.

"I am truly an ill-fated person," sighs Guo Yunfang, an elderly neighbor of Zhao's, as she carefully strips the thin outer leaves off the onions. "We women in this village are made to suffer, worked to the bone, oppressed, and given no freedom!" She tosses the dirty leaves on the brick farmhouse floor.

Guo's words are harsh, especially for a woman in her seventies. But they flow from years of abuse beginning when Guo was a girl in the 1920s. She was born in 1919, the daughter of a rich landlord in nearby Yanjin County. In the 1930s and 1940s, her father, a stern disciplinarian, served as an official of the Nationalist regime. Guo's simple but perfectly tailored clothing hints of her wealthy past. Her snow-white hair is neatly held back with combs. She wears gray trousers, black cotton shoes, and a white short-sleeved shirt that buttons at the shoulder. But the most telling sign of Guo's past status—and suffering—are her tiny pointed feet, which look grotesquely out of balance with her rotund figure.

"My feet were wrapped up when I was ten years old," Guo recalls. "First, all my toes were broken and forced under. It hurt terribly. Then, they were wrapped in long cloth strips eighteen inches long and five inches wide," she says, remembering every agonizing stitch of the cloth that bound her feet, day after day. After some time, the flesh of her feet atrophied, leaving only shrunken, misshapen appendages of skin and bone.

"Why did they do it? Well, when a girl married in those days, everyone looked at her feet, not her face," Guo says. "If she teetered along, 'ta-ta-ta,' on dainty feet she was considered pretty. Big feet were ugly."

Foot binding was one of the cruelest, most flagrant forms of subjugation of women in China's old society. Euphemistically called "lilies" and meant to give erotic pleasure, bound feet crippled millions of Chinese women like Guo. The tiny deformed stumps made even simple movements painful and awkward for the women and forced them to stay close to home.

In any case, Guo, like other girls, was barred from leaving her family courtyard without permission. Girls were to stay at home, sewing, embroidering, cooking, and keeping house. According to Confucian tradition, Guo was essentially the property of her father until her marriage. Then she became the subject of her husband, whom she addressed as *zhangfu* (master). In Henan, a man still calls his wife "the person inside the room" after this ancient tradition. Even when her husband died, a woman was not free from the domestic tyranny. She was obligated to obey her son.

"My sister's marriage was arranged when she was only two years old. She couldn't even talk," says Guo. "Mine was settled when I was fourteen. Of course, I hadn't set eyes on my husband before our wedding day. That night, we were two strangers in one bed!" she says with a loud laugh, drawing chuckles from her neighbors.

Zhao's brother-in-law, a gray-haired man in his late fifties, peers in the open farmhouse door with a quizzical grin.

"Who invited you?" Zhao asks him. "Go on, now," she says. Reluctantly, he shambles away.

When the laughter subsides, another village woman with short steel-gray hair and a squarish face turns to Guo. "You suffered a lot, for sure. But what about me? I had twelve children!" says the woman, a peasant in her sixties named Wang Shenglan.

"My goodness! Twelve children. She just couldn't control herself. Those two together, all they did was make babies!" says Guo loudly. Laughter again bursts from the peasant women.

Wang, who is one of the village's 200 Christians, blushes deeply. But she recovers and goes on with her story. "I had twelve children, but only seven of them survived, five boys and two girls. Those were considered lucky numbers. But it was not lucky for me. It was a lot of trouble and hardship. Every year I had to spin and weave to make shoes and clothes for them. I felt so irritated with all the children crying."

Like all Chinese women, Wang had an unshirkable duty to bear sons, the more the better. Beyond that, though, her life and the lives of other women often seemed to have little value. In Chinese kinship rites, women were treated as fleeting vessels made of flesh. Their bodies served to perpetuate the all-important male line before melting away, soon to be forgotten. Only men, whose essence was symbolized by the enduring bones, had the hope of attaining immortality if their descendants worshiped them long enough. When Wang was young, as today, a woman who failed to produce a boy was often harshly chastised by her husband and in-laws. Adding to the insult, her husband almost certainly took a concubine if he could afford one.

Although men yearned for sons, they usually left all the care of children to their wives. Wang's husband refused even to pick up their youngsters. "After giving birth, I could only rest three days before getting up to work again," Wang says. "I couldn't even eat eggs to get my strength back. Once, we had a few eggs. But my husband told my son to sell them at the market and buy him tobacco. My son argued that I should have the eggs. But my husband refused. I still remember that." Her face darkens.

"My husband is ill-tempered, too," says Guo. "He is always beating me and cursing at me. He hardly allows me a mouthful to eat. I've had to accept a sack of grain from my [married] daughter." Guo winces at the humiliation.

Women like Guo and Wang had little recourse against such abuses once they moved into their husbands' households after marriage. Traditionally, a husband had the right to virtually complete control over his wife. Indeed, according to one interpretation, the Chinese character for woman, *nü*, is based on an ideogram of a woman kneeling. For centuries under ancient Chinese law, a man who murdered his wife faced no punishment; if she committed adultery, he was legally free to kill her. Yet a woman who injured or killed her husband, even in self-defense, was severely punished or beheaded. In the Qing dynasty (1644–1911), women belonged to a legal category of subjects called the "petty and low." They were routinely held responsible for crimes committed by their husbands, who were categorized as the "elder and better." As late as the 1940s, a man in financial straits could sell his wife. Or, he could engage in *dianqi* (wife mortgaging), lending his wife to another man for a few years.

Worst off were the young girls from poor families, like Zhao's mother, who were often sold by their fathers as child brides, servants, concubines, or prostitutes. Their lives of slavery started in girlhood. "My mother's life was miserable," Zhao tells the neighbors gathered in her farmhouse. "When she was nine years old, her parents died. They were very poor, so her uncle sold her as a *tongyangxi* to a family with some money."

Tongyangxi (daughter-in-law-to-be) was one of the lowliest of social rankings. An ingenious invention of China's patriarchal system, it allowed a family to train its son's future wife to be submissive and obedient from childhood. For girls like Zhao's mother, this meant giving up the relative freedom of her parent's home for years of servitude. "The family bound her feet. She was just like a slave in their house. She was very unhappy," Zhao says.

Zhao's mother was not alone. She was born in 1920, the first year of a devastating famine caused by severe drought in Henan and neighboring provinces. At least 500,000 people died in the famine, and nearly 20 million more were left destitute. Deadly epidemics plagued survivors. Refugees filled the roads, trying to escape the disaster. Unable to feed themselves and their offspring, adults sold tens of thousands of children like Zhao's mother.

One day, however, Zhao's mother managed to escape her mother-in-law's watchful eye and flee. At first she ran to her uncle's house, but he was away. Inside, there was no food. In desperation, she ground up some old peanut shells she found on the floor. For several days, she hid in a ditch, eating the ground shells, weeds, and anything else she could scavenge. But soon the family found her and dragged her back to Le village, not far from Xiaodian.

Each day, Zhao's mother was put to work milling flour, cooking meals, spinning and weaving cloth, or stitching shoes. She hated the tedious work, especially the long hours sitting cross-legged and rocking to and fro as she spun cotton on a hand-rotated wooden spinning wheel. Her outstretched arms ached as she turned the wheel with one hand and drew the other back and forth spinning wad after wad of cotton into one long thread. But as the years wore on, she accepted her fate, glad simply to have food and shelter.

In 1938, when Zhao's mother was eighteen, the family fled Le village during a massive flood of the silt-laden Yellow River, some thirty miles to the south. The flood was triggered by Nationalist leader Chiang Kai-shek, who had ordered his engineers to blow up the river dikes to slow the advance of Japanese troops. Full-scale war between China and Japan had erupted the year before. The huge flood wiped out more than 4,000 Chinese villages and shifted the course of the Yellow River south nearly 300 miles. But it merely stalled the Japanese for three months. Before long, the family found itself again on the run as Japan's army moved deeper into China's heartland. "My mother and her family were always running from here to there, but somehow they lived through the war," says Zhao.

The widespread atrocities of Japanese troops terrified Zhao's mother and her in-laws. During the 1937 massacre in Nanjing, Japanese invaders raped an estimated 20,000 women and murdered some 12,000 civilians. Zhao's mother told Zhao the tragic story of one young mother she knew who hid behind a door petrified as Japanese troops stormed into her house. To keep her baby from crying, she pressed it hard against her breast. Finally, the soliders left without detecting the woman, but her baby had died of suffocation. Zhao's mother knew other women who had babies while fleeing in 1938 and were forced to abandon them.

Zhao's mother did not have a child until after the Sino-Japanese War ended in 1945. In about 1946 she gave birth to a son, the first of six children. At the height of China's civil war between the Nationalists and Communists, she bore her second child, Zhao. Zhao was born on April 12, 1948, as Communist armies in Henan seized the nearby city of Luoyang. In a little more than a year, the Communist victory was complete and Zhao's mother and father settled down to a life of farming back in Le village. During the land redistribution campaign in 1950, Zhao's parents were classified by the Communists as "middle peasants," which meant they escaped the beatings meted out to landlords and rich peasants but also received none of the land and property reallocated to poor peasants. Still, they were allowed to keep what land they had.

Zhao grew up in a period of relative calm in China. But domestic battles raged inside her mud-walled home. Although Zhao's parents had been raised together, they had a stormy relationship. Zhao's father was a coarse man with a fierce temper. Although he never beat his children or derided them, he fought constantly with their mother. For her part, Zhao's mother had always resented being sold as a *tangyangxi*. As she grew older, her resentment over the thankless role grew. She went about her chores muttering to herself. "These lazy, good-for-nothing men! I'm tired to death!" she complained over and over.

Zhao remembers her mother busy from dawn until dusk as she single-handedly cared for six children, cooked the meals, spun, wove, and hand-stitched cotton clothes, and also did a little farmwork. "My father would come back from the fields with his pant legs rolled up and squat on his heels, smoking tobacco,"

Zhao recalls. "The household was chaotic and my mother was frantic trying to get things done, but he just sat there.

"Now, it's the same," Zhao swats a chicken with the back of her hand and sends it flapping out the farmhouse door. "The men all want to squat on their heels, play cards, play mah-jongg. They are all alike. 'Every crow under Heaven is as black as the other,'" she says, quoting a Chinese adage. "This is the reason for most of the conflicts in the countryside today: The men are lazy and the women are tired."

As a girl in Maoist China, Zhao grew up in a world radically different from her mother's. Mao Zedong advocated women's equality under the slogan "women hold up half the sky." Shortly after taking power in 1949, the Communists announced a program that promised women equal rights and pledged to end their "bondage." In 1950, a new law banned compulsory arranged marriages and the sale of women and girls as brides. It promoted the freedom of Chinese to choose their spouses and allowed women to seek divorce. Also, the law gave unmarried, divorced, and widowed women the right to hold land in their own names. (Married women were still denied that right.)

Communist propagandists campaigned against footbinding, concubinage, prostitution, and other traditional practices that oppressed women. "Big feet are good. Big feet are steady. Big feet won't let you slip and leave you muddy!" went the propaganda ditty Zhao sang as she played in the village as a little girl.

Although the Communist revolution promised Chinese women some new political and legal protections, it fell far short of liberating them. Old prejudices lived on for girls like Zhao, especially in rural villages, where the subordination of women had been ingrained for centuries. Many peasants like Zhao's father still viewed girls primarily as household labor and hesitated to educate them. Zhao went to primary school for only two years before dropping out because her father and grandfather withheld tuition. When she was only seven, Zhao was put to work spinning cotton. By the time she turned thirteen, Zhao could manage all the domestic chores and often did.

Moreover, it quickly became apparent that Maoist policies were dictated less by the aim of freeing women than by the necessity of tapping female labor for radical economic programs. Beginning in the 1950s, the government aggravated the burden of peasant women by forcing them to take part in often grueling collective farm labor. In 1958 China launched the Great Leap Forward. Under the slogan "release men and substitute women," millions of men were drawn off the fields to smelt steel and build irrigation works. Rural women, meanwhile, were enlisted for field labor on an unprecedented scale, with some 90 percent of able-bodied women taking part. Zhao was only ten years old, still too young for strenuous farmwork. But her mother and millions of other Chinese women were organized into rural production teams in Henan as the province led China's drive to abolish private plots and create people's communes. In order to free women from domestic chores, the communes set up mess halls, nurseries, shoemaking shops, laundries, and other services. But this pooling of household work quickly broke down as the Great Leap collectivization movement brought starvation.

"At first, we had the big rice pot," Zhao said. "We all took our bowls to the canteen, where workers ladled out gruel from a big basin. Then we carried the bowls home to eat. But later the gruel became thinner and thinner. All the peasants started to complain. 'The big pot of rice is too watery!' they said."

The Great Leap ended in a severe nationwide famine. Zhao and her family struggled to fight off starvation. The village grain supply was exhausted, some of it shipped out to fulfill state quotas and feed China's cities. The family subsisted mainly on carrots and other root vegetables. Meal after meal, they ate steamed buns made of carrot flour, broth of carrot tops, and sweet potatoes. Sometimes Zhao, driven by hunger, crept into the communal fields to dig up carrots and turnips. She stuffed them into her mouth, dirt and all. But later, even these disappeared. Zhao and her family ate wild leaves and weeds.

The famine was hardest on women like Wang Shenglan, the mother who bore twelve children. Wang had her first baby when she was only eighteen. By the peak years of food shortages she was in her late twenties and already had several more children. Wang, like most peasant women at the time, was ignorant about methods of contraception and could not refuse her husband's advances. Even if she had known how to prevent conception, Communist Party policy during the Great Leap discouraged her from doing so. The party declared that due to the success of people's communes China faced a labor shortage. In 1958, Mao declared that China could manage not only 800 million people but 1 billion. As a result, countless undernourished women like Wang suffered the agony of becoming pregnant, giving birth, and lacking enough breast milk to keep the weak infant alive. "I had no milk, so the babies got sick and died," Wang said. Some peasants, realizing the bleak prospects that awaited their newborns, resorted to infanticide.

In 1962, when Zhao was fourteen, she was assigned to a women's production team. By then, the party had reversed many of the disastrous Great Leap policies. Local officials had decentralized the commune's powers and redistributed small individual plots in Le village. Communal mess halls had shut down, and domestic labor was no longer pooled. But as women once again shouldered the household chores, they were not free to quit working the communal fields. Maoist radicalism combined with traditional prejudices had locked peasant women like Zhao and her mother in a double bind: They were compelled at once to be revolutionaries on the farm and wifely at home. "If we didn't work, we didn't eat," Zhao said.

Shoulder to shoulder with other peasant women, Zhao labored to earn the work points that were converted into grain at the end of the year. At first Zhao found the farming awkward and difficult. Food remained scarce in the village, and she was still weak from malnourishment. She earned only seven or eight work points a day. Later, as she grew stronger and more skilled, she received the women's daily maximum of fifteen points, worth about 40 Chinese cents. "I pulled a plow and harrow, work an animal should do," she said.

But no matter how hard they worked, Zhao and her teammates on the women's production team could never earn the maximum of twenty points reserved for men. A man was always considered a more able farmhand than a woman. Rural communes claimed to liberate women, but discrimination was built into the work point system.

The outbreak of the radical Cultural Revolution in 1966 heightened pressure on rural women like Zhao to emulate Mao's "iron girl," the unadorned, sturdily built peasant woman with short-cropped hair and baggy clothes glorified by propagandists. Already in the early 1960s, millions of women like Zhao were organized into "red women's shock brigades." They underwent basic military training, marching into the fields with crude rifles as well as hoes on their shoulders. The iron-girl model forced women like Zhao to suppress any display of femininity, as if womanliness itself was at odds with the revolution.

Women were also masculinized by their mandatory role in political violence during the Cultural Revolution. Many rural communities were spared severe turmoil in the decade-long movement, but Le village saw its share of "class struggle." Maoist extremists recruited Zhao and other women for mass struggle sessions against peasants accused as enemies of the people. As Red Guards dragged victims before a packed-dirt square in the center of the village, Zhao had to scream out charges with the crowd or risk being accused as a sympathizer. Often, the hapless peasants were twisted into the torturous "airplane position," their arms pinned behind them and heads jerked forward. If a victim failed to confess his or her "crimes"—often something as minor as stealing vegetables from communal fields—he would be beaten.

But even as Cultural Revolution fanatics smashed ancestral shrines, preached revolutionary puritanism, and painted life as an endless struggle between class enemies and the people, relations between peasant men and women remained essentially traditional in Le village and across rural China.

One summer day in 1968, as Zhao was pruning cotton, a teenage girl in a straw hat ran up to her through the rows of green shrubs. Breathlessly, the girl said that her mother's younger brother, Ran Wenli, had just returned to nearby Xiaodian Village after four years in the People's Liberation Army. Zhao perked up but said nothing. She knew a hint of courtship when she heard one. The girl had been instructed by her mother to draw Zhao's attention to Ran. Not long afterward, the girl and Zhao had occasion to go together to the local market town. "Oh, there's my uncle now," the girl said, squeezing Zhao's arm as they walked past the local wheat station.

Zhao glanced over and saw a tall, handsome young man hoisting sacks of grain. She instantly turned away again, feigning a lack of interest. But in spite of herself, she felt her heartbeat quicken. "He caught my fancy. He was good-looking. And as a returned soldier, he had a good class status."

A matchmaker for Zhao's parents conducted a detailed inquiry on the family and character of their prospective son-in-law, just as Ran's family had checked on Zhao's background in advance. From Ran's friends and relatives, a picture emerged of an even-tempered young man of twenty-two. As a former soldier from a poor peasant's household, his revolutionary credentials could not have been "redder." Soon, in the traditional fashion, the go-between arranged for Zhao to be formally introduced to Ran.

On the day of the meeting, Zhao's stomach was taut. She and her parents met with Ran's parents, according to tradition, in the eastern room of his family's home. After some polite small talk by the elders, Ran and Zhao were left alone briefly. "Do you have any complaints?" he asked simply. It was the first time he had ever addressed her. "If not, then it's settled," he said.

Zhao felt the blood rushing to her face. Her heart leaped upward and blocked her throat. She shifted in her chair, stared down at her cotton shoes, and said nothing.

Finally, she looked up. "I don't have any complaints," she replied.

Smiling, Ran unfolded a pretty yellow scarf and tied it gently around Zhao's neck. In accordance with the local custom, Zhao also gave Ran a scarf as a token of her affection. They were engaged.

In 1969, the wedding was set for an auspicious day in the second lunar month. That morning Zhao dressed in her best shirt, a red, white, and green plaid. She wore matching plaid cotton shoes and also the yellow scarf from Ran. When all was ready, she stepped into the back of a wooden horse-drawn cart accompanied by two women relatives. Six men followed behind carrying her dowry of a cabinet, a table, and a dresser containing a wadded-cotton quilt and mattress. As the driver clucked to the horse, Zhao's parents firmly shut the door of their house and climbed into the cart. Tradition dictated that from this day, Zhao would belong to her husband's household in Xiaodian.

Zhao sobbed all the way to her wedding. She cried out of shame because she thought her dowry was too small. She cried from a lingering fear of Ran and his four brothers. She cried as Chinese women had for centuries on their wedding days, because there was no going home.

The ceremony was an odd mixture of traditional ritual and worship of Mao. When they arrived at Ran's home, the two mothers met alone for a customary chat. Then, as friends and relatives gathered, the bride and groom paid their respects to cosmic and earthly authorities.

"First we prostrated before Heaven. During the Cultural Revolution that meant we kowtowed in front of Mao's portrait," Zhao explained. Next, Ran and Zhao bowed to the northern wall of the simple courtyard home, where Ran's parents stayed, to show their obedience. They bowed to each other. Finally, amid the crackling of firecrackers bunched on long strands, they bowed to the guests.

At the wedding feast, the hosts toasted everyone with cups of rice wine. The guests sampled eight plates of cold dishes and eight bowls heaped with fragrant meat and vegetables and gave Zhao and Ran small packets of money as gifts. After nightfall brought the festivities to a close, the newlyweds withdrew to their room behind doors marked with the red-painted Chinese symbol for "double happiness."

For seven months, the couple lived with Ran's family. Zhao was happy, although her workload was heavier than that of men in the household. Every morning she rose early to prepare meals and wash clothes. Then she left for work in the fields to earn her grain ration. In the evening, Zhao often had to attend political meetings. She had been put in charge of her women's production team in 1969, and the meetings were mandatory for a low-level cadre. However, like many younger Chinese women who became cadres in the Maoist era, Zhao had little real power. Although far more women served as officials under Mao, their jobs tended to be menial, low-ranking, and therefore unattractive. Many women quit after a brief time or once they bore children. Zhao resigned in 1970 after being criticized for arriving late at meetings.

Zhao's double burden in the home and fields was by now not only accepted but glorified as politically virtuous by the party leadership. The party badly needed women's labor as it launched a campaign to achieve agricultural self-sufficiency in the early 1970s. But it lacked the resources to set up collective nurseries and cafeterias to relieve women of their household chores. So party propagandists created a new female paragon to encourage women like Zhao to work harder. Known as the mother with "four goods," this superwoman excelled at collective labor and opposing revisionism as well as bringing up children and keeping house.

After less than a year of marriage, Ran left Xiaodian to accept a job as a state worker in a leather shoe factory run by the county. As a returned soldier, he qualified for the coveted state job, which offered financial security even though it paid only 40 yuan a month. A few months later, he was offered another job in a coal mine on Henan's northwestern border. The couple knew the job would mean years of separation before Ran would be allowed to retire. But it also offered him an urban residence permit, along with state grain rations, medical care, and other lifelong benefits. "All the peasants wanted to get urban residence. Workers ate much better than peasants. Peasants exhausted themselves in the fields every day and still ate poorly," Zhao said. "We believed the urban residence was worth it."

One day not long after Chinese New Year, Zhao watched Ran hoist his bedroll and knapsack onto a crowded provincial bus and squeeze through the doors. As the bus rattled away, she waved goodbye with her yellow scarf and tears ran down her cheeks. She did not imagine, though, how deeply she would regret his absence.

In the spring of 1971, after one of Ran's home leaves, Zhao began feeling queasy. It was a busy farming time, and she had to rise at dawn and join her production team in the fields before breakfast. Several times, she returned home at midmorning dizzy and with her stomach heaving. Exhausted and yet too nauseated to eat, she lay on the bed, her face pale and drawn. She "had happiness," as Chinese say.

Despite her pregnancy, Zhao had no respite from fieldwork. But fortunately, she was healthy and suffered no complications. Harsh working conditions and a lack of even crude medical care meant that the maternal death rate was high in China. The loss of infants was also common. When it came time to give birth, Zhao was attended only by her mother, who came from Le village to help. The baby was a ruddy boy. Because he was born just before the lunar New Year in 1972, Zhao named him Fachun (Bringing Spring).

Zhao would give birth to two more sons, Fatai and Fayang, whose names together mean "Bringing Sun," in 1975 and 1979. By that time, she had moved out of Ran's parents' home and lived with her children in a simple thatched dwelling. Her mother helped with the second birth. But Zhao delivered her third baby alone. Her mother had died a few months earlier at the age of fifty-nine. "My mother died too young. She died of exhaustion."

The period after her mother's death was one of the hardest in Zhao's life. She felt an intense loneliness. More than anyone, Zhao's mother had supported her in Ran's absence. Now, she needed that support more than ever. With a baby and two small children to care for, Zhao found it hard to do much fieldwork. Her work points fell to seven or eight, and so her grain allotment dropped sharply. The family received some cash from Ran each month, but the food still fell short. With her children hungry, Zhao often had to hide her shame and ask for handouts of grain from relatives.

In 1980, China's market-oriented reforms began alleviating poverty in Xiaodian and thousands of other Chinese villages. Collective fields were broken up. The revival of family farms spurred huge gains in productivity. As farms nationwide reaped record harvests with fewer hands, millions of peasants began quitting the land for factory jobs.

Ironically, however, the reforms only compounded Zhao's difficulties. In 1980, she received her own small plot of land when she was least able to farm it. Still, she had to till the land in order to feed her family. "I had three children and no one to help me," Zhao said.

Zhao dreaded most the strenuous jobs of harvesting, hauling, and threshing the wheat. Each day before dawn in the summer of 1980, Zhao walked the mile to the field with her baby, Fayang, tied to her back and two other sons dawdling behind. Because of the constant bending and stooping, Zhao could not carry Fayang as she harvested the wheat. "I had to lay the baby in the dirt and let him cry."

Later, in desperation, Zhao sometimes locked her children in the house while she did the farming. Her overwork and lack of vigilance proved tragic. When Fayang was about twelve months old, he crawled over to the stove and toppled a pot of boiling corn gruel. He screamed as the hot gruel spilled on his face, badly burning it. Zhao rushed the howling child to the neighbors and borrowed some ointment. The cream did little good, however, and within days the burn was seriously infected. Fayang grew feverish. Zhao carried him to the nearest hospital, which was several miles away. With treatment, his infection slowly healed. But Fayang's left eye and most of the left side of his face were grotesquely disfigured for life.

✼

In the early 1980s, Zhao was unusual as a woman single-handedly running a farm. Today, she is the norm. Every day in Xiaodian, peasant women like Zhao shepherd their children down dusty tree-lined paths to the fields. As the mothers farm, their youngsters play, throwing rocks, chewing on twigs, or digging up clumps of soil. At the end of the day, the women head home, often with a sleeping child on one shoulder and a hoe on the other.

Scenes in Xiaodian reveal how China's market-driven reforms have been a mixed blessing for rural women. A walk through the village at harvesttime leaves no doubt that the reforms have ended hunger for Zhao and most other villagers. Golden wheat lies piled on the village's only paved road, to be threshed by tractors and other passing vehicles. In the village market, peasants buy swirly flat breads called *huo shao* as a vendor browns them on an iron skillet. A young married woman walks past with her arm hooked through a basket filled with fragrant fried dough twists, a customary harvesttime gift for her mother back in the home village. Zhao's family is now self-sufficient in grain, and by selling cotton, goats, and chickens, Zhao earns a cash income of about $550 a year.

Yet as reform has brought greater productivity and prosperity to Xiaodian, it has been almost exclusively the men who have seized the opportunity to escape the drudgery of farming. As fewer of Xiaodian's 1,000 villagers were needed to farm its 800 acres of land, men left in droves to seek higher-paying jobs in construction, manufacturing, carpentry, and mining outside the village. Peasant men also occupied most positions of power in China's newly emerging rural enterprises and commercial networks. In contrast, only a few young women have ventured out of Xiaodian. They work mainly as babysitters and maids or at menial factory jobs. Many rural enterprises pay women workers less than men, retaining the assumption of the collective work point system that any man will do more than a woman. Virtually all of these young women return to Xiaodian to marry, raise children, and till the land. Older and married peasant women like Zhao have stayed in the village. For them, any fleeting leisure enjoyed as a result of the reforms ended with the departure of their husbands. "When the man leaves home, he leaves all the farming to the woman," said Wu Cuilan, a stout middle-aged matron who runs Xiaodian's agronomy station.

Women like Zhao handle all the painstaking work of growing Xiaodian's annual 640-acre cotton crop. They fertilize the soil, apply pesticide, and carefully clip off the twigs of cotton plants that have not borne heads of cotton. In the fall, women pick the cotton and also harvest corn, peanuts, beans, and vegetables. During the summer wheat harvest, some men who work in nearby factories take leave for a few days to help. Otherwise, bringing in the grain is also left to women. "Now, the women's burden is relatively heavy. Every day they bury their heads in hard work," said Wu. "When they return from the fields, from the moment they enter the door they have to cook, wash clothes, and care for the children."

As Zhao knows well, a husband's absence adds nagging loneliness to the hours of toil. Although Zhao is convinced her husband has remained faithful to her, many migrant men are promiscuous, according to Chinese experts and the official media. "Peasant women today have a big problem," said Ren Qingyun, a Chinese professor of women's studies in Henan. "After the reforms began, a lot of their husbands went out and found work, earned money, and took lovers. These women are brokenhearted when they discover their husbands with other women.

They face great hardship on the farm. Without some sort of moral support, they really can't handle it."

Although their lives on the farm are physically and emotionally taxing, Zhao and other rural women can at least take pride in their new farming skills. Zhao finds satisfaction in the easy, graceful way she swings a hoe, in her deftness at pruning cotton, and in the two kids born to her herd of white goats one summer morning. She tends a brood of thirty chicks. In addition to the staple crops of wheat, corn, and cotton, she grows cash crops of peanuts and vegetables. With the help of villagewide broadcasts by Wu, Zhao and many other Xiaodian women have learned about modern farming technologies, seeds, and pesticides. "How can I afford not to be skilled? I have farmed this land for so long just to feed a few mouths!" Zhao says as she squats in her field of sprouting cotton, inspecting the plants. "We depend on the land to survive."

Even if Ran returned today, Zhao said she would still manage the farm. "He doesn't know how!" she exclaims. "My husband is good to me, but he can't handle anything here. Women these days have more ability than men," she says, standing up and brushing the dirt from her hands.

In the company of other women, Zhao describes her husband as an honest, gentle, and simpleminded man. With an earthy, irreverent affection typical of Chinese peasant women, she calls him a "big, dumb dick" (*da sha diao*).

Zhao's confidence suggests that rural women are gaining self-esteem as they master the once male-dominated occupation of farming and prove their economic worth outside the home. In a few cases, peasant women have risen from threshing grounds to boardrooms, launching highly successful rural enterprises and leading whole villages to prosperity.

Ten miles from Xiaodian, a large, headstrong woman named Liu Zhihua has transformed the village of Jinghua into a rural corporation with yearly profits of over $500,000. Jinghua's 360 villagers now earn double the average per capita income of Chinese peasants. No one had believed Liu could succeed in 1971 when she and a few other women took over the village production committee. At that time, Jinghua's impoverished villagers were almost completely dependent upon resold state grain.

"The first day we organized people for work, peasants came from all around to watch. It was as if we were a local opera troupe," she laughed. "The party branch decided to let us try. Their attitude was 'If the pot is cracked, why not smash it to pieces?' But I had confidence. I knew the men we were replacing were terribly incompetent."

Liu recalls one day asking a group of men to thresh some wheat. This was heavy work. It required pulling a half-foot-thick stone roller over the wheat to remove the husks from the grain. Defying Liu's authority, the men refused. They thought the women would be helpless without them. But Liu organized the women cadres in the village to do the work; they finished by late afternoon. "Those men were put to shame," Liu recalled with a smile of satisfaction. "After that, I asked all the village women to learn such methods of farmwork."

By 1973, thanks to Liu's promotion of fertilizers and other farming techniques, Jinghua was no longer short of grain. Over the next decade, Liu launched a variety of rural factories making products ranging from rope and dried tofu to asbestos shingles. By 1987, Liu's Jinghua Industry Corporation was recognized nationally as a leader in rural enterprise. Her latest goal is to raise the incomes of Jinghua's villagers to equal those of people in middle-income developed nations.

To a degree, Liu has succeeded in changing the status of women in Jinghua. Her corporation is something of a matriarchy, with more than 90 percent of the workers and managers women. So eager are men to move into the wealthy village that a full third of Jinghua husbands have "married in" to their wives' homes. In Xiaodian, in contrast, only the poorest bachelor will stoop to become a *nüxu*, or son-in-law in his wife's household. Still, Liu's female workers are beaten by their husbands, and Liu herself faces sexual discrimination and hostility.

"In more than twenty years as village production team leader, people have never stopped cursing me," Liu said. "The village party branch didn't make me a member until 1983 because all the male cadres were afraid I would fire them! Other people claim that my husband is behind everything I do. They don't want to give me credit."

Despite some striking achievements, the vast majority of rural women—from talented entrepreneurs like Liu to common peasants like Zhao—are still restrained by lingering, ancient prejudices in China's patriarchal society. For many, this means a lack of opportunities to move beyond the dirt and toil of the farm. For some, it means a life of virtual imprisonment and cruel abuse. In Xiaodian today, discrimination against women is widespread, many-faceted, and at times severe.

✻

Chen Wensheng squats on his heels in the doorway of his run-down brick home in Xiaodian, slurping a bowl of noodles. As he eats, the shirtless young laborer idly watches people passing on the dusty dirt road out front. Above Chen in the doorway hangs a ribbon of red, the Chinese color symbolizing happiness, announcing the birth that morning of his first child.

In a dimly lit back room of the filthy, cluttered dwelling, Chen's wife lies on a bed wrapped in a quilt, perspiring in the summer heat. Her hours-old newborn lies swaddled beside her. She smiles weakly as she shows off the baby, greeting a visitor in the thick accent of her native Sichuan Province.

"It's a boy," Chen says, flashing a proud smile.

In his delight over fulfilling his Confucian obligation to father a son, it makes no difference to Chen that he bought his wife as he would a mule or sow. Indeed, Chen is one of several Xiaodian men who have bought brides from Sichuan in recent years amid a resurgence of China's traditional trade in young rural women. The trade was widespread before 1949. It was revived after Beijing began to unleash market economic forces and loosen social controls in the 1980s. Now, China each year reports at least 10,000 cases of rural women being abducted and sold, mainly as brides but also as prostitutes. More than 50,000 abductions of women and children were reported in 1991 and 1992, according to official figures. The actual number of sales is believed to be far higher, especially as cadres and police increasingly assist the tens of thousands of "people mongers" (*ren fan*).

Abductors often lure women from poor mountain villages in Sichuan, Guizhou, and other hinterland provinces with promises of jobs. Most are sold as wives for less than $1,000 to farmers in slightly better-off areas like Henan who cannot afford the exorbitant cost of formal weddings. Thousands of women are sold to Henan men each year, according to Chinese experts in women's studies. The trade is so widespread and accepted in Henan that one party secretary listed the number of women sold into his village to "solve marriage problems" for local men as one of his main achievements.

Villagers in Xiaodian, like many rural Chinese, take a pragmatic view of bride-buying. "Here, the men from rich households who are handsome and have good class status all find local wives," explained Zhao. She lives a ten-minute walk from Chen's house. But "men from poorer families who are short, old, or have bad class backgrounds take Sichuan wives."

Chen is short. He is also the fifth son in a poor family. He admits that he lacked the more than $2,000 required to build a new house and host a respectable wedding in Xiaodian. So in 1991, he paid only $200 to a matchmaker who delivered his twenty-one-year-old bride from Sichuan's Mianyang district. Chen was pleased with the trade. "She's pretty, she can till the land better than a northern man, she's a good housekeeper, and she saved me a lot of money," said Chen. He earns $1 a day doing odd jobs.

At first, Chen and his family kept a close watch on his new bride to make sure she did not run away. Some farmers beat wives who disobey or try to flee. Others threaten to resell them to older bachelors, according to official reports. Once the women bear children, as Chen's wife did, they are often ashamed to go home. Many of them resign themselves to their lot. In the end, Chen's wife stayed. "Not many run off," said Zhao. "The Sichuan women want to come here. They come here because the work is lighter. They are poor. In the mountains they eat corn. They want to come down to the plains where they can eat wheat and rice. It is a good thing," she said.

Zhao's attitude toward the Sichuan brides shows how greatly the mistreatment of women is tolerated by both sexes in China's countryside. Millions of rural women like Zhao are so molded by Confucian customs, and so inured to lives of hardship and humiliation, that they are blind to even the most glaring injustices. Although they complain about their difficulties, Zhao and her neighbors passively accept many traditional beliefs that lie at the heart of sexism in China. In Xiaodian, such old biases have reemerged widely along with the easing of social controls under reform.

Boys, for example, are preferred by couples in Xiaodian and throughout rural China because of the importance in Confucian culture of carrying on the male line. Women are largely held responsible for the sex of their offspring, as many peasants are unaware that sperm determines a baby's gender. According to Chinese superstition, even what a woman eats and does during pregnancy can decide the sex of the child in her womb. The pressure on women to produce sons has grown since China imposed its "one couple, one child" birth control regime in the 1980s, as each additional child brings the risk of greater sanctions by the state.

"If people have boys, they are happier," said Zhao. "If they have no son, they think of all possible ways to have another child, even running off to join the 'guerrillas,'" she said, referring to Chinese couples who take to the road to dodge family planning authorities.

As Zhao speaks, her year-old niece, the second child of her sister-in-law, plays on the floor. Across the room the child's mother, Wang Shijie, makes wheat noodles with a hand-rotated press. The toddler was born secretly and is a "black child," one of an estimated 1 million over-quota children who have not been registered with the government because their parents fear official retaliation.

Many women like Wang are caught in an emotional vise between the conflicting demands of family members and birth control officials. If they resist trying repeatedly for a son, they will face the wrath of their husbands' families. But if they become pregnant without approval, they are likely to be forced to undergo the physical and psychological trauma of sterilization or abortion, sometimes as late as the third trimester. "If I have another child, they will tie my tubes at the township hospital," says Wang. She speaks in a dull tone, without emotion. The procedure is common enough not to cause excitement in Xiaodian.

Women in Xiaodian suffer greatly from the family planning regime and preference for boys, but young girls stand to lose even more. "Here, girl babies are not killed, but some people give them away or abandon them for others to find," Zhao said. Girls in rural villages like Xiaodian are several times more likely than boys to fail to enter school or drop out to work, according to Chinese statistics.

The pervasive custom of girls "marrying out" of their home villages into their husbands' households perpetuates discrimination against women of all ages in Xiaodian. Girls are less valued in their own homes since they will leave upon marrying. Unlike sons, they are not expected to care for their elderly parents. They rarely inherit land or houses and therefore only by marrying can they secure a livelihood and place to live. Yet as outsiders in their husbands' homes, they are vulnerable to mistreatment, especially if they do not bear sons.

Zhao's own efforts to find a suitable match for her eldest son, Fachun, reveals how strong remains the practice of the *popo* (mother-in-law) dominating the *xifu* (daughter-in-law)—the custom that so oppressed Zhao's own mother. "Here it costs about 10,000 yuan [$2,000] to get a *xifu*, and it's not easy to find a good one," Zhao explained. "My son courted five or six girls. But many of them were too fierce and sharp-tongued. I was afraid I couldn't manage them, so I refused to give my approval. In the countryside, parents still have a lot of power over their children's marriages."

Eventually, Fachun was introduced to a girl his mother liked. He married her one early spring day in 1992 at the age of twenty, as Zhao and her husband proudly looked on. "She says what she should and does what she should," said Zhao approvingly as she hurriedly swept out her house on the day before the wedding. "And she's quiet." Although Zhao is not as tyrannical as many Chinese *popo,* she clearly expects her son's wife to heed her.

Even in old age, some women cannot escape the miseries inflicted by he system of marrying out. Guo, the snowy-haired grandmother with bound feet, is often beaten and cursed at by her husband, a factory watchman. Her grown son, who lives at home with his wife, is equally cruel, refusing to give his mother grain to eat unless she cooks and cleans the house. Often, Guo must eat cornmeal given to her by a sympathetic daughter, who is married and living in another village. Guo would like to move in with her daughter, but she is bound by deep-rooted Confucian mores to stay with her abusive husband and son.

"If I moved to my daughter's house, the other elderly people in the home would say, 'How unlucky!' And if I died there, I would bring insults upon my daughter," said Guo. According to custom, Guo's daughter must devote herself to caring for her parents-in-law, and Guo must rely on her own son in old age. "When I'm old and sick, I have no choice but to depend on my son to take care of me," Guo said, tears welling up in her eyes. "In the end, the leaf must fall at the base of the tree."

❋

After hoeing all afternoon in her cotton field, Zhao returns home to make supper. She uses a hand pump in the courtyard to fill a large bucket with water and carries it to a brick hearth that stands in an open shed. She pours the water into a large iron pot sitting on the hearth. Fachun sits on a wooden stool, stoking the fire with wheat stalks and kindling.

Back in the house, Zhao beats a spongelike dough of wheat flour and water called *mian jin* (wheat cloth). Her two-room brick-and-tile dwelling is an eclectic jumble of new and old. Guardian spirits glare fiercely from the double doors at the courtyard gate. Chinese New Year couplets at the entryway celebrate the coming of peach blossoms and fragrant grass. In the larger room, old newspapers and Henan opera posters cover the wall. A small white bust of Mao sits on a wooden table. An electric ceiling fan whirs overhead, while a soap opera plays on a new television set, a wedding gift for Fachun and his bride.

When the dough is ready, Zhao walks outside and plunges it into a peppery stew of eggs, vinegar, fungus, and other ingredients now boiling on the hearth. "You take a bowl, I take a bowl, and we all squat on our heels and talk together. This is how we eat here," Zhao tells a visitor, a wide smile crinkling the corners of her large bright eyes.

For a woman who has shouldered as much as she has in life, Zhao seems fairly content. She often laughs and jokes, poking fun at herself and others. "We peasant women are comfortable. We sit here and do some cooking, watch the children. We are happy," Zhao says in a tranquil moment after dinner. Things are easier for Zhao now that her boys are in school and old enough to help a little on the farm. Her husband is kind compared with other men. But there are other reasons for her sense of satisfaction. Zhao contrasts her life, no matter how harsh at times, to that of her mother and other women of the older generation. "My mother suffered much more bitterness. I am better off than my mother," Zhao says.

Zhao's own life hints that the worst abuses against rural women will be alleviated only by slow, generational changes in attitude. For example, Zhao out of necessity raised her three sons to cook and sew as well as to till the fields. Unlike many men of his father's generation, Fachun helped mind his younger brothers and now delights in caring for his one-year-old cousin. Fachun, Fatai, Fayang, and many rural boys now being reared by their mothers alone are less likely to become aloof, traditional fathers.

As for Zhao herself, her low expectations, limited education, and traditional peasant values keep her from moving beyond the boundaries of home and farm. Instead, she is resigned to her demanding life as a full-time farmer and mother.

"Here on the farm, you work for a year's worth of grain. Sometimes it is busy. Sometimes there is not much work to do. You can manage to farm with children; you just put them on the ground. How could a woman with children work in a factory? If she put her child on the factory floor, it would be crushed! And how could she nurse her baby?

"I believe a woman's most important task is to raise her children and take care of her husband," Zhao says. "Let the men go out and earn money."

As Zhao looks back on her life, she derives a sense of well-being from the knowledge that she has fulfilled her traditional womanly obligations. As for the future, she looks forward to Ran's retirement in a few years and return home from the mine. But most of all, she said with a smile, "I want to find brides for my sons and hug my grandchildren."

While impeding peasant women like Zhao Xinlan, economic reform has also set back many urban workers. More than any other sector of the workforce, the 110 million laborers at mammoth state factories face increasing job insecurity because of greater competition under reform. Many bold workers, primarily at bankrupt Stalinist enterprises, are organizing to protect their rights. Today, Chinese laborers are staging more strikes and other job-related protests than ever before under Communist rule.

Undaunted by past imprisonment and torture, activist Han Dongfang struggles to organize an independent labor movement. The former state railway worker races against time; he fears that without free unions, the scattered brushfires of worker unrest will explode in nationwide turmoil.

Han Dongfang and his wife, Chen Jingyun

Photo by Ann Scott Tyson

SEVEN

"Walking on Fire":
The Railway Worker

HAN DONGFANG CAN'T RECALL whether it was on the rail line that inches across the crackling Gobi Desert or on the tracks snaking through the misty bamboo forests of Sichuan, but somewhere on China's vast railways he found the inspiration to become one of the country's most forceful labor activists since the Communist Party took power. Han rode the state railroad for five years with a team of workers who maintained refrigeration freight cars. Often railway bosses ordered the team to labor amid a gas of ammonia that leaked from the ramshackle freight. Some workers choked and had to be carried by their workmates away from the searing gas. All of them coughed and their eyes streamed with tears. When Han and his crew complained, the bosses scoffed at them and insisted that the chemical was harmless.

It was not just the sight of his fellow railwaymen hacking and weeping that moved Han to political action; it was the irony of a socialist state blinding and exploiting the laborers it claimed to champion. Han's comrades were unaware of the harm from the invisible gas even as they toiled behind a veil of tears.

Enraged by the official abuse of workers, Han helped lead China's first unofficial trade union during the 1989 democracy movement in Tiananmen Square. After the army massacred hundreds of protesters on June 4, Han was jailed and tortured. During twenty-two months in prison he nearly died as tuberculosis induced by his jailers gutted his right lung. Thanks in part to international pressure, Han was allowed in 1993 to go to the United States for medical treatment. While overseas Han solidified the support of foreign leaders and unionists, winning the backing of President Clinton and befriending Lane Kirkland of the AFL-CIO.

Since then, Han has fought to return to China and renew his struggle for workers' rights. He could not be banging on China's gate at a more politically charged time. Discontent among the 110 million workers at state enterprises is at an all-time high as the Communist Party rushes China toward a market economy. The state workers are the biggest losers from economic reform. Tens of millions of them face layoffs and cuts in bonuses and wages. When the workers look ahead, they see only the prospect of more harm to their livelihood. Two-thirds of the firms that employ them lose money. Also, double-digit inflation is rapidly eroding their incomes. The last time inflation suddenly surged, in 1988, Chinese rushed to the stores in a frenzy of panic buying. The economic instability helped provoke the nationwide protests of 1989.

The party leadership has forced the suffering on the state workers. It is thrusting them from a repressive socialist system into the raw exploitation of a crude market economy—from the grip of Marxist dictators into the grasp of primitive capitalists. While advancing economic reforms, the party has withdrawn the "iron rice bowl" guarantee of a job and the paltry benefits that it had offered workers for decades. It has also condoned the rise of the factory boss. In an effort to streamline industry, Beijing has steadily granted managers greater control over hiring, firing, wages, and benefits, allowing them to extract weighty concessions from workers. In many factories, workers stand alone against tight-fisted, antagonistic managers.

As the party has encouraged the profit motive among managers, it has failed to grant laborers adequate institutional protections in law, social security, and other areas. It bars workers from forming independent labor unions. It denies them the right to strike, engage in collective bargaining, and exercise other universally recognized rights. Such freedoms for workers would threaten party control.

Han believes that as millions of Chinese see their slim assets erode they will demand a political voice and the right to unionize freely. Barred from redressing their grievances within factories, workers will probably try to do so in the streets, as they did in 1989. Their unrest will demonstrate to the Communist regime that strife is inevitable as long as it promotes economic prosperity but denies political pluralism. Han aims to meet the millions of state workers at the agonizing crossroads between socialism and capitalism. He will urge them to organize, demand their rights, and bring democratic change.

China's leaders are trying to bar Han from his native country because he embodies their worst nightmare. Few other Chinese combine his grit, eloquence, foreign support, and impeccable working-class origins. Wei Jingsheng and other dissidents similar to Han are either behind bars or severely restrained by the police. Even the steeliest survivors among China's old guard have found their match in Han. Although repeatedly threatened with execution in prison, Han refused to admit to any crime. He disarmed one torturer with a wry smile. And after nearly two years, a prison system that treats political prisoners as harshly as any other in the world failed to break Han even as he lay immobilized with tuberculosis.

Han criticizes China's leaders as articulately as many students and intellectuals. But he goes a big step further than the scholarly elite. Students and intellectuals represent just a thin, usually aloof social strata. Han speaks for the millions of workers at the bedrock of Communist power. He openly refutes the party's claim to rule in the name of the working class. Han is an incurable carrier of the "Polish disease," the term Beijing applies to independent labor solidarity. And he is the only free, internationally known dissident from mainland China holding the pure and powerful title of "worker."

Han has been dubbed "China's Lech Walesa." But the label understates the task before him. Unlike Walesa, Han is trying to rally workers whose tradition of labor activism is largely limited to the organizing by the Communist Party this century. The Confucian emphasis on harmony and submission to authority discourages Chinese workers from dissent. Unlike Walesa, Han cannot count on the support of the church and other social groups. He must organize more workers across a far larger country than Walesa did. He must inspire workers divided by a babble of dialects, whereas Walesa and Poland's workers are united by a single tongue. He is defying a more brutal and intrusive regime than Walesa did. And unlike Walesa, Han was jailed for an extended period and tortured.

Despite the obstacles to a free labor movement, Han is determined, as he says, to "walk this road to the end." He returned to mainland China on August 13, 1993. Within hours police arrested him, beat him, and accused him of subversion. When Han refused to walk back over the border, the police hurled him over a barrier and out of China. Other dissidents have returned to China and been deported. But among this handful of die-hard liberals, Han is by far the most dogged.

Since his expulsion, Han has remained on China's doorstep in Hong Kong speaking out about cases of worker abuse and publicizing foreign labor laws to encourage Chinese to organize independent unions. He could start by telling workers about his own life. Many Chinese laborers could understand the mistreatment and disillusionment Han endured on his path from dirt-scrabble peasant to Communist adherent and labor camp guard to railwayman and worker activist. They know such suffering firsthand. By sharing how he grew aware of injustice and resolved to combat it, Han could bring to workers the dawn of understanding vital for a free labor movement.

Han's courage and intolerance for injustice are largely a legacy of his late mother, Zhang Sandou. (Zhang followed Chinese tradition and retained her maiden name after marriage.) Han's mother nurtured his outlook and conviction; she did the hard labor of a man and the parenting of both a mother and father, he said. She was proud, giving, and fiercely hostile toward wrongdoing. Not long before she died in 1988, her good qualities clashed with her blind faith in the party. Han believes she died prematurely because of disillusionment over the abuses of Communist officials. Through activism, Han said he is avenging her death.

Like her son, Zhang was motivated by the death of a parent. The only time Han ever saw his mother weep was when she described how in 1932, when she was eight, her father patted her on the head, told her to obey her mother, and walked out of Nanweiquan village in Shanxi Province on a distant errand. Some villagers said invading Japanese troops pressed him into a labor gang. Some of them said he died in Hebei Province; others said he perished in Manchuria. Zhang never saw him again.

With her father gone, Zhang did the farmwork for her poor family. She had no choice. Her two older sisters had bound feet. They tottered about on their pinched extremities, unable to do heavy work. Zhang's parents had bound her feet too, but she had protested and removed the cloth after only a few days. She paid a price in hard labor for her refusal to bow to tradition. She had to hoe the fields, fell trees, chop wood, fetch water—do all the heavy tasks. She had always been a tomboy; now she was head of the family.

When she was ten, Zhang established impeccable political credentials as a revolutionary by joining a women's armed regiment mustered by the party branch in the county. Zhang and other local militia were armed only with hoes, sickles, and other farm tools. But they provided regular troops with intelligence, shelter, food, water, fuel, and other material support. After six years with the local regiment, Zhang quit to care full-time for her mother and tend the family's plot of land.

The Communists considered Zhang's poor native region an ideal "base area," or fertile ground for mobilizing downtrodden peasants. In 1938, the 129th Division of the Eighth Route Army, a forerunner of the People's Liberation Army, set up its headquarters not far from Zhang's village. Deng Xiaoping, China's paramount leader, served with the division. Zhang's two older sisters went to work at the headquarters, earning a small but steady ration of millet for the family. After the revolution they parlayed their positions into comfortable jobs as cadres with the Agriculture Ministry in Beijing. Forever the family workhorse, Zhang went with them to the capital as their maid.

Zhang gave birth to Han on August 19, 1963, in Beijing. Her husband, a traditional farmer, ordered her to return his only son to the village to till millet and wheat like his ancestors. Zhang refused, insisting that Han be educated in the capital and forever leave the dust and lassitude of the countryside behind. When her husband objected, she sealed her decision with a divorce. But before Han could enter school, Mao Zedong impelled millions of Chinese youth to the disastrous ultraradicalism of the Cultural Revolution. Zhang's relatives were branded as "capitalist roaders" and exiled to the countryside.

Zhang was forced to return with Han to Nanweiquan. But she refused to shift her official residence registration from Beijing back to the native village. She did not want to deny Han the chance to return to the capital for an education. Without a residence registration, however, Zhang was denied grain in Nanweiquan. Even when she recounted her revolutionary credentials, village cadres turned a deaf ear. They also barred her from the politically taboo endeavor of growing grain herself. Although friends in the village gave her grain, she and Han were always dogged by hunger.

After the harvests, Zhang often led her son out of their thatched dwelling at dusk and slipped into the fields to glean ears of corn and grains of wheat. The young boy silently helped his mother stuff the wheat in pockets and small bags. They braided the ears of corn, slung them over their shoulders, and hid the chains under their clothing. Local cadres banned scavenging for the otherwise wasted grain, calling it theft from the commune. As Han and his mother stole their way back home in the darkness, they had to pass several checkpoints where the People's Militia frisked passersby. The militia often confiscated the gleaning. When she made flour, Zhang mixed any grain she spirited by the checkpoints with husks of millet in order to lengthen the precious nourishment. "It was wonderful then just to eat one steamed corn flour bun," Han said.

Soon after Han entered the village grade school, he became a favorite target for bullying. Word had reached the villagers that Han's cadre relatives were in political disgrace. Moreover, without a grain ration, Han and his mother had fallen among the hungriest and poorest residents of the village. Han was abused in keeping with the old saying "Rage at the wealthy, ridicule the poor." At school the children often grabbed whatever Han held in his hand. Shy and introverted, he never fought back. One day after the harvest, a dozen children hustled him into an empty field, slung around his neck vines bound to a heavy stone, and paraded him around. Mimicking their parents and other villagers who were still enthralled by Maoist fanaticism, they called Han a "bad element" and "capitalist roader."

By 1970, Zhang was severely weakened with hunger. She foresaw only famine for her in the village, so she left her five-year-old daughter and took Han back to Beijing. After several months searching for work, she won the sympathy of a cadre who helped her land a job with a team of laborers repairing buildings and homes. She labored hard, mixing concrete and hauling bricks. She earned only 30 yuan a month, but she had a steady income and a place to live. She brought her daughter back from the village.

Han was glad to have sufficient food but was still miserable in Beijing. His classmates made him a prime source of amusement, tormenting him for his rough Shanxi tongue. Even his teachers mocked him. When Han came home with poor grades, Zhang beat him. The cold treatment gelled Han's introverted, quiet nature. As a migrant squeezed by the long-standing hostility between peasants and city-dwellers, he was a misfit in both village and city. His fellow villagers saw him as a politically suspect urbanite; the people of Beijing mocked him as a bumpkin. He withdrew into his own thoughts and in self-defense grew indifferent about how his peers and teachers viewed him. At the same time, he developed a fiercely independent mind. After mastering the Beijing dialect, he lashed back at some teachers by pointing out their mistakes in class. Unlike most Chinese parents, Han's mother did not discourage defiance in her son. Although she was strict about study, she allowed him to talk back when he felt he was unjustly criticized.

One spring day when he was thirteen, the free-thinking youth was drawn to a sudden outpouring of dissent in Tiananmen Square. In his first overtly political act, Han rushed to the giant plaza on April 4, 1976, as thousands of common Chinese gathered there to denounce the brutal excesses of the Cultural Revolution. The demonstration preceded the traditional Qingming holiday to honor the dead. The protesters flooded into the square on the pretext of mourning the death in January of Premier Zhou Enlai. They posted poems expressing grief over Zhou and sharply attacking Mao and other ultraleftist leaders behind the Cultural Revolution. Many protesters shouted out the poems to the crowd and copied down the words to share with family and friends. The directors of several work units in

Beijing defied a party directive and led their workers to the square behind a vanguard of wreaths and bright factory banners. The unruly surge in popular unrest was unprecedented in Communist China. Its aims paralleled those of Han. Like his mother, Han venerated the party but could not forget his suffering during the "ten years of turmoil."

Although local officials told Han not to go to the square, he pushed his way through the throng to the Monument to the People's Heroes where he copied down as many poems as he could. The next night police cleared the square with an onslaught of flailing truncheons. Han's teacher asked Han and his classmates to turn in any poems they had copied, but for several years Han kept the tattered, inspiring sheaf of papers.

Han took the national exams for university entrance but, as he expected, fell far below the standard for admission. After graduating from high school in September 1980, he could only find a job as a guard in a new unit of the People's Armed Police, the national paramilitary security force. The future political prisoner was assigned to watch the wall at the Tuanhe reform-through-labor farm in Daxing County south of Beijing.

Still believing in Communist ideals, Han applied for membership in the party. But while working as a frontline agent for the party, he grew increasingly angry as he saw evidence of its corrupt and brutal ways. One warm autumn evening just before the harvest, Han and his platoon leader were walking from their sentry post after duty dressed in T-shirts with their uniforms slung over their arms. Six inmates assigned to guard the cornfields suddenly rushed from among the tall stalks and fell upon them with iron bars and clubs. The inmates had mistaken Han and his superior for local thieves. The platoon leader held them off with a pistol as Han disarmed them. Then they walked the prisoners back to headquarters and recounted the episode to the commanding officer and his staff. As Han was leaving, the officers began to punch and kick the inmates. The prisoners knelt and begged to be spared, but the officers redoubled the beating. Han walked back to the commanding officer.

"They mistook us for thieves and surrendered right away; it's not necessary to beat them," he said.

"This is the only way to treat such people," the officer replied.

As a squad leader responsible for a dozen guards, Han saw every facet of the systematic way in which camp officers abused common Chinese on both sides of the labor camp fence. Camp officers led a comparatively silken life, but Han and other guards were given only 60 cents each day for living expenses. Their daily diet was not much better than that of the inmates: two meals of *wotou* (steamed corn flour buns). They were rarely given meat.

One day Han could no longer contain his rage. He was especially vexed that he and his men lacked even a desk and had to read and write on their cots. He roused a few of his men and led them to the quarters for five officers who had seven desks. Han and his men removed a desk despite the shouting of an officer who accused Han of disobedience.

Back in the squad's tent, Han opened the drawers of the desk and found a cornucopia of choice victuals: green vegetables, steamed wheat flour buns, chicken, sausages, and wine. He grabbed two fistfuls of the food and stormed back to the officers' quarters, his men trailing behind him. "Look at what you eat and compare it to what we eat!" Han shouted at the company commander. "I'm sure you didn't buy this food with your own salary!"

Before long, Han again showed his defiance when a political commissar of the regiment visited the unit as part of a campaign to wipe out "unhealthy tendencies" and the abuse of rank. In preparation for the visit, Han wrote a long account detailing how the company commander stole the food and pay of the guards and frequently beat them. A platoon leader, Han's immediate superior, ordered Han not to present it to the meeting. But Han refused to comply. As he quietly read his statement before the large gathering of guards and officers, he noticed the faces of his superiors turn a soft shade of gray.

Two days later the platoon leader was summoned to the company headquarters. He returned and said the vice commander had torn up Han's party application in front of him. "'You go back and tell Han Dongfang that as long as I'm here, he can forget about joining the party,'" the platoon leader quoted the vice commander as saying.

Han laughed. "I've never done anything just to join the party; I've done it because I should," he told the platoon leader. But Han's vain effort to hold the party to its own lofty standards ultimately led him to doubt the organization. Later, the company commander denied him a promotion and, as part of a routine demobilization in September 1983, discharged him.

Back in Beijing, Han withdrew from people into books. He befriended the librarian at the Beijing Teachers College and took a temporary job as an assistant librarian. Amid the stacks of books, Han voraciously read whatever he chose. He was the happiest he had been in many years. He was especially taken by the spare, forceful style of Hemingway. And he relished the philosophical writings of Zhu Guangqian, a professor at Beijing University. At the library he plowed through other books on philosophy. But at home, behind a small redoubt of books, Han faced the hostility of his elitist relatives in the party establishment who scoffed at a common worker who read. "Why are you reading books about society and politics?" asked one of his aunts one day. "You're only a worker. Just go to work every day and do your work well; don't be concerned about these ideas."

Han shrugged off his aunt's remarks. Still, after six months at the library, he had to give up his hope of becoming a librarian. He realized that with a modest salary and no guarantee of a permanent position, he could not fulfill his duty to support his mother and sister. So he accepted a job with the national railway that offered much higher pay, the socialist guarantee of lifetime work, and full medical benefits.

In March 1984, Han entered the grime and clamor at the Fengtai railway yard in Beijing. He was assigned to a mobile team of workers in the locomotive maintenance section. He and his workmates labored in monthlong shifts, crisscrossing China and tending around the clock a group of ten diesel refrigeration cars that carried meat and produce. Although Han often had to work late at night amid the burning gases and jarring noise, he had plenty of time to read when work was slow.

As Han passed through China's major cities, he heard of countless protests by railway workers. They staged work slowdowns, braking the trains to a plodding-oxen pace. Or they found excuses like the failure of a lone railway signal to halt all the trains on the line for hours. The members of Han's crew bristled with griev-ances that the railway managers refused to consider. Corruption was widespread. The only pay raises went to workers with *guanxi* (connections), regardless of their skill or performance. While on the job, Han and his crewmates each received a daily subsidy of about $1, far too little to improve their spartan life or help build savings. Their diet was just a small helping of vegetables and either rice or noodles with a thimbleful of soy sauce. They envied workers from the railway branch at the booming southern city of Guangzhou who enjoyed a far higher subsidy and a rich, varied diet. "The food Guangzhou workers threw away was better than what we could afford to buy!" Han said.

Angered by the poor conditions, Han approached his supervisor in Beijing on behalf of his crew. He appealed for better benefits, such as compensation for the earsplitting din on the train and other health hazards. But in an ironic statement in socialist management, the supervisor brushed Han aside by saying it was not the place of workers to ask for compensation. Such benefits were only handed down by the "upper levels." The party-run All China Federation of Trade Unions (ACFTU) and the perfunctory workers' congresses also proved indifferent to Han and his crew.

Han found greater cause for bitterness and defiance right at his doorstep. In March 1984, the Agriculture Ministry took over the apartment house where Han's family lived with plans to turn it into an office building. The ministry evicted Han and his family in May and moved them into a dark, dilapidated warehouse. A tall building next door blocked all sunlight. The floor of the warehouse was three feet below ground, so when it rained, up to a foot of water flooded the room. That winter, even with a coal stove burning around the clock, Han could not raise the temperature of the dank one-room cellar above thirty-eight degrees. The ministry promised Han and his family that when it had completely renovated a wing of their former apartment building, they could move back into their old lodgings until they found permanent housing.

As the chill north winds swept into Beijing in late September 1985, Han learned that the ministry had built a large apartment house elsewhere in Beijing to per-manently house other families evicted from their original building. The ministry had apparently favored the other families because they were members of the cod-dled bureaucratic elite. The ministry had not offered Han and his working-class family an apartment. Worse, it reneged on its promise and barred them from their former dwelling. Han and his family finally had to force their way back into their old lodgings in the renovated but unoccupied building.

After repeated attempts to bully Han and his family from their apartment, the ministry sued them in the nearby district court in December 1986. The judge asked Zhang why she had forcibly occupied a public building and lectured her on the great harm to society from selfishness. He denied Han and his mother an opportunity to present their case. Then on April 27, 1987, the judge ordered that Han and his family be evicted although they had nowhere else to live.

Han and Zhang appealed the decision and won. The Beijing Intermediate Court decided on June 10, 1987, that the warehouse cellar was unfit for human habitation. It ordered the ministry to find a new home for Han and his family by September 30.

Zhang was elated. After so much hardship, the court's decision offered sweet vindication for her faith in the party. A few days later, the intermediate court judge summoned her and told her to sign the court decision. Zhang was illiterate, so she asked that the document be read to her. The judge refused, saying the statement was identical to what he had read earlier at court. When Zhang declined to sign, court officials grabbed her hand and forced her to do so. Later, when her daughter read the statement at home, Zhang learned the new lodgings would be far smaller than what her family needed and what the judge had described in court.

The eviction and the ensuing official abuse and deception cast Zhang into total disillusionment. Since ranging the dry hills of Shanxi with the People's Militia in her youth, Zhang had believed in the propaganda depicting the party as the world's shining champion of justice. She had always clung to what Han calls the "blueprint": The party will reward Chinese for their complete submission with the steadfast promotion of economic progress and social justice. "When I was young my mother would often say, 'Only with the Communist Party could there be a new China,'" Han said. "The party painted a beautiful blueprint for her, but she discovered before her death that it had only led her to suffering."

Zhang had long been weakened by high blood pressure. She grew sicker as she fought the Agriculture Ministry for her home. She died of stomach cancer less than a year after the judge forced her signature. "My mother had a blind faith in the party. She died because the party betrayed her," Han said.

Han was devastated by his mother's death. "I badly miss my mother. Sometimes when I feel weak, I think of her. I have an image of her greeting me with open arms that will always stay in my mind," he said. Zhang's death sharpened his anger and disillusionment over official injustice. From childhood to his posting as a labor camp guard, Han had also clung to the party's blueprint. "I was a complete believer in the religion of communism."

But Han's faith turned to slow-burning fury after the death of his mother. At the same time, he seized on Western ideas about democracy and individualism that he had pondered since taking the job at the library. The ideas helped him to recognize how absolute power had corrupted the party. Emboldened by Western political theory and embittered by official abuse of his family and workmates, Han threw himself into the prodemocracy protests in the spring of 1989. "To a great extent, I went to the square in 1989 out of hatred for the party's blueprint," Han said. He first spoke out in a speech near the Monument to the People's Heroes in the square on April 17. He voiced his rage over the wrongdoing by the court. He deplored how China lacks an effective legal system and criticized the courts for trampling the rights of common individuals and following the arbitrary whims of powerful officials.

"Think of your own lives," Han said. "Haven't the leaders of your work unit encroached on your rights? Of course they have. I know each of you has suffered these abuses countless times!" he said.

"*Hao! Hao!* [Good!]," his listeners clapped and yelled. Han showed his identification card to prove he was taking full responsibility for his words. His message contained nothing new for many of his listeners. They clapped simply because Han had the courage to speak out. "All I did was to say what listeners felt in their hearts. They wanted to say these things, but they didn't dare."

For more than a week, Han spoke several times in and around the square to students, professionals, workers, and even police. When not addressing a crowd, he sought to advise student activists and hunger strikers. Over several weeks he urged students to rent trucks, acquire loudspeakers and megaphones, and drive to the neighborhoods and factories in Beijing. He told them that they would never bring lasting change unless they broadened the base of the demonstrations by rousing workers. But the students disregarded Han, showing the deeply rooted bias against workers in Chinese society.

During the 1989 Beijing Spring, student leaders often excluded Han and other labor leaders from meetings and rallies or assigned them to a subordinate role. For weeks they barred Han, other activists, and common Chinese from the monument by organizing students to stand arm in arm in concentric rings around the site. While talking of democratic reform, the student leaders perpetuated the ancient hostility of the scholar-official toward members of the working class.

Like many Chinese, students believed that workers like Han could not offer any useful ideas. They viewed workers with a mixture of distrust and fear. They saw labor as a wild force bent on violent revolution and sure to provoke the party into a brutal backlash. Finally, student leaders spurned workers because as they defied the world's largest Communist Party, they wanted the limelight and power all to themselves, Han said.

If Han had set out in 1989 to humiliate himself rather than promote democracy and workers' rights, he would have succeeded remarkably. He was repeatedly rebuffed and belittled by students and intellectuals. Still, he continued to make impromptu speeches and backed up his words by showing his identity card.

In late April, as the waves of student marchers began to sweep up the support of common Chinese, Han recognized both the power and danger of the movement. He wanted to continue his activism but knew he was likely to be arrested. So like a good filial son, he went home to seek the blessing of his father.

Han's father, a contented farmer, shouldered his hoe and walked out of his millet field to greet his son. The villagers peppered Han with questions about the riots in Beijing described in the official press. Han assured them there were no riots, just peaceful student demonstrations.

"If I took part in what was going on in Beijing, what would you think?" Han asked his father.

"Don't do it; it's too dangerous!" his father replied. "Our family only has you, our one son, and if something happens to you, our family would be finished." Both Han's father and grandfather were also only sons.

"All right," Han replied. But as he climbed aboard the bus for Beijing after his weeklong visit, Han knew the Confucian ideal of perpetuating the family line would not stop him from speaking out.

Back in the capital, Han resumed his speeches in the square. Again he urged student leaders to go to the neighborhoods and factories in Beijing to organize working-class Chinese. Han also offered more down-to-earth advice. As a hunger strike begun by thousands of students on May 13 dragged on, Tiananmen Square became a fetid squatters' camp reeking with garbage, sodden blankets, and human waste. Under a baking sun, weak, tired, and thirsty students lay on the concrete shoulder to shoulder. Doctors feared an outbreak of disease. The government repeatedly decried the filth and chaos in the square. Han warned that it could use the threat of widespread illness as an excuse to move in and resume control. He vainly advised students to clear wide passages in the crowds for ambulances and refuse trucks.

Han spent much of the hunger strike in the van that strike leaders used as their headquarters. After three days without food, dozens of students began to faint. Medics and ambulances rushed to the square. The plaza seethed with sympathetic citizens: Workers beating cymbals, gongs, and drums roared around the plaza and along adjacent avenues in open trucks; gray-haired grandmothers hustled bread and soda to the striking students and implored them to eat; bureaucrats quit their desks and sternly marched beneath banners declaring their ministry affiliation.

As rumors of government reprisals rose, Han grew more desperate to see the students act on his suggestions. He spent hours waiting in the van in the afternoon of May 18 and the early morning of May 19, assured he would soon be able to speak to a strike leader. Finally, he left in exasperation but later in the day went to the monument in search of the main student leaders. He muscled his way through the many human barriers student leaders had laid around the monument and at last gained an audience. "You have to state your case in factories and Beijing neighborhoods far beyond the square. Most Beijing residents are workers. They should be the core of your movement, and you should rally them behind you," Han told the leaders.

After Han spoke, an energetic, chain-smoking man also rose. He wore a visor with the words "Beijing University Constitutional Law PhD" displayed above the brim. He echoed Han's assertion that the support of workers was vital for the student movement to grow and triumph. The young scholar was Li Jinjin, the legal adviser for the recently established Beijing Workers Autonomous Federation (BWAF). Standing together, the two like-minded activists appeared to be one another's alter ego: Han tall, dignified, and reticent; Li short, bubbly, and gregarious. They hit it off immediately.

Both Han and Li failed to move the students. Their message was lost as rivalries among student leaders intensified, clouding the limited focus the student movement had at its inception. Students were increasingly reacting to events rather than shaping them.

The declaration of martial law on May 20 jolted students, workers, and activists with a sudden sense of urgency. After several days of squabbling and division, demonstrators in the square seemed finally to agree on one thing: The army would soon try to put them to rout. Amid the sense of mounting crisis, the protesters set aside their differences and sought strength in unity. Han visited the headquarters of the BWAF to the northwest of Tiananmen Square. He spoke with Li for two hours and found Li's views and concerns nearly identical to his own. Li assured him that the federation complied with the constitution and aimed to uphold workers' rights without breaking the law. The two set to work immediately drafting an urgent appeal for an alliance between students and workers. Han was no longer a lone protester. He began identifying himself with the fledgling labor organization.

Li and Han held a press conference on May 20 in the van that served as the headquarters of the hunger strikers. Appearing with them in a rare gesture of cooperation were two student leaders. Li read over loudspeakers the "Joint Declaration of All Workers and Students in the Capital," one of the most militant written statements of the spring. The activists urged students and workers to unite and solidify the popular uprising. They also demanded that the standing committee of the National People's Congress, China's rubber-stamp parliament, recall Premier Li Peng, President Yang Shangkun, and paramount leader Deng Xiaoping. Finally, they called for a special court to try the leaders and urged military officers to turn their guns against party headquarters.

The declaration was one of the few tokens of unity between students and workers. The young intellectual elite extolled popular democracy but left the workers' federation largely to fend for itself. The snub helped guarantee that the federation left little more than a symbolic imprint on society.

As the first public unofficial union in Communist China, the BWAF was a landmark. But as an organization, it was little more than a shell. No worker, including Han, knew firsthand how to lead a union. Even the concept of a union was alien to much of China's poorly educated, easily intimidated workforce. The federation had scores of "members" but no organization on factory floors. Without a systematic way to mobilize members and recruit new ones at the grass roots, it lacked a solid base of support. Although its ranks included workers from large institutions like the Capital Iron and Steel Company and the Beijing Bureau of Railways, it could claim to represent only small pockets of Beijing workers. It made no formal contacts with workers outside Beijing. It had scant funds and few clear-cut aims. The appointment and responsibilities of its leaders were vague. Indeed, the only true strength of the federation was the powerful mix of courage and resentment among its membership.

Although other prodemocracy groups had frequently rebuffed them, the workers under martial law redoubled their efforts to ally with other protesters. On May 24 the federation began to send representatives regularly to meetings of the Capital Joint Liaison Group, a forum in which representatives of students, citizens, workers, and intellectuals tried to coordinate strategies for protest. On the urging of Li, Han addressed the group's May 26 meeting. Noting that the government would likely soon suppress the prodemocracy protests, he called on the group to bind together students, workers, and other parts of society in a powerful organizational model for future liberal movements. He said that peasants, workers, and other low-level tiers of society would probably suffer most as income disparities widened in the coming years. Consequently, peasants and workers would benefit most from effective organization. They would be especially eager to see the birth of an open and just government, he said.

"If we could create a foundation for a large workers' organization and spread the word about it, we could leave a deep impression on the Chinese people," Han told the group. He urged the students and other activists to subordinate their private interests to the collective need of founding a broad-based workers' organization. The twenty people at the meeting approved a motion to act on Han's advice. Still, Han might as well have addressed an empty room. "An hour after I spoke, it seemed that no one remembered a word of my comments." Han decided that his first meeting with the group would be his last.

The following day some federation members visited ACFTU, the party-run trade union, without seeking formal approval from the federation leadership. They hoped to engineer a measure of cooperation with the official body. They had reason for optimism. Zhu Houze, a moderate reformer and acting head of ACFTU, had donated about $25,000 on May 18 for the medical care of the hunger strikers. Nevertheless, union officials refused to meet with the workers. Han condemned attempts to reach out to the official union, saying the federation should be completely independent of the government.

Rebuffed by students, the joint liaison group, and ACFTU, federation leaders on the afternoon of May 28 took their organizing to the workers. They drove to the gates of several factories in the Dongcheng district of Beijing. Workers flowed from the factories and applauded the activists' declaration of the need to build a broad-based political movement.

That evening the federation leaders called a full meeting of the organization and read its constitution drawn up by Han, Li, and other leading figures in the federation. Several dozen workers clumped around the jerry-built headquarters at the Western Reviewing Stand on the edge of the square as Li Jinjin read the constitution. The federation will be totally independent and function democratically, Li said. It will serve the role of "monitoring" the Communist Party. And it will observe the bounds of China's laws as it seeks to defend all the rights of workers. The federation approved the document. Although bold in principle, the constitution skirted the issue of workers' rights. Both Han and Li shied from putting on paper labor tactics like strikes, collective bargaining, and anything else that smacked of illegality. Their chief aims were to win legal registration for the federation and show common workers that they could independently organize.

The federation made Han a standing committee member and its spokesman to the foreign media. He was given no other title. Inaccurate foreign reports saying that he was given a title like "convenor" or was made the first among equals on the standing committee worsened schisms within the federation, Han said. Members envious of Han's charisma and eloquence claimed that he was trying to promote himself through the media. They urged the standing committee to reassign him to the tasks of either writing federation statements or thwarting efforts by the army to enforce martial law. The standing committee rejected the suggestions.

The next day the government made its first direct move against the federation. A plainclothes officer from the Public Security Bureau appeared at the headquarters and told members their encampment at the Western Reviewing Stand was illegal. A few hours later the police seized three leaders of the federation. The unlawful arrests offered Han an ideal opportunity to show his potent mix of charisma and discretion. He rounded up nine federation members on May 30 and marched on the Public Security Bureau. Avoiding a direct confrontation, Han and his comrades unfurled a banner protesting the seizures some twenty yards from the door of the Beijing police headquarters on Qianmen Street. A policeman approached, asked what they wanted, and led Han and two other members through the back door of the police station to a reception room.

Han repeatedly asked the officer three questions: Were the three men seized, were the arrests legally carried out, and what were the legal grounds for their detention? Each time police replied that the workers were defying martial law. After a twenty-minute standoff, an officer rushed into the room. "These people's supporters are attacking the police station!" he said.

Some 500 students and workers had rushed from the square and massed at the gate of the police station. One of the protesters identified a police jeep driving through the rear gate as the one used in the seizure of a federation leader. Dozens of students and members of the Citizens and Workers Dare-to-Die Corps fell on the jeep, banging its doors and smashing its windows. Police barking through bullhorns threatened the crowd and it fell back. Han left the building to restore order. "The people seized are not students. They are leaders of the Beijing Workers Autonomous Federation," Han told the crowd in an even tone. "This is a problem workers can handle themselves, so please disperse."

The crowd slowly began to break up. Although Han had calmed the protesters, the police refused to resume their stalemated dialogue. Han took up the megaphone again and announced that the workers would stage a sit-in in front of the Ministry of Public Security until the three federation leaders were set free. Within hours, police released the activists.

In an effort to gain official recognition and forestall more arrests, the federation on June 2 resolved to go to the Beijing municipal offices on the coming Monday, June 5, and press for legalized status. They also decided to quit the square on the fifth but leave only a broadcasting station intact and to set up a small permanent office in a storefront.

On June 3, in the lull before the storm of army killing, Han was vindicated in his belief that students and workers must unite in a strong alliance. As he lay resting in his tent on the square, three student leaders visited the workers' encampment and asked him to mobilize the federation in a last-ditch effort to bring the city's workers into the streets.

"We don't have enough people to do that. All we can do is try to rally people around the square," Han said, unable to hide his exasperation. "I advised you before to organize in the neighborhoods and factories, but you didn't listen to me." Still, he agreed to offer the meager help of the federation. The only trucks the federation could use were those "borrowed" by its members from their workplaces. None of those were available. Han glanced around the federation tents and saw just a handful of workers; they came to the square haphazardly, not according to a plan. Even if all members of the federation were there, few of them were eloquent enough to move people into defiance. Han patiently repeated the advice he had made several weeks earlier. He asked the students to borrow several trucks and loudspeakers and divide them among teams of students. The teams would fan out to the factories across Beijing and urge workers to take to the streets in the first act of a broad-based alliance between students and workers.

One of the students drove Han to Beijing University in the northwest district of the city to meet with a student leader who he said could muster the trucks, loudspeakers, and manpower. He asked Han to wait in a dorm room. Han waited more than an hour. The student never returned. Once again Han had watched a blaze of student enthusiasm die out with a pathetic fizzle. Exhausted, sick, and disgusted, Han lay down on a dorm bed and fell asleep.

While China's leading labor activist slept, security forces launched the prelude to the Beijing massacre. Protesters and police scuffled outside the northwest corner of the Great Hall of the People and at Xinhuamen Gate. Han was jolted awake by student-controlled loudspeakers declaring that the police had fired tear gas at demonstrators outside the leadership's compound at Xinhuamen. Fearing the army and workers had come to blows, he rushed out of the dormitory to the main gate of the university and hitched a ride to the square with a journalist from Hong Kong.

Han greatly underestimated the resolve of both Beijing's citizen protesters and the army. He doubted citizens would stand in the way of resolute troops. And he never thought the army would lower its rifles on common citizens. He expected troops to fire tear gas and water cannons, not machine guns. He remained in a federation tent at the northwest corner of the square for the rest of the day. After the brief battles earlier in the afternoon, the tension eased, and curious residents milled around a staff car and bus that troops had abandoned in front of Xinhuamen. The citizens kept away from the leadership compound and the Great Hall of the People.

Still convinced there would be little violence, Han tried to calm members of the federation who feared an army assault. By 10 p.m. he felt totally exhausted. His gut ached from what he suspected was a liver disorder. Practitioners in *qigong*, a traditional regimen that combines controlled breathing with methods in charismatic healing, had vainly tried to cure him over the previous days. Han lay down in his tent to sleep. Chen Jingyun, his wife, watched over him. Soon after he shut his eyes, a federation member burst into the tent.

"Soldiers have shot and killed several people at Muxidi!" he said as other workers peered into the tent or rushed around outside. Han was growing annoyed at the workers and what he felt were their groundless fears. He got up, wincing from the pain, and walked out of the tent.

"The army will probably enter the square and drive all of us away, but don't be nervous. Soldiers won't shoot us, and it won't be that bad," Han said. "I'm too tired and I've got to get some sleep. There's no need for you to call me again." Then, with a slight grin and a dash of sarcasm meant to chasten the anxious workers, Han said before turning back into the tent, "Don't wake me up unless the tanks come."

Han was awakened later by the sound of machine guns. He emerged from the tent and saw tracer bullets streaking from the Avenue of Eternal Peace to the east over the workers' encampment. Han was shocked. He had no idea what to do; he had made no plans for how to react to a violent crackdown. He never considered battling the army. Workers hustled him back into the tent.

"You have to leave the square. We can't let you be killed," one of the federation members said.

"If China is ever to have a free labor movement like Poland, it needs a Walesa like you," another worker urged.

Still dazed, Han impulsively decided to stay in the tent. But the workers surrounded him and two of them put his arms over their shoulders and carried him outside. Four workers led Han and his wife east along the northern edge of the square away from the tanks and troops. Other workers stayed close behind Han. The square and avenue were a maelstrom of shouting and screaming protesters rushing helter-skelter on foot and by bike. The terrified demonstrators seemed only to respond rationally to each burst of machine gunfire: They froze and then ran east away from the fiery blitz. The workers passed an armored car blazing near the portrait of Mao. It was 1 A.M., June 4.

As the workers approached Nanchizi east of the square, a young protester sped by on a bicycle shouting, "The People's Liberation Army is killing people! The Communist Party is killing people!" The youth held on to the handlebars with just one hand. Above his head he raised his other arm covered with blood. The workers spirited Han to a hideout. For the rest of the night and for many hours into June 4, Han heard constant rifle fire and people's shouts and screams.

✳

The police arrested at least 200 members of the federation in the days after the Beijing massacre, Han said. The federation had failed to destroy its lists of members' names, addresses, and employers. Police used the rosters in their dragnet, methodically seizing workers in their homes or workplaces.

The short-lived federation was in many ways a failure as a labor organization, Han said. Time, money, and experience were all too limited and political uncertainty was too great for it to thrive. However, it was a workers' protest group, and the accomplishments of the federation were momentous. Through their courageous audacity, federation members ensured that millions of workers nationwide learned of their capability to organize freely, even under the most hostile political order. Laborers in several cities were inspired by the Beijing federation and formed their own independent unions.

After the massacre, Han dodged the police sweep by resuming his identity as a common laborer. Like millions of Beijing workers, he climbed onto a plain black bicycle and wheeled into the river of commuters that flows along the capital's boulevards. But he kept on pedaling south out of the city and into neighboring Hebei Province. Showing once again his theoretical bent, Han decided to embark on a one-man survey of the livelihood of peasants and workers throughout China.

One day as Han rode deeper into Hebei, he stopped at an eatery in a small village. There he heard a radio announcer report that the police were looking for the leaders of the workers' federation. The first name the announcer read was Han's. Han froze. Suddenly he felt that everyone had turned to stare at him. He walked out of the eatery, climbed on his bicycle, and pedaled to a riverbank. He realized his research plan was plain folly. The police would eventually nab him. He decided that running from inevitable arrest would not be as honorable or beneficial to workers as going straight to the police.

Han returned to the capital on June 19, wheeled his bike through the gate of the Beijing Public Security Bureau on Qianmen Street, and strode into the reception room. He identified himself at the desk and sat down to wait. Nothing happened for several minutes. Exasperated, Han rose to leave.

"Hey, aren't you Han Dongfang?" a passing officer said.

"Yes," Han said.

"What on earth are you doing here?" the officer said.

"All the television and radio broadcasts and newspapers report that the Public Security Bureau is looking for me. So, here I am," Han said.

The officer's face brightened. "Oh, you've surrendered yourself!" the officer said.

"Excuse me, but please don't use the word 'surrender.' 'Surrender' is a word used for criminals. I've come to dispute the claim in the newspapers and the broadcasts that I was the member of an illegal organization and involved in counterrevolutionary incitement. I've come to reason with you and to clarify the matter," Han said.

"Oh, never mind. It's good that you came, whatever the reason," the officer said. He politely led Han to a room used for receiving guests and offered him a chair.

After forty minutes, several policemen drove Han to a two-story brick jail in the Dongcheng district at 21 Paoju Lane. The jail is built in the shape of a cross with a short horizontal line at the base. Its design is poetically fitting. Intentionally or not, the chief jailers for China's despots laid out the prison in the same shape as *shi*, the Chinese character denoting the piece in Chinese chess known as the bodyguard.

Prison guards pushed Han into a cell of thirty square feet. Its wooden floors were painted a scuffed and faded color of revolution red. Opposite the door was a small window. It had a tap, sink, toilet, and weak lightbulb but nothing else. Two other prisoners were put in the cell to keep Han under constant surveillance. Twice a day he received a scant meal of *wotou* and a watery soup with shreds of vegetables.

Daily interrogations began immediately. Some ran as long as fifteen hours. Guards came for Han at 8 A.M. and he was grilled with short breaks until as late as 2 A.M. Each time, guards hustled Han into a room of fifty square feet with a couch on one side and a long table in the middle. They pushed him onto a low wooden box in a corner of the room. The interrogator, an officer from the Ministry of State Security, sat on the couch with a scribe next to him.

Han was prepared for a contest of wills. He knew that if he buckled before the pressure of the interrogator early on, he would be on his knees throughout the grilling. If he stood firm, he would discourage the worst sort of abuses and keep an advantage, however small. The interrogator began by leaving the initiative to Han. Han quickly seized it.

"Han Dongfang, why did you give yourself up?" the interrogator said.

"I've already said that I have not surrendered. You said I have committed a crime. You labeled the student movement a 'counterrevolutionary rebellion.' As someone who went through the movement from start to finish, I have the responsibility to clear things up."

"So you came to the Public Security Bureau to reason with us?" the officer said.

"Yes," Han replied.

"The PSB is not a place to reason. Your problem is very serious. If you admit to your surrender, then perhaps at least you can save your life," the interrogator said.

"I can't let go of my principles," Han said.

"Han Dongfang, a few days ago one batch of counterrevolutionaries was already executed. I think a bullet can burst your brain too," the officer said.

"Well then, I guess there is nothing I can do about that. That's your affair. I can only hold on to my principles," Han replied.

Han was determined to repulse the interrogator by showing defiance in any way possible during the first session. As the hours dragged on, with the interrogator firing questions from the couch, Han decided to make a small statement of resistance. He put a leg on one of his knees and leaned back against the wall.

"Put your leg down!" the officer said.

"While we talk do you need to make demands on how I situate my leg?" Han said.

"I told you to put it down, now put it down!" the officer yelled.

Han slowly put his leg down. After a few minutes he said, "Excuse me, but these days I've felt rather tired, and I need to put one of my legs up on the other one to rest. Is that all right?"

"Of course you can," the interrogator spat, not looking at him.

During interrogations spanning most of his twenty-two months in prison, Han maintained the cross-legged posture as one of several gestures of defiance. The strategy apparently worked. The interrogator gradually granted him a small space of dignity.

The aims and wiles of the interrogator were clear. He first asked Han several detailed questions about what he and other activists did during various times of the democracy movement. Then he constantly needled away at actions he believed Han was trying to conceal, especially those the state could call criminal. He was particularly interested in a joint declaration on May 20 in which students and workers had called for the trial of Premier Li Peng and other leaders and urged the army to revolt against the party leadership. Han described only what happened in public, never revealing what was said and done in private.

The interrogator repeatedly tried to deceive Han into making a confession. For instance, he bitterly criticized the Communist Party in an effort to coax Han into admitting a crime.

"Many people already verify that you did these things. Why don't you just admit it?" said the interrogator. He once took out a written document, waved it about, and said, "Look, this was written by another federation leader. He wrote what happened every day. Why won't you admit your crimes too?"

In another blatant effort to wear Han down to surrender, prison guards for the first few days awakened Han repeatedly in the middle of the night.

"We're trying to help you. What are you trying to accomplish by resisting?" the interrogator said. "Come on, save your own life and you can do anything you want," he added.

At the end of each session, after Han was again thrust before the gaze of the two informants in his cell, he reviewed in his mind everything he had said, agonizing over the possibility he had made a mistake. Each time guards came for him, he grew extremely tense, thinking to himself, "This time will I not be able to bear it any longer? Will I tell them everything?"

Han was convinced from the moment he entered prison that the police would execute him. He would die the standard death for enemies of the party: A bullet would be fired from close range at the back of his head. The image strengthened him by making him determined to die honorably. Had he believed that he had a hope of living, he would have been more likely to give in to the interrogator, he said. Rather than fear death, Han became obsessed by the idea that before the police shot him, they would force him to his knees. "I absolutely must not die that way," Han thought to himself. He resolved to bolt upright rather than die kneeling.

As Han constantly turned these thoughts in his mind, he became suicidal. His eyes wandered around his cell but always arrived at the porcelain sink on the far wall. "If I lunge across the room, could I hit my head on the sink hard enough to kill myself?" he thought to himself. After a few days pondering the question, he decided the answer was no.

Han's two cellmates must have guessed his thoughts and tipped off the warden. After a week at the jail, Han was moved with the two observers into another cell. The walls and floors of the small room were covered with blue rubber padding five inches thick. A ray of sunlight shone from a small window high up on the far wall. There was no sink, toilet, or anything else in the room, only a single lightbulb far beyond reach. Guards allowed Han and his two cellmates to leave the padded room to wash and use the toilet. His interrogations were reduced to three or four days during each week.

In an effort to humiliate and soften up Han, the interrogator constantly tried to make him say he had surrendered to police. Finally, in an effort to rebuff the interrogator for good on the question, Han seized on a historical allusion, a powerful rhetorical tool in China. He raised the memory of Tan Sitong, a hero of a brief, desperate campaign in 1898 to promote political and economic change known as the Hundred Days' Reforms. Tan, a philosopher and martial arts expert, fearlessly awaited arrest and certain death at his home after Dowager Empress Cixi staged a coup and aborted the reforms. On her orders, the imperial executioners beheaded him.

"I wouldn't say my bones are harder than Tan Sitong's, but when I came to your door I knew I was risking my life," Han said. The interrogator never again accused Han of surrendering.

After ten days, the warden moved Han and his cellmates back to their original cell. Han was not allowed any contact with people outside the prison, although his wife was able to get a blanket and some clothing to him. Occasionally, he was able to see a newspaper, and he was enraged by the propaganda. The claim by the leadership that the democracy movement was a conspiracy by a few people to overthrow the party infuriated Han. He began to argue frequently over politics with his interrogator. His taut nerves steadily exhausted him. He began to vomit everything he ate and grow weak and sick.

The prison warden accused Han of faking an illness and in early September moved him into a small cell jammed with twenty-four other prisoners. Most of the inmates had been arrested since the massacre. The cell had a window, a lone lightbulb, and two small sinks. It had no toilet; the inmates used a bucket in the corner. Lice infested the bedding and cockroaches crawled from the cracks in the wooden floor. At night the vermin skittered over the faces and bodies of Han and the other inmates. When not in interrogation, Han lay on the floor.

After two weeks the warden shifted Han again, this time back into a cell like the first one with a worker and a student arrested for taking part in the democracy movement. Over the hours as Han mulled his condition, his sickness grew doubly painful. It reminded him of his mother's long illness and the wrongs that had brought her down. Before dying of stomach cancer, she too had often vomited after eating. The sickness was thwarting his vow to avenge her death. The party's vast machine of systematic injustice was wearing him down as it had his mother.

Han demanded to see a doctor. His cellmates and even some guards said they believed he was sick. But the warden repeatedly said that he was feigning an illness. He claimed Han was vomiting on purpose. Desperate for medical care, Han began a hunger strike on September 28, 1989, refusing the two daily meals of buns and soup. In the morning two days later, the warden appeared. He ordered a group of prisoners to hold Han down while a guard forced a rubber feeding tube up his nose. As Han resisted and writhed with pain, the tube crimped in his pharynx, the cavity in the head through which air and food pass before entering the windpipe or gullet. The guard switched on the feeding pump. Han convulsed and bellowed out in pain as the machine shot a jet of milk and rice gruel that exploded in his pharynx and sprayed up into his nasal cavities and down his gullet. Han passed out.

That afternoon the warden ordered the same treatment. Han ran up a fever and his heartbeat accelerated. He drifted in and out of consciousness but still refused food. During the next few days he felt so weak and feverish he was convinced he would soon die. In a lucid moment he asked his cellmates to memorize his last words to his wife. He then drifted off to sleep, thinking he would never awaken.

The next morning, the warden entered the cell and again pressured Han to eat.

"I won't," Han said. "I never asked you for anything extraordinary. All I asked was to see a doctor."

"All right. We agree," the warden said. He turned and quickly walked out of the cell. Han accepted a meal, ate it, and vomited.

About a week later Han was taken to the infirmary. The warden was waiting for him with an acupuncturist.

"Set your heart at ease, I can cure your illness in one stroke," the acupuncturist told Han, taking his hand. "I've cured a lot of people before and after I cure them, they never get sick again," he said in a warm, sing-song tone.

The acupuncturist spread Han's hand, picked up a needle seven inches long, thrust it in just below the thumb, through the palm, and out beneath the little finger. Han winced. The pain was so intense that he was too shocked to cry out. The acupuncturist cranked the needle in the wound. The warden apparently thought he could stop Han from feigning sickness by making him face the prospect of undergoing such "medical treatment" again.

"How about it, are you cured yet?" the acupuncturist said as he plunged the needle back and forth and glanced at Han with a grin. The shock had transported Han beyond pain. He looked up at the acupuncturist and smiled back at him. The eyes of the acupuncturist widened and his grin vanished. He pulled out the needle, turned away, and walked from the room.

Han was returned to his cell. Again, he could only lie amid the filth and vermin on the floor and feel a slow, rising tide of daze and weakness engulf him. After a few days, when it was clear the ingenious cure had failed, the warden ordered guards to take Han to the infirmary. Although Han was too weak to walk and his vomiting continued, the doctor said he could find nothing wrong with him. Convinced that he was locked in a contest of wills, the warden returned Han to his cell for a few more weeks. Then, toward the end of November, the warden entered the cell with a group of convicts.

"I've decided to let you exercise your legs," the warden said with a smile.

Han's fellow inmates lifted him up, carried him out the cell door, and propped him against the wall of a hallway. Supported by the inmates, Han struggled to lift his head. His knees buckled.

"Let's see if he can walk. Let him go," the warden said.

"He's too weak. He'll fall," said a prisoner holding Han.

"Let's give him a chance. Let him go," the warden said. The prisoners backed away and Han, too weak to raise his arms, watched the floor rise up and slam him in the face.

Weeks passed with Han unable to stomach little more than small amounts of rice and boiled water. He drifted in and out of consciousness. Then in early January 1990, a guard entered Han's cell with another gang of inmates.

"We've been too kind to you," the guard said, looking down at Han. "We didn't want to humiliate you and so we kept you out of the contagious diseases unit. But that's where we're putting you. You're afraid of illness and that's what we're going to give you now." The inmates lifted Han and carried him into a cell crowded with more than a dozen other sick prisoners. Han looked around at his languishing cellmates and estimated that at least half suffered from tuberculosis. The air was stagnant and sour. Day and night there was no end to the sound of loud coughing and hacking. Han spent more than three months in the cell. Doctors never bothered to diagnose his illness.

In the spring, the interrogator from the Ministry of State Security determined that his questioning was complete. The police gathered up Han and took him to Banbuqiao, a jail for prisoners facing trial. Not long after passing through the high electrified walls, Han was thrust before a new interrogator. Still weak but no longer bed-ridden, Han again was determined to show his adversary from the start that he was neither a "soft bone" nor a grunting laborer. Using high-brow propriety and a soft voice as rhetorical smokescreen, Han went on the offensive.

"Excuse me, but may I say a few words to you?" Han asked before the interrogator had said anything.

"Of course you may," the interrogator said, grinning to hear such deference and geniality from a notoriously uncooperative "black hand" of the 1989 democracy protests.

"I hope that we can cooperate well, understand this case as quickly as possible, and not delay in arriving at what sentence should be given," Han softly said. The interrogator nodded and his grin broadened a bit.

"So please don't tell me over and over again to have a good attitude so that I can receive a lighter sentence. I don't need any of that. I will only tell you what I know. What I don't know, I just don't know. I won't weave any tale for you for more lenient treatment. Also, please only ask me a question once. I will only answer it once. If you think I answered incorrectly, you can ask someone else about it. Don't ask me over and over again and say I'm speaking nonsense because I won't change my answer."

The interrogator leaped to his feet and slammed his fist on the table. "Han Dongfang, do you know what your identity is, what your plight is?" he shouted. "How dare you put on a show of force before an organ of public security!"

Still, Han's gambit worked. The interrogator did not repeatedly ask Han to consider his "crimes" or describe his attitude.

Although Han was formally charged as a counterrevolutionary, he knew at least he was not alone. Not long after Han entered Banbuqiao, he and many other inmates contracted the highly contagious skin disease known as scabies. The malady is torturous: A parasitic mite burrows under the skin to lay its eggs, causing intense and incessant itching. Prison officials reckoned that exercise would help clear up the ailment, so they let Han and the other sufferers walk around the prison yard for a spell each day. One day, as Han leaned against a wall, he noticed the Roman letters "LJJ" scrawled there. He knew immediately his friend and fellow activist Li Jinjin had written them. Underneath, Han hurriedly wrote "HDF VVV," the three "Vs" a declaration of victory.

After holding Han in Banbuqiao for nine months, the police moved him to Qincheng prison to await trial. The move was a bitter distinction: The party reserves the jail north of Beijing for its most menacing political prisoners. There, Han began to suffer from the worst legacy of his abuse at Paoju. He lost the little weight he had regained. He developed a fever and at night endured uncontrollable shivering and sweating. Gradually, he suffered from the same symptoms that he had seen overwhelm many of his cellmates at the contagious-diseases unit in Paoju. He coughed up a phlegm resembling slime. He felt cutting pains in the chest. Worst of all, he often felt a sudden onrush of imminent suffocation, a clawing need for air. By the winter of 1991, Han suffered from a full-blown case of tuberculosis. Although much of the time he was semiconscious and could walk and talk only with great difficulty, prison doctors ignored him.

In April 1991, however, the police suddenly showed compassion for the young railwayman. The party had hustled many leaders of the democracy movement to trial in January as the world focused on the Persian Gulf war. But by the spring, Beijing knew the world would not overlook indefinitely the abuse of Han and other jailed dissidents. Washington had begun debating whether to make special trade status for China contingent on its human rights record. Han exploited the party's vulnerability. He refused medical care and met his interrogators with stubborn silence. "You know, if I die you'll be in big trouble," was all he told them.

Han triumphed in the high-stakes brinkmanship. The police apparently decided that if he were to die, he would best do it at home. On April 28 a police officer phoned Chen and told her to fetch her husband. He took pains to stress that the charges against him still stood; Han was being temporarily dismissed on medical grounds. Chen rushed to the hospital to find the tall, robust activist of the Beijing Spring little more than a pale, broken skeleton. He could barely move. When he did, he seemed to be struggling to hack out his lungs. He lay in bed with eyes shut, a still, silent figure. But then his savage cough possessed him, suddenly turning him into a macabre puppet of convulsing flesh and bone.

Even under the treatment of a physician, Han's cough and fever steadily grew worse. Desperate for competent care, his family sought the help of a friend in Hong Kong and contacted a specialist in the United States. The doctor arranged tests that confirmed Han had tuberculosis. At last, Han began receiving proper care.

By the early spring of 1992 Han was still often seized by the cough. Occasionally he succumbed to a bad fever. Still, he felt well enough to renew his activism. In mid-March, he submitted an application at the Beijing Public Security Bureau to stage a demonstration. His one-man protest by bicycle on March 24 would coincide with the opening of the National People's Congress; the parliament meets for three weeks each spring. He sought chiefly to urge delegates to ensure that a draft labor law complied with the constitutional right to freedom of assembly. He also wanted to spread word that he was again speaking out. Then when the time for mass protest came, restive workers would know Han would march with them.

The day after submitting the application, Han went back to the police headquarters. An officer returned the application, saying police would not consider it because a one-man bicycle ride is not a protest. Without explicit official approval, Han decided not to demonstrate. But on March 23, the eve of his proposed demonstration, plainclothes police began blatantly following Han wherever he went. The officers moved into a room in a factory adjacent to the small courtyard home of Han's in-laws, where he was staying with his wife. They closely tailed Han's wife and her family. The police also tried to plant a bug in the basement of Han's home. Han discovered the technician trying to set up the device and drove him away.

Han did not have to search for another opportunity to battle the party. In May, the authorities abruptly began to worry his oldest, deepest wound. Han went to his one-room apartment outside the offices of *Beijing Daily* and found an eviction notice slapped on the door. He was furious. The authorities' unjust treatment of his family over housing had worn down the health of his mother and stoked the fury behind his own activism. Han's mother had lived in the same apartment and received an identical eviction notice from the local court just before she died. Han had ignored the notice and held on to the apartment.

The Dongcheng District People's Court summoned Han to an "informal" meeting on May 14. Han told officials that the notice was illegitimate; it applied only to his mother.

"My lawyer advises me that your effort to evict me is not in accordance with legal procedure," Han told a court official.

"Your lawyer is a bastard," the official said.

"Please don't curse my lawyer," Han replied mildly.

"Did I curse your lawyer? He *is* a bastard!" the official said.

Feeling his rage rise, Han decided to leave rather than argue and damage his health.

"Excuse me, but I don't want to talk any further today," he said and walked from the room.

"Come back at once!" the official shouted, but Han walked out of the building and onto the street. Suddenly, he was seized from behind by several police and court officials. They hustled him back into the "people's court" and hurled him down into the basement. The assailants kicked and beat Han, handcuffed him, and shoved him into a small cell. After an hour the police and officials returned. They punched Han and repeatedly jabbed him with an electric prod. Han ran up a high fever. His breathing was shallow and rapid. He could not stand. After several hours the officials called Han's sister and told her to collect him.

Han attempted a legal counterattack, filing civil and criminal suits at the district, city, and national judiciaries. He learned later that the party's political and legal committee, the ultimate judge on legal matters in China, barred an investigation into the assault. Soon the district court seized on another way to harm Han. Along with the police, the district withheld permission for Han to go to the United States at the invitation of the AFL-CIO and receive treatment for tuberculosis. He secured a passport only after submitting a statement to the court on August 10 saying that he was abandoning his property in his apartment. He denounced the court for its lawlessness and never surrendered his claim to the dwelling. Soon thereafter, Han and his wife flew to the United States.

In America, Han found renewal in mind and body. A New York doctor removed the wasted upper part of his right lung and put him on an eighteen-month course of medication. His wife gave birth to a son, their first child. Han had more opportunity for free reflection and inquiry than at any time since his job working among the stacks at the library. He studied techniques for training labor leaders at the George Meany Center of the AFL-CIO. In meetings with U.S. lawmakers and officials he discussed U.S. policy toward China and the systematic abuse of workers' rights there. He traded ideas with delegates to the World Conference on Human Rights in Geneva and addressed a conference of the International Labor Organization in Vienna. The strongest foreign endorsement came in the form of a prize in April 1993 from the National Endowment for Democracy, an organization established by Congress to promote democratic movements abroad. In a clear sign of U.S. support, President Clinton attended the award ceremony and met briefly with Han.

Buoyed by the foreign encouragement, Han felt a renewed sense of confidence and purpose as he prepared to return furtively to China. He flew to Hong Kong and on the morning of August 13 boarded a ferry for Aotou, a small port in Guangdong Province. Lowering his eyes in an effort to hide his nervousness, Han handed his passport to a guard at the small border post. The guards lacked computers and access to up-to-date immigration information, so they quickly stamped Han's passport and let him pass.

"This is incredible! How can it go so smoothly?" Han thought to himself as he clutched his passport and held in a surge of exhilaration. Soon after climbing aboard a bus for Guangzhou, he felt doubly convinced that he was right to return to the mainland. As the bus rattled and lurched northward, Han watched unfold before him what he later likened to a live documentary on labor exploitation.

Guangdong has been broadly hailed as China's bellwether—the wealthiest, boldest, most advanced region. For several years the province has logged double-digit industrial growth, sometimes exceeding 20 percent. It is the most robust province of the fastest growing economy in the world, attracting some 10 million migrants, or the greatest concentration of the 70 million to 100 million workers on the road in China today.

But the Guangdong that Han saw differed dramatically from the widely celebrated province. As he gazed at one of the region's main arteries from the perspective of a worker, Han saw income disparities and hardship for laborers that made

Guangdong the country's shame. He saw signs from the bus window indicating that although migrants in Guangdong find jobs, they also confront cruel working conditions. Many of them must labor long hours for low pay at dangerous factories and work sites. They may be fired at will and in most places there are no laws ensuring them a minimum wage. They receive no health insurance or other benefits. At least 500,000 of the itinerant workers in Guangdong are child laborers, according to government surveys.

At several places along the road, Han saw migrants dressed in filthy clothes and laden with stacks of bricks or clinging to scaffolding. The scrawny workers were building factories in dusty lots marked by signs declaring "Development Zone" or "China–Hong Kong Joint Venture." At times traffic on the congested road forced the bus to a standstill, offering Han a view of the shacks and huts of leaky scrap wood or asbestos boards in which the migrants slept. Inside large dwellings were long platforms the workers shared as a bed. The jammed sleeping quarters reminded Han of prison.

Han saw more Mercedes-Benzes during the few hours en route to Guangzhou than during his entire stay in the United States. The bus passed through towns where new, brightly colored dance halls, karaoke bars, restaurants, and hotels lined the streets. "What migrant worker has the time and money for singing, dancing, fine eating, or lingering at resort hotels?" Han wondered to himself. In Guangdong, capitalism had returned to China in its rawest, cruelest form, he concluded. Such convictions made Han's return especially dangerous for China's leadership.

Once in Guangzhou, Han went immediately to the airport. After learning that all flights to Beijing were fully booked, he checked into a hotel in the city. At 6 A.M. on August 14 he was awakened by a knock on the door, and a dozen police muscled their way into his room. They rifled through his suitcases and hustled him into another room, where they interrogated him late into the afternoon about his activities abroad and reasons for returning to China.

"Please don't make a mess of this incident," Han told the interrogators. "If you decide to expel me, the damage will be extremely great, not only for me but for the government. Could you relay my suggestion to the upper levels so that they don't do such a foolish thing?" he said in the measured tones that are his trademark under fire.

At 4 P.M. police gathered his bags. "While overseas you participated in anti-government activities and violated the constitution, and therefore it has been decided that you are to be expelled from the country," a policeman said.

"Please tell your superiors that I'm willing to go to jail. You can arrest me, try me, and sentence me. But you shouldn't drive me out and mar public opinion," Han said. The police ignored him. As they walked him out of the hotel, Han broke away and bolted down the street. Eight police ran him down on the sidewalk.

"I don't want to leave my country! I want to return! If I've broken the law, sentence me to jail! You can't expel me!" Han shouted as the policeman yanked his arms, bent him double, and shoved him into a car. Han felt part of the scar tissue from his May lung operation tear.

Police gagged Han and pinned him to his seat for the entire ride to Shenzhen. The car pulled up to the port-of-entry building at China's busiest border post. The massive square structure is plain, gray, and faceless but for the ersatz, traditionally upswung corners of its tile roof. Each day tens of thousands of travelers funnel through a serpentine channel of metal barricades into the building, past immigration officials, and across a narrow bridge into Lo Wu, the border town in the New Territories of Hong Kong.

The police stamped Han's passport and cleared the area of some 4,000 travelers by detaining them in a large hall. More than a dozen plainclothes police, uniformed officers, and troops of the People's Armed Police bundled Han to the foot of the bridge and around a metal railing. Then they backed away.

"Cross over to Hong Kong!" a police cadre yelled. But Han forced his way back around the railing and into China. When they blocked him from moving further, he held fast to a post.

"Get moving, get him out of here!" the cadre yelled. The police surrounded Han.

"This is my country! What right do you have to force me to leave? I want to return to my country!" Han shouted.

"You aren't qualified to be a Chinese!" the cadre yelled as the police picked up Han, heaved him over the barricade, and backed away.

Han ran back around the barricade; the police threw him over the fence again. He ran back in a third time, and again the police hurled him back toward Hong Kong. Thinking that he could find an entry elsewhere, Han calmly walked twenty yards down the bridge toward Hong Kong, quickly swung his legs over the railing, and jumped onto an embankment. Immediately Han was seized by Hong Kong border police and taken to an office on the Hong Kong side of the bridge. He refused to undergo entry procedures and spent the night in the office.

When the border opened the next morning, Han walked down the bridge toward China. Several troops of the People's Armed Police were waiting for him. Recognizing the futility of his effort, Han walked back to the Hong Kong border post and submitted to a seven-day visa. Within days the New China News Agency in Hong Kong, China's de facto embassy in the territory, informed Han that his passport had been revoked.

The expulsion was a Pyrrhic victory for Han, a tacit acknowledgment by the party that it could not break him through jail and torture. Still, Han was enraged. Through Zhou Guoqiang, his lawyer in Beijing, Han sued the government on October 5 seeking a public apology and permission to return to China. After Beijing courts refused to accept the suit, Han tried to fly to Beijing on November 11 but was turned back before boarding the jetliner.

The next day Han tried to return to China by land at Lo Wu. He passed through Hong Kong immigration, walked across the bridge, and again faced a harsh welcome from a small force of the People's Armed Police. He turned on his heel, walked several yards away, and camped on the bridge for the night.

After slipping into a sleeping bag, Han took out a pen and wrote down thoughts that help explain his extreme tenacity: "I've knocked on all the doors but all the doors were shut in my face. God has taken away all the easy roads and left me with a narrow path—faith."

❋

Han welcomes hardship because he believes it is a test by God. He became a Christian in July 1993 after befriending members of a Chinese-American church in the United States. Since then, he said, he has tried to love his oppressors. "I believe very much that people should love their neighbors and their enemies. God is always with me, telling me what to do," Han said. "I often report to God about my life," he added.

Han believes his conversion makes him a greater threat to the leadership. Because of faith, Han is driven more by the uplifting desire to champion abused workers than by the corrosive obsession to avenge his mother's death. Also, faith has given spiritual power and sanction to his long-standing yearning for justice. Finally, it has convinced him that if Chinese hope to bring lasting change, they must reform their hearts first. "China's problem is that people's hearts must be saved; they must have love. Dictatorship and autocracy thrive in a society of hatred, so by changing this hatred to love, autocracy will not be able to exist."

Han intends eventually to pry his way back into China. But his forced exile has some advantages. In Hong Kong, he can promote labor education without interference from Beijing. Meanwhile, he can maintain stronger relationships with international labor organizations than if he were in China's capital.

Han works as a researcher at the Christian Industrial Committee, a Hong Kong labor organization. He aims to plot the best course for China's labor movement. In addition, he publishes *China Labor Bulletin,* a monthly newsletter on workers in China. Some 1,000 copies are mailed or carried into the mainland every month. Through the bulletin, Han tells workers that the party denies them universally recognized economic and political freedoms. He shows them how Beijing prevents them from freely organizing, striking, engaging in collective bargaining, and exercising other basic labor rights. He describes working conditions abroad and tells how unions overseas defend their members. He also outlines foreign laws granting workers social security, unemployment compensation, medical care, and other benefits. "Chinese workers will begin to think, if 'exploited workers' in capitalist countries have these rights and benefits, then why can't the 'vanguard class' in China have them too," Han said.

Although Han carries an incendiary agenda, he is not a revolutionary. He is a reformer who seeks to promote workers' rights openly, peacefully, and strictly according to the law. So before he tries to establish an independent union, he plans to agitate for the repeal of China's law banning free workers' organizations. After rallying a free union, Han will focus on defending workers' economic interests. He believes labor organizers who use covert, violent, and illegal methods risk perpetuating autocracy rather than advance the cause of achieving lasting democracy and worker rights.

Although the party might continue to bar Han from China, it is unlikely to halt the forces that will compel Chinese workers to unionize. Laborers will organize in desperation as China continues its painful transformation from a socialist to a market economy, Han said.

Already Chinese workers are growing increasingly resentful as the party fails to control inflation, widening income disparities, and corruption—all causes of the 1989 protests. Inflation in the cities that often surges above 20 percent gnaws away at the livelihood of laborers. Factory bosses granted greater power under reform are exploiting defenseless workers. Thousands of massive state enterprises that operate in the red are cutting laborers' salaries and benefits and laying off millions of their 110 million employees. The dismissals are breaking the paternalistic guarantee of lifetime employment and benefits. Although strikes are illegal, the number of walkouts each year since the 1989 crackdown has steadily increased, according to Labor Ministry statistics.

"China's reformers are creating an unadulterated, predatory capitalism, not a modern capitalism but one in its primitive stages. In this transition, workers and peasants are the biggest victims. The factory owners use violence and raw power to accumulate wealth, and their appetites are inexhaustible," Han said. "Inflation and declining living standards will provoke jealousy and discontent among workers, and the social consequences are hard to predict," he added.

Han believes that the party risks provoking mass unrest as it bans independent unions that would safely channel the rising tide of workers' resentment. Rather than enacting sweeping reforms to placate workers, the party is using intimidation and sheer force in an attempt to stem their discontent. Police routinely jail organizers of free labor movements nationwide. The workers are virtually defenseless. They find the party-controlled legal system, the official labor union, and withering state enterprises more hostile than helpful. Labor organization is the best answer for workers and the best hope for peaceful change, according to Han.

"If free unions exist, perhaps the workers' protests can be fairly moderate," Han said. He views his attempts to establish a free union as an effort to prevent a ruinous whirlwind of unrest. "My fundamental goal is not to organize independent unions; that is just a means to an end. My goal is to better equip China to make a stable transition from socialism to a market economy. When workers realize they can use collective bargaining, unions, and other methods to solve their problems, China will be less likely to face turmoil."

To the party, however, dissidents like Han are harbingers of chaos, not stability. The party has expelled several activists who attempted to return home from overseas. But Han will not accept forced exile. He is determined to return to China even if it means returning to prison. He entered the Paoju jail in June 1989 expecting to die. Ultimately, though, all that perished was his fear. Quoting a Chinese adage, Han said, "A dead pig does not fear a scalding in boiling water."

PART FOUR

Chinese Challenge the State

"The Tree Craves Calm but the Wind Rages On"

樹欲靜而風不止

As labor activist Han Dongfang campaigns for Chinese workers, dissident journalist Zhang Weiguo strives to help millions of ordinary Chinese gain the power to speak for themselves. The affable Shanghai-born journalist is one of China's most dogged and outspoken advocates for a free press. Years of jail and official harassment have failed to silence him. Zhang's life shows how young, independent-minded Chinese intellectuals have become a potent force for democracy.

Zhang Weiguo   *Photo by Ann Scott Tyson*

EIGHT

"Touching the Scales of the Dragon's Throat": The Dissident

EVERY DAY AT THE Shanghai Number 1 Jail, journalist Zhang Weiguo led his dozen cellmates on an escape. Zhang roused the men from out of the stench of urine and excrement and led them in circles along the walls of the dark, cramped cell. As the inmates shuffled along, heavy leg irons that bound the accused murderers among them scraped noisily on the concrete floor. Under the cover of the clanking shackles, Zhang and his cellmates sang.

"I'm nothing but a northern wave, / Rolling in a boundless expanse, / Blown by the wailing, shrill north wind," the men sang, walking to the slow beat of the melancholy Taiwanese song. As they walked and sang together, the prisoners briefly fled the memory of regular beatings and other abuse. Amid the demeaning squalor, they staked out a small circle of dignity.

Zhang sang the loudest. Charged with counterrevolutionary crimes for his role in the 1989 democracy movement, he was awaiting trial and expected a sentence of ten years or more. But Zhang was determined to maintain his self-respect. Every morning, in defiance of the prison regime, the gregarious, heavyset reporter led his cellmates in doing exercises: handstands, push-ups, and martial arts. His cell became known as "the gym." And, day after day, he led the circling chorus of alleged thieves, corrupt officials, and murderers in rounds of karaoke to the rattle 'n' roll of chains.

One day, after a dressing-down by guards for an outburst of karaoke, the prison warden summoned Zhang for interrogation. Zhang walked into the room of pale gray walls and sat as usual in a wooden chair under the glare of a lamp. The warden approached, his fat face twisted in a grimace.

"You are a Communist Party member! How can you behave like a common criminal?" he yelled, slamming his fist on a table.

After six months behind bars, Zhang knew better than to let the warden anger him.

"It's comical that at this moment you say I am a Communist Party member! You falsely accuse your own Communist Party member, lock him up, and then demand that he not act like a criminal. Isn't that full of contradiction?" he replied coolly.

In fact, Zhang had never felt so vehemently opposed to the Communist regime. He had quit the party in revulsion on June 4, 1989, the day of the Beijing massacre. His own jailing as a political prisoner had further convinced him to shun any association with the dictatorial state. The slam of jail doors marked the finality of Zhang's radical break with his youthful faith in communism.

Zhang had been a model Communist during Mao's 1966–1976 Cultural Revolution. As a Red Guard, he was compulsively obedient to Chairman Mao, his idol. One utterance from Mao, as the slogan went, and Zhang would "scale a mountain of knives and plunge into a sea of fire." His fervor won him fame in Shanghai, a hotbed of radicalism during the ten-year upheaval. One bright spring day in 1975, the eighteen-year-old Red Guard leader headed a parade honoring Mao before hundreds of thousands of onlookers. Zhang rode through the densely populated city, past his family's tiny working-class apartment on Tibet Road. As crowds cheered him on, he basked in the party's favor before his parents, teachers, and peers.

Back then, Zhang believed that by obeying Mao and the party whole-heartedly, he too would become all-powerful. But in later years, he gradually realized that his worship of Mao had enslaved him, making him the party's tool.

Through defiance, Zhang landed in jail. Ironically, though, he felt freer in prison than ever before. Just as Zhang discovered prison karaoke amid the grim rhythm of fetters, he found a new magnitude of freedom in a head-on confrontation with the repressive Marxist regime. Faced with the party's total betrayal of his trust, Zhang felt for the first time entirely at liberty to speak his mind. The authorities, by jailing Zhang, had unwittingly sealed his transformation from a minion of Mao to an independent intellectual, from a cog-in-the-wheel Communist to a citizen demanding his rights, and from a pawn of the party to a political activist.

Zhang's emergence as a dissident epitomizes the birth of a new generation of young, independent-minded Chinese intellectuals. More than any past generation, these young thinkers are challenging the invasive controls of the Marxist state on their lives. Like Zhang, they are increasingly outspoken in their demands for intellectual autonomy and political rights.

This maverick generation is breaking with the ancient Confucian tradition of scholars kowtowing to the state. For hundreds of years, Chinese scholars aspired to serve the emperor by offering advice, supporting his judgments, and propagating one orthodox school of thought. Communist leaders exploited the tradition and strengthened it with fear by systematically persecuting dissenters. Most older Chinese intellectuals obey the Communist regime. Like scholars in imperial China, they often act as loyal, behind-the-scenes critics of the leadership. But they rarely challenge the party's basic creed or revolutionary right to rule.

Unlike their elderly counterparts, many young and middle-aged Chinese thinkers were raised not as obedient Confucian servants of the state but as Maoist rebels. Moreover, their experience under Mao has left them deeply disillusioned with the Communist state. Many of them are from a lost generation of intellectuals whose talents and youth were squandered in the folly of Mao's Cultural Revolution. Like Zhang, they came away from those years feeling angry and cheated by Mao. Their rejection of Maoism left them thirsting for a new way to make sense of the world. Many looked to the West and Japan for alternatives and began agitating for democratic reforms. They see their activism as justified by the needs of China's modernizing society with its millions of aspiring individuals.

Outspoken young intellectuals like Zhang risk less than past generations when they challenge the regime. Unlike their mentors, they must no longer rely on the state for jobs and funding. Since the early 1980s, China's market-oriented economic reforms have offered them broad opportunities outside the state-run system. They have drawn on the resources of a growing market economy to found private or nongovernmental think tanks, political salons, newspapers, and publishing houses as well as businesses to support their activism.

These young intellectuals must refrain from open political dissent or face brutal and swift suppression by the police state. Their nascent unofficial groups cannot yet play a direct political role. The party's monopoly on political power ultimately limits their influence by forcing them to rely on the support of a faction or leader within the Communist establishment.

In the future, however, this bold generation of intellectuals promises to help lead China toward a more democratic civil society in which unofficial citizens' organizations take part in political decisionmaking. The story of Zhang—his years as a young Red Guard, his crisis of faith in Maoism, and his ensuing journey of self-discovery and political action—illustrates the emergence of this potent force for change. His odyssey begins in a rickety working-class tenement in the thronging heart of Shanghai.

✳

One of Zhang's earliest childhood memories is of sitting at home with his legs dangling out between the iron bars of a second-story window, watching children play and cyclists pass on the city lane below.

It was the spring of 1961. Shanghai, like the rest of China, was suffering through the three hard years of shortages caused by Mao's ill-conceived Great Leap Forward. Food rations had dwindled and starvation was claiming millions of lives. The economy was in chaos. Workers were exhausted from toiling on giant dams and other overly ambitious public works projects. Closer to home, economic austerity had forced the neighborhood nursery to close, and Zhang's worker parents were too poor to pay the monthly fee of 5 yuan per child for another kindergarten.

Every morning before leaving for work at a cardboard box factory, Zhang's mother corralled the four-year-old Zhang and his two younger siblings into the tiny apartment, locked the door from the outside, and took away the key. The three children, led by Zhang, immediately scrambled up a ladder to the "pigeon coop," a tiny wooden loft that formed half the family's living space. There, they sat on the windowsill, their legs hanging down and hands gripping the bars. Neighbors passing below sometimes took pity on the forlorn, hungry children and tossed them a bun of steamed bread.

Zhang's family was needy by Shanghai standards. Crowded into two small, dingy rooms on the first and second floors of a decrepit wooden row house, the family had only the crudest furnishings. They cooked over a single-burner coal stove. They shared a cold-water tap with several dozen inhabitants of the house. A wooden chamber pot was the only alternative to a filthy public toilet more than 100 feet down the lane.

Zhang's mother, Ying Zhuhua, scrimped in every way possible. She cut the children's hair, sewed all their clothing, and stitched their cotton-soled shoes by hand. When the money still fell short, she sold her blood.

No matter how depleted she felt after selling her blood, Ying always beamed when she walked through the door and pulled 100 yuan from her pocket, a sum three times her monthly income. For Zhang and the other children, it was a gleeful occasion, too. It meant they could taste a little pork, chicken, or egg. They usually survived on a bland diet of wheat buns, carrots, and small rations of rice. Of course, Communist authorities never spoke of people "selling" blood; it was always "contributed." The money authorities handed out was not "payment"; it was a "nourishment fee." But no matter what it was called, the giving of blood allowed the Zhangs to scrape through in hard times.

When difficulties mounted, Zhang's parents often reminded their children how much worse life had been in the oppressive "black society" of prerevolutionary China. Zhang's father, Zhang Dianzhi, was one of nine children born to peasants in the hinterland province of Shaanxi. As a teenager in the 1940s, he was pressed into the Nationalist army of Chiang Kai-shek as it battled Mao's straw-sandaled guerrillas. In the chaos of civil war he lost touch with his family in Shaanxi and never saw them again. He fled the army at the first opportunity and spent the next few years wandering the country, dodging the war, and working at odd jobs. In 1948, on the eve of Mao's rise to power, he arrived in Shanghai. He was twenty-two and penniless. He found temporary work at a bicycle repair shop. A quiet, diligent man, he eventually landed a full-time job at a bicycle repair and assembly plant.

It was there that he met Ying, who worked at the box factory nearby. A peasant from Zhejiang Province, Ying made her way to Shanghai in 1949 at the age of fourteen. Unskilled and illiterate, she first worked as a babysitter and maid for a worker's family. She sent almost all her earnings back to the home village in Zhejiang to support her widowed mother and younger brother. During the Sino-Japanese War (1937–1945), Japanese occupation troops had seized her father as a coolie. He had a fiery temperament and resisted Japanese officers; he paid for his defiance with his life. A few years after her father's death, flooding in the village pushed Ying's family to near starvation. Her older sister drifted to Shanghai seeking work, and Ying followed soon afterward. Ying had lost most of her hair during a childhood illness, and in Shanghai she grew embarrassed about her appearance. She adopted the habit of always wearing a white cotton worker's bonnet. Ying still wears the bonnet as well as the mental trappings from years of deprivation. "My children have never suffered real hardship," Ying says as she recalls her girlhood.

Both Zhang's parents were grateful to the Communists for a relatively secure life in Shanghai in the 1950s and 1960s. Because of their poor origins, the two workers had almost nothing to lose and everything to gain from the "victory of the proletariat." Lacking formal education, they readily embraced Communist claims to have founded a shining "new China." So when their first child was born on an upper floor of the tenement on November 9, 1956, they named him Weiguo (Mighty Nation) in honor of the Communist state. From that day on, they raised Zhang to serve the party and Mao. "My parents taught me that Mao and the Communist Party were supreme," said Zhang. "So from birth I was under the influence of Mao."

In his early years, though, it seemed Zhang listened to little anyone said. He was a curious, headstrong, and naughty boy. People often hammered on the door in a fury over his pranks. Neighbors said he broke things. Children said he wounded them in fights. Irate teachers stormed over to lodge complaints and demand he write self-criticisms. Ying often beat Zhang for his misbehavior. Once she grabbed his arm as he tried to flee, inadvertently dislocating his shoulder. When he was in third grade, Zhang had a run-in with his teacher, nicknamed Fatty Hu. One day at lunchtime he propped a garbage pail and dustpan on a broom above the classroom door. When Fatty Hu walked in, the foul debris spilled onto her head. The students laughed uproariously. Zhang's mother dragged him home and beat him severely. "You are my oldest child, and you won't obey me! What can I do?" she yelled, bursting into tears.

Partly in desperation over his behavior, Ying often sent Zhang to her parents' village in Zhejiang. Zhang loved the countryside. He felt freer among the paddy fields and fishponds of the village than in Shanghai's crowded lanes. He chased the chickens and gobbled up crunchy green cucumbers as they ripened on the vine, earning himself the nickname Little Cucumber. Zhang's maternal grandmother curbed his mischief by putting him to work taking meals to relatives laboring in the fields.

During one stay in the countryside, Zhang learned to swim in a village pond. Thrilled with his accomplishment, he spent hours in the water. Soon, the Shanghai boy swam farther and faster than his rural cousins. In the strange sort of twist of fate common in China under Mao, Zhang's newfound skill changed his life.

Back in Shanghai, Zhang was recruited by authorities for Shanghai's first annual "commemorating Mao swim" in the Yangtze River. Mao, too, had learned to swim as a boy in his father's fishpond, and virtually every Chinese city dweller, including Zhang, knew about his celebrated swim in the Yangtze River on July 16, 1966. Photographs of the chairman bobbing among the waves were splashed across the nation's newspapers along with articles hailing Mao's leadership. At the ripe age of seventy-three, Mao wanted to appear vigorous as he defied the party establishment and launched his most ambitious political campaign, the Cultural Revolution. Only a month later, Mao had stood atop Beijing's Tiananmen Gate mobilizing crowds of up to a million student Red Guards. Mao intended to purge the party of moderates whom he accused of steering China onto "the capitalist road." But within a year, the Cultural Revolution had disrupted almost every facet of life as it spiraled into modern China's bloodiest, most destructive political campaign. Millions of Chinese were killed, beaten, or driven to commit suicide.

It was in this frenzied atmosphere that Shanghai authorities staged the first swim in July 1967 as a tribute to Mao. Shanghai at the time was a radical stronghold of Mao's wife Jiang Qing and her leftist allies, later dubbed the Gang of Four. The Shanghai leadership touted the swim as one of its prime "commemorating Mao activities."

Zhang, at the age of eleven, was among the youngest of the more than 1,000 people rallied for the Yangtze swim the following year on July 16, 1968. Early in the morning, tingling with excitement, he arrived by bus at Bao Shan, a point several miles upstream of the river's mouth on the East China Sea. Zhang yanked on a swimsuit hand-sewn by his mother and lined up on the bank. He felt intimidated next to the burly peasants, militiamen, and Red Guards beside him. But his fears were overwhelmed by the thrill of blaring loudspeakers, fluttering red banners, and hundreds of cheering onlookers.

"Long live Chairman Mao!" Zhang and the others shouted in unison. "Long live our great teacher, great leader, great supreme commander, and great helmsman!" they yelled, and plunged together into the swirling, brackish Yangtze waters flowing toward the sea. Braced by the wind and waves and encouraged by the shouts of other swimmers, Zhang plowed through the water with all his might. An hour flew past. But the swim was long, nearly fifteen miles. Zhang found himself struggling numbly through the water pulled along by the strong current. All he could think of was making it to the end. Suddenly, after more than four hours, a squall blew up waves that capsized some of the naval landing boats following the swimmers. Lifeguards signaled to the swimmers to board the boats and carried them through the driving rain to the end point at Gaoqiao. Zhang's legs were so weak that he could barely make it up the bank to the bus carrying his clothes and towel. But he was euphoric over his feat. "I felt very proud. It was extremely glorious."

Zhang felt his esteem rise dramatically in the eyes of his classmates, teachers, and neighbors. Overnight, the class prankster had become a school hero. On the first day of fifth grade in September 1968, classmates greeted him with a mixture of awe, envy, and admiration. Party officials at school invited him to take part in special projects. Zhang, like all his peers, had already joined the Young Pioneers, the party-run children's organization. As a Young Pioneer, he wore a red kerchief that represented a corner of Communist China's flag. Now, he donned a red armband, tossed back his shoulders, and entered the ranks of the "little Red Guards."

Zhang had learned a vital early lesson from the Yangtze swim: Loyalty to Mao brought honor, and those who went to the greatest extremes to demonstrate their loyalty won instant popularity and adult approval.

From that day on, Zhang channeled all his unruly energies into Cultural Revolution activism, turning from boyish mischief to Red Guard witch-hunts and from juvenile egotism to feverish worship of Mao. Just as he had plunged into the Yangtze River, Zhang delved into the radical movement, outdoing his peers time after time and winning ever greater popularity and official acclaim.

One of Zhang's first lessons in revolutionary activism came at the start of the Cultural Revolution in 1966. Thousands of Red Guards were swarming through Shanghai chanting Mao's quotations, ransacking homes, and persecuting people. Zhang watched as their factions competed to prove their loyalty to Mao's cause. Erecting makeshift platforms at major intersections, the teenage zealots carried out public inquisitions of accused "landlords, rich people, reactionaries, bad elements, and rightists." The Red Guards scoffed at their victims' weak replies and beat them viciously with their Sam Browne leather army belts.

Zhang often joined the huge crowds of onlookers that gathered to jeer at the victims. He didn't flinch at the beatings. He imagined the victims were truly the evil "class enemies" reviled by Mao. Like most Chinese, Zhang believed Mao knew everything. As he watched the beatings, a quote of Mao's ran through his mind: "Sweep away enemies like leaves in autumn wind, / Embrace comrades with the full warmth of spring."

After entering fifth grade, Zhang began waging his own political struggles in imitation of the older Red Guards. He led other primary school students in attacking teachers as spies and capitalist roaders. Zhang's enthusiasm impressed Maoist authorities at his school, who named him a head of the little Red Guards. From then on, whenever Mao made a speech, Zhang immediately led his troops on a march through the city that often lasted into the middle of the night. Holding Mao's portrait high, they banged on drums and shouted slogans to publicize the chairman's words, reverently lauded as "the latest instruction."

Zhang excelled at memorizing Mao's writings, which along with a handful of Marxist classics made up the school curriculum. For three years, he was the school's representative to a citywide congress on "The Lively Study and Use of Mao's Works." At the congress, Zhang took the stage and mechanically recited Mao's quotations. "No one must remain outside of the revolution!" he yelled in a high juvenile voice as the other youths applauded.

In only a few months, Zhang had gone from being a nobody to being one of the most popular boys at school. He was cocky with success. At the primary school graduation ceremony, he achieved the height of revolutionary fashion by wearing a genuine People's Liberation Army cap given to him by a family friend in the air force.

Zhang's parents, too, were proud of their son. Like a good little Red Guard, he helped them cook, clean, and go to market. He took charge of his little brother, sister, and a new baby girl. In a "Red Diary," he diligently recorded his "revolutionary" deeds. And in keeping with Maoist self-sacrifice, he saved money. He filled each page of his composition books three times over, first in pencil, then in ink pen, and finally with an ink brush. When he practiced calligraphy, he didn't use paper at all. He brushed the characters on his desk and wiped it clean with a wet rag. Zhang's mother stopped beating him and praised him instead.

With growing self-confidence, Zhang ascended to new heights of Maoist activism when he entered secondary school in the fall of 1970. Almost at once, he was recruited as a full-fledged Red Guard and put in charge of a platoon of fifty others. He often led his teenage platoon into Shanghai's busy intersections to inspect the clothing of passersby. Frumpy olive PLA uniforms were the politically sanctioned dress code; snappier fashions such as pointy-toed shoes or tapered trousers were "bourgeois." When Zhang and other Red Guards spotted someone wearing fitted pants, they halted the person and slit open the pant legs with scissors. When they spied dainty shoes, they ripped them off their wearer and flung them away, drawing riotous cheers from the mob. "Everyone was terrified," said Zhang. "No one dared oppose us."

Zhang's status as a Red Guard leader won him not only popularity but also political privileges. For example, he was allowed access to classified party documents. One day in late 1971, he was summoned to hear a crucial announcement on Lin Biao, a PLA commander and Mao's designated successor. According to the party, Lin perished in a plane crash in Mongolia in September 1971 after a failed plot to assassinate Mao. Zhang listened solemnly as Lin was condemned for "betraying the party, betraying the country, and destroying himself."

By 1973, China was convulsed by a mass campaign against "the swindler," Lin Biao. Leftist authorities put Zhang in charge of the school's campaign, choosing him out of 600 students to head a "great criticism writing group" directing propaganda for the entire school. Zhang wrote several articles attacking Lin. One day, his teacher announced that one of his articles would be aired by the Shanghai People's Broadcasting Station at 7 P.M. Zhang flushed with pride as he sat in his family's run-down apartment listening to the radio announcer read his article to more than 1 million listeners. Once again, his pure faith in Maoism had been rewarded with public acclaim.

Zhang's identity and his outlook were increasingly defined by his role in Mao's revolution. Nevertheless, even as he swore to follow Mao to the end, the ardent Red Guard retained an innate curiosity. Every so often, his inquiring mind encountered some glimmer of unorthodox thought. The mystery of a banned book, the strange-sounding language of a censored foreign news report, a whispered account of a "revisionist" Soviet film—all of these held strong appeal for a teenager thirsty for knowledge. More important, a series of enlightened mentors showed Zhang glimpses of a reality beyond the Alice-in-Wonderland world of Mao. None of these alone would shake Zhang's bedrock faith in Maoism. But they encouraged a natural inquisitiveness that would lead him, years later, to confront the party's machinations and the monstrous lies of Mao's rule.

Ironically, it was often Zhang's privileged status as a Red Guard leader that gave him exposure to ideas and mentors that flouted Maoism. For example, Zhang gained rare access to a library. All Shanghai's libraries were officially closed by 1967. But school authorities allowed Zhang to visit the library in Huangpu district to research his propaganda essays.

Every week, Zhang would mount the steps of the neoclassical brown brick library to check out Marxist texts and help maintain the collection. One day, he was sent into the stacks of banned books to inspect each volume for insects. Alone in a roomful of forbidden writings, he found the sheer force of curiosity overwhelming. When he spotted a dusty book of verse by the romantic English poet Lord Byron, he quietly tucked it under his arm and later hid it in his satchel.

That evening, Zhang hurried from the stuffy library. As he stepped into the crisp autumn air and headed down a tree-lined street filled with factory workers cycling home, he felt his anxiety ease. But the knowledge of the book in his bag preoccupied him. His impatience grew until late that night at home when he was finally alone. As his brother and two sisters slept nearby, Zhang lowered a bare lightbulb suspended from the ceiling by an electrical wire. He covered the bulb with a newspaper to soften the glow and turned it on. Then he quietly removed the book from his satchel and opened the musty cover. For the rest of the night, he reveled, wide-eyed, in the feats of Byron's swashbuckling brigands. Byron's defiant heroes, like the Spanish adventurer Don Juan, tantalized the young Red Guard.

From then on, the library stacks captivated Zhang's young mind as irresistibly as hidden treasure. With the tacit consent of sympathetic library staff, he smuggled out dozens of other literary gems. He discovered the French novelist Stendhal and was drawn to the young protagonist in *The Red and the Black*. He delved into Chinese classics such as the Qing dynasty (1644–1911) epic *The Dream of the Red Chamber*. Finally, he read banned novels by modern Chinese authors.

Each time Zhang got a new book, he read it all night. The next morning, he lent it to his friends. Soon, he set up an informal exchange of banned and classified literature. Unlike many fellow Red Guards, who had access to their parents' personal libraries, Zhang found no books at home. His mother was illiterate. His father, a bicycle repairman, lacked the time, money, and inclination to buy books or read.

Through the exchanges, Zhang had a rare chance to read *Reference News*, a classified Chinese newspaper that carried foreign press reports. Zhang studied articles on the opening to China in the early 1970s by U.S. President Richard Nixon. The reports were heavily censored, but they offered a radical contrast from the formulaic propaganda of the party-run press. "It was a completely new way of seeing things and considering problems. Even the language was different," Zhang recalled. "The more the authorities forbid knowledge, the greater our appetite."

Zhang's awakening interests were further fueled by a series of well-educated mentors, who offered insights and encouragement absent in his working-class home. Throughout Zhang's life, these mentors introduced new ideas and ways of thinking that defied the intellectual drone of Maoism. The older men enjoyed the traditional Chinese teacher-student relationship with Zhang, who treated them with respect. But all of Zhang's mentors eventually disappointed him. Because they were traditional intellectuals, their willingness to speak out was limited by a moral compulsion to remain loyal to the state. One by one, Zhang outgrew them.

It was in the darkness under a stairwell behind his family's apartment that the youngster found his first guide to enlightenment. There, in a windowless hovel barely big enough for a bed, lived Mrs. Wang. Wang Mama, as Zhang called her, was completely paralyzed on her left side, but she was kindhearted. Zhang liked to visit her after school before his parents came home from work. He often ran small errands, fetching a little rice, soy sauce, or pickled vegetable for her, and she always rewarded him with a few pennies. But what Zhang treasured most were the crippled woman's stories. Whenever she wasn't busy laboring to cook and keep house, she captivated Zhang with ghost stories and legends of martyred generals, scheming eunuchs, and willowy beauties. On summer nights, she lay on a cot under a dim street lamp entertaining Zhang and other neighborhood children who gathered around.

Unlike Zhang's parents, Mrs. Wang had *wenhua* (culture). She read newspapers and stroked a fine ink-and-brush calligraphy with her good hand. During the political inquisitions of the Cultural Revolution, she often wrote self-criticisms on behalf of illiterate neighbors who had fallen victim to attack. Zhang admired her talent and generosity and looked up to the paralyzed woman.

Once Zhang reached secondary school, his prominence as a Red Guard leader won him new mentors. Attracted by his energy and enthusiasm, some of the more open-minded teachers subtly initiated him to ideas beyond the strict confines of Maoist ideology.

Zhang got to know one teacher, Mr. Zhang, during the summer of 1971 when his entire class was sent to the Shanghai suburbs for a month of military "camp and field training." The school was heeding Mao's call on Chinese to "prepare for war" and learn from the PLA in the wake of clashes along the Sino-Soviet border in 1969. Like millions of intellectuals, teacher Zhang had been persecuted by Maoists for thinking independently. He lost his job as an engineer and was assigned to teach junior high physics. A slight, unathletic man, teacher Zhang was grateful to Zhang for shouldering his pack on the long march to Hangzhou Bay. As the two trooped down rural trails, teacher Zhang enthralled his student with accounts of banned Soviet films and rich capitalists in Shanghai's pre-Communist heyday. As he listened to the stories, Zhang began to realize how much he was missing in the stale Marxist classroom. "I saw that knowledge was something inexhaustible. This increased my thirst for it even more," Zhang said.

Zhang's most influential early mentor was a mild-mannered man named Zhu Songqiao. Because of a slight deformity—one of his arms was shorter than the other—Zhu was not assigned a job by the state. He took advantage of years of unemployment to become a self-styled renaissance scholar. His impressive grasp of ancient Chinese literature, language, archaeology, and history won him acceptance in a circle of prominent Shanghai intellectuals. Finally, he landed work as a calligraphy teacher at Zhang's school. Calligraphy was a popular fad among

Shanghai youths, and in the fall of 1973 Zhang asked Zhu for tutoring. For three or four hours a day after school, Zhang and Zhu brushed bold characters in preparation for competitions. As they worked, Zhu introduced Zhang to China's most illustrious writers and historical figures, people rarely mentioned in Marxist textbooks. The elder man further nurtured Zhang's intellect by taking him to art exhibits, museums, and calligraphy shows. Zhang quickly came to worship Zhu, in whom he found a paternal figure more inspiring than his own father.

Zhang and his mentor often strolled through Shanghai's sleepy lanes talking, sometimes until 2 A.M. One spring night in 1974 as they were out walking, a sudden cloudburst emptied the streets. The two friends took cover under the cloistered walkways of Shanghai's Jinling Road and continued on. After a lull in the conversation, Zhu turned to Zhang.

"Isn't it true," he asked, "that if a man is running a race along a very narrow track, the only way he can take the lead is to break a new path?"

"That's so," Zhang replied.

"If you are always following others, imitating others, you will never succeed. On the well-trodden path, others ahead will block you. To succeed, you must find a new road," Zhu said.

Only years afterward did Zhang understand the full heretical meaning of Zhu's subtle advice to rise from the rut of Maoism. At the time, he remained completely devoted to the Great Helmsman. But Zhu's emphasis on individual initiative persuaded Zhang that it was not enough to be a cog in the revolutionary wheel. From that time on, he was determined to break new paths in serving Mao.

When Zhang graduated from high school in July 1974, he decided to forgo a secure job assignment at a state farm or factory. Instead, heeding Mao's command to "learn from the peasants," he volunteered to lead a team of Shanghai youths to live and work in a remote rural village.

Zhang's bold gesture delighted Shanghai's radical leaders, who exploited his naive enthusiasm for their own political ends. They wanted to bolster Mao's drive to send city youths "down to the countryside and up to the mountains." More than 16 million urban youths were sent to work on rural production brigades during the Cultural Revolution, 1 million of them from Shanghai. But by 1974 the flow of youths from Shanghai had slowed to a trickle as reports spread of bitter hardship on the communes. Shanghai's ultraleftists seized on Zhang's decision as a way to revive the campaign.

A few weeks after graduation, Shanghai officials dispatched Zhang on a special trip to Jiangxi Province, which along with Yunnan, Heilongjiang, and Anhui provinces were controlled by leftists. Upon his return, the officials named him head of the "educated youths down-to-the-countryside and up-to-the-mountains Mao Zedong propaganda team" and organized rallies at Shanghai schools to drum up support. "The countryside is a great, vast expanse—ripe for youths who want to temper themselves and contribute to the revolution!" Zhang told his audiences. His zeal persuaded hundreds of youths to give up Shanghai's comforts for a politically pure life on remote provincial farms.

Zhang's activism won him celebrity status in Shanghai. Local newspapers printed his speeches and photograph. For months, his picture hung alongside those of propaganda film stars and other "advanced" figures at the Huang Kai Photo Studio, Shanghai's largest, on bustling Nanjing Road. The photograph showed Zhang standing before an artificial backdrop of terraced rice paddies and an ox pulling a plow. Sporting a PLA uniform and the Red Guard armband, the eighteen-year-old Zhang was a model for Shanghai teens.

But Zhang's day of glory was yet to come. On the clear, sunny morning of March 18, 1975, the Red Guard and more than 200 recruits were honored at a massive send-off staged by city authorities. With bright red paper flowers pinned to his uniform, Zhang marched into a huge rally of several thousand people at the municipal government auditorium. The vice director of Shanghai's revolutionary committee, Wang Yiping, led a drove of officials in hailing the youths. Amid warm applause, Zhang's mother, flushed with pride, took to the stage and spoke a few sentences. Then Zhang mounted the podium.

"Doesn't Chairman Mao say we must become one with the peasants?" Zhang's voice boomed over the loudspeakers. "Let's go throw ourselves into peasant life!"

Then, to loud clapping, Zhang led his recruits outside and into awaiting minivans. "Chairman Mao waves his hand and I march forward," they yelled, chanting a favorite Red Guard slogan.

The motorcade slowly started off from Waitan Park on the quay of the Huangpu River, led by a corps of marchers beating drums and banging gongs. The loud procession inched through the heart of the city, bringing traffic to a standstill. Zhang and his entourage waved to the hundreds of thousands of residents who lined the parade route to the Shanghai train station. They rode along Nanjing Road and up Tibet Road, right past Zhang's house. "Of course, my parents felt very glorious," Zhang said. Never before had Zhang felt so intensely devoted to Mao. Never before had his devotion won him such vast recognition by his family, friends, and society. But the clanging gongs and jarring drums of the spectacular send-off could just as well have marked the beginning of the end of his worship of Mao.

Ironically, it was the sheer strength of Zhang's trust in Mao that ultimately shattered his faith. He stepped aboard the train to the rural backwater of Jiangxi Province because he believed unswervingly in Mao's leadership. But as the train lurched out of Shanghai's cavernous station, Zhang embarked on a discovery of the China that Mao's propagandists never wrote about. In the countryside, he came face-to-face with the brutal toll of Mao's campaigns on human life and the insidious lies that underpinned Communist rule.

Night fell as the steam engine chugged past the dormant rice fields of Zhejiang Province and began a slow climb into the rolling hills of Jiangxi. Zhang and his six young team members were too excited to sleep. He looked out the window as the sun rose over the red earth and rugged pine-scrub landscape of Jiangxi. Already, he felt closer to Mao. The train was heading southwest toward the Jinggang

Mountains on the Jiangxi-Hunan border. As a young guerrilla fighter, Mao had arrived at the foot of the Jinggang cliffs in October 1927. He held out in the rugged mountains for more than a year, but his 8,000 peasant recruits suffered heavy casualties in raids against Chiang Kai-shek's Nationalist forces. By the time Chiang's forces drove them from the mountains in December 1928, only about 4,000 men were left. Zhang had listened to stories of Mao's heroism in the Jinggang Mountains since he was a boy. Now, he thought, he was following Mao's footsteps.

The next day, the train jolted to a stop in the city of Xinyu, just seventy-five miles from the Jinggang peaks. Zhang and the other youths loaded their bedrolls and rucksacks into the back of a truck, which rumbled down a dirt road on the three-hour trip to Nangang commune on the hilly border of Jiangxi's Shanggao County.

When Zhang and his comrades arrived at the commune's tea farm, the villagers came out to welcome them with food and sorghum liquor. In a symbolic gesture, the youths planted pine saplings, which they called "taking-root trees." As a commune official snapped their photograph, the youths swore to stay in the countryside forever. "That day marked the climax, the high tide of my faith in Mao," said Zhang.

On the tea farm, Zhang immediately took a post on the revolutionary committee, the administrative organ that ran each level of government during the Cultural Revolution. Zhang was vice director of the five-man committee. The director, a forty-year-old peasant cadre, felt his power threatened by the upstart educated youth from Shanghai. The farm's twenty peasant laborers were also suspicious. But unlike most Shanghai youths, Zhang knew something about the Chinese peasant mentality from his time in the countryside as a child. To head off resentment, he mimicked the earthy ways of the villagers.

Zhang ate with the peasants. Squatting on his haunches, he shoveled down rice and bland vegetables doctored with fiery peppers. He often talked and joked with the peasants, but most important, he worked with them and worked hard. Zhang knew peasants judged strangers by how they labored, not by what they said. Every day he rose at daybreak and farmed for two hours. He gulped a bowl of rice gruel for breakfast, then headed back to the fields. He worked until dark, resting only briefly at lunch. Zhang opened up wasteland, dug irrigation ditches, hoed, picked weeds, and spread manure. He learned to make green and black tea, to boil the leaves and roll them with his bare hands. He also farmed rice, peanuts, vegetables, and watermelon. In summer, he went barefoot like the peasants. On the hottest days, he stripped down to a pair of shorts, with a straw hat to shield him from the sun. Despite a huge effort, Zhang was humiliated at first to earn only eight work points a day. But he exerted himself until he collected the full ten points expected of an able-bodied male farmer. By the end of each year, Zhang's points earned him between 100 yuan to 300 yuan, which he sent to his needy family.

Zhang's solid work and endurance impressed the peasants and local leaders, who had rarely seen a city youth who labored as if "gambling his life," as they put it. Commune officials named Zhang a "model" youth and gave his father an all-expenses-paid tour of the commune.

A propaganda photo showing Zhang Weiguo (seated, center) at the Nangang commune tea farm in Jiangxi Province in 1975 discussing Mao's works with other rusticated city youths.

It was only at night, in a brick dormitory shared with another youth, that Zhang reverted to a city Red Guard. He lay on a bed of wooden planks padded with rice husks and read for hours. He read indiscriminately, picking up books on animal husbandry, meteorology, and Marxism from a jumble of volumes beside his bed. Mao had declared that "man can conquer nature," and Zhang wanted to prove there was nothing he could not do. The village had no electricity, so Zhang read under a kerosene lamp. He strained his eyes, permanently damaging his vision. Each morning, he wiped off a telltale black beard left by the kerosene smoke before heading to the fields.

Zhang adapted easily to village life, but his comrades from Shanghai had a harder time. Dismayed by the coarse peasant diet, they wrote home asking for gifts of dried meat and biscuits. Unable to shoulder heavy farm labor, they complained and dragged their feet. Partly as a result of their poor work, the tea farm faced a crisis in the summer of 1975. Young tea bushes on two of the farm's hills were overrun by weeds and tall grass. The plants also needed fertilizer. But the farm lacked the manpower to sustain the crop.

One day, commune officials offered to round up the commune's "class enemies," the perpetual scapegoats in Mao's political campaigns, and force them to do the work. About 150 of the commune's 10,000 peasants were categorized as class enemies. Many of them wore political "hats" only because some official bore a grudge against them. They were at the mercy of local authorities. No one dared defend them.

Zhang and the other farm leaders were delighted at the prospect of free man-power. In their minds, Chinese who had committed "crimes against the people" deserved to be "reformed through labor." Zhang was put in charge of supervising the political outcasts on the farm.

One morning a few days later, the class enemies trudged down the dusty road leading to the farm. They wore broad hats of straw and bamboo and loose black tunics and trousers, the traditional summer garb of peasants in the area. On their shoulders they bore long wooden hoes. They clutched small bags of dry rice; the tea farm would not feed them. Some of them were seventy years old. Many of them had to rise before daybreak to reach the farm, and some walked ten miles from their home villages. They moved along slowly, their faces blank.

When he spotted the spiritless group, Zhang felt a pang in his chest, but he quickly put on the mien of Mao's loyal foot soldier and barked commands at the political pariahs. "Come on! Get going!" he shouted, gripping a wooden rod and motioning toward the plantation.

The outcasts set to work pulling weeds, hoeing, and spreading manure around the young tea bushes. As the sun arced higher, the heat grew suffocating. One of the Shanghai youths fainted from exhaustion. But the forced laborers, all peasants tempered by years of hardship, maintained a steady, graceful tempo. At noon, Zhang gave them each a ladle of water and allowed them to cook their meal of rice and searing hot peppers. After a short rest in the shade, Zhang set them to work again. If the laborers failed to work "cleanly," removing every weed and tuft of grass, he loudly berated them. If they chatted or joked, he denounced them se-verely. It was forbidden to "speak or act carelessly." Zhang's harshness was a way of demonstrating his own devotion to "class struggle." He forced the victims to toil until sundown, then sent them on the long walk home.

This routine continued for about two weeks. But as the days wore on, Zhang grew uneasy about the class enemies. He noticed that they worked much harder than the city youths. They rarely loafed and never complained or grumbled. Zhang felt a twinge of sympathy, especially for the elderly peasants. He began to let them rest more and gave them extra water. For the first time, doubts about Mao's teachings crept into his mind. "They were human beings like me. Mao, in his little red book, talked about revolutionary humanism. But the way we treated these people didn't seem to jibe with what he said."

Zhang looked around and realized none of the local peasants were attacking the "bad elements." It dawned on him why—they knew the victims personally. Suddenly "class struggle," which had long been only abstract words to Zhang, be-came painfully concrete. From then on, he no longer abused class enemies but treated them with tolerance or even with distant sympathy.

As Zhang's radical outlook softened, he felt his ties with the peasants deepen. One friend, an amiable basket weaver named Old Pan, often invited Zhang to visit his home in the mountains on the commune's edge. Old Pan often traveled the countryside peddling his straw baskets, hats, and mats, and Zhang enjoyed listening to his gossip. Old Pan's business, like all private enterprise, was illegal. In the heat of political campaigns, he often fled into the hilly no-man's land along the provincial border to evade punishment.

From offhand remarks of friends like Old Pan, Zhang began to discover the peasants' true feelings about Mao's 1949 revolution. To Zhang's surprise, much of what they said flew in the face of party propaganda. Many of them seemed to prefer life under the old order. Peasants contended that landlords, the party's arch-villains, had treated them better than Communist cadres, who constantly persecuted them. Before 1949, the peasants said, they lived as they pleased. Now, they complained, "if you want to sleep late you have to ask the production brigade for permission."

One day while chatting with Zhang, Old Pan motioned to a naked hillside across from the doorway of his mountain hut. He said that when invading Japanese troops reached the area in the 1930s, he and other villagers hid in a dense pine forest that covered the hills. "Now, the trees are all gone," he sighed.

Old Pan explained that most of the trees were chopped down during the Great Leap Forward in a mad rush to raise industrial output. Whipped up in the 1958–1960 campaign, peasants razed forests in Nangang and across China, using the wood to fuel some 1 million backyard steel furnaces. Zhang was shocked to learn the Great Leap had caused such devastation. He had never questioned official statements declaring the campaign a success. Zhang's encounters with Old Pan and other rural Chinese lent a bitter irony to Mao's dictum to learn from the peasants. He had learned a great deal indeed.

Despite these early misgivings, Zhang remained fundamentally committed to Mao and the party. On December 26, 1975, Mao's eighty-second birthday, Zhang stood before a group of peasant cadres and solemnly took his vow of initiation into the Communist Party. But the longer he remained in the countryside, the more mistrustful Zhang became of his party and ultimately of Mao himself.

In early 1976, Zhang decided to leave the tea farm. He had fallen out with the other Shanghai youths, who threw their energies into petty political squabbles instead of peasant life. Zhang still intended to settle in the countryside. But he felt the malice of his peers, who were resentful of his success, had poisoned the atmosphere on the farm. Commune authorities approved his request for a transfer to a reservoir project a few miles away.

Dug out basketful by basketful by 20,000 peasants, the Long Tunnel Reservoir in the mountains bordering the commune was typical of the massive works projects ordered by Mao. Zhang lived and worked with the ordinary laborers. Every day from dawn to dusk, he hauled large baskets of sand, sludge, and rock on bamboo shoulder poles. He learned to walk with short lilting steps and balance swaying loads of up to 200 pounds. He competed with the other peasants to see who could carry the most. Zhang also helped tunnel through a mountain to create a channel for overflow from the reservoir. Using a pick and mallet he chipped out a hole for dynamite, placed the sticks inside, and ran back while the blast ripped through the mountain valley. Once an explosion accidentally killed several workers.

Zhang Weiguo and a friend at the coal mine in Jiangxi Province in 1976.

After a few months at the reservoir, Zhang was assigned to a local coal mine. There, he found worse hazards than at the reservoir site. Miners were frequently poisoned by the seepage of underground gas or killed by blasts when the gas was carelessly ignited in the pit. Nearby, a deserted mine was filled with rainwater. When the miners accidentally broke through into an old shaft, the water rushed in and drowned them. There were few safeguards at the primitive mine. The shafts were so narrow that the colliers had to crawl into them and haul out the baskets of coal with ropes held between their teeth. Their ragged clothes, secured with straw belts and black with coal dust, steadily shed cotton stuffing from rips in the cloth.

Wearing a headlamp and tall rubber boots, Zhang often labored with the miners. The coal pit reminded him of the propaganda film *Liaoyuan* (Set the Prairie Ablaze). In the film, Mao visits a dilapidated coal mine in the 1920s to rally workers to strike and join the revolution. Zhang believed that after 1949 China had eradicated such oppressive work conditions. But at the Jiangxi coal pit, he saw miners who in 1976 were far worse off than the on-screen colliers rallied by Mao in the 1920s. Zhang was especially distressed by how eager peasants were to work at the mine despite the cruel and hazardous conditions.

For the first time, Zhang began to see peasant life for what it was, rather than as the rustic utopia painted by Mao's propagandists. He understood the desperation with which many peasants sought release from the hardship and monotony of the farm. "I realized how it was for peasants who spent their entire lives sweating on the land with no chance to break away from the bitterness and poverty," Zhang said. "They wanted to work in the coal mine, even though it meant risking their lives, just so they could earn a salary and escape tilling the fields."

Zhang stopped short of viewing the peasants' suffering as an indictment of Mao or the Communist system. Rather, he saw it as evidence of misguided policies or the incompetence of local party officials. He clung to an old Chinese saying about Buddhism: "The scriptures are not wrong; only the monks recite them incorrectly." Mao was still Zhang's god, and communism his religion. But Zhang saw that, at a minimum, the party's economic policies had failed miserably to curtail poverty and backwardness in the countryside.

Zhang's rising doubts over the party's programs made his new job as a propagandist increasingly difficult. He was assigned to a commune work team that indoctrinated peasants in the party line. He led political study groups, put up posters, and staged rallies. After three months at the coal mine, Zhang's work team moved to a village. At the time, a nationwide campaign was raging against Chinese leader Deng Xiaoping, who had been stripped of his posts by Mao in April 1976 and accused of plotting a capitalist restoration. As documents denouncing Deng blared from the village loudspeakers, Zhang and his team were ordered to "link theory with reality" and attack Deng-inspired evildoers. Zhang's team targeted the "capitalist tails" among the villagers: peasants who used their tiny family plots to grow cash crops for sale on the market. Zhang's team members discovered one peasant growing garlic. They thrust a dunce cap on his head, draped a wreath of garlic bulbs around his neck as evidence of his "crime," and marched him around the village to the bang of a gong. As Zhang watched the farmer being humiliated, his heart sank. "The peasants' lives are bitter, so they grow some cash crops to improve their lot, and then we attack them for being capitalist," Zhang thought. "Socialism is supposed to be better than capitalism. But we are depriving the peasants of the power to get rich! How are they supposed to prosper?"

Zhang decided he had to quit the propaganda team and find a way to help the peasants rise out of poverty. When the party announced a plan for educated youths to set up rural factories, Zhang jumped at the idea. He proposed starting a factory to make and repair farm machinery. Eager to groom Zhang as a local cadre, commune officials agreed and named him factory director and party secretary.

In the summer of 1976, Zhang returned to Shanghai for the first time to try to obtain equipment for his factory. Ma Tianshui, Shanghai's leftist party secretary whom everyone called Ma Lao, or "the revered Comrade Ma," authorized a load of used machinery for Zhang's factory. Zhang rushed back to Jiangxi with the gear, two trucks, and five tractors. He recruited twenty youths and eighty peasants and started work.

One afternoon in early September, Zhang was at the factory when the public loudspeaker began crackling from its pole on the road outside. It was 4 P.M., too early for the usual evening news broadcast, Zhang thought. Then he heard the solemn voice of a male announcer: "Comrade Mao Zedong, our esteemed and beloved great leader, passed away at 00:10 hours today, September 9, 1976, in Beijing."

Other factory workers, hearing the news, rushed from their workshops to the loudspeaker. A woman student from Shanghai burst into tears. Zhang was stunned. His initial reaction to Mao's death was disbelief. "How could Mao die?" Zhang asked himself. On a purely emotional level, Zhang had never wholly rejected propaganda claiming that Mao was "all-powerful and omnipresent," a god-man who would live "10,000 years." Yet however inexplicably, the Great Helmsman was gone. Zhang felt that he and all of China were cast adrift.

Mechanically, Zhang began supervising the mourning. He halted production and lowered the factory flag to half-mast. The single-story brick factory was quickly transformed along with other workplaces across China into a mourning hall. Workers hung a huge portrait of Mao, under which they laid wreaths of white paper chrysanthemums. They draped black cloth on the walls in the workshops, dormitory, and canteen.

Mao's funeral was scheduled for 3 P.M. on September 18. The day was sweltering. At noon, Zhang got into a factory car and rode down a bumpy dirt road toward the next brigade. After picking up the commune's top party cadres, the car drove an hour to Shanggao, the county seat, and pulled up in front of a large sports arena. Zhang and the other cadres elbowed their way into the stadium. The air was stifling. All around, people were waving bamboo fans and mopping sweat from their foreheads. Already, more than 10,000 people stood wearing the traditional black armband of mourning, awaiting the nationwide radio broadcast of the funeral from Beijing. As the broadcast started, people all over China were asked to stand at attention, in silence, for three minutes. In Shanggao stadium, though, violent sobbing broke the quiet. As the half-day ceremony and eulogies wore on, many people fainted and were carried out. Zhang stood watching in a daze, his heart drained of feeling, his mind numb.

That night, Zhang kept a lone vigil in the factory. China's leaders, paranoid over the possibility of a military invasion after Mao's death, had placed the country on a first-level war alert. Across China, party secretaries at every *danwei* were ordered to await a call to arms. Zhang sat beside a wooden crank phone that connected him to the local operator.

There was a surreal quality to that night. Under the brilliant white light of a full autumn moon, the fields of late-ripening rice and the surrounding hillsides shone as if covered with frost. Dark shadows filled the contours of the land and stretched out behind every tree and village dwelling. The scene was so striking that despite the war alert Zhang's girlfriend urged him to take her on a walk in the nearby hills. In those days of revolutionary puritanism, one had to be discreet about girlfriends. But a stroll after dark never drew much attention. And Zhang was fond of Little Zhang, a peasant-born girl from Nanchang who had graduated from a worker-peasant-soldier university. He agreed to meet her at 8 P.M.

Still, Zhang felt uneasy and preoccupied. After accompanying Little Zhang on a stroll of only half an hour, he excused himself and rushed back to the phone. He was afraid the commune's party secretary would call. Everyone feared secretary

Ya, a dwarfish, bespectacled man of about forty with thick lips and thin patience. Ya was known as an ultraleftist and fierce critic of anything smelling of capitalism. He was also very smart and made speeches without using any notes. Whenever he spoke, he never looked at his audience but rolled up his eyes so only the whites showed.

Secretary Ya never called. The wooden crank phone sat mute. No foreign troops invaded. And Zhang sat up in solitude all night, watching the harvest moon rise into brightness and then slowly sink and fade into the blue dawn.

As occurs with many profound losses, Zhang's feelings of denial over Mao's death soon turned to anger—only his was directed against Mao and was prompted by a dramatic political twist. On October 6, Mao's widow Jiang Qing and the rest of her Gang of Four were arrested. The four were accused of myriad crimes ranging from fabricating Mao's statements to inciting fighting among the masses. Zhang also heard that Ma Tianshui, the Shanghai leftist who authorized equipment for his factory, had been purged along with other allies of the gang. Ma returned home to Shandong Province and later went insane.

The precipitous downfall of the gang startled Zhang by exposing the dark recesses of Chinese politics. Only days earlier, Jiang Qing had figured prominently in the broadcast of Mao's funeral. Moreover, after watching Mao and the gang together for years, Zhang found unbelievable the party's claim that Mao was merely a victim. He recalled reading some leaflets vilifying Mao and other Cultural Revolution leaders in Shanghai earlier in the year. The pamphlets had proliferated after the April 5, 1976, Tiananmen Square incident in Beijing, when some 100,000 Chinese gathered to pay their respects to the late moderate premier, Zhou Enlai. Now, Zhang believed the leaflets; he finally accepted Mao's mortality and fallibility.

Zhang felt deeply betrayed. For years, he had modeled his life after Mao's. He had planned to move up the party ranks from the grass roots to become a leader in Mao's image. Now, Mao's death had discredited much of what Zhang believed in: the Cultural Revolution, Red Guards, the down-to-the-countryside movement. Zhang's zeal for power evaporated. The part of him that had thrived on being a Red Guard commander, model youth, and party secretary faded. His dream of a political career appeared utterly naive. "One day, you could be in a high political post. The next day, you were in prison, a scapegoat," he said. "Chinese politics was brutal and black, very black. I knew I wasn't suited for that kind of career."

The party's deception pushed Zhang to turn inward. His trust in Mao shattered, he had to rely on himself. But he felt hampered. Years of indoctrination had left him ignorant. Zhang realized that he vitally needed knowledge in order to cast off Maoism completely and forge a new career. Amid this introspection, another side of Zhang's personality emerged: his curiosity and intellectual drive. The same spirit that drove Zhang to smuggle banned books from the library in 1974 now spurred him on in a single-minded quest for learning. He vowed that as long as he remained in the countryside, he would devote himself to study.

In the summer of 1977, Zhang left the factory. He returned to the tea farm and took a job overseeing an agricultural research institute. The institute tested new hybrids of rice and breeds of duck and conducted other experiments aimed at boosting the farm's output. Zhang found the practical, scientific work of the institute refreshing after years of impulsive political activism.

Meanwhile, Zhang watched as pressure mounted among the millions of displaced urban youths for a massive exodus from the countryside. Zhang lingered longer in the village than most youths. He genuinely liked the peasants and their easygoing ways. But eventually he, too, decided to pull up his rural roots and start anew in the city.

As Chinese New Year approached in early 1979, Zhang left the farm to spend the holiday with his family in Shanghai. One chilly afternoon, a green Soviet-made Volga sedan pulled up to the mouth of Tibet Road a few doors from his home. Out stepped a tall gray-haired official in a military uniform. It was Li Donglu, a member of Shanghai's party committee and a high-ranking PLA commissar. Flanked by a coterie of bodyguards and secretaries, Li made his way down the lane and knocked at Zhang's door. Leaders like Li still considered Zhang a model youth, and Li had come to extend a traditional New Year greeting.

After Zhang invited him in for tea, Li inquired about Zhang's future plans. Zhang replied that he was one of the last city youths left on the Jiangxi commune and wanted to return to Shanghai to study. "*Hen hao* [Very good]," Li said in a Shandong accent.

Zhang was elated. With Li's backing, he could easily persuade commune authorities to release him. More important, Zhang thought Li's attitude reflected a new open-mindedness among China's post-Mao leaders. Zhang had read about the pragmatic changes initiated by Deng Xiaoping and other reformers at a party plenum in December. The reformers criticized a dogmatic adherence to Mao's policies and instructions, urging Chinese instead to "emancipate" their minds. They banned the use of Mao's slogan "take class struggle as the key link" and shifted the country's main agenda to economic modernization. Realizing that China required scientists, skilled managers, and technocrats to modernize, the reformers also began rebuilding an educational system decimated by the Cultural Revolution. They rehabilitated teachers persecuted by Red Guards, reopened schools and libraries, and reinstated a national entrance exam for universities. They also removed some ideological barriers to learning, reviving many disciplines that had been "forbidden zones" under Mao.

After the New Year, Zhang returned to Jiangxi for the last time. He gained permission to leave the tea farm to teach at the commune's primary school. Zhang and ten other teachers instructed 600 students at the one-story red-brick school. In his spare time, Zhang studied for the university entrance exam. He repaired a broken shortwave radio from the commune broadcasting station and at night practiced English by listening to the Voice of America (VOA). He wrote to the VOA's Hong Kong bureau and received a free program schedule and English study guide. Years later, the correspondence would be used against Zhang in his first real conflict with Communist authorities.

After the school year ended in July 1979, Zhang packed his bags and traveled to Shanghai for the national university exam. A few weeks later, Zhang was making repairs on the home of one of his old teachers when his mother, Ying, rushed in. "You've passed!" she cried, her eyes brimming with tears.

Ying was overjoyed that her son would enter the university, a high honor for a Chinese parent. She was even happier that after five years in a remote provincial outpost, Zhang was home to stay. Zhang read her thoughts, and his mind raced back to Jiangxi's lonely hills with a fleeting sentimentality. But Zhang knew college was his only hope for a new life. So vivid was his memory of feasting on books from the Huangpu library that he had asked to study librarianship. As fate would have it, though, the Communist regime opted to educate Zhang in politics and law, a decision it would later regret.

On September 1, 1979, Zhang walked through the gates of the East China College of Politics and Law in northwestern Shanghai. The college had been shut down during the Cultural Revolution, and Zhang's class was the first to be admitted since its reopening. Living conditions were spartan. Zhang arrived at the concrete dormitory room and found he would share it with fourteen other young men. They had already piled their books, bedrolls, and other belongings along the walls.

Zhang's reputation as a Communist activist followed him to campus. Not long after classes started, school authorities asked Zhang to head a party branch for students. To their annoyance, Zhang refused, saying he needed more time to study. Zhang's decision underscored his repugnance for the vagaries of politics and his growing desire for intellectual freedom. "Party politics had lost all meaning for me. Whatever knowledge I gained would be my own."

During his freshman year, Zhang studied well, earned high marks, and ranked first or second in his class. But by the second year, he had grown dissatisfied. The college, he discovered, was a bastion of hard-line Marxists. The mission of the college was to train cadres for China's party-controlled legal apparatus, and hostility toward free thinking pervaded the classrooms. All students were required to take the same dry courses heavily laden with Marxism and party history. The teachers, mainly educated in the Soviet Union in the 1950s, forced students to learn by memorizing outdated textbooks.

The regimented atmosphere also imbued campus life. As future officials, students were expected to obey a strict code of discipline. Military drills were mandatory. A nightly curfew meant lights out at 10 P.M. At midnight, the college gate was locked. Another regulation warned sternly: "Love affairs are impermissible." "For the first year we were relatively well behaved," Zhang said. "After that, we made our own arrangements."

The heavy-handed indoctrination and boot-camp discipline fired defiance in Zhang and his spirited roommates. When the lights went out at night, Zhang reached up and screwed in a bulb wired to a wall socket that he had secretly installed. The bulb was rigged up under the mosquito netting that draped over his bunkbed, so Zhang could read as late as he liked. When Zhang and his roommates returned after midnight to find the college gate locked, they boosted each other over the wall. Zhang's room became known on campus as a "hot and noisy" (*renao*) place. By day he and his roommates played soccer or visited friends. At night they sat up debating ideas, listening to foreign shortwave broadcasts, and drinking. They threw back the cheapest rice wine and Shanghai's notorious Brightness Beer. As for dating, Zhang and his friends creatively skirted school rules.

Zhang also rebelled against the formulaic teaching. He refused to do more than the minimum of coursework, joining other students in declaring "Long live sixty points!"—a pun on the Red Guard mantra "Long live Chairman Mao." Sixty points was the lowest passing mark on exams. To Zhang, anything higher represented a wasted effort. He often skipped class altogether to explore sources of learning outside the college walls.

Zhang didn't have to look far. Beyond the college gates, intellectual ferment was bubbling in Shanghai and cities across China in 1980. Under Deng and his protégés, Communist China was opening its doors to foreign influence, freeing market forces, and relaxing social controls on an unprecedented scale. Emboldened by the changes, Chinese were drinking in ideas from Western political theory, psychology, and other fields of thought banned under Mao. In late 1978 and early 1979, hundreds of Chinese in Beijing had mounted posters on a wall west of the Forbidden City calling for democracy and human rights. The party shut down Democracy Wall and arrested its leading activists by that spring. But in Shanghai and elsewhere, Chinese continued to make speeches, print unofficial journals, and put up posters demanding greater freedoms.

Zhang often biked to Shanghai's more liberal campuses to listen to speakers and scan wall posters and "blackboard newspapers." It was during a visit to East China Teachers College that he encountered Professor Lei Zhenxiao, whose thinking would have a huge impact on Zhang. Lei, a short man with deep-set eyes, was a self-proclaimed expert in "talent studies." Lei had bolted to intellectual prominence soon after Deng took power by coining the controversial slogan "Reform needs human resources, not slaves." A former Red Guard like Zhang, Lei had gone through a similar crisis of faith after Mao's death. He emerged fiercely critical of the conformism Mao had imposed on Chinese society. Lei especially detested Maoist campaigns that urged Chinese to emulate selfless martyrs like PLA soldier Lei Feng, who aspired to be a "screw" in the revolutionary machine. Lei asserted that success came not through blindly obeying Mao but through "designing oneself."

For Zhang and other Chinese who had lived through Mao's closed, oppressive reign, Lei's advocacy of independence for the individual held explosive appeal. "You are a screw! You do whatever the government assigns you to do! This is wrong!" the peppery Lei told the enthusiastic audience at the teachers college. "To succeed in modern society, you must design yourself, you must realize yourself, you must take the initiative!" Lei preached to Zhang and others in his heavy Sichuanese accent.

Zhang left Lei's lecture with his mind reeling. He flew through Shanghai on his Eternity-brand bicycle, racing past young workers as they slowly pedaled home from state-run factories. When Zhang arrived back at his room, he flopped down on his bunk and stared up at the ceiling. "I finally realized that the great trouble with China under Mao was that there was no 'self,'" Zhang said. "Now I knew I had to realize my 'self' through my own design. I had to become an independent, free person. But how?"

To Zhang, Lei's ideas resonated with the advice of his old calligraphy teacher, Zhu Songqiao, as they strolled one rainy night in 1974. Like Zhu, Lei was urging Zhang to get off the beaten track of Maoism and use his unique strengths as an individual to break a new trail. For the first time since Mao's death, Zhang felt he was regaining a sense of direction and personal worth.

Zhang discussed Lei's motivational talk with his roommates, who were equally enthralled. Eager to learn more, Zhang began corresponding with the editors of a new magazine entitled *Talent* that drew on Lei's theories of self-improvement.

At the same time, Zhang was attracted to Lei's democratic political beliefs, which stemmed naturally from his faith in the individual. Lei was convinced that by investing power in the citizenry, democracies would always be superior to Communist regimes. As a former Beijing Red Guard, he stumped for Western democracy using colorful terms that Zhang and ordinary Chinese could understand.

Lei used a Chinese saying, "A new official must make three contributions," to explain the advantages of the U.S. electoral system. Mao ruled China for decades and ónly had to make three contributions, he said, but American presidents must make three contributions in every four-year term. "So of course China is backward compared to America!" he concluded.

As simplistic as Lei's analysis was, it helped Zhang begin to understand the deeper problems of China's political system. Why had China undergone such catastrophes as the Great Leap Forward and the Cultural Revolution? The answer lay not only in Mao's fanaticism or the viciousness of the Gang of Four but in the system itself. China's entire party apparatus was not accountable to the people. From Beijing down to the grass roots, leaders enjoyed lifelong tenure. With a monopoly on power, the party easily muzzled popular criticism.

Inspired by Lei and others, Zhang began to look for democratic alternatives to the dictatorial system that had devastated China and deeply wounded him personally. In the goal of democratic reform, Zhang found a new mission as well as an opportunity to realize himself as a free-thinking intellectual.

From 1980 on, Zhang expanded his contacts with Shanghai's circle of independent-minded intellectuals. Along with some former teachers, including the calligrapher Zhu, Zhang organized a reading group of eight scholars. He was the youngest member. Every month, the group gathered in the cramped two-room apartment of one of the teachers to sip green tea and "discuss Heaven and earth." Books discussed ranged from Confucian classics such as the *Spring and Autumn Annals* to the memoirs of Zhang Guotao, a revolutionary veteran and onetime rival of Mao. The sessions convinced Zhang that the best learning came not from classrooms and textbooks but through informal, free-ranging dialogues with genuine scholars. "One conversation with a prince is worth ten years of reading," thought Zhang, recalling a Chinese adage.

Through his group, Zhang discovered the democratic ideas of Sun Yat-sen, a key leader of China's 1911 revolution and a founding father of the Nationalist Party. Zhang found merit in many of Sun's ideas on how to bring democracy to China. But because the Nationalists lost the civil war against the Communists for control of China, party historians and official textbooks gave Sun short shrift. Zhang wanted to fill in this blank in China's official histories and promote Sun's democratic and constitutional theories as an alternative to totalitarianism.

Determined to spread Sun's ideas, Zhang for the first time openly challenged school authorities and, indirectly, the Communist Party. He set up the first unofficial student-run organization at the college, the Sun Yat-sen Research Society. Overnight, the society became the talk of the campus. It broadcast articles over school loudspeakers, ran an influential newspaper posted on walls entitled *Explorations,* and edited a book on Sun's political thought. Sun's widow, Soong Ching-ling, agreed to pen the society's name in her calligraphy for a plaque on the college gate. As Zhang's success emboldened others, unofficial student groups proliferated on campus.

College authorities, however, worried that Zhang's maverick group was weakening their control and undermining the Communist Youth League and party-run student council. In 1982, a conservative backlash gave authorities an excuse to attack the group. The nationwide campaign to check the spread of "spiritual pollution," broadly defined as "decadent" Western culture and ideas, saw thousands of intellectuals criticized and unorthodox works suppressed. Zhang's hero, Lei Zhenxiao, was silenced when the party banned his writings and attacked him in internal documents as an "individualist." The campaign signaled Beijing's intent to restrict expression even as China freed market forces and opened to the outside world.

In early 1983, the school's party secretary denounced Zhang's group as a nest of "liberalism" and "bourgeois thinking" and closed it down. Using the classic Chinese tactic of "killing the chicken to scare the monkey," he singled out Zhang for criticism as a warning to the rest of the student body.

Zhang's first clash with party authorities delayed his mandatory state job assignment for more than three months after his graduation in July. Finally, he was assigned work as a lawyer at the Shanghai Petrochemical Factory. He was the last member of his class to get a job.

Zhang learned that the party had barred him from many government legal jobs because of "black materials" in his personal dossier. The Communist regime keeps secret files (*dang an*) on all Chinese citizens. Most people never see their papers. But Zhang learned from a sympathetic school official that his file showed he had "bourgeois tendencies." What shocked and angered Zhang most was that the evidence cited included his correspondence with the Voice of America in 1978. "I had trusted the party so totally, but even back then it didn't trust me."

In November 1983, Zhang started work as deputy legal counsel of the Shanghai Petrochemical Factory. By practicing law, he intended to find ways to advance China's legal reforms and use the law to promote social justice and democracy. But his hopes soon dimmed.

The sheer size of the factory, which was the biggest in Shanghai and an archetype of China's mammoth state-run enterprises, gave Zhang little room for innovation in his work. A sprawling compound situated some forty-five miles south of Shanghai on Hangzhou Bay, the factory was like a small self-contained city. It housed 70,000 workers and family members and boasted its own schools, hospital, movie theater, fire station, post office, bank, retirement home, police, courts, customs, and docks.

Moreover, Zhang's boss, the legal counsel, was a man in his fifties with little vision or interest beyond the day-to-day work of shuffling documents, posting regulations, and collecting stamps of approval from China's fickle bureaucrats. Frustrated by the cautiousness of his boss, Zhang often acted independently and the two clashed. Fortunately, the factory's more forward-looking director, Gu Chuankun, liked Zhang's gumption and gave him opportunities. Director Gu came to trust Zhang and his advice, jokingly calling him Lao Ye (Master Zhang).

Zhang enjoyed his camaraderie with Director Gu and the prestige of the job. He wore a sleek Western suit and silk tie and carried a leather briefcase. Every weekend, he rode home to Tibet Road in a chauffeur-driven factory car. On most weeknights, Director Gu and a dozen factory cadres and staff crammed into Zhang's dormitory room to drink beer and listen to music on a big Japanese boom box. Zhang was named head of their informal "beer-drinking society." After years of quaffing spirits with the peasants, he held his liquor better than most.

Despite these diversions, Zhang grew increasingly troubled by what his job was teaching him about China's legal system. Almost no one, he discovered, had any faith in the judiciary, which was tightly controlled by the party. The party, in turn, was above the law. Court deliberations were farcical. The real battles were fought behind the scenes, where bribery and corruption were rampant. Whoever could best manipulate the court by pulling strings with high party officials won.

In a sign of how far corruption had penetrated China, Zhang's factory in 1985 got involved in the country's biggest profiteering scandal under Communist rule. From January 1984 to March 1985, officials on the freewheeling island of Hainan had illegally resold on the mainland 89,000 imported motor vehicles and other goods worth more than $1.5 billion. But long after Beijing seized the vehicles, mainland officials kept reselling them.

Zhang's firm wanted to buy sixty of the contraband cars worth over $1 million. But customs officials in neighboring Jiangsu Province blocked the shipment in hopes of extorting profits. Immediately, officials at Zhang's factory resorted to *guanxi* (connections). They rang up Liu Bochao, a revolutionary veteran from Jiangsu who had served as the factory's vice party chief and vice head of the Shanghai police. A factory car chauffeured Liu straight to the docks at Nantong where the shipment was held. Customs officials released the cars within hours. "I wasn't directly involved in the car incident, but I enjoyed the consequences," Zhang said. Afterward, he rode home each weekend in a silver-gray Toyota luxury limousine with eight seats and a fold-down bed.

Still, Zhang realized that amid such flagrant official corruption the law could never be a noble profession in China. In a last-ditch effort to preserve his integrity, Zhang used the factory's auspices to set up a law office to handle civil and criminal cases on his own. Even then, he had to go through the *hou men* (back door) to win. Increasingly, Zhang saw himself as an accomplice to injustice.

Disillusioned with his practice, Zhang decided to confront more directly China's failure to reform its political and legal system. He persuaded the factory to sponsor two national conferences on legal reform and invited the brightest young law scholars from Beijing, Shanghai, and around the country. There, Zhang met Chen Xiaoping, a far-sighted young expert in constitutional law; the two became close friends. In his spare time, Zhang also began writing articles on legal reform for university law journals and edited an official magazine called *Shanghai Courts.*

In the summer of 1986, Zhang had a call from Xu Xiaowei, a friend and reporter at the Shanghai-based *World Economic Herald.* Xu asked Zhang to edit the newspaper's legal page while the regular editor was abroad. In a decision that would change his life, Zhang agreed.

A few weeks later, the *Herald*'s editor in chief, Qin Benli, asked to meet Zhang. So one hot, sunny morning Zhang accompanied Xu as he delivered the weekly proofs of the paper to Qin's apartment in Shanghai's old French Quarter. The two bicycled to Qin's building on the corner of Ruijin Road and Nanchang Road and climbed the stairs to room 301. Qin's wife answered the door and led them into a spacious old apartment with high ceilings. A balding, white-haired man with thick black eyebrows emerged from a back room, smoking a cigarette. It was Qin.

On first impression, Zhang thought Qin an amiable but ordinary old man. Qin's casual manner belied the fact that he was one of China's most extraordinary newsmen.

Qin was born in 1918 in Jiangsu Province to a Mongolian merchant and his Chinese wife. Like Zhang, he studied law, enrolling at Chaoyang University in Chongqing, Sichuan, during the Sino-Japanese War. Also like Zhang, Qin enraged school authorities with his democratic beliefs. He was expelled for joining a prodemocracy student movement. In the 1940s, Qin joined the Communist underground and became a party member in 1948. He believed the Communists would end the rife corruption and inequality of Chiang Kai-shek's Nationalist regime and bring democracy to China. After the 1949 revolution, Qin became a party cadre, holding senior jobs at Shanghai's *Liberation Daily* and the party mouthpiece *People's Daily* in Beijing. In 1956, Qin returned to Shanghai to run the newly revived *Wenhui Daily.*

Qin believed deeply in the aims of communism, but he opposed dictatorship by the party or Mao. He was a traditional Chinese intellectual whose highest calling was to serve the state. But he was also a loyal critic, determined as a newsman to air popular complaints to help the party correct its mistakes. When Mao urged Chinese to speak out in the Hundred Flowers campaign of 1957, Qin and other intellectuals seized the chance to vent their grievances against the party. Qin opened up the pages of the *Wenhui Daily* to a stream of critical articles. But Mao saw the tide turning against him. He launched an abrupt, sweeping crackdown in which

Qin Benli, editor in chief of the World Economic Herald, *in the newspaper's Beijing bureau in March 1989. Reuters/Bettmann.*

hundreds of thousands of Chinese intellectuals were persecuted as rightists. Qin was the target of a July 1, 1957, article written by Mao himself entitled "We Should Criticize the Bourgeois Orientation of the *Wenhui Daily.*" Qin was immediately fired as party secretary of the paper and exiled to the Shanghai suburbs to labor as a peasant. After several months on the farm, he returned briefly to Shanghai with the aid of a sympathetic leader for a low-level job on an internal party publication. He was spared the label of rightist. During the Cultural Revolution, however, Qin was again attacked and sent to one of the thousands of prisonlike May Seventh Cadre Schools set up for intellectuals and cadres suspected of harboring anti-Communist beliefs. Qin underwent years of hard labor and constant indoctrination in Maoism at the camp. Once, after seven months of solitary confinement in a cowshed, he temporarily lost the ability to speak. The constant persecution broke the health of Qin's first wife, Gu Xiaolan, the *Liberation Daily* reporter, who died of an illness as the campaign drew to a close.

Qin was finally rehabilitated in 1979 and sent back to Shanghai. The party assigned him a job as deputy director of the World Economic Research Institute at the Shanghai Academy of Social Sciences. But Qin was eager to return to journalism. In 1980, he gathered a group of veteran newsmen, many of whom had also fallen afoul of Mao, and launched the *World Economic Herald.* From his old paper, the *Wenhui Daily,* Qin was able to borrow $10,000 and some newsprint. On June 21, 1980, the first *Herald* edition appeared.

The *Herald* was Communist China's first aboveground unofficial newspaper. It was neither funded nor directly controlled by the state. In name, the paper fell under Qin's institute and the Beijing-based China World Economics Society, but in practice it was relatively independent. Qin decided what to publish and ran the paper's day-to-day operations and staffing with little interference from its two academic parent organizations.

The *Herald* further evaded government censorship by slipping through the cracks in the Chinese bureaucracy. Beijing usually relegated control of the *Herald* to local authorities in Shanghai, where the paper was based and registered. But Shanghai hesitated to assume responsibility for the *Herald* because its reporting and circulation were national and international in scope.

Qin's powerful connections in Beijing also helped shield the *Herald* from political meddling. The paper's most prominent patron was Qian Junrui, an influential economist and the former secretary of Premier Zhou Enlai, as well as an old friend of Qin's. In 1980, Qian, who headed the China World Economics Society, agreed to cooperate with Qin in founding the *Herald*. He became the paper's publisher. Qian was close to Deng's two key protégés at the time, party secretary Hu Yaobang and Premier Zhao Ziyang. When the *Herald* came under attack, Qian often wrote self-criticisms on its behalf to assuage the leadership. "Whatever happens, I can handle things up here," Qian reassured Qin from Beijing in tense times. "You people down there [in Shanghai] just write for all you're worth," he said.

Although Qian was the paper's most influential backer, many others ran interference with the leadership. The support came from a broad range of the party's powerful: Huan Xiang, a top Chinese diplomat and adviser to the Foreign Ministry; Li Hao, then vice secretary of the State Council, China's cabinet; and Wang Daohan, a former mayor of Shanghai. Moreover, the *Herald*'s masthead and bylines read like rosters of the children and spouses of high-ranking Chinese cadres. They included Chen Lebo, the son of Shanghai party leader Chen Tongshen; Ruan Jiangning, the son of a high-ranking PLA political commissar; as well as the wives and daughters of ministers, cabinet officials, and government advisers.

Thanks to its unique status, the *Herald* enjoyed far greater editorial leeway than the state-run press. Qin stretched the limits of journalistic freedom just as he had during the Hundred Flowers campaign thirty years earlier. He was still determined to make the media a loyal critic of the Communist regime. The *Herald*'s pathbreaking reports were rare in China in the early 1980s and quickly attracted readers. Subscriptions grew, and in 1981, after only a year of operation, the paper began turning a profit. By 1983, circulation hit 300,000. The *Herald* expanded to sixteen pages and widened its range of reporting from international economics to China's economy, society, culture, and politics. It tapped its powerful connections for a steady stream of inside information. Before long, it was breaking the news on controversial economic and political reform policies and airing major intellectual debates.

As it pushed back the frontier of press freedom, the *Herald* came to symbolize the irreversible momentum of China's reforms. The paper emerged in 1980 as a product of the leadership's easing of totalitarian controls. It pioneered a strategy whereby Chinese intellectuals used the market to fund nongovernmental newspapers, publishing houses, and research institutes. By the mid-1980s, the *Herald* was an established force for independent intellectuals agitating to accelerate China's tentative liberalization.

Repeatedly, the *Herald* fulfilled Qin's mission of "playing a critical role at a critical time" by printing reports that swayed the leadership in favor of faster, more profound reforms. The paper had a valuable channel to the top leadership: its *neican* (classified report). Most Chinese newspapers compiled *neican* on topics considered too sensitive for open publication, but only the most explosive of these reached China's top leaders. A handful of privileged state news organs, however, sent all their *neican* directly to Deng and other top leaders. Thanks to Qian Junrui, the *Herald*'s internal report achieved this rare status.

By the time Zhang walked into Qin's apartment in the summer of 1986, the *Herald* was recognized worldwide as China's boldest, most outspoken newspaper. After the men chatted for a while, Qin told Zhang he was pleased with his editing of the legal page. Then he took a long drag on his cigarette, looked at Zhang, and in his heavy Jiangsu accent asked whether he would join the *Herald* as legal editor. "Our benefits are not as good as at your current job, so you'll have to be psychologically prepared," Qin added with a smile.

Sensing the tremendous opportunity at the *Herald,* Zhang agreed. He had grown deeply frustrated as a lawyer trying to reform China's legal system from within. As a *Herald* reporter, he thought he could bring vital, popular pressure to bear on the system by informing Chinese about the law and their civil rights. Zhang envisioned his personal quest for intellectual freedom and democracy merging into something far more powerful, public, and concrete.

Soon after meeting with Qin, Zhang started work. He found the *Herald*'s atmosphere friendly, even familylike. Qin shunned the stiff formalities imposed by many Chinese in senior positions. He enjoyed the convenience and comfort of working at home, where he lived with his second wife and two stepchildren. Every Friday night, he summoned the editors to a meeting in his bedroom. They debated the paper's contents late into the night, with the editors sitting on a sofa and Qin presiding from a worn writing desk. The editors and all *Herald* staffers called him Lao Ban (Boss), an appellation used cordially among intellectuals in pre-Communist Shanghai. When Qin was in the office, female reporters would often sidle over, casually reach an arm around his shoulder, and feel his shirt pocket for a packet of cigarettes. Finding a pack, they would slip it out and offer it around. Qin didn't mind. He was a chain-smoker and often bummed cigarettes. Kents were his favorites. He amused reporters by putting the imported Kents in one pocket for himself and a pack of ordinary Chinese cigarettes in the other pocket to give away.

But there were also tensions at the *Herald.* As the son of a bicycle repairman, Zhang was one of the few editors from a working-class background. He felt uneasy surrounded by so many high cadres' children and bridled at their cliquish ways, constant name-dropping, and other subtle displays of elitism. By relying on their parents' connections and little else, these privileged offspring were ensured good jobs and salaries. In contrast, Zhang had to work very hard, knowing only the caliber of his reporting would determine his success.

Zhang quickly set out to prove himself. As legal editor, he stirred public debates on a range of major cases. For example, he covered a dispute between Shanghai authorities and a Hong Kong businessman who had a joint venture on Nanjing Road. Zhang broke with the official line by running articles defending the Hong Kong investor's rights.

One day at a staff meeting in early 1987, Zhang was startled when Qin abruptly laid into him. "Zhang Weiguo! *What* are you doing?" Qin roared.

Zhang flushed. He had seen Qin criticize staffers before, slamming his fist on the table and picking articles apart. He stood up, prepared to be acutely embarrassed. He felt that everyone in the large meeting hall, some seventy or eighty people, was staring at him.

"There was an important conference last week. Why didn't you cover it?" Qin demanded.

Zhang hesitated. "I'm in charge of legal news. That conference had nothing to do with law," he replied.

"I never pigeonholed you [as a legal reporter]. Why have you pigeonholed yourself?" Qin asked, then broke into a smile.

Zhang realized that Qin was not criticizing him at all. He was encouraging and praising him. Qin was saying he no longer wanted Zhang to restrict himself to legal reporting. "I was very happy," Zhang said. "In essence, Qin was giving me freedom to report on whatever interested me."

After the meeting, Zhang struck an agreement with Qin on his new status as a general reporter. "I never want to be made an official on the paper," Zhang said, again swearing off politics, "or have any special title or earn a higher wage than others. Those things will only create 'red-eye disease' and cause trouble for me. But whenever I want to go somewhere to cover a story, I would like you to grant me approval. I guarantee I won't go for nothing. I'll bring back a story the paper can publish."

After a moment, Qin nodded. "*Hao* [All right]."

Although Qin and Zhang were very different, each had qualities that complemented the other. As time passed they grew increasingly close.

In mannerism, character, and outlook, Qin epitomized the traditional Chinese intellectual. He was thoughtful and unhurried, cautious and circumspect. He walked in a shuffle. From a long way off, Zhang knew Qin was approaching by the slow scraping of his heels on the newsroom floor. When Qin spoke, he measured his words. He read slowly, often pondering the usage of a Chinese character. Even in crossing a road, he craned his neck to look left and right before stepping into the street.

Qin was cautious politically, too. He had strong democratic principles but also a powerful aversion to head-on conflicts with the regime. Like many elderly intellectuals, Qin had been reared on the Confucian doctrine that a man should submit to his ruler for the sake of social harmony. As a party member, Qin sought to preserve at least the illusion of deference to the Communist leadership. Instead of confronting Beijing directly, he relied on his connections to lobby quietly for the *Herald* and placate the leadership when he came under fire.

In journalism, Qin was renowned for his skill at publishing critical or sensitive news in an unprovocative way. So successful was Qin's technique that it earned a colorful nickname, *ca bian qiu*. In table tennis, *ca bian qiu* means hitting a ball so it nicks the table edge and is impossible to return. In Chinese journalism, it means using oblique yet legitimate ways to disclose controversial news, leaving the authorities no pretext for retaliation.

Unlike Qin, Zhang was impulsive, extroverted, and blunt. He spoke his mind. Zhang had never adopted the polite restraint and meticulous ways of the Shanghainese. Instead, he inherited the frank peasant style of his rural migrant parents. As a child of Mao's era, Zhang belonged to a generation of Chinese intellectuals raised on iconoclasm instead of Confucian ethics. Zhang eventually lost faith in Mao, but he retained something of his radical antiauthoritarian outlook. Zhang felt no obligation to serve the state. He mistrusted people in power. And as a worker's son, he shunned reliance on elite connections. Compared with Qin, Zhang was more individualistic, more independent, and ultimately more of a threat to the regime.

Still, Qin and Zhang each had something unique to offer the other. Qin gave Zhang an opportunity very rare in totalitarian China in the mid-1980s: the space to explore, debate, and sometimes publish controversial ideas without fear. Qin had carved out a small but significant realm of free expression, and he welcomed Zhang to exert his talents there. Qin understood Zhang. He admired Zhang's youthful idealism, curiosity, and integrity. At the *Herald*, Qin nurtured these traits, which would have been stymied at almost any other job.

At the same time, the sixty-nine-year-old Qin relied on Zhang to bring him new ideas and keep him abreast of the latest currents in China's rapidly changing society. Unlike most other Chinese in senior posts, Qin had the virtue of being open-minded enough to accept advice from younger people. Instead of simply issuing orders, he cultivated good counsel from his underlings and let them inform his decisions. Qin found wisdom in an old Chinese saying: "Choose what is good, and follow good advice as naturally as a river follows its course."

Zhang's relations with Qin grew closer but also more conflictual as the *Herald* encountered its first major crisis in early 1987. In the winter of 1986, China experienced what were then its largest unofficial student protests under communism. Some 3,000 students rallied in Hefei, Anhui Province, in December against government manipulation of local elections. On December 20 the protests spread to Shanghai, where tens of thousands of students and citizens joined marches for freedom and democracy. It took three days for local officials to suppress the Shanghai protests, whereupon new demonstrations broke out in Beijing, Nanjing, and other cities. The *Herald* indirectly supported the movement by publishing the articles of Fang Lizhi, the astrophysicist whose calls for democracy sparked student protests in Hefei.

In early January, party hard-liners in Beijing cracked down on the protest movement and purged Professor Fang and other leading prodemocracy intellectuals. In an ominous move, Deng Xiaoping also forced the resignation on January 16 of party secretary Hu Yaobang, sacrificing his close protégé as a scapegoat for the unrest. Premier Zhao Ziyang, who also criticized Hu, was named acting party secretary and a few months later became the new party chief. Hu's sudden ouster affirmed Zhang's belief that despite economic and social reforms, Chinese politics remained a savage, unstable arena ruled by men not law.

Qin worried as Beijing's crackdown broadened and threatened the *Herald*. Party conservatives had ordered tougher controls on the media as part of a new campaign against "bourgeois liberalization" and Western ideas. Qin knew conservatives would grab the first opportunity to silence the *Herald*, so he shifted to his *ca bian qiu* strategy. Instead of commenting on politics outright, Qin and his editors let foreigners do their talking for them. They printed interviews with ambassadors in Beijing and compilations of the overseas press. By cleverly restating the views of foreigners, the *Herald* addressed controversial topics while minimizing its vulnerability to attack. But one day, the *Herald* went too far.

On February 23, 1987, the *Herald* ran on its front page a compilation of foreign reports praising Mikhail Gorbachev's efforts to speed political reform in the Soviet Union. Headlined "The Kremlin Again Blows Forth a Tornado of Reform," the story quoted Gorbachev as saying "democratization is the decisive force of reform." It also noted, in the last line, that Moscow had recently granted amnesty to 140 political prisoners and was planning to convene an international human rights conference. No one, least of all China's diehard Marxists, could interpret the article as anything but a scathing attack on political repression by Beijing. However, because the article summarized foreign reports, party conservatives had trouble finding a pretext to crack down. In the end, they seized on a single unattributed line implying that Romanian leader Nicolae Ceauşescu was unenthusiastic about Gorbachev's reforms. The Foreign Ministry issued a circular accusing the *Herald* of violating "diplomatic discipline." "Wantonly publishing opinions on fraternal Communist states has a very bad influence," the circular said, citing several other infractions by the *Herald*.

Two powerful party hard-liners, propaganda czar Deng Liqun and Marxist theoretician Hu Qiaomu, penned angry comments on the document. "What 'Economic Herald'?" Hu wrote. "This is a 'Political Herald'!"

Shanghai party secretary Rui Xingwen ordered the city's propaganda committee to dispatch a working group to "rectify" the *Herald*. The group decided to fire Qin as editor in chief and replace him with a deputy editor named Chen Yang. It had already printed new business cards for Chen and an order to remove Qin when a powerful friend of the *Herald* intervened. A Chinese businessman living in the United States with close ties to Zhao Ziyang flew to Beijing and met with one of Zhao's chief aides, Bao Tong. The businessman gave Bao a letter for Zhao urging him not to let Qin go. "Newsmen like Qin Benli are hard to find. He has contributed a lot to reform," the letter said. Zhao intervened and allowed Qin to stay on. Qin, who had been resting with a "sore throat," suddenly improved and returned to work.

Soon afterward, in April, the *Herald* won praise from Zhao for a series of articles on enterprise reform. Zhao ordered the State Council to reprint the articles as an official document and distribute it to every ministry along with his personal instructions to study it carefully. Zhao's intention was to support the *Herald*, but he did so indirectly to avoid coming under attack himself.

Zhao's astute praise for the *Herald* made the rectification team look ridiculous. Its members disappeared from the newsroom, and the political pressure eased. Still, the incident left Zhang uneasy. It demonstrated the clear limits to the paper's independence. Despite all its advantages, the *Herald* remained vulnerable to the political shifts and ensnaring factional struggles in Beijing. Zhang was especially uncomfortable over the personal debt Qin now owed Zhao Ziyang. In China, such debts are deadly serious. Zhang rightly guessed that before long, Zhao would ask a favor in return.

In mid-May, one of Zhao's personal secretaries, Li Yong, walked into the *Herald*'s Beijing office and passed on two verbal messages from Zhao. The first was that Zhao "cared greatly about" the *Herald*. Second, Zhao believed that China's problems of corruption, price hikes, and education were long-term difficulties that couldn't be resolved overnight. To avoid inciting social instability, the *Herald* should tone down its reporting on these problems. Zhao's unspoken message was clear: I will protect the *Herald*, but the *Herald* must support me politically.

When Zhang heard of Zhao's remarks, he went immediately to Qin. "Boss, you mustn't 'hang yourself on one tree,'" Zhang appealed, quoting a Chinese adage. "We can't let the *Herald* become Zhao Ziyang's newspaper or the mouthpiece of the reformist faction. If we do, we'll be just like *People's Daily*." A degree of political independence, he told Qin, was vital to the *Herald*'s mission and long-term survival. Qin nodded, but Zhang saw he had reservations.

"Boss," Zhang began again, on a different tack. "The biggest help we can give Zhao is to tell the truth. If we don't do that, in the end, we will be harming him," he said. Qin nodded again. Still, Zhang sensed he was torn.

From mid-May on, the *Herald* continued to report on corruption, inflation, and other pressing problems. But Zhang noticed that Qin avoided highly sensitive topics that could reflect badly on Zhao or fuel hard-line attacks. As a traditional intellectual, Qin was more comfortable than Zhang with the idea of Zhao as a political patron. As a party cadre, he saw Zhao as the best hope for reforming the Communist Party. Pragmatically, he estimated that Zhao's support was worth the awkward compromises. "Qin had to show gratitude for Zhao's protection and also be faithful to the facts. Sometimes, it was very contradictory," Zhang said.

As Zhang grew more confident and bold as a reporter, he often challenged Qin's editorial caution. In 1987, for example, Zhang defended dissident Fang Lizhi, the astrophysicist purged for allegedly advocating China's "total Westernization." "What 'total Westernization'? China is totally Sovietized!" Zhang quoted historian Li Su as saying. Qin deleted the quote.

Not long afterward, Zhang landed an interview with a deputy foreign minister. In the interview, Zhang asked pointedly why Chinese citizens were less free than foreigners in voicing their views on diplomatic affairs. Infuriated, the official flushed and refused to answer. Zhang described the whole scene in his article, including the official's crimson face. Again, Qin cut out the exchange.

Qin's censoring of Zhang revealed a fundamental divergence between the seasoned editor and the maverick reporter. Qin was willing to practice restraint, both for the sake of sheer survival and to support what he believed were sincere efforts by China's reformers to revitalize the economy and curb party abuses. Zhang was less willing to pull his punches. He distrusted the party. He placed higher value on his rights as an individual, the *Herald*'s rights as a paper, and the rights of the Chinese public to be informed. Qin was more the pragmatist, Zhang the idealist. As the saga unfolded, they both ended up partially right.

Nevertheless, the tensions between Qin and Zhang were held in check by a growing mutual respect. Qin increasingly admired Zhang's ambitious reporting and forthrightness. Zhang, in turn, learned to appreciate Qin's editorial restraint for keeping him out of trouble.

In late 1987, Qin demonstrated his trust in Zhang by appointing him to the *Herald*'s seven-member editorial committee. The committee was the *Herald*'s highest body and charged with deciding editorial direction. Zhang, who was out of town when Qin made the promotion, was surprised and flattered. But he reminded Qin that he did not want a special title. Qin brushed aside Zhang's protest with feigned gruffness, claiming the appointment was strictly for his own convenience. Qin said he was tired of having to okay all of Zhang's air travel. As a member of the editorial committee, Zhang could fly without his approval.

In early 1988, Qin promoted Zhang to what was arguably the most critical reporting job on the *Herald*: chief of the Beijing bureau. Zhang maintained a collegial mood at the bureau. As long as the reporters turned out decent copy, Zhang rarely gave orders. The government already hobbled journalists enough, he reasoned. Yet despite his easygoing style, the magnitude of Zhang's responsibility and influence as Beijing bureau chief was clear to everyone on the *Herald*.

The Beijing bureau was not just another reporting post. It was the *Herald*'s hold on the political pulse of Beijing. Zhang's most important job was to "gather intelligence" on the direction of China's reforms and party policy. Based on this information, Zhang and the editorial committee decided how best to promote individual reforms, including controversial experiments with privatization and democracy. The *Herald*'s excellent sources enabled it to stay one step ahead of other media in unveiling new reforms. Known as the "quick-to-publish faction," the *Herald* aired the most forward-looking debates on reform, printing articles by not only the economists, scholars, and officials who designed the experiments but also their critics.

Zhang constantly cultivated new sources for the *Herald*. Before long, he was as attuned to the capital's political intrigues as any Beijing pundit. Every one or two weeks, Zhang wrote "Beijing Shujian." His accounts of behind-the-scenes politicking, which often disclosed the views of top leaders, were immensely popular among Beijing insiders.

Zhang's success in running the Beijing bureau increased his influence with Qin. Most nights, Qin telephoned Zhang for the latest news and rumors circulating in the capital. "Some people joked that I was a bigger heavyweight on the paper than Qin Benli, because Qin listened to Beijing, and that meant he listened to me," Zhang laughed.

In late 1988, Zhang got hold of an explosive speech delivered by Marxist scholar Su Shaozhi at a conference marking the tenth anniversary of China's reforms. Reviewing the decade, Su eloquently summarized the misgivings of many Chinese intellectuals about the party's failure to promote democratic reforms. He harshly attacked the hard-line campaigns in 1983 and 1987 against spiritual pollution and bourgeois liberalization and denounced the fact that certain fields remained off-limits in academic research.

Zhang faxed Su's speech to Qin. A few hours later, Qin telephoned Zhang and they discussed it at length. Qin said he and the Shanghai editors considered Su's critique the best they had come across in the *Herald*'s eight-year history. Qin stressed that some of Su's pointed wording had to be toned down. For example, he deleted a reference to party conservative Bo Yibo, whom Su attacked for his role in ousting party chief Hu Yaobang. But he retained the bulk of the address.

The speech was rushed to press, appearing on December 26, the ninety-fifth anniversary of Mao's birth. Instantly, Su's daring critique became the talk of Beijing. The hard-line reaction was also swift. Four days after the article appeared, the propaganda department issued a directive forbidding other media from reprinting or broadcasting any of it. Bo Yibo, spotting the thinly veiled attack against him, took a copy of the article to Deng Xiaoping and lodged an angry complaint. Bao Tong, Zhao Ziyang's chief secretary, was standing at Deng's side. Sensing the danger if Deng spoke against the *Herald*, Bao jumped in first and called for the paper to be "sternly dealt with."

Zhao was in fact the leader most hurt by Su's article. As the *Herald*'s main patron, Zhao was the obvious scapegoat for the newspaper's audacious attack on the party leadership. Zhao was already vulnerable to hard-line criticism. Since mid-1988 his economic experiments had badly faltered. That summer, as double-digit inflation sparked panic buying in Chinese cities, conservatives had stripped Zhao of his de facto position as China's chief economic policymaker and launched a stringent austerity drive. Zhao had also drawn fire from ideologues for attempting to dilute the party's "four cardinal principles" (Marxism, socialism, the proletarian dictatorship, and Communist Party rule). Zhao stressed only party rule.

Jiang Zemin, the urbane but hard-line Shanghai party secretary and one of Zhao's rivals, relished the chance to denounce his political foe. Jiang had already mobilized Shanghai's veteran cadres to condemn Zhao's waffling over party principles. Jiang now realized that continued outspokenness by the *Herald* would hurt Zhao even more. So, in the kind of double-dealing often seen in the warped world of Chinese factionalism, the conservative Jiang temporarily sided with China's most liberal newspaper. In early 1989, Jiang approached Qin at a Chinese New Year gathering of senior Shanghai newspapermen.

"Don't worry," Jiang said, patting Qin on the back. "Whatever happens, the Shanghai party committee will help you keep your post." He continued in an unctuous, paternalistic tone. "We'll handle things with the propaganda department," he added and sat down to advise Qin on how to write a self-criticism for the department. Propaganda officials in Beijing had issued a directive calling on Shanghai to discipline the *Herald* severely.

Qin left the gathering in high spirits. He was delighted that Jiang, a politburo member, had sympathized with him. He felt his basic trust in the party reaffirmed. Once again, Qin was deluded into thinking he could rely on party leaders.

Zhang, however, suspected that Jiang was using the *Herald* in his rivalry with Zhao. Worse, he feared the newspaper was being sucked into a far broader power struggle. Signs of discord between conservatives and reformers had intensified since the annual summer gathering of party leaders at the Beidaihe resort on the Bohai Gulf. Zhang knew the ultimate goal of China's conservatives was to purge Zhao altogether. He sensed the danger to the *Herald* and groped for a way to free the paper from the sticky political web.

In the early spring of 1989, Zhang lit on a plan that might bolster the *Herald*'s independence: He would garner support for the paper from the overseas Chinese media. On April 5, he hosted a gathering for journalists from Hong Kong and Taiwan who were in Beijing covering the annual session of the National People's Congress (NPC). That gathering, one of the first of its kind, led to discussions of formal cooperation between the *Herald* and Taiwan's *Independent Evening News*. The two papers agreed to become sister publications, cooperate on coverage, and promote journalists' exchanges across the Taiwan Strait. Zhang hoped the accord would increase the *Herald*'s freedom and objectivity by linking it with a publication outside of Communist control. The signing ceremony was set for the evening of Saturday, April 15.

Earlier that day, however, an unexpected event intervened. Johnny Lau, a Beijing correspondent for the Hong Kong newspaper *Wen Wei Po*, telephoned at midday to tell Zhang about a rumor that Hu Yaobang had died of a heart attack. Could Zhang confirm it?

"Can do," Zhang said and hung up.

Zhang dialed the office of Hu's son, Hu Deping, but no one answered. Next he phoned Hu's home and got Hu Deping on the line. Zhang addressed him using a polite formula.

"Friends are very deeply concerned about the health of your father and wonder how he is," Zhang said.

"This morning, after 7:30, he already passed away," Hu replied somberly.

Zhang offered to go to Hu's home, which was on Nanchang Street not far from the *Herald*'s Beijing bureau, to assist the family.

"There's nothing you can do for the moment," Hu said. "If something arises, I'll notify you."

Zhang phoned Johnny Lau with the news. Then he called Qin to discuss the *Herald*'s coverage. Qin, like many Chinese intellectuals, admired Hu as a moderate leader and strong proponent of reform. He wanted to play up the mourning for Hu. Zhang agreed. But with the *Herald*'s weekly deadline just hours away, Qin could insert only a small announcement on the front page. For the next edition, though, Zhang had an idea. He would invite Beijing's leading intellectuals to attend a memorial for Hu and then publish a summary of their speeches. Zhang called up his friend Ge Yang, the seventy-three-year-old editor in chief of the liberal *New Observer* magazine. Ge, a strong-willed woman and revolutionary war veteran, agreed to organize the memorial jointly with the *Herald*.

That evening, Zhang and his colleagues had dinner with reporters from Taiwan's *Independent Evening News* at the Beijing bureau and afterward signed the cooperation agreement. Still, Zhang was preoccupied with news of Hu's death. As soon as the ceremony ended, he left the bureau by bicycle for a look around Beijing with a younger colleague, Fei Xiaodong. They headed first for Tiananmen Square. It was about midnight when the two rode into the sprawling concrete plaza in the heart of the capital. The square was empty except for a few plainclothesmen. One spoke into a cordless phone, and the other held a megaphone. The night felt eerily calm.

Zhang and Fei slowly circled the square. As they passed the Monument to the People's Heroes, the towering white obelisk at the southern end of the square, Zhang spotted a few wreaths resting against the chain barrier at the monument's foot. The two reporters rode closer and dismounted. The wreaths bore white paper chrysanthemums, the traditional Chinese symbol of mourning. On strips of paper hanging from the wreaths, hand-stroked Chinese couplets affectionately addressed Hu by his given name:

"Rest eternal, Yaobang!"

"Yaobang, don't die!"

Standing before the shadowy wreaths, Zhang had a sense of foreboding. "The memorials for Hu won't be very tranquil," he said to Fei. But he never imagined the massive popular uprising that was to come.

The next morning, Zhang and Ge Yang began organizing their memorial for Hu, inviting Beijing's most prominent liberals. That afternoon, the two went together to Hu's home. In the family mourning hall, a large photograph of Hu, bordered in black, hung on the wall with flowered wreaths clustered below. They offered their condolences to the family, and Zhang gathered some black-and-white photographs of Hu for the *Herald*. As they left the house, Ge vented her bitterness over Hu's political disgrace and death. "Hu Yaobang died from bullying and deceit!" she muttered under her breath.

Many Chinese liberals like Ge were angered by what they saw as the party's unjust treatment of Hu. A fiery, elfish politician who punctuated his speeches with arm waving and jokes, Hu endeared himself to intellectuals with his enthusiastic calls for Chinese to "emancipate their minds." An outspoken critic of Maoist excesses, Hu was also a key backer of Chinese liberals, such as the investigative reporter Liu Binyan. But Hu's ideas as well as his blunt off-the-cuff style had ruffled party conservatives.

On April 19, about 100 intellectuals gathered for the memorial for Hu. The meeting was held in a conference hall of the Ministry of Culture on North Shatan Street, just north of the Forbidden City and Tiananmen Square. Outside, students rallied in growing numbers and covered campus walls with posters critical of the leadership. The students praised Hu and vilified other Chinese leaders. "Those who should have died live, / Those who should have lived have died," read one elegiac couplet posted at the time.

First to address the meeting were the "old democrats" like Ge Yang, economist Yu Guangyuan, scholar Su Shaozhi, newsman Hu Jiwei, and other contemporaries of Qin Benli. One by one, these elderly supporters of Hu stood up, some with tears streaming down their faces, and railed against the grave injustice dealt a good leader.

Next spoke the younger liberals. They dwelt less on Hu's mistreatment than on the political system that caused it. Political scientist Yan Jiaqi criticized China's lack of a rational, legal procedure for succession. *Guangming Daily* reporter Dai Qing noted that in the entire history of China's Communist Party, not a single party secretary had come to a good end.

Zhang spoke last. He focused on the potential for channeling the flood of support for Hu into popular backing for a new wave of reform. "China's reforms have entered a very difficult stage. Chinese must transform their grief for Hu into a force for pushing reform forward," he urged.

That night at about 9:00, Zhang and some friends arrived at the gates of Zhongnanhai, the party compound about a quarter mile west of Tiananmen Square. The compound is the main locus of party power, housing the offices and living quarters for most of China's top leaders. Xinhuamen Gate, the ceremonial main entrance to the compound, was packed with scores of students agitating for democracy. A row of armed police blocked them from entering through the crimson gate.

Watching the scene, Zhang found his excitement as a reporter quickly overrun by concern. He sensed a crisis. In the strained faces of the students, Zhang saw how urgently China's younger generation desired freedom. Yet as the students chanted in vain for Chinese leaders to come out, he also knew their demands for change would go unmet; no leader dared risk his career by negotiating with the demonstrators.

At midnight, Zhang cycled back to the empty *Herald* bureau to write his report on the Hu memorial. As usual, he first phoned Qin to ask how much space he could have. Qin listened to Zhang relate what people said at the meeting. "Brilliant!" Qin exclaimed. "The more the better. I'll give you as much space as you can fill."

Zhang was thrilled. Never in the *Herald*'s history had Qin given a reporter such leeway. "For a journalist, it was an opportunity that comes once in a thousand years," Zhang said.

He wrote furiously through the night and all the next day describing the bitterest laments of the old democrats and the most cutting criticisms of the young liberals. On Friday morning, April 21, Zhang faxed his report to Shanghai. It ran to 30,000 Chinese characters, or six full pages of newsprint. Within hours, the report sparked events that would thrust the *Herald* to the center stage of China's political crisis.

The first sign of trouble came late Friday morning with a phone call to Qin from the head of Shanghai's propaganda bureau, Chen Zhili. "We are a little curious to see the contents of the next edition," Madame Chen said calmly. "Please send over the final page proofs so we can have a look." She had learned from a Hong Kong report that the *Herald* planned to dedicate several pages to Hu.

Qin hesitated. Until then, he had never been required to submit proofs for official scrutiny before the paper went to press. Nevertheless, he thought, the circumstances were extraordinary. "I'll send them over tomorrow afternoon," Qin agreed. He wasn't too worried. After all, Chen's boss, Shanghai party secretary Jiang Zemin, had patted him on the shoulder and promised to back the *Herald* only a few months before.

The next day, April 22, as the party leadership gathered for Hu's state funeral in Beijing, Qin sent the proofs of issue 439 to Chen. A few hours later, Qin was at the Jinjiang Hotel entertaining a Taiwan reporter when he received another call from Chen. This time, there was a hard impatience in her voice as she summoned him to the Shanghai party headquarters for a "discussion."

When Qin arrived at Chen's office, she explained that student protests in Beijing made this *Herald* edition "sensitive." Pointing to Zhang's report, she singled out several hundred words, including Dai Qing's ascerbic remarks on the fate of party secretaries. She suggested Qin delete those sections.

"Don't worry, I'll accept the responsibility," Qin said.

"It's not a question of personal responsibility but rather of social effect," interjected one of Chen's underlings.

"Excuse me," Qin said, "but I won't delete it."

Chen refused to back down. She called in party chief Jiang and Wang Daohan, a former Shanghai mayor and chairman of the *Herald*'s board. Jiang was furious with Qin for his insubordination. He curtly ordered Qin to revise Zhang's article and left. Wang stayed on, reading the article until about 1 A.M. Unwilling to back the paper, Wang warned Qin to change the article or face the party's "discipline."

This time, Qin's allegiance to the party prevailed. He agreed to drop the offending paragraphs. As Chen looked on, he called the printing factory to halt the press run. But it was too late. Thousands of copies of issue 439 were printed, and a few hundred had been picked up by postal workers for distribution. Again obeying party orders, Qin ordered the undistributed papers "locked up." But with hundreds of copies of the uncut version soon to hit the streets, the task of revising issue 439 suddenly became increasingly awkward. Still fuming, Jiang demanded to see Qin again the next afternoon, Sunday, April 23.

In the middle of the night, Zhang was awakened in Beijing by a phone call from Shanghai. On the line were four of the *Herald*'s senior editors: Fang Jun, Xu

Xiaowei, Ruan Jiangning, and Lu Yi. They had just left Qin's apartment and were calling from the post office. Speaking rapidly in urgent tones, they described Qin's predicament. Knowing Zhang's advice carried weight with Qin, they asked him to intervene before Qin met with Jiang again later that day. "Weiguo, you've got to call Qin and persuade him to stand firm," Ruan told Zhang.

Zhang agreed to call Qin the next morning. He hung up, flicked off the light, and went back to bed. But for what seemed like hours, he lay awake wondering what to tell Qin. How could he persuade the veteran party member to defy the party? Zhang rehearsed his arguments until he finally drifted into a light slumber.

At dawn, Zhang awoke with a start. He filled an enamel basin with cold water and splashed it on his face. Then he dressed, collected his thoughts one last time, and dialed Qin's number.

From the first strained tones of Qin's voice, Zhang knew he was angry, which was good. But Zhang also sensed that the whole episode had badly rattled Qin. The editor in chief had been caught completely off guard by Jiang's brusque rebuff. Ever since his encounter with Jiang at Chinese New Year a few months earlier, Qin had clung to the illusion that the party boss was behind him. Now, Qin felt stunned and betrayed by Jiang's 180-degree turn. "They spoke to me very rudely," Qin complained, his voice shaking. As a traditional intellectual, Qin was almost as upset by the authorities' disrespectful tone as by their orders.

Qin asked Zhang for his opinion. Zhang said that if party authorities insisted, Qin could agree to revise the article in one of three ways. He could insert brackets showing where text was deleted, remove the article entirely and leave the pages blank, or fill the pages with black-rimmed photographs of Hu. Qin said the ideas were good, but from the hesitation in his voice Zhang knew his proposals were too radical for the old man.

Zhang then went straight to the heart of what he knew was tormenting Qin. Ironically, he began by quoting Mao, appealing to Qin in the political jargon the long-serving party member knew so well. "Boss, you shouldn't 'use class feelings to replace revolutionary principles,'" Zhang said, alluding to a popular Cultural Revolution slogan. Qin's devotion to the party, he meant, should not supplant his belief in the principles of democracy and press freedom. "Boss, this time you can't obey the party."

Qin was torn. He didn't want to revise Zhang's article. But even stronger was his aversion to defying the "party central." That afternoon when he met with Jiang, Qin reluctantly agreed once again to revamp issue 439.

When he heard the news, Zhang realized that his friend and editor had reached a political chasm he could not cross. For too long, since the 1940s, Qin had served the party with the conviction that despite its many failings it was China's best hope. With a Confucian sense of duty, he had devoted his life to the organization. He couldn't bring himself to break ties with it now.

Zhang felt no such loyalty to the party. A child of Maoist China, he never chose the Communist regime and felt no Confucian obligation to support it. As a youth, he embraced the party not out of any moral conviction but because of peer pressure, indoctrination, and the charisma of Mao. Once he lost faith in Mao, his compulsion to serve the party vanished. Along with a generation of young Red Guards, Zhang emerged from the Cultural Revolution far more irreverent and individualistic than party veterans like Qin. Now these qualities freed him to act when Qin could not.

Zhang phoned Qin again the next day, Monday, April 24. "Boss," Zhang advised, "this time you should let us young people handle things. Withdraw behind the front lines. Don't step in unless we get into a big quarrel that we can't manage."

Qin seemed relieved. Zhang's advice offered an escape from possibly the most difficult dilemma of his career. That evening, according to colleagues, Qin "was taken ill due to exhaustion" and left for Shanghai's Yinghua resort "to rest."

❋

The *Herald*'s future now lay in the hands of Zhang and his young fellow editors. They saw the *Herald*'s struggle against party censorship as a decisive test for press freedom in China, and they staked the paper's fate on that principle. Moreover, they decided to take their case directly to the Chinese people. "The stakes were very high," said Zhang. "When fighting for press freedom, if you advance one step, you advance ten years. But if you retreat one step, you retreat ten years."

By noon on Monday, April 24, when the *Herald* failed to appear, word spread rapidly in Beijing, Shanghai, and overseas that issue 439 had been banned. Meanwhile, the few copies that had slipped out made their way into readers' hands, only to be photocopied and posted on streets and campus walls for a much larger audience.

Under the circumstances, Zhang and the other editors decided that a censored *Herald* would be nothing more than a public mockery of the ideal of press freedom. At 6 P.M. on Tuesday, April 25, they delivered an "urgent report" to the Shanghai party committee, stating that they would stick to publishing the original version.

Shanghai party authorities were outraged. Madame Chen and others were particularly incensed because the editors had not requested approval but simply announced their decision under the heading "for your information."

The ax fell one day later, on April 26. At a 3 P.M. mass meeting of 14,000 party cadres at the Shanghai gymnasium, Jiang Zemin announced that Qin Benli was dismissed as the *Herald*'s editor in chief for "seriously violating [party] discipline." Moreover, he said a "rectification group" had been appointed to occupy the *Herald*'s offices, reorganize the paper, and take over its operations.

The rectification group, led by Liu Ji of the Shanghai propaganda bureau, entered the *Herald* on April 27. The same day, under the orders of the party committee, a revised edition of issue 439 finally appeared. Zhang's entire article had been deleted except for a four-paragraph summary of the memorial meeting on the front page.

Jiang's crackdown on Qin and the *Herald* appeared to Zhang cleverly calculated to establish his hard-line credentials with Beijing. At the cadres' meeting, Jiang had joined the conservative war cry against *dongluan* (turmoil), the party's new inflammatory label for the student movement. In hindsight, Zhang suspects Jiang was even more Machiavellian, deliberately using harsh tactics to fuel the unrest, speed its suppression, and justify a purge of the party's reformist wing. Jiang clearly wanted to get rid of Zhao; he knew student protests had been decisive in the fall of Zhao's predecessor.

Jiang trumpeted his removal of Qin. He requested public support from Beijing, which obliged. China's state-run television network and the official news agency Xinhua carried the news the same day. The following day, all the major Shanghai dailies led with the story.

Jiang's attack on the *Herald* provoked a sharp and immediate outcry in Shanghai, Beijing, and other cities, where protesters rallied behind the maverick paper as a symbol of press freedom and intellectual openness. Posters demanding a free press proliferated. In Shanghai, the *Herald*'s headquarters became a focal point of demonstrations. Thousands of phone calls and hundreds of letters and telegrams from supporters flooded into the editorial offices. Qin Benli's dismissal became a cause célèbre for students, journalists, and liberal intellectuals throughout China.

At the same time, Zhang and the other editors refused to back down. Their determination helped galvanize the official Chinese media and a growing segment of the public behind the cause of press freedom. On May 3, Chinese journalists spoke out for the *Herald* for the first time. Within days more than 1,000 journalists had signed a petition calling for a dialogue with the party central committee. The first item for discussion: Qin's dismissal and the reorganization of the *Herald*.

Anger over the "*Herald* incident" broadened into a general protest for press freedom on May 4. Hundreds of journalists joined the march on the seventieth anniversary of China's May Fourth Movement, which championed democracy and science. As the journalists marched along the Avenue of Eternal Peace to Tiananmen Square, thousands of onlookers cheered them on, with some of them moved to tears. "Our mouths can't say what we want to; our pens can't write what we want to!" the journalists' banners declared.

Never in China's Communist history had members of the state-run press openly demonstrated against the regime. The next day, in a daring display of openness, the *People's Daily, China Youth News,* and other official newspapers and television stations spread the news of the protest nationwide. The reports helped speed the broadening of the student protests into a genuine mass movement. "It was a turning point in the 1989 movement," said Zhang.

Zhang covered the march. "The people's government vitally needs supervision by the people and the press," he wrote in an article in the *Herald*'s May 8 edition. He also used the occasion to take a jab at Jiang. "I am grateful to Mr. Jiang Zemin," Zhang told Hong Kong's Asia Television in an interview. "If he had not dealt with the *World Economic Herald* as he did, China's press circles would not have the awakening they are having today."

Shanghai officials tolerated Zhang's article on press freedom, but they were furious over his ridiculing of Jiang. Liu Ji, the head of the rectification group, attacked him as "reckless and irresponsible." Liu ordered Zhang to return to Shanghai to "study central documents" and "rectify" his outlook. Zhang replied that he would answer only to his editor in chief. "If Qin Benli calls me back, I will return immediately," he said. He stayed in Beijing.

The protests over the *Herald* and expansion of the democracy movement as a whole further polarized the party leadership. The *Herald* incident in particular provided ammunition for a bitter duel between Jiang and party secretary Zhao Ziyang. As the conflict between the men escalated into all-out factional warfare, the *Herald* was caught squarely in the line of fire.

Zhao, who was visiting North Korea when Jiang announced Qin's dismissal, issued a stern rebuke soon after returning to Beijing on May 1. "Jiang has made a mess of things. He has added fuel to the flames," Zhao stormed during a politburo meeting. "Let the one who ties the bell on the tiger take it off," Zhao warned, quoting a Chinese saying.

Jiang defended his decision. "I'm a politburo member! Can't I fire a bureau-level cadre?" he ranted to the Shanghai party committee in early May. Jiang secured a committee resolution that both backed his handling of the *Herald* and effectively diluted his personal responsibility.

While Jiang allied with party conservatives, Zhao gambled his career on the high-risk strategy of conciliation toward the protesters. In a nationally broadcast speech on May 4, he called the students "patriotic" and said their demands should be resolved in a legal, democratic manner. He calculated that by riding the wave of student activism, he and fellow reformers could make a political comeback.

Zhang watched with growing anxiety as the *Herald* was dragged deeper into the factional struggle. He cursed the paper's one-sided reliance on Zhao. Zhang and his colleagues wanted the *Herald*'s future determined by the public's sense of justice, not by the fortunes of one political faction. They stepped up their campaign to bring the *Herald*'s case to China's public.

In Shanghai, the paper's editorial offices became a center of activism. Staffers converted the newsroom, which was draped in black as a memorial hall for Hu, into a gallery displaying hundreds of letters and telegrams sympathetic to the *Herald*. Editors posted news of the *Herald* incident and student movement in the glass display window at the main gate, near busy Huai Hai Road, drawing large crowds of readers.

Editors churned out copies of the banned issue 439 until they estimated its circulation was double the usual press run. They also transformed the paper's *neican* into an open tabloid. They blacked out the words "secret" and "reference for comrade party leaders" from the *neican* heading, expanded the number of pages from two to ten or more, and increased its frequency from monthly to weekly. Next, they filled its pages with messages of protest and support from across China and overseas, including the United States, Europe, and Japan. Chinese from all walks of life poured out their sympathy for the *Herald*. Tens of thousands of copies of the *neican*, which was still officially licensed, reached the public.

In Beijing, Zhang mainly worked to shunt news about the *Herald* and the protest movement to the Chinese and foreign press. He also gave information and advice to student leaders. Often, a group of students would hire a taxi, ride to the gate of the *Herald*'s Beijing bureau, and ask Zhang to come out and make a speech about the "truth of the *Herald* incident." Zhang joined activists Wang Juntao, Chen Ziming, and Chen Xiaoping in some dialogues with student leaders at the Jimen Hotel. Still, he kept a low profile. He wanted to deny the party a pretext for claiming that older "bearded men" or "black hands" were manipulating the movement.

Zhang and his fellow editors also tried to defend the *Herald* on legal grounds. On May 1, they publicized a protest telegram from the China World Economics Association contending that Shanghai authorities had acted illegally by firing Qin without first consulting the *Herald*'s two parent organizations. Meanwhile, Zhang drafted a lawsuit demanding that the Shanghai party committee compensate the paper for economic losses and damages to its reputation. Although both efforts at litigation failed, the lawsuit and protest telegram circulated widely among demonstrators, bolstering the *Herald*'s cause.

The campaign by Zhang and his colleagues to muster public support for their newspaper's defiance of the party was unprecedented under Communist rule. Party leaders, like Chinese rulers for millennia, strove systematically to unify and control intellectuals under a monolithic state. All scholarly groups and institutions, from universities and journals to calligraphy societies, were bound to the state through *danwei*. In the 1980s, the *Herald* pushed the limits of state control and achieved a rare degree of autonomy. But in important ways it remained a newspaper tied to the ruling elite, dependent upon Qin's liberal connections and the patronage of Zhao and his reform-minded brain trust.

Now, Zhang and his fellow editors were trying to break all remaining ties between the *Herald* and the Communist hierachy. They turned completely to society for support, resources, and legitimacy. For a brief time, they succeeded. Along with a handful of other organizations that gained prominence during the democracy movement—student federations, workers unions, unofficial think tanks—the *Herald* drew its strength from below, not above. Zhang and his colleagues set a precedent for Chinese intellectuals seeking to take their place in an independent civil society.

Zhang and the other editors felt their control over the paper slipping dangerously, however, as the party's crackdown grew more aggressive. When the working group rejected their demands to publish the protest telegram in the May 15 edition, the editors were left with one drastic recourse. "We can't give way and let the authorities put out the *Herald* as they wish," Zhang said from Beijing in a telephone conference with editors Zhu Xingqing in Shanghai and Pan Muping in Washington, D.C. Vowing never to let the *Herald* become a party mouthpiece, the editors agreed to halt the paper themselves. The May 15 edition was canceled. No more issues of the *Herald* would appear.

On May 18, the *Herald* staged its last major act of defiance against the regime. That evening, the staff held a press conference at the auditorium of the Shanghai Academy of Social Sciences. About 300 reporters and intellectuals attended. At about 7:30 P.M., Qin Benli walked onto the auditorium stage, stirring applause from the audience. In response, Qin waved a bunch of red carnations given to him by a well-wisher.

It was Qin's first appearance since his dismissal. Emboldened by the recent flood of popular support for the *Herald*, he had emerged from seclusion ready to stand by his principles as Zhang had urged him to. When he spoke, he attacked the party for suspending political and press reforms.

But Qin made his stand too late. The political tide had already turned. Hardliners in Beijing had moved to crack down on the protests and halt the brief flourishing of press freedom. Ominously, not a single report of the news conference appeared in the Shanghai press the following morning. Two days later, at 10:00 A.M. on Saturday, May 20, martial law was imposed on all the main districts of Beijing.

On Sunday, students in Shanghai reacted by staging a huge march to protest martial law. They tried to muster a similar turnout the next day but were impeded by a heavy spring rain. A few marchers took to the city's streets despite the downpour, however, including a contingent from the *Herald* led by Qin Benli. Their banners wet and sagging, Qin's bedraggled group was cheered on by onlookers shouting "Long live the *Herald*! Long live Qin Benli!" It was Qin's last public appearance.

❉

In Beijing, meanwhile, Zhang watched as citizens rushed to blockade truck convoys carrying tens of thousands of martial law troops toward the city. Party hard-liners had underestimated the strength of opposition from common Chinese. After holding off the troops for three days, Beijing residents rejoiced on May 23 when the convoys retreated to the capital's outskirts. Meanwhile, tens of thousands of students and a smaller number of workers still occupied Tiananmen Square.

At the time, Zhang often bicycled down Beijing's poster-strewn streets, talking with residents, meeting with sources, and attempting to gauge the course of the high-level power struggle. Zhao Ziyang was now fighting a rear-guard battle against hard-liners. His effort to rescind martial law by convening an emergency session of the National People's Congress failed when party elders ordered NPC chairman Wan Li detained in Shanghai. Zhao's only option was to await the next regular NPC session, scheduled for June 20.

Zhang watched the end of May arrive without a crackdown. Thousands of students had already left Tiananmen Square. He began to think the leadership would try to resolve the conflict peacefully at the June 20 NPC session. Expecting few events in Beijing until then, he decided to use the time to write a detailed account of the *Herald* incident.

On the evening of June 1, Zhang packed a bag of documents, grabbed a few pens, and flew to Shanghai to a quieter place to write. He spent one night at the home of his friend Xu Xiaowei. The next day, he took a taxi south of the city to the petrochemical factory on Hangzhou Bay. A friend from the factory was in West Germany and had offered Zhang his room. Immersed in his writing, Zhang worked late into the night and rarely went out. But by habit, he listened to radio newscasts several times a day.

Early on the morning of June 4, Zhang heard news of the massacre in Beijing come crackling over the airwaves. Hundreds of people, perhaps thousands, were gunned down or crushed in the onslaught of troops and tanks. Zhang was horrified by the cruel, calculated blitz. Like many Chinese, he had expected some arrests, perhaps some accidental deaths. But he never imagined that the army would indiscriminately fire on citizens. Faced with such an enormous setback for China, he groped for a way to respond. Almost immediately, he realized that he had to quit the party. He took up a pen and wrote his resignation.

Soon, Zhang began hearing scattered reports from friends of arrests in Beijing. Some of his closest contacts were detained, and many others had gone into hiding. Friends urged Zhang to leave Shanghai and travel south to the bustling commercial city of Guangzhou or beyond, perhaps to Shekou or Shatoujiao, the freewheeling trading posts on China's border with Hong Kong. Many dissidents eventually fled China's police dragnet via this southern escape route, which became known as the "underground railway."

On impulse, Zhang decided not to flee. He reckoned he had done nothing wrong. He had not led protest marches or called publicly for overthrowing the regime. Moreover, the reporter in Zhang urged him to stay to witness the fallout from the movement. "This, too, is a kind of life experience," he told himself.

Still, Zhang's actions betrayed a profound disquiet. For days, he lived as if under siege. He rarely left his friend's room. He bought a bag of rice and cooked for himself. He didn't even change his clothes. "I was trying to keep something in my life constant, to 'use one unchanging thing to respond to 10,000 changes,'" said Zhang, quoting a Confucian saying.

During the day, Zhang read and listened to the radio. It was only at night that he ventured out, walking along the shore and breathing the salty sea air. On June 19, Zhang's close friend from the *Herald*, Xu Xiaowei, came to see him. That evening, Xu joined Zhang on his seaside stroll. Xu had been on the road since June 4. He told Zhang all he had learned about the bloodbath in Beijing and the suppression of protests in other Chinese cities.

It was nearly midnight when the two journalists headed back to Zhang's room. Xu was asking Zhang to join him on another trip around the country when a car and van suddenly pulled up and stopped on the road beside them.

In the darkness, Zhang could just make out the characters for *gong an* (police) on the car. More than a dozen men got out, one of them shouldering a video camera. At first, Zhang didn't realize they were plainclothesmen. He thought they were factory workers recruited by the police to make routine patrols.

"State your names and *danwei!*" one of the men barked.

Zhang and Xu weren't alarmed. Both knew that every Chinese city had tightened security after the massacre. They each replied with their names, followed by "the *World Economic Herald.*"

"Show us your *zhengjian,*" the man said, demanding to inspect the state-issued identification card that every Chinese citizen must carry.

Neither Xu nor Zhang had his card with him. Xu calmly pulled out his monthly bus pass, which bore his photograph. Zhang had nothing but a name card, which he handed to the plainclothesman.

"Come with us," the man ordered, leading Zhang and Xu into the van.

They rode a short distance to the factory's police station on the seaside. Xu was led into one room, while two men took Zhang into another. Once inside, one of the men, named Dong, opened a briefcase and removed a document. Standing stiffly behind a wooden table, he addressed Zhang.

"In accordance with the Ministry of Public Security Wanted List and an arrest warrant, we are taking Zhang Weiguo in for investigation," he announced. The second man, Li, clapped handcuffs around Zhang's wrists.

Zhang saw that the document was a certificate for "detention and investigation," a power that the security police were notorious for abusing. Even worse, Zhang knew, "detention and investigation" carried no statutory time limit.

"Since you are detaining me in accordance with an arrest warrant, I have a right to see it," he protested. As a trained lawyer, Zhang was far better equipped than most detainees to defend himself.

"The warrant is 'internal.' You can't see it," Dong said.

"Then you are detaining me illegally; you have no legal standing," Zhang said.

Dong's face darkened. "You are guilty of inciting counterrevolutionary propaganda!" Dong shouted, pounding the table.

"What is your evidence?" Zhang pressed.

"That is precisely what we want to interrogate you about," Dong snapped. "Frisk him," he said, turning to Li.

Li took everything out of Zhang's pockets while Dong recorded the items on a list. Next, Dong ordered Zhang to lead them back to his friend's room. The police tore the room apart, rifling through every drawer and cabinet. Zhang hadn't taken precautions to hide his belongings, so the police took everything: notebooks, photographs, a camera, a tape recorder, and writings.

The next day, Zhang was taken to the Shanghai Number 1 Jail. As he rode in a police van toward the hulking Japanese-built structure in downtown Shanghai, Zhang wondered what had befallen Qin Benli and other close colleagues. For many months thereafter, Zhang heard nothing of them.

Much later Zhang learned the details of the party's nationwide witch-hunt and subsequent mass arrests and executions. According to the U.S. State Department and human rights groups, between 20,000 and 40,000 people were arrested in the post–June 4 suppression. Among them were many of Zhang's close friends and associates, including legal scholar Chen Xiaoping and activists Chen Ziming and Wang Juntao. The party labeled many of them, including Zhang, "black hands" of the student movement, making the absurd claim that the disorderly Tiananmen protests were manipulated by a handful of conspirators.

The *Herald* was officially accused of inciting the "turmoil." Its offices in Shanghai and Beijing were thoroughly searched. Many materials were confiscated, including, Zhang learned later, all his notebooks, photographs, and personal diaries. Zhang's colleagues, the young editors Chen Lebo and Ruan Jiangning, were detained. Many other *Herald* staffers were harassed by security police, tailed constantly, photographed meeting foreigners, and blacklisted for new job assignments for months after the crackdown. Qin, as a veteran party cadre, was spared jail and put under house arrest.

The *Herald*'s fate was shared by dozens of other nongovernmental publications, research institutes, student groups, and workers unions that flourished before and during the short-lived Beijing Spring. The *New Observer* magazine was closed down. Ge Yang, its editor in chief, chose exile in the United States after being labeled a "heroine of the turmoil" by Beijing. The outspoken newspaper *Economics Weekly* and the Bejiing Social Science and Economics Research Institute, both run by Chen Ziming, Wang Juntao, and others, were banned and their substantial research materials and electronic equipment confiscated. The suppression of the *Herald* and other unofficial groups demonstrated the vast political and historical barriers in 1989 to the emergence in China of a full-fledged "civil society."

In many ways, the *Herald* was a paragon of the kind of semiautonomous organization that could help foster a democratic society in China. It was profitable and financially independent of the government. It was energized by relatively young, free-thinking intellectuals willing to break with constraining Marxist dogma. Above all, the *Herald* strove to respond to the broad interests of Chinese people, refusing to blindly serve the ruling party.

Despite its strengths, the *Herald* and its editors lacked the broad-based, sustained backing from China's public to challenge the party successfully. Their dramatic eleventh-hour appeal to win popular support was too little, too late. Even if the appeal had come earlier, the democratic tradition among China's citizens remained too weak, and the political monopoly of party factions too strong, for the *Herald* to prevail.

Ultimately, the paper's fate rested on Qin's high-level connections and the party's reformist wing, represented by Zhao Ziyang. Although over the years these ties to the elite had greatly helped the maverick newspaper, in the end they hurt it more. On June 24, four days after Zhang entered prison, Zhao was formally stripped of all his powers. Zhao's fall doomed the *Herald* and many other unofficial proreform groups. Zhao's replacement as party general secretary was the *Herald*'s nemesis, Shanghai party boss Jiang Zemin. Jiang was favored by hard-liners in part due to his stern handling of the *Herald*.

Still, the weeks of activism by *Herald* reporters and other bold journalists in 1989 left behind a vital legacy for democracy in China. By upholding their ideals against all political odds, Zhang and his colleagues inspired thousands of Chinese to rally for press freedom for the first time under Communist rule. As they embraced their right to free expression and other basic liberties, Chinese began calling themselves "citizens," spurning their party-designated title, "the masses." Although the newspaper was silenced, the *Herald* survived as a powerful symbol of democracy and press freedom in the minds of Chinese.

The *Herald*'s legacy also lived on in Zhang. As the police van carried him through the gate of the jail on June 20, Zhang knew his fight for the paper was over. But he was determined to defend his individual rights as a journalist and Chinese citizen.

❋

At the jail, guards first assigned Zhang the prison designation "857" and ordered him to forget his real name. Then they put him in a cell less than twelve feet square with three other prisoners. The dank space was empty of furniture or fixtures except for a tap and a urinal. Zhang and his cellmates slept on a cement floor covered with wooden boards. During his first nights in jail Zhang rested only fitfully. Cockroaches infested the dark slits in the floor and often awakened Zhang when they scurried over his face and arms. Zhang was also disturbed by the dim glow of a lightbulb left burning all night to allow guards to see into the cell. Inmates resorted to black humor in calling it a "long-life lamp"—the lamp Chinese Buddhists keep lit over the dead before burial to expiate their sins and free their souls from purgatory.

The cell had one high narrow window. Through it, Zhang could hear the din of traffic on Nanchezhuang Road. A few blocks farther south flowed the Huangpu River. Sometimes as he lay awake at night, Zhang listened to the horns of ships and river barges as they plowed through the brackish waterway toward the mouth of the Yangtze and beyond to the East China Sea.

During his first weeks in jail, Zhang faced long, frequent interrogations. Prison officials woke him before dawn, took him to a separate room, and forced him onto a wooden chair bolted to the floor under blazing lights. Several men grilled Zhang late into the night about the *Herald*, his activities, and his contacts. They sometimes offered Zhang a bowl of weak broth. But he was so tense from constant arguing that he couldn't eat. When he dozed off, they shook him awake.

Back in his cell, Zhang's three cellmates watched his every move. They told Zhang they were awaiting trial, but in reality they were convicted criminals assigned to spy on Zhang and draw information from him. One cellmate, an elderly Shanghai cadre, often encouraged Zhang to talk by dropping the names of people he claimed were mutual friends. Such "meritorious service" could earn him a reduced sentence.

Zhang grew suspicious as his cellmates fawned over him, scrubbing the pan he ate from, mopping the floor for him, and helping him wash his clothes. He knew that by custom newly arrived prisoners should do more routine work. At night, with feigned concern, the cellmates had Zhang lie with his head to one wall and then completed a box around him with their three bodies. They aimed to prevent Zhang from attempting suicide.

Zhang's misgivings were confirmed one day when his interrogator accused him of plotting an escape. "Don't try to hide it!" the official snapped.

Incredulous, Zhang denied the charge. But later he recalled joking with his cellmates about trying out the jailbreaks they had seen in movies. Immediately, he realized his fellow inmates were reporting back everything he said and did. Prison officials used Zhang's alleged plans for a "jailbreak" to deny him outdoor exercise.

During his entire imprisonment he was let out only once for twenty minutes of "fresh air."

Zhang was outraged. The Number 1 Jail was a detention center for suspects who had not stood trial; it was illegal for them to be jailed together with convicts. The next day, he confronted his captors. "*You're* the ones committing a crime against *me!*" he burst out. "You detain me without evidence. You refuse to show me the wanted list. You violate my rights."

Zhang's anger fueled his defiance. During interrogations, he answered only the most benign questions. Most of the time, especially when pressed for the names of his sources, he refused to respond on the grounds that as a journalist he was responsible only to Qin Benli. Exasperated, the authorities tried a new tactic.

On the night of August 4, prison guards abruptly ordered Zhang to gather his belongings and led him outdoors to a waiting car. The car left the city and drove west into Shanghai's suburbs. As they approached what in the darkness appeared to be a large gateway, the guards covered Zhang's head. Soon, the car stopped. Zhang learned later that he had been taken to a top-secret jail, sometimes called the Shanghai Number 3 Jail.

Zhang discovered that much like the famous Qincheng prison in Beijing, the Number 3 Jail primarily held political prisoners. The rolls of past and present inmates read like the cast of a black satire on Communist Party rule. Victims from virtually every party campaign since the 1949 revolution had resided at the jail at one time or another. Ma Tianshui, the ultraleftist Shanghai leader who approved equipment for Zhang's rural factory, was held there until he went insane. When Zhang arrived at the jail, its cells were filled with victims of the party's latest purge—prodemocracy activists and their sympathizers. To Zhang, the problems of China's political system seemed embodied in the ugly thick-walled structure and its hollow-eyed inhabitants.

The jail, Zhang learned, was located in the western outskirts of Shanghai somewhere off Hami Road. Zhang knew Shanghai's Hongqiao Airport was nearby because from his cell window he often saw low-flying planes. Sometimes, he saw swans overhead, which confirmed he was not far from Xijiao Park and the Shanghai Zoo. A state-run pig farm was also nearby. On hot summer nights, the heavy stench of pig manure permeated the air in Zhang's cell.

Zhang remained under intense surveillance at the Number 3 Jail. Despite his efforts, he found it impossible to hide a prison diary he was keeping from the ever watchful eyes of his new cellmates. One day prison guards came in and searched all his belongings, inspecting his clothes and ripping open the seams of his cotton quilt. They found the diary and took it away. After that, their searches were more frequent.

Still, physical conditions were far better than at the Number 1 Jail, which housed common criminals. Authorities apparently believed they could win confessions by sparing political prisoners some of the worst deprivations. Zhang's cell at the Number 3 Jail was spacious. Sunlight sometimes glanced through the window. Outside, he could see plots of vegetables growing. The food was more flavorful and better prepared. Sometimes in summer, guards put a fan near the door to cool the cell. Once a week, Zhang was permitted to watch state-run television. He could also read Shanghai's official newspapers. "We want you to talk with us, to cooperate with us," Zhang's new interrogators appealed. "Reform your attitude; consider your future," they urged. Still, Zhang resisted.

Then one day after lunch, while he was standing looking out the window, Zhang suddenly collapsed and passed out. For several seconds, the guards couldn't find his pulse. He broke out in a sweat, and his body felt cold and clammy. When he came to a few minutes later, he felt exhausted. A prison doctor gave him a cursory exam and suspected a heart problem. Zhang asked to go to the hospital for a checkup, but prison officials refused.

Zhang's weakness continued for a few days. As he lay in his cell resting, he couldn't forget the sensation of blacking out. He took up a pencil and wrote an article entitled "I've Already Died Once." "I felt that I already knew what it was like to die," Zhang said. "It was as though I was living for the second time. Nothing from the past mattered; I was starting a new life."

Zhang felt immensely liberated. He saw his life with a fresh, uncanny clarity. All his past uniforms—as Beijing bureau chief, party member, and Red Guard—were stripped away. Now, he stood naked as an individual against the state. At the most vulnerable time in his life, he felt freer than ever. He confronted his captors with new resolve.

Over the weeks that followed, tensions steadily mounted between Zhang and prison authorities. They peaked on December 20 when the authorities announced that they were formally arresting Zhang on charges of "counterrevolutionary propaganda and incitement," a crime that carried a maximum sentence of life imprisonment. The same day, authorities sent Zhang back to the Number 1 Jail—as punishment, he guessed.

From then on, Zhang kept silent. He ignored his interrogators. He refused to answer questions or sign anything. He was confident that he could accept responsibility for his actions. All he wanted was to be tried in accordance with the law.

"Whatever I have to say to you, I will say in court," Zhang told his interrogator.

"You must rectify your attitude, Eight-five-seven," the interrogator began, "admit your mistakes—"

"Don't talk to me about my attitude," Zhang interrupted. "At issue now is whether I committed a crime. You say I committed a crime; now show me your proof."

Zhang found conditions at the Number 1 Jail even worse than during his first stay. Typically the jail had about 500 to 600 detainees packed into forty cells. Zhang was jammed into a cell with fifteen other detainees, including accused robbers, murderers, embezzlers, and rapists. It was so crowded that Zhang's cellmates often quarreled or broke into fistfights over a spot of floor to sleep on.

Despite his innocence, Zhang realized that China's party-controlled courts could convict anyone on trumped-up charges. He expected his defiance would earn him a long sentence, maybe ten years. As if mentally preparing for the worst, he settled into the prison's grim routine.

Zhang quickly adapted to the informal rules of the street-toughened inmates, and on the whole, they respected him as a university graduate and lawyer. The better Zhang got to know his cellmates, the more he sympathized with them. He often advised them on their cases and offered concrete suggestions for their defense. He was intrigued by the prisoners' stories.

One cellmate, a sixty-seven-year-old peasant named Gu Genxiang, came from a village in Shanghai's Nanhui County, near where the Yangtze River flows into Hangzhou Bay. Like most Chinese peasants, Old Gu was used to being pushed around by the "local tyrants" as village cadres are often called. But he grew enraged when a village cadre forcibly occupied part of his farmland to build a house. One day, the cadre's wife started cursing Old Gu as he sat drowning his humiliation in a bottle of spirits. Gu grabbed his hunting rifle and shot them both, blinding the cadre and wounding his wife.

Zhang found many of the detainees highly intelligent. They showed their cleverness in the handicrafts they made in jail. To mend their clothes, they fashioned needles out of slivers of wooden chopsticks. Using old newspapers and a paste of water and leftover rice, they made strong suitcases as well as delicate papier-mâché crafts. They also taught Zhang how to use levity and camaraderie to make the best of the dreary prison regimen.

The revolting food was a constant source of jokes. The pound of rice that made up the bulk of the prisoners' daily diet was full of grit that cracked between their teeth. The muddy outer leaves of boiled vegetable that accompanied the rice were so old and tough that the prisoners labeled them "dishrags." The eggplants were dubbed "plastic jars" because they were little more than hard shells. The meat served once or twice a week was almost all fat (*feirou*), so the prisoners called it "soap" (*feizao*).

The only relief from this bland diet came on the fifteenth of each month, when inmates with "good attitudes" were allowed to receive a small parcel of food from their kin. Families were permitted to supply one or two pounds of crackers, one package of malted milk powder, and other daily necessities such as toothpaste. If a detainee showed "bad behavior," the goods were confiscated.

Every month, as the fifteenth approached, a giddy anticipation filled Zhang's cell. Inmates began talking about their families and guessing who would deliver the package. Zhang thought about his family, too. He felt guilty about causing them so much worry. "People on the outside suffer more than people on the inside," he thought.

The worst-off inmates received nothing from beyond the jail walls. They were known as the "three withouts" (*san wu*) because they had no known family, home, or material aid. For clothing, some of them had to borrow grimy blue prison uniforms. Most inmates abhorred these "dead men's clothes," which were thought to be left behind by prisoners who were executed.

When their loneliness and frustration mounted, Zhang and his cellmates vented it in song. Amid the scraping and clanging of leg irons, the band of prisoners belted out popular tunes. Zhang found comfort in the lusty, off-key crooning.

To pass the time, he began copying down lyrics on the wrapping paper from bars of soap provided by his family.

Prison guards often responded to the loud outbursts of karaoke in Zhang's cell by cursing and beating the inmates. The guards routinely struck inmates with cattle prods for petty reasons.

The jail authorities had many other, more insidious ways of abusing Zhang and his cellmates. On hot summer days, they sometimes denied prisoners water. On a daily basis, water was rationed to small amounts a half hour before each meal. Inmates were also regularly denied medical care. Each week, a prison doctor made a round, sliding open the tiny metal window in the cell doors.

"Any problems here?" she would ask. About a dozen men crowded each cell, but the doctor refused to examine more than three on each visit. Any more than that and she would impatiently slam the window closed. "Shut up, you bastards!" she told the sick men, turning her back on their pleas. She refused altogether to treat "minor ailments" such as the contagious skin diseases that constantly plagued inmates in summer.

Zhang sometimes had to listen for hours to the wails of ailing inmates who were denied medical care. Those who received treatment found it so crude and slapdash that they dubbed prison doctors "veterinarians." Indeed, Zhang often felt that prison authorities treated the detainees as beasts. He was shocked one day to hear the prison warden admit as much in a lecture to inmates over the prison broadcast system.

"You are human, and you are not human," boomed the warden's grating voice from the loudspeaker built into the cell wall. "You are human because you have the thoughts and feelings of normal people. You are not human because you have deviated from social ethics and broken the law."

Zhang shook his head. "Conclusion: Detainees, who have deviated from social ethics and broken the law, are not human," he thought. "Why protect the human rights of a person who is not human?" The warden's lecture reminded him of the Cultural Revolution, when people were locked up in cowsheds and denounced as "monsters and evil spirits." Now, China had courts and laws, but prison authorities still acted like Red Guards. Little wonder, Zhang thought, that detainees viewed prison authorities with a mixture of hostility, distrust, and mocking defiance.

"Confess and you will be treated leniently. Resist and you will be treated severely," went the official slogan constantly repeated over the prison broadcast system. Inmates had their own ditty:

> *Confess and you will be treated leniently?*
> *You'll spend your entire life in here!*
> *Resist and you will be treated severely?*
> *You'll be home for Chinese New Year!*

Far from being "reformed," Zhang's cellmates and other detainees often swore to take revenge when they got out. "I'll commit worse crimes until the shot is fired!" one inmate vowed to Zhang. In other words, he would be a criminal until his execution. In China, condemned prisoners are forced to kneel and then shot in the back of the head.

As a political prisoner, Zhang suffered less than the average detainee at the Number 1 Jail. In tacit recognition of his status, prison officials often summoned Zhang for interrogation when his cellmates were being beaten. Moreover, Zhang defended himself more aggressively than ordinary inmates. He knew that under Chinese law a detainee should retain all his basic rights while under investigation. Over the months, he doggedly challenged every infraction by prison authorities.

Zhang harangued officials for denying him exercise in the prison yard and barring him from the jail's reading room. When another of his diaries was seized after informers tipped off the guards, he retaliated with sarcasm: "While in a czarist prison, Lenin wrote a monumental classic. In this prison, even my diary is seized. Whose human rights record is better?"

Zhang learned that the use of convicted criminals to spy on detainees was widespread and systematic at the jail. Informers were placed in most of the cells. Nicknamed "hooks" and "spoons," the informers were convicted criminals who here handed over to the jail by Shanghai's Labor Reform Bureau. Their task was to report on other inmates and pay special attention to "important criminals" like Zhang. In return, informers could receive more food and longer prison visits by their families. In addition, each week they were released from their cells to smoke a cigarette on the pretext of being interrogated. Smoking, Zhang knew, was considered the height of enjoyment by inmates. When the warden deemed an informant had performed "meritorious service," he cut his sentence. So attractive were these benefits, that most of the convicted criminals working as hooks and spoons in the jail had pulled strings to get there.

Zhang had known for years that China's legal system was corrupt. But he was still shocked by the blatant abuse of the law at the Number 1 Jail. If convicts were systematically bribed to incriminate political prisoners, he thought, how could justice ever be done?

After several months at the jail, Zhang grew anxious that prison authorities would keep him in limbo indefinitely. The legal time limit for trying his case had long passed. He knew of prisoners who had been "taken in for investigation" and held for more than three years without charges or trial. He warned the authorities that they were violating the criminal procedural law. "Don't worry," the official in charge of Zhang's case replied in a well-rehearsed voice, "there is a document approving an extension for closing your case."

After that, Zhang drafted a letter of appeal criticizing the prison authorities to China's parliament. But the warden refused to mail the letter. "What is the use of writing this stuff? Will they get it?" one prison official asked Zhang.

What amazed Zhang most was the prison authorities' indirect admission that China's legal system was a farce. Over and over, Zhang's interrogators told him that "leaders at higher levels will determine the nature of your case."

If "leaders at higher levels" would determine Zhang's fate, then what was the use of evidence or trials? If China had an authority higher than the law, who but those in power could rely on the legal system? Zhang was astounded by the openness with which the officials acknowledged that the Communist Party leadership was above the law. China was still a nation ruled by men (*renzhi*), not by law (*fazhi*).

One night in June 1990, Zhang was again hustled into a car and driven to the secret Number 3 Jail west of Shanghai. Again, the authorities sought to entice Zhang into "cooperating" and making a confession. As before, they pampered him with better food, a sunlit room, and a fan to blow in fresh air. But this time, they also dangled before him a tantalizing reward: freedom.

"Eight-five-seven, did you know that gradually other people are being granted amnesty?" his interrogator asked one morning. "Why don't you cooperate this time? Don't try to be a hero," he said, forcing a smile. The authorities were apparently prepared to release Zhang. Beijing had freed many other leading dissidents in a bid to clinch renewal of most-favored-nation trade ties with the United States. But first, they wanted to extract all the information they could from Zhang. By October, however, it was clear that Zhang would not cave in. He was abruptly returned to the Number 1 Jail.

❋

For four months, Zhang waited for news on his case. Then, on February 12, 1991, the warden entered Zhang's cell along with two officials from the Shanghai Public Security Bureau (PSB). "Eight-five-seven, the Shanghai Municipal Procuratorate has completed its investigation of your case. It has determined that your activities did not amount to the crime of counterrevolutionary incitement and propaganda. It has authorized us to free you."

Zhang didn't hear what the PSB official said next. "They are freeing me! I have won!" he thought. He had stood up to the state as an individual citizen and prevailed. Many factors in addition to Zhang's defiance contributed to his release. Certainly, foreign pressure and China's eagerness to renew favored trade ties with the United States played a role. Also important, Zhang believes, was the desire of Shanghai's new, moderate party chief, Zhu Rongji, to distance himself from Beijing hard-liners. Apparently at Zhu's request, Zhang was released as Beijing announced lengthy sentences for other prominent dissidents. Still, Zhang felt a powerful sense of relief and vindication. His elation vanished, however, with the news that followed.

"You must be psychologically prepared," said the PSB official. "Qin Benli is dying of cancer. He is near the end. He wants to see you. Foreigners might try to exploit the situation to write articles," he warned.

"I am one of Qin's *laobuxia*, his longtime troops," Zhang replied. "I have an obligation to him. I will meet that obligation."

Later that afternoon, Zhang's younger brother and sister came to the jail to pick him up in a neighbor's taxi. On the way home, they broke another piece of bitter news. In August 1989, citing his involvement in the "turmoil," the Shanghai Justice Bureau had permanently disqualified Zhang from practicing law. Zhang stared blankly ahead. He was no longer a lawyer. His newspaper had been disbanded. He was leaving jail at the age of thirty-four as an ordinary, unemployed Shanghai citizen.

That night, Zhang was heartened when many of his law school classmates, colleagues from the *Herald*, and old mentors came to celebrate his release. He was especially moved to see the elderly well-wishers, who had their own rich encounters with political persecution. Some who had dared to criticize Mao's rule were purged in the 1957 antirightist campaign and jailed or ostracized for more than twenty years. Others had been "struggled against" during the Cultural Revolution. When they finally got out of Mao's labor camps, almost no one was brave enough to speak to them, let alone welcome them home. But in a sign of changing times, they now came openly to greet Zhang. "History will prove you right," they said.

The next day, Zhang and some colleagues bicycled to Shanghai's East China Hospital to visit Qin Benli. The air was raw, the sky overcast. Zhang thought of Qin, hoping the hospital ward was warm enough for his old friend.

At the hospital, Zhang found that Qin had been assigned a private room with not only heating but a bath and balcony in a ward reserved for high cadres. But the room was no more than a luxurious prison cell for Qin. Party authorities, worried about the political sensitivity of Qin's declining health, had ordered the special room, number 402, equipped with surveillance gear. They also controlled Qin's medical treatment, ruling out as too risky the use of the newest drugs from abroad. Later, they dictated who could see Qin, using police to bar from the room anyone but his immediate family.

When Zhang entered room 402, Qin looked over and immediately smiled. He tried to sit up but winced and fell back on his pillow. "Weiguo … you've come to see me … good," he said haltingly in his rural Jiangsu dialect.

Zhang went to Qin's bedside and took his frail hand. "Don't get up, Boss. I'll sit here next to you." Qin nodded.

Zhang sat quietly. For a long time, neither spoke. Zhang looked at Qin, his eyes sunken under bushy black eyebrows, his body atrophied by the cancer. Qin, too, detected thin lines of worry on Zhang's young face. Their fates had been wound into one by the *Herald* crisis in the spring of 1989. The silencing of the paper had oppressed them in different ways, but the root of their pain was the same. It united them. With Zhang and Qin, it was no longer a question of two separate lives but more of a continuum, of who came before and who went after.

Over the next few weeks, Zhang spent many hours at the bedside of the veteran editor, listening to his reflections, his regrets, and his final wishes. With a notebook and fountain pen, Zhang carefully recorded everything Qin told him. He knew that Qin had held on, struggling against the cancer, waiting for Zhang's release from jail. He only dreaded the thought that Qin, after telling him everything, would find no reason to live on.

Zhang listened to Qin recount his decision to join the party in the 1940s and his purge by Mao in 1957. They talked about his lifelong effort to foster a Chinese press that would point out the party's failings, promote democratic reform, and play "a crucial role at the crucial time." The two joked about Qin's trademark technique of finessing state controls with *ca bian qiu.* Zhang raised the possibility of writing a book about Qin, and Qin brightened at the idea. "You must gather all the materials," Qin said, briefly reverting to his tone as *Herald* editor in chief. "I want you to write this book yourself!"

But as their conversations deepened, Qin began to talk less about his life's successes and more about what he saw as its final, devastating failure.

"I awakened too late, Weiguo ... too late!" Qin lamented one day. Qin, Zhang learned, had undergone a sudden, wrenching change of heart after the PLA opened fire on Beijing citizens on June 4, 1989. The massacre shattered his faith in the party. From then on, the bloodbath had haunted Qin as a symbol of a life of delusion and betrayed trust. He sank into a deep depression and within months was diagnosed with stomach cancer.

Although Qin had "awakened too late," he found solace in knowing that it was not too late for Zhang. On the evening of March 9, as Zhang sat at Qin's bedside, the veteran editor asked him for his pen and notebook. With effort, Qin took the pen and, his hand shaking, scrawled these characters: "For young Weiguo, the spirit of the *Herald* will never die."

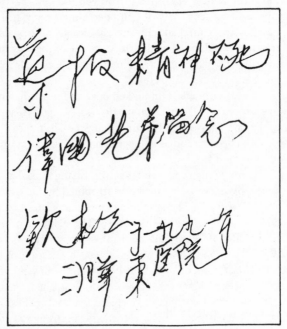

Qin Benli's inscription for Zhang Weiguo: "For young Weiguo, the spirit of the Herald *will never die."*

After that, Qin spoke as passionately and as often as he could to Zhang of the need to advance press freedom. In early April, Qin summoned Zhang, Zhu Xingqing, and other young editors of the *Herald* for his final behest. "My last wish is for you to go on running newspapers, to push forward the cause of press freedom in China," Qin said.

"Put your heart at ease, Boss," Zhang said. "We will do what you ask."

❉

On April 15, 1991, exactly two years after Hu Yaobang's death sparked China's largest protests ever against Communist rule, Qin passed away at the age of seventy-three. On hearing the news, Zhang's first thought was of his promise to Qin. "What the dead cannot do must be done by the living," he told himself. The *Herald* was gone. He had to find new outlets for his reporting, new ways to promote press freedom in China. Blacklisted from China's media organizations, he decided the best channel for his writing was the overseas press.

Ignoring official warnings, Zhang passed on information about Qin to the foreign press and Chinese-language papers in Hong Kong and Taiwan. Qin's death was itself news, all the more so because it occurred on such a sensitive anniversary. It was widely played overseas.

Soon after that, Zhang began freelancing for the Hong Kong and Taiwan press. It was risky. To his knowledge, no mainland Chinese since 1949 had openly freelanced for foreign publications. But there was no law forbidding it. At first he wrote interpretive pieces on Chinese politics, press reform, and other news. His essays filled an important niche in the Hong Kong and Taiwan press, which lacked commentators skilled at analyzing mainland news. Initially, Zhang used a pen name. But soon he switched to his own byline except in cases where he might imperil his sources.

Party hard-liners were outraged at Zhang's boldness. Shanghai police redoubled their surveillance of him. His phone was tapped; his mail was crudely opened and resealed or never delivered. Authorities interrogated his friends and warned them to stay away from him. Whenever Zhang went out, he was shadowed. "Is there a *weiba* [tail]?" friends whispered to Zhang. Invariably, at least one plainclothesman hovered nearby.

The official harassment failed to intimidate Zhang or scare off his contacts. On the contrary, he was encouraged by a growing chorus of Chinese intellectuals, who quietly applauded his defiance. By openly expressing his views despite the oppressive post-Tiananmen atmosphere, Zhang set an example for independent-minded intellectuals all over China, they said. Inspired by Zhang, other intellectuals began freelancing, although none of them used their real names. "What is important is not what you write but that you are writing at all," said a friend.

Sympathizers began leaking stories to Zhang. As his sources multiplied to include party cadres, PLA officers, and frustrated journalists, so did demand for his articles. Zhang became a regular contributor to the Taiwan papers *United Daily News* and *China Times Weekly* and the Hong Kong publications *Ming Pao*, the *Mirror* monthly, and *Zheng Ming* magazine. Several publications offered to hire Zhang as a "special correspondent" for an attractive salary. But he declined, knowing he could never get the required Foreign Ministry accreditation.

Soon, Zhang's freelance career kept him busier than he had ever been at the *Herald.* "My room was like the headquarters of a small independent news agency," Zhang laughed.

Every morning, Zhang woke up at 6:00 and began listening to shortwave radio newscasts. After the crackdown, the overseas broadcasts became an especially vital source of objective news for dissidents, intellectuals, and many ordinary Chinese. Zhang recorded important news on a cassette tape to exchange with friends.

After eating breakfast and scanning Shanghai's official press, Zhang began writing, churning out page after page of handwritten copy. Then he decided how to get the story out of China. If it was urgent he secretly faxed it, aided by friends working at hotels, companies, or government offices. Less timely stories he mailed in hotel stationery. His safest course was to give articles to contacts to carry out of the country. In the afternoon, Zhang met with sources, often in Shanghai's small noisy streetside eateries. Once in a while, to let off steam, he joined friends for an evening at a karaoke bar, crooning the pop songs he had learned in jail.

Late at night, Zhang returned home to begin writing again. He stayed in a separate room in the tenement next door to his family's apartment, which was now occupied on the street level by his younger brother's one-table private restaurant. Zhang would climb the unlit, creaking wooden staircase that was blackened from the smoke of a communal coal stove in the hallway. Year-round an ancient teakettle sat on the stove slowly simmering. At the end of the narrow hallway, a door led into Zhang's second-story loft. The room was only big enough for Zhang's desk and the fold-out couch that he slept on. Books and papers were stacked high on the arms of the couch. On the wall hung a large photograph of the Statue of Liberty.

Zhang pulled a stool out from under his desk and sat down to write. The desk, which was flush against the north wall, faced two large windows overlooking the lane off Tibet Road. In warm weather, he left the windows open to the cacophony of the city. Zhang wrote with a fountain pen on cheap onionskin paper. Each sheet was printed with rows of squares. For clarity, he placed one character in each square, continuing a practice from his days at the *Herald* when printshop workers had to set the metal type word by word. Like many Chinese reporters, Zhang lacked both the money and desire to write by computer. Habitually heavy smokers, a lot of Chinese journalists shunned computers because they found it hard to concentrate without a burning cigarette in one hand. Zhang didn't smoke, but he found computers cumbersome. His pen softly scratching the paper, he wrote late into the night, often listening to jazz. Sometimes, he put his feet up on the couch for a rest until he grew too drowsy and fell asleep.

❋

By May, Zhang had established himself as an independent freelance writer, an unprecedented feat in Communist China. At the same time, he emerged as China's most outspoken dissident. In frequent interviews with foreign reporters, he advocated press freedom, judicial independence, and political reform. Unlike most dissidents, he agreed to be quoted by name. He was testing his belief that openness was the best way to advance his principles and guarantee his own protection. His refusal to remain silent marked another breakthrough in post-Tiananmen China. Since the bloody crackdown two years earlier, no other Chinese dissident had dared to speak out publicly for human rights.

Chinese leaders, especially party leader Jiang Zemin, were vexed by Zhang's outspokenness. But Zhang had won international sympathy, so officials shied from jailing him again. Beijing wanted to minimize foreign criticism and improve its image abroad. Moreover, Jiang opposed new actions against Zhang that would rekindle images of his cruelty to Qin and repression of the *Herald,* Zhang's sources told him. After Qin's death, many Chinese intellectuals had privately denounced Jiang. Fearing that the official verdicts on the democracy movement and the *Herald* "incident" might one day be reversed, Jiang sought to distance himself from the crackdown while still in power.

Still, as the June 4 anniversary approached, nervous Shanghai authorities moved to restrain Zhang. On the afternoon of May 29, Zhang's phone rang. An officer summoned him to the police station near his home on Tibet Road. He went down to the street, unlocked the old Eternity bicycle his father had pieced together for him, and pedaled over to the police station, parking his bike outside.

"You have been subpoenaed by the Shanghai Public Security Bureau," the officer informed Zhang. "Come with us."

Zhang boarded a small police van, which drove to the Shanghai Public Security Bureau's branch office in Luwan district. There, Zhang was taken before three plainclothes PSB officers waiting for him in an interrogation room. They were all in their mid-thirties and casually dressed in slacks and brightly printed shirts. Zhang later confirmed that they were members of the PSB's political security section. As he came closer, Zhang immediately recognized two of the men as Li and Dong, the officers who had detained him at the petrochemical factory early in the morning of June 20, 1989.

"We've already met," Zhang said.

"That's right, please sit down," Li said, taking out a subpoena for Zhang to sign. As he did so, Zhang noted that it was 5:45 P.M. "We'll eat first and then talk," Li said.

"Don't trouble yourself," Zhang replied. "Let's talk business. Anyway, I'm expected for dinner."

But from the look Li gave him, Zhang could see that he had no choice. He was in for a long interrogation. A woman brought in the meal. Four different dishes and one soup, he observed, not bad. "It would be ungracious of me to refuse your hospitality," Zhang said with polite sarcasm.

After they finished eating, Li held out a pack of Marlboros to Zhang. Famous brand-name cigarettes, along with fashionable clothes, were vital to the smooth image cultivated by the PSB political agents. When Zhang refused, Li lit up and began the questioning.

"Today, we've called you in to discuss the case of Gu Bin. Do you know him?"

So that's their excuse, Zhang thought. Gu and eight other activists had been detained in April for trying to run an underground publication, a compilation of reports from Hong Kong and Taiwan. Zhang knew from his sources that Gu was an undercover agent.

"I've met him, but he left no deep impression on me," Zhang answered.

In response to questions, Zhang told his interrogators he had met Gu once about a month after his release from jail. Over coffee at a restaurant on Tibet Road, Gu asked Zhang to join the group. Zhang declined. He said he sympathized with Gu but wanted no part in an underground publication. He had decided to keep his actions legal, independent, and in the open.

"All my friends know that I want to be a free intellectual and nothing more," Zhang told Li. "As for Gu's case, I have nothing whatsoever to do with it."

After several more questions about Gu, Zhang grew impatient and pressed his interrogators to get to the point.

Li obliged. He held up a list of overseas journalists. "Do you know, apart from being journalists, what the identity of these people is?" Li asked, raising the old scare tactic that all foreign reporters are spies.

"I don't know, and I don't want to know," Zhang said.

One by one, Li quizzed Zhang about how he had met the reporters and what he told them. Zhang knew he had a right to keep silent. But he answered all the questions. He saw the interrogation as an excellent opportunity to gauge how the leadership was reacting to his outspokenness, and to explain his standpoint to the authorities.

"In one interview, you said 'in China, whether you're inside [jail] or outside, it's about the same except for the height of the wall.' But now you go wherever you want; you say anything you like to foreign journalists. Aren't you free?" Li asked.

"My firsthand experience proves how free I am," Zhang said. He ticked off his complaints over the harassment of his friends, the phone tapping, mail tampering, and constant shadowing.

Finally, the interrogators began pressing Zhang on his ties with Qin Benli. "During Qin's last days, you often went to the hospital to see him. What did he tell you? Did you write it down? Can you let us have a look at what you wrote?"

This time, Li had hit a raw nerve. "If you really think I have the freedom you just spoke about, then I'll use that freedom to refuse your request," Zhang shot back.

"As for my notes and other materials, I've already copied them and scattered them around in different places. Even if you search my home, you'll never find them," he continued. "But I know as a matter of fact that Qin Benli's room at the East China Hospital was installed with hidden recording equipment. All you have to do is request the recording from the relevant department and listen to it. Why do you have to take such great pains to ask me for it?"

"No need to make things so tense. Let's not have a defiant mentality," Li said in an artificially soothing tone.

"A fall in the pit, a gain in your wit," Zhang quipped. "I remember vividly something a high-ranking cadre told me before my detention in June 1989: 'Weiguo,' he said, 'you should be extremely careful. The Communist Party will dare to do anything.' At that time, I didn't pay much attention to him. But after two years of learning the truth of that statement, I've begun to cultivate a habit: Whatever I'm thinking of doing, I always prepare for the worst, or I won't do it at all. Perhaps in that way I'm a little tense. But as long as what I'm doing is for freedom of the press, for democracy, for the rule of law, I'm not one bit nervous."

The interrogation lasted until 11:30 P.M., then Zhang was allowed to leave. At midnight, he got home and found his mother, brother, and youngest sister up waiting for him. But the next morning the police called again and told Zhang to return for questioning at 3:00 that afternoon.

When Zhang arrived at the branch office, he was taken to the same interrogation room, where the same three officers sat waiting for him with their flowered shirts and Marlboros. The tension from their last encounter also remained.

Li aggressively started the questioning, pressing Zhang hardest on the location of his materials on Qin Benli. Chinese authorities, Zhang knew, were eager to stop him from writing about Qin. More than any other, Qin's life and death symbolized the Chinese yearning for press freedom and the state's brutal repression of it. Zhang refused to change his position.

"There is no law or regulation saying that I can't write a book on Qin Benli," he said.

Li's tone was threatening. "We summoned you here today to give you an opportunity—"

"I treasure all my opportunities," Zhang interrupted, "but I've said all I can. As to how the authorities deal with me, I am not free to choose. The Communist Party is irrational. Before coming here today, I made preparations for not going home."

After about three hours of questioning, Zhang noted that the twenty-four-hour subpoena had expired. The police freed him. But before he left, they advised him to "continue considering" their orders and asked him for a written summary of his statements.

"I won't consider their demands, but I will definitely write something," Zhang thought as he joined the rush-hour crowd of Shanghai workers pedaling home.

The next morning, he wrote a detailed account of his interrogation. A week later, a contact carried the article to Hong Kong, where it appeared in *Ming Pao* on June 24 and 25. Meanwhile, on the anniversary of June 4 he gave a long, candid interview to the BBC, which was rebroadcast in Chinese to millions of mainland listeners. Zhang wanted to signal clearly to China's leaders his determination to defend his right to speak out. "Openness is the basis for my survival," Zhang told an American reporter at the time.

From then on, when police interrogated him about his conversations with foreign journalists, Zhang warned them: "Whatever I told them, I'll tell you. But whatever you tell me, I'll also tell them."

In late June, Zhang took his crusade for basic rights one step further in a direct appeal to the leadership. This time, he focused not on press freedom but on legal reform. In a 10,000-character letter to Wan Li, chairman of China's parliament, Zhang detailed the blatant abuse of the law that he witnessed during twenty months as a detainee of the Chinese penal system. "If China's legal system had been sound and met real social needs, the June 4 events would not have oc-curred," he concluded.

Yet even as Zhang wrote, Chinese authorities were plotting their revenge. For two days, Zhang had noticed an unmarked limousine with five PSB agents inside parked in the lane outside his window. He ended the letter with the closing "Zhang Weiguo, a Shanghai citizen, written in haste, 28 June 1991."

That night, while Zhang was out at dinner, the PSB agents stormed into his family's apartment and demanded to interrogate him. They waited for him for several hours. But they were too late. Zhang, thanks to a tip-off, had disappeared.

For three days, as police scoured Shanghai looking for him, Zhang hid out at a friend's home. The third night, he slipped out of the city by bicycle, riding several hours to a provincial train station. He caught a train to Yangshan village in Zhejiang Province, where he took refuge at the home of his mother's relatives. For weeks afterward, he relished life in the countryside and the respite from the con-stant harassment in Shanghai. He relived his boyhood, swimming with a cousin in the streams and fishponds.

But at 2:00 A.M. on July 30, Zhang was awakened at his uncle's farmhouse by shouts and pounding on the door. Police broke down the door and rushed in. Re-fusing to produce a warrant, they handcuffed Zhang and led him outside the house before a ring of about thirty police and a dozen vehicles. Several police hus-tled Zhang into a car and sped through the night back to Shanghai.

For twenty-four hours, Zhang was again held at the Shanghai Number 1 Jail. Authorities interrogated him around the clock about his letter to Wan Li, alleged underground groups in Shanghai, his contacts with foreigners, and his plans to write about Qin Benli. Then, to prevent news about Zhang from leaking out, au-thorities drove him north out of the city to a large PLA camp and listening post near Bao Shan. For three weeks, Zhang was held in solitary confinement in an army compound under the constant watch of PLA guards. On August 21, Zhang was released only after his mother guaranteed he would not leave Shanghai. Of-fering no legal justification, authorities told him he was "on bail awaiting trial" and that his case was still unresolved. They ordered him to remain in Shanghai and report to police whenever they asked. He could be rearrested at any time, they warned.

❋

Undaunted, Zhang walked out of jail and immediately gave detailed accounts of his detention to foreign and Hong Kong reporters. Articles on his ordeal ap-peared overseas, including one in the Hong Kong monthly *Bai Xing* entitled "The Persecution of Zhang Weiguo." To Zhang's surprise, however, the authorities re-mained silent, which signaled that his strategy of openness was working.

"In China, you first of all have to stay alive and not be engulfed by the threats and machinations of the government," Zhang told a Hong Kong journalist. "Then you begin to test the limits of its tolerance. After you have pulled off your outra-geous acts once, twice, and three times, a pattern is established, a small victory is achieved."

From then on, it seemed Shanghai authorities would grudgingly tolerate Zhang's contributions to the overseas media. Over the next several months, despite regular interrogations by police, Zhang's freelance career flourished. He wrote prolifically on myriad topics, but his most powerful articles were arguments for a more open mainland press. He published a series on Qin Benli in the Hong Kong magazine *Dang Dai*. In March 1992, Zhang revealed in *Ming Pao* that subscriptions for the main state-run newspapers had plummeted after the 1989 crackdown. "Without press freedom, all other freedoms are illusory," he wrote.

Even in the dog days of summer, when ninety-degree weather sent many Shanghainese fleeing into the doorways of air-conditioned department stores, Zhang sat at his desk, stripped down to his shorts, writing. Sometimes, when the heat grew unbearable, he left his cluttered loft-turned-news-bureau and walked down to the lane below to buy a slice of watermelon from a farmer's stall. Or he splashed himself off in the old wooden tub his family used for bathing. He also drank beer, which doctors advised was good for his heart. "I can't stop writing; it's an illness of the profession," he told a friend one sultry Shanghai afternoon.

Zhang's success as a freelancer was a tribute to Qin Benli, whose words often sustained Zhang through his worst ordeals with the security police. Yet his personal triumph had far greater significance. It showed the millions of mainlanders who heard him interviewed or read his reports that a Chinese citizen could defy the state and survive. More broadly, it affirmed that despite the brutal crackdown in Tiananmen, party hard-liners had failed in the end to rein in China's newly assertive society.

Defiance remained especially strong among young intellectuals after the crackdown. By mid-1992, a few others were speaking out just as boldly as Zhang. Even dissidents in jail continued to write. Some of them published their works overseas. Zhang's friend Chen Ziming, who was sentenced in February 1991 to thirteen years for sedition, wrote a book in prison on China's economic reforms and had it smuggled to Hong Kong for publication in 1992. Under pressure from the United States, Chen and his colleague Wang Juntao were released in 1994.

Moreover, scores of young liberals, once out of jail and beyond intense police scrutiny, began quietly reviving their research, scholarship, and writing. Members of unofficial think tanks began as early as 1990 to gather scattered manuscripts and research plans and renew work aborted after the massacre. With old sources of funding cut off, they turned increasingly to the marketplace. Aided by sympathetic entrepreneurs, they set up private businesses to help finance new research in progressive political, economic, and social reforms. Ironically, the hardship imposed by the crackdown pushed them toward a new level of autonomy and freedom.

To varying degrees, Zhang's willingness to skirt or defy state controls was shared by Chinese of many other professions. From peasant entrepreneurs and grassroots officials to urban scholars and artists, Chinese of all walks of life single-mindedly pursued their private interests after June 4. They turned deaf ears to leftist propaganda on class struggle. They quietly boycotted a nationwide campaign to punish Chinese protesters and their sympathizers. The campaign fizzled out after a few months because in many *danwei* supervisors chose to protect rather than antagonize those below them. Similarly, they blocked conservatives' efforts to roll back vital market-oriented economic reforms. Profit-hungry entrepreneurs and local officials along China's prosperous coast were especially combative in defending the reforms. One by one, Deng Xiaoping and other Chinese leaders reboarded the reform bandwagon and began subtly distancing themselves from the 1989 crackdown.

Even party chief Jiang Zemin joined in the reversal to a degree. In late 1991, he attempted to revive the *Herald*. Jiang dispatched its former board chairman, Wang Daohan, to discuss the possibility with former *Herald* staff. The journalists snubbed the overture. In early 1992, Shanghai authorities also responded to the new political climate by dropping their hard-line tactics and holding out a carrot to Zhang.

"We know that you have plans to go abroad," a PSB officer told Zhang one day during a routine interrogation. Zhang had been invited to go to the University of California, Berkeley, as a visiting scholar. "We think that might be possible."

Convinced of the futility of their efforts to silence Zhang, the authorities now hoped to be rid of him. They expected that Zhang, like other Tiananmen activists, would quickly fade from public prominence once overseas. Moreover, Zhang's departure would enable party propagandists to malign him, as they did other dissidents abroad, as a self-interested schemer intent on "selling the country."

"It would be best if you stopped writing sensitive articles for the time being," an interrogator advised Zhang. "That way, we can speed the approval of your passport. Once you are overseas, of course, you can write whatever you want," he added, glancing up to gauge Zhang's reaction.

Zhang understood clearly the motives of Shanghai police. But he had his own reasons for wanting to go abroad. He knew that to grant him a passport the authorities would have to drop their case and lift the internal travel ban against him. By going overseas, Zhang could eventually regain his freedom of movement in China. Moreover, Zhang believed that by going abroad he could better advance his goal of setting up an unofficial newspaper in China. In the United States, he could learn firsthand how to run a private, profit-making, technically advanced newspaper. He could also rally the international contacts and support that he felt would be crucial to the financial and political viability of an independent media venture in China.

After several delays, Shanghai authorities finally lifted Zhang's parole on December 11, 1992. Zhang immediately traveled to Beijing, meeting many friends in the capital for the first time since June 1989. Then he returned to Shanghai, collected his passport and U.S. visa, and boarded a flight to Hong Kong. On February 11, 1993, Zhang arrived at the University of California, Berkeley, as a visiting scholar at the Center for Chinese Studies.

✳

Zhang has plunged into life in the United States with characteristic energy. He has rented a loft near Berkeley and learned to drive. He frequently travels to cities across the United States to give lectures, join conferences on China, and cover news. Zhang writes extensively about China for English- and Chinese-language publications in the United States, Hong Kong, and Taiwan. He also contributes to the New York–based magazine *Human Rights in China* and serves on its editorial board.

Zhang's journey from his tiny, closely watched "news bureau" in Shanghai to the broad vistas and footloose lifestyle of the United States is only the latest episode in a life of extremes. Indeed, Zhang's life so far has been a string of profound transformations—from prankster to Maoist zealot, from barefoot rural laborer to chauffeured corporate lawyer, and from liberal reporter to political prisoner and champion of a free press.

Still, there is a continuity within the chaos of Zhang's young life. Again and again, Zhang's relentless curiosity drove him to live out ideas to the fullest and hence discover their flaws. This pattern of probing and testing, especially his fanatical embrace and total rejection of Maoism, led Zhang to break the passive mold of his traditional mentors in one brief generation. Through his irrepressible questioning, Zhang came to know himself—his individual worth and purpose. Over the years, Zhang found within himself the conviction and independence of mind that he needed to defend his rights, and those of all Chinese, against the intrusions of the Communist Party. Bent on serving society rather than the state, Zhang and other young intellectuals have an antiauthoritarian, public-spirited outlook. Their views will help them fight for democratic reforms in China more boldly and effectively than have Qin Benli and other old democrats.

Zhang's most urgent goal is to promote a free press in China. He believes that long before a pluralistic political system emerges, an independent media could offer a voice to the Chinese public as well as to a range of opposition forces. He sees titanic obstacles to his task. Most Chinese today have never read a politically independent newspaper or voted in a truly free election. Despite a growing awareness of individual rights, many citizens are afraid to speak out and lack confidence in the unfamiliar ways of democracy. They are accustomed to strongman rule and fear that without it China will slide into chaos.

Zhang is confident, however, that press reform in China will accelerate along with the rise of a market-oriented, trade-driven economy. Growing economic freedom will offer liberal Chinese journalists more opportunities to set up unofficial, autonomous media enterprises. Already, many small, privately owned trade and cultural newspapers are thriving in China. Zhang believes that competition from such ventures will gradually erode the state-run media monopoly. Inroads by foreign broadcasters are another source of competitive pressure on the state media. Today, millions of Chinese are shunning state-run stations as they tune to overseas radio programs and foreign television shows beamed in by satellite.

In his first effort to set up an independent publication, Zhang launched a Chinese-language newsletter in November 1993 to promote constitutional reform in China. Entitled *China's Constitution After Reintegration,* the newsletter has stimulated a debate over the kind of constitution that would work best for a Chinese federation composed of the mainland, Hong Kong, and Taiwan. Zhang has circulated the newsletter in all three areas. But he won't be satisfied for long promoting Chinese press freedom from afar. "As soon as the conditions are ripe, I plan to return to China to have a direct impact on the changes there," Zhang said.

Zhang has broken with the submissiveness of older intellectuals to embrace free thinking and activism in a society under reform. Still, he appreciates lessons from the past and venerates the mentors who have gone before him. As he drives around San Francisco in his rusty red 1984 Nissan, or walks through an airport on assignment carrying a flightbag stuffed with clothes and handwritten news copy, Zhang often finds inspiration in the words of his old editor: "The spirit of the *Herald* will never die."

Shortly before the second anniversary of Qin's death, Zhang wrote an article for the Chinese-language newspaper *World Journal*. In the article, which appeared on the April 15, 1993, anniversary, Zhang posed a question to his readers.

> Qin Benli left the world of the living, bearing with him the regret that China's mainland had not yet realized press freedom. … Yet imagine for a moment, if he had awoken earlier, would Qin Benli still have chosen the Communist Party? If he had awoken a little sooner, would Qin Benli have run the *World Economic Herald* as he did? If he could choose a second time, what would he do? Questions like these are already superfluous for Qin Benli, but for each of us, the living?

As Chinese awaken to their rights, China will one day have a free press, Zhang wrote. Then, "the spirit of the *Herald* will never die, and Qin Benli, in the nether world, will close his eyes, fulfilled."

$\mathbf{A}$lthough *Zhang Weiguo and other intellectuals are staking out new ground for thought and action free of government control, they are not necessarily the social force that will spark a movement for political change in China. If modern history is any guide, the social tinder for decisive reform will probably be ignited by China's bold, capricious army of activists: students.*

University students have helped lead every major political struggle in China during the twentieth century. Moreover, since the Communist Party assumed power in 1949, students have grown steadily more organized and pragmatic in their intermittent movements for progressive change.

The life and activism of Gao Qinxin illustrate the potent role of students in political movements. From his peasant beginnings, to 1989 Tiananmen activism, to the black aftermath of the Beijing massacre, Gao's life shows how reform is empowering students to help free China from its torturous cycle of rebellion and repression.

Protesters and the Goddess of Democracy on June 2, 1989, in Tiananmen Square

N I N E

Conclusion: "Truth New Born"?

Youth of delight, come hither,
And see the opening morn,
Image of truth new born.
Doubt is fled, & clouds of reason,
Dark disputes & artful teazing.
Folly is an endless maze,
Tangled roots perplex her ways.
How many have fallen there!
They stumble all night over bones of the dead,
And feel they know not what but care,
And wish to lead others when they should be led.

—William Blake, "The Voice of the Ancient Bard,"
from *Songs of Innocence*

A NIGHTTIME SCENE in Tiananmen Square occasionally returns for Gao Qixin: Amid leaping flames he runs and takes cover as advancing tanks spit fire and bullets ... a phalanx of soldiers raise their AK-47 rifles ... the guns sound in a soft, surreal "pop" ... a fellow protester falls and wriggles on the concrete before lying still.

The image of the slaying has stayed with Gao since he fled the Monument to the People's Heroes in the square that night as soldiers advanced swinging iron truncheons. It enthralled his mind's eye three days later when, in a blind alley in Beijing, he declared his plan to take up captured army rifles and grenades against the Communist leadership. "I've never been a soldier, but I know how to fight and I'm a good fighter," Gao said. "We'll avenge blood with blood!" he proclaimed before striding away down the dark Beijing alley.

Gao laughs today when he recalls his flamboyant declaration of guerrilla war. He has left behind the intense, selfless devotion of Tiananmen Square. A few months after the June 1989 massacre, he accepted a job as an editor at an official newspaper. He is no longer the restless, exuberant, and lean student activist. He has married. His cheeks and waistline have filled out. He is calm and slow-talking as he clings to a measure of contentment.

Gao reconciles his survival with the death of his fellow activists by asserting that rising prosperity and economic development will eventually give Chinese the wherewithal to dismantle Communist tyranny and achieve democracy. He believes he and other Chinese will slowly avenge the victims of the massacre by continuing to take advantage of economic reform, eased restrictions on their day-to-day lives, and openness to foreign ideas. As common Chinese grow richer and less constrained, they will break the ancient cycle in which authoritarian regimes continually rise and fall on the backs of common people. Once the aging Communist leadership dies and Chinese are willing and able to take to the streets, Gao plans to resume open political activism.

But while Gao marks time as a silent offstage activist, he cannot dismiss the image of the protester slain by his side. Sometimes, the memory makes him feel that since fleeing the square he has betrayed his fallen classmates—that by working for the government, he has become an accomplice to the tyranny his peers died to end. Just as disturbing, he sometimes imagines that the crackdown was not the beginning of the end for China's autocratic tradition but just one more tide of blood in the rhythmic ebb and flow of tyrannical regimes. He wonders whether the student protest was merely an episode in another cyclical grassroots rebellion that will topple one repressive regime only to impose a new oppressive order. In dark moments, Gao fears that he and others among Tiananmen's "youth of delight" have not helped to bring progressive change and halt a history of authoritarianism. Rather, the historical cycle of repression has acted on them. They have pursued an "image of truth new born" that is just an old, recurrent illusion.

Gao's life story suggests, however, that his worst fears may prove unfounded. From his barefoot peasant beginnings, to lamblike idealism, to Tiananmen carnage, and then to marriage and government work, Gao illustrates how Chinese who are becoming increasingly prosperous and exposed to outside ideas are a growing force for progressive political change. Chinese like Gao have started to unshackle themselves from the painful wheel of political history. They are not turning in place, locked in an ancient dynastic cycle, but are trudging on a slow upward spiral away from tyranny. They are probably not headed immediately for democracy. But they are more aware of their own economic and political interests and so are likely to gradually demand a more humane and responsive government.

Already, Chinese like entrepreneur Zhang Guoxi, clan leader Wang Bao, cosmopolite Harold Xu, and migrant Jin Xiulin are pursuing their distinct interests more aggressively than at any other time under Communist rule. In fields, factories, and marketplaces nationwide, they have seized the initiative for change from the party. Now, helter-skelter, they are claiming social, economic, and political freedoms that go far beyond the reformist leadership's original intent.

The groundswell for progress has made society highly turbulent. Chinese are increasingly at odds as they discard Mao's dogma of socialist cooperation and seize on Deng's creed of market competition. Day by day, society splits further along the lines of class and region: Jin and other enterprising migrants face the hostility of destitute, envious peasants too diffident or tradition-bound to take to the road; Tibetan nomad Sonam and other members of minority groups in borderlands decry the exploitation of their natural resources by the wealthy, thriving coast. Moreover, state workers who depend on the failing socialist economy for their livelihood resent those prospering in the growing private sector. Bureaucrats at state industries clash with maverick businessmen like Zhang Guoxi, whose private companies rival their own.

Fearing unrest, the party has ruled out democratic reforms that would help Chinese reconcile the conflicting demands of their increasingly complex society. Instead, it seeks to repress citizens' clashing interests. Unless the party gives way and grants Chinese the political representation they need to vent their varied demands, society will probably grow increasingly divided and tumultuous.

Although the current leadership is unlikely to hand down democratic reforms from above, citizens are no more likely to construct them in an orderly way from below. After years of totalitarian repression, common Chinese lack both the will and the organizational strength to stage a coherent movement for political change. Traditionally submissive and parochial, most Chinese only challenge the government with extreme caution. Rather than openly protest, they tend to confront officials within the narrow channels of work units and bureaucracies controlled by the party. When chastened by the party, citizens usually back down.

Such is not the case for students. When it comes to activism, university students are far bolder and more openly idealistic than any other group in China. Although the views of students and intellectuals like Gao are not representative of all citizens, their political aspirations have frequently inspired common Chinese. Indeed, students have helped spark every major progressive movement in modern China. Consequently, the change in outlook of a former student activist like Gao might foreshadow the coming changes in the political consciousness of the larger society.

Gao also shows how the political views of young Chinese activists have matured under communism. His opinions radically changed from the time he helped lead the first march to the square, to the seven weeks of demonstrations and hunger strikes in the massive plaza, to his bloody expulsion and retreat to a government job. His evolution from peaceful protester, to urban revolutionary, to reformer-in-waiting exemplifies the spiritual passage described by Blake: from wide-eyed innocence, to jarring experience, to a wise innocence. It also shows how, with each generation since 1949, young dissidents under communism have tempered and focused their political aims and strategies. Since the death of Mao, students have grown increasingly pragmatic and down-to-earth in their public demonstrations.

From his childhood to his entrance into a university in Beijing, Gao was a paragon of Mao's peasant ideal. His farming family lived in a destitute mountainous area of western Shandong Province. As if following a revolutionary script, his mother bore him at a time of great hunger for the village. Her diet was severely lacking in grain and sources of protein. Like other villagers, she tried to end constant hunger by eating wild herbs, sweet potato vines, and the flower of the scholar tree.

Gao was born in 1965 in a small three-room home made of stone, mud brick, and thatch. Weak and malnourished, he did not muster enough strength for even a feeble cry until twelve hours after his birth. His father was overjoyed to have a firstborn son, although the legs of the baby were no thicker than his father's thumb.

Gao relied on the commune from the moment of his birth. His mother was too weak and thin to nurse him, so each day he was passed around the village from one mother's bosom to another. Because of his small size and dependence on neighbors' milk, Gao was always surrounded by fussing villagers. He became the village darling: at first sustained, then pampered, then spoiled, then cheered on in his education. Although his father was strict, Gao confronted few limits as a child along the village footpaths and in his neighbors' homes. "I was spoiled by my neighbors and teachers when I was young, and I felt superior to my schoolmates—I always wanted to be the winner in whatever I did," Gao said.

Gao usually ate just wild herbs and *wotou*. His father rarely grew enough wheat, sorghum, or vegetables and could not purchase much staple food at the village market because he had to pay the heavy medical expenses for his wife's parents. Sometimes Gao ate only what he could pick or unearth from nearby mountainsides. The family regularly had to rely on relief grain from the government to get through the year.

Gao slept with his younger brother in a tiny dwelling made of stone and thatch at the entrance to his family's home. Despite persistent cold and hunger, he earned excellent grades in elementary school. The commune in 1975 advanced him two grades and assigned him to a special school for outstanding students two miles from his village. The opportunity signified the high social approbation for Gao's peasant origins, bedrock values, and hard struggle. Gao returned the praise with an intense devotion to Mao. Like many Chinese, Gao identified himself with the Great Helmsman. He embraced the belief that Mao was a paragon of virtue who promised to bring Chinese justice and prosperity. In party lore, Mao epitomized the simple peasant who brings China great good through self-reliance, lofty principle, and sacrifice. Gao wept when Mao died and felt a deep affection for him for many years thereafter. On the tenth anniversary of Mao's death in September 1986, when Mao's popularity was at a low, Gao was one of the few university students to lay a wreath at Mao's mausoleum on the southern side of Tiananmen Square.

Gao's attachment to Mao was largely sentimental. He was enthralled by the charisma and political romance of the peasant leader, but his understanding of Mao's thought was very limited. So in 1985, when Gao entered a university in Beijing, he was easily swept up by the rising enthusiasm over liberalism, even though it contradicted Mao's ideas.

Gao had his first run-in with party officialdom after he began embracing liberal views at the University of Politics and Law. As vice chairman of the university's student union, he invited the outspoken liberal scholars Yan Jiaqi and Hu

Ping to give lectures on democracy in late 1986. (Yan was a figure in the 1989 democracy protests and is now a leader of expatriate dissidents.) Gao was a bold advocate for a "campus culture," a vague phrase for free expression and independent political participation on campuses. As part of the movement, he wrote a series in the university's Communist Youth League journal entitled "I Am None Other Than Myself." The articles championed individuality and basic liberties.

"I have my own experiences and thoughts, my own background, and my own education. These elements all form me alone," he wrote. "One's own experience, background, and education are unique and different from those of others; I am not anyone else." He did not hide the fact that activism was the logical offshoot of individualism.

"I will initiate reforms here and there, but often I run into snags and receive many warnings," he wrote. "Still, I have no regrets and I will continually try until the day I am off the stage. I will neither cater to the likes or dislikes of certain people nor go along with some temporary tendencies at the cost of my conscience."

Gao's feelings were shared by thousands of students at China's elite universities. Early in December 1986, some 3,000 students at a university in Hefei demonstrated against party manipulation of local and university elections. The surge in student activism quickly spread to Wuhan, where about 5,000 students marched with similar grievances. In Beijing, students tacked up posters written in bold Chinese brush strokes. Then 30,000 students in Shanghai, joined by an equal number of city residents, defied a government ban on protests and took to the streets in an impassioned but scattered outcry for basic liberties. Students in at least seventeen other cities also staged rallies. The protests provoked a crackdown by hard-liners in the leadership. They purged Hu Yaobang, the moderate general secretary of the party. They also imposed a mass campaign against "bourgeois liberalization" and expelled from the party intellectuals who had inspired the students.

Because of his naive and somewhat narcissistic articles, Gao became an easy target for the defenders of Communist purity during the crackdown. Hard-line zealots emerged in full force at the university and in the Communist Youth League. They called his thoughts corrosive, labeled him "untrustworthy," and dismissed him from the student union in April 1987. "The 'anti–bourgeois liberalization' campaign first showed me the dishonesty of politics. I realized that the official media just told lies and most officials were just trying to get ahead politically. I felt I had been cheated," Gao said.

As punishment, the university sent Gao and many of his classmates to the countryside in the summer of 1987 to "educate" them to peasants' hardships. The party intended to show them that the demand for political freedom is absurd in a society dominated by millions of farmers fettered by hunger. But the party's scheme backfired with Gao. Discussions that summer with peasants in his native province of Shandong merely reinforced his conviction that despite their ignorance and impoverishment, peasants also resented intrusions by the party. They also felt that corrupt, heavy-handed officialdom was keeping them down. "I realized that summer that if Chinese were ever to get enough to eat, the government would first have to respect their freedoms and not restrain their ingenuity and drive in any way," he said.

By the spring of 1989, Gao was eager to follow the lead of more than 120 intellectuals who called on Deng Xiaoping and other leaders to ease restraints on political expression. In several petitions, the intellectuals urged the leadership to free Wei Jingsheng, who had been sentenced to fifteen years in jail for his outspoken protests during the Democracy Wall movement of 1978–1979. They called for greater funds for education. And they urged tolerance for freer expression, arguing that it would speed economic growth and scientific progress.

The sudden death on April 15 of the ousted Hu Yaobang electrified Gao and other students at his university. In their view, Deng had made heir-apparent Hu the scapegoat for the 1986–1987 demonstrations. The students mourned Hu as a political martyr for greater freedoms, even though he had shown a penchant for pragmatism and moderation rather than for liberalism. By demanding the political rehabilitation of Hu, students aimed to strike a blow for economic and political reform.

On the afternoon of April 17, two days after Hu's death, Gao helped lead 900 of his schoolmates out the gates of the University of Politics and Law in the first student march of the 1989 Beijing Spring. At the head of the protest, a student held a bamboo pole flying a red banner bearing the university's name in yellow lettering. Behind him, students shouldered a large crepe-paper wreath of white, pink, yellow, and blue pastels. In the traditional form of mourning, two long strips of white paper inscribed with couplets extolling Hu fluttered from the wreath.

"Long live democracy!" Gao and his schoolmates shouted in unison as they marched toward Tiananmen Square. The students closed shoulder to shoulder in tight ranks and walked east down the Avenue of Eternal Peace toward the high imperial-red walls of the leadership's compound called Zhongnanhai. Plainclothes police and agents from the Ministry of State Security videotaped and photographed the demonstrators but did not interfere. Before Xinhuamen Gate, the ornate entrance to Zhongnanhai, the students slowed to short mincing steps and shouted slogans for freedom, rule by law, and an end to corruption. The loud demands encapsulated the basic themes students would struggle and die for during the next fifty days. Having issued their message, Gao and other leaders guided the students into the square and laid the wreath at the foot of the gray stone Monument to the People's Heroes.

The bold march by Gao and his schoolmates inspired other campuses in Beijing. Several hours later, after midnight on April 18, hundreds of students streamed out of Beijing University in what is erroneously depicted as the first march by students that spring. On the way, the protesters swept up hundreds more students at People's University and marched on to the square.

The well-orchestrated protest by Gao and his classmates contrasted with the chaotic ragtag demonstrations of 1986–1987. The students had learned from the failure of those pell-mell outbursts. Indeed, initially, student leaders were more unifed and pragmatic, and their demands more concrete, than in any previous demonstrations against Communist abuses. They were not militant revolutionaries seeking to eradicate socialism and overthrow the party; they were radical reformers using moderate, nonviolent tactics to goad the leadership toward political reform, especially clean government and eventual democracy. In the most potent challenge to Chinese communism since 1949, they mixed political passion with political reason and high spirits with high learning. Only after several days did extremism, folly, and internal strife tear apart their organization.

The moderate goals, peaceful tactics, and legitimate demands of the students were not the only reasons the leadership was anxious. Since the nineteenth century, when China began to cast off its imperial traditions, students have been the bellwether for public expressions of discontent and progressivism. They have criticized Nationalists and Communists more than has any other social group. The current leadership has been on both sides of the barricades: Deng and many of the founders of Communist China were students when they first began organizing for the revolution.

Many old guard Communists were drawn into politics in the aftermath of the May Fourth Movement beginning in 1919, in which students enraged by foreign aggression and by the ineffective republic rallied society around the ideas of democracy and science. As part of an overall effort to revivify China, the youthful May Fourth activists sought to rebuff imperialism, shake up an exploitative landlord system, and halt the splintering of China into various warlord realms.

Throughout the twentieth century, student activism has repeatedly flared into open conflict with those in power. Thousands of students rallied in Beijing against Japanese colonialism and the weakness of the Nationalist government on December 9, 1935. Police responded by firing water hoses at the protesters and clubbing dozens of them. The courage of the "December Ninthers" inspired a march by 30,000 activists a week later and demonstrations in five other major cities, including the Nationalist capital of Nanjing. Then in July 1948, thousands of students from northern China who were forced out of school by advancing Communist troops marched on the home of the president of the municipal council in Beijing. Nationalist authorities called out the police, who turned machine guns on the students, killing fourteen of them and wounding dozens more.

After taking power, Mao Zedong, Deng Xiaoping, and other party leaders systematically exploited the idealism and courage of students. Mao harnessed students for many of his pet political campaigns. At his command, many students in 1949 and 1950 went directly from their campuses into the ranks of cadres implementing his program of land redistribution by seizing property. In the spring of 1957, students innocently heeded his call for lively debate and criticism in the Hundred Flowers movement, only to be slapped down and jailed by Mao a year later. Mao also manipulated students into supporting the Cultural Revolution, whipping millions of Red Guards into a destructive whirlwind. When the youths became disillusioned and denounced Mao and his leftist allies at Tiananmen Square in 1976, police violently crushed the demonstrations. Two years later, Deng Xiaoping also exploited the idealism of students and intellectuals by winking at liberal criticism plastered on Democracy Wall. After using the calls for democratic freedom to further his political comeback, Deng coolly quashed the movement.

From the beginning of the 1989 protests, Gao and other students were keenly aware that party leaders, both in the ouster of Hu in 1987 and in previous incidents, had exploited their youthful activism to defeat rivals in factional infighting. Still, Gao and many other students believed that this time they would goad leaders into subordinating their self-interest to the nation's crying need for political reform. They would compel reform of the party itself. The party would then free China from the old cycle of autocracy and lead it toward democracy.

"Without the Communist Party, China couldn't be governed; we need the party," Gao said as he trudged back to the university after the April 17 demonstration. "But without a reformed party—an end to corruption and democratic freedoms—our nation can't survive."

"Newborn calves do not fear the tiger," according to an old Chinese saw. Because of their naive trust in the party and confidence in their ability to spur democratic reform, Gao and many students were completely surprised by the bloody blitz that began not long after dark on June 3. As Gao and his schoolmates huddled together at their university's encampment on the east side of the Heroes' Monument, they dismissed reports at about 11 P.M. that troops had opened fire on demonstrators a few miles west at the Muxidi Bridge. "Nobody believed it; our schoolteachers had told us that even the Nationalists had only used water cannon and truncheons against student protesters," Gao said.

The first sign of the approaching violence jarred Gao at about 11:30 P.M. An armored personnel carrier roared north by the Revolutionary Museum along the eastern side of the square and turned away to the east. Many students, shaken by the clamor and speed of the vehicle, emerged from the squalid squatters' camp of tents scattered across the southern half of the square. They sat in a large circle around the monument. Clutching his camera, Gao ran for the northwest corner of the square, where he reckoned heavily armed troops shooting their way from Muxidi Bridge were likely to appear.

Like other eyewitnesses, Gao found in the massacre more than the fear, suffering, and deliberate cruelty that roil China's classic version of hell. China's aged revolutionaries thrust Beijing citizens into an underworld lacking even the order of the traditional hell of Buddhism with its king, malicious but obedient devils, and soul-saving Buddha. In the name of "stability," the leaders had created perfect chaos, a perverse firestorm of extreme and opposite feelings: full-throated elation and crushing grief; giggling jollity and wailing sorrow; buoyant hope and downcast despair; warm pity and cold savagery.

On both sides of Tiananmen Square, the Avenue of Eternal Peace running east and west seethed with the conflicting emotions of tragicomedy. To the west, troops slowly advanced in a black spectacle of raw pain and power. To the east, the so far invincible citizens of Beijing continued their fifty days of fantastic, high-spirited defiance, their profound and appalling springtime comedy. They reveled in the mirth and collective bravado that had bound them together since they first flouted the world's largest army by thwarting martial law on May 20.

Like Gao and other students, Beijing residents denied until the end that their passionate claim to China's political future would provoke a bloody backlash and end in tragic folly. They were confident they could shape China's future; party leaders would not try to regain control by ordering the "People's Army" to attack the people. Boys and old men laughed as they together pulled concrete and steel dividers across the road. Many citizens crowded atop buses and cars blocking the avenue. They waved and cheered with each explosion and leap of flames around the advancing soldiers to the west. A young couple wearing slippers and bathrobes strolled toward the square, the man occasionally puffing on a cigarette.

"*Hao le! Hao le!* [Good! Good!]," said an old gap-toothed woman wearing a gray T-shirt and black pants as she waddled toward the approaching soldiers and tanks. By her side a grinning mother in a light cotton dress of pastel yellow pushed a red metal stroller. Her toddler leaned forward toward the fiery onslaught with wide eyes.

At the northwest corner of the square, Gao saw victims of the assault appear from out of a distant darkness broken by flames, flitting shadows, and orange tracer bullets. A young man shot at Xidan Avenue lay senseless on the back of a speeding flatbed pedicab, his body jostling as blood oozed from his belly. Bullets whistled overhead. The rumble from exploding firebombs rolled down the boulevard. Slowly and methodically, the troops plowed before them a chaotic mass of wounded, wailing, and frenzied protesters.

"*Bu pa! Bu pa!* [Don't be afraid!]," many students and workers said after each rapid volley of machine gun fire. Gao and many protesters in the square still refused to believe the troops were systematically firing at the unarmed demonstrators.

But then one of Gao's classmates appeared, running toward him from the carnage, his face twisted in a grimace, his eyes welling up. "Get out of here! A lot of people are dead!" he shouted. He had helped several of the wounded withdraw, and the entire front of his torso, from Adam's apple to loins, was covered by a slick crimson drenching of blood. The familiar face crying above the gore persuaded Gao that the leadership had abandoned all restraint.

Gao turned and watched his classmate sprint eastward down the avenue. The leaping orange flames from an armored car abandoned at the Gate of Heavenly Peace lit up the portrait of Mao Zedong with a flickering, lurid glow. The serene gaze of Mao on the killing recalled the arrogant inhumanity of the party leaders during their many previous debacles: the antirightist campaign and the Great Leap Forward in the 1950s, the Cultural Revolution in the 1960s and 1970s. It was about 2:30 A.M.

Gao wheeled at the sudden sound of a nearby machine gun firing from the west. Four main battle tanks were slowly rumbling abreast into the northwest corner of the square with heavily armed troops and supply trucks in their wake. Soldiers sitting in the turrets of the tanks repeatedly fired short bursts into the air from mounted machine guns. Gao and two other activists, a man and a woman, ran behind the concrete base of a lamppost on the northern edge of the square just east of the Mao portrait. The troops halted just west of the portrait, raised their automatic rifles, and without warning fired on the protesters in the square who had not taken cover. They let loose three bursts of about ten shots each.

Three people near the flagpole within the northern edge of the square were hit and fell. Other demonstrators tried to crawl away from the troops. One protester about twelve feet away from Gao was shot in the chin.

After the gunfire had stopped for about a minute, several demonstrators jumped up and rushed back toward the guns in an effort to drag away their three wounded comrades. The troops fired again, hitting in the head a student trying to aid the activist wounded in the chin. The bullet knocked the student off his feet. He fell close to Gao. His legs and feet twitched rapidly for several seconds before he lay still. The shooting stopped again, and Gao and some twenty other remaining activists rushed south, dragging the four casualties. After running about forty yards, Gao stopped and turned back toward the portrait. The soldiers fired once more. Several bullets whistled above his head. He turned and dashed southward again.

Gao watched from the middle of the square as two public buses appeared speeding west on the avenue directly toward the troops. In a suicidal bid, the drivers of the vehicles apparently aimed to block the tanks' advance. The soldiers quickly shot out the windows of the two buses, apparently killing the drivers. The lead bus lurched to a stop several yards shy of the portrait. The battle tanks rumbled east. As the tanks and troops exited the northeast corner of the square, they let loose another fierce fusillade of machine gun fire. Gao realized the army aimed to close off the square at all costs. So he ran east and moved north under the cover of trees and the Revolutionary Museum.

"Are you looking to die?" one of two protesters said from the shadows around the north side of the museum as Gao stepped from the cover of the building and raised his camera. Despite the danger, Gao felt driven to document the party leadership's butchery.

The tanks slowly advanced, clearing the way ahead of them with a steady stream of machine gun fire. Several people unable to flee in time were hit and fell in the street. After snapping several photographs, Gao returned to the middle of the square. At about 3:40 A.M., some of the doctors stationed in hospital tents dotting the square crossed the avenue and began negotiations aimed at trying to ensure a peaceful withdrawal of the protesters from the square. Army commanders were drilling and psyching up their soldiers along the northern edge of the avenue outside the high wall of the Forbidden City. Wearing dark green fatigues and steel helmets, the soldiers jogged back and forth in tight ranks, barking in unison and banging metal truncheons on the street. A doctor in one of the hospital tents in the square told Gao that the military commanders considered anyone in the square a "thug."

"Everyone in the square is a thug. You must retreat to the steps of the military museum or we can't guarantee your safety," they told him. The doctors from Fuxingmen, Xiehe, and Shoudu hospitals had the wounded taken to Fuxingmen Hospital. They left their medical supplies and tents and withdrew to the museum steps.

The shouting by the soldiers and the sharp ringing of their weapons on the concrete rose as the clusters of spherical lampposts across the square flickered off at 4 A.M. Gao began to run back through the growing darkness to the safety of other students gathered around the monument. "The troops are going to enter the square, get out of here!" he shouted into several tents on his way.

"We're too tired," yelled one of several students lying in the dozens of canvas or cloth shelters. They were exhausted after weeks of demonstrations that had flung them from giddy jubilation to crushing defeat. Although the wave of carnage crested above them, they too believed the army would do them no harm. Meanwhile, some students proclaimed their willingness to die fighting tanks and guns with wooden staves and sticks. But whether students denied or defied the army blitz, most of them acted out their tragic drama to the end. They clung to the same romantic delusion that had characterized the fairy-tale democracy movement all along. Despite the ever present danger, everything would turn out right in the end. Indeed, compared to workers and other groups of Chinese, students suffered far less in the crackdown. The Beijing massacre affirmed how students, members of the social elite, enjoy a charmed political status. Although scores of students died in the army onslaught, many more common Chinese were killed; although many students were later jailed, many more workers who protested were executed.

Some 3,000 students huddled together around the monument. They slumped on the concrete of the plaza, on the monument's steps, or on the tiers of its base. They held one another with heads downcast. Some of them sobbed, others wept without a sound, while others with blank faces watched the army advance. Their faces seemed to flicker in the dim orange-yellow glow from fires burning between the monument and the Great Hall of the People to the west.

"Our lives and blood are bound to the future of our country," a young student with teary eyes said to her schoolmates, reading one of countless political poems written by activists that spring.

"On our shoulders, to our death, we will carry the weight of the nation and the Heroes' Monument," another student read. Around the monument several maudlin poets told of loss, martyrdom, and their certain vindication by history.

Two of four activists involved in a seventy-two-hour hunger strike, including the rock star Hou Dejian, had tried to secure the peaceful withdrawal of the students. They returned to the monument and went among the protesters, arguing that to resist was suicidal and urging a withdrawal. They persuaded some of the activists to surrender their bottles, wooden staves, and other crude weapons. Yet many activists remained combative, denouncing Hou as a coward although he and the hunger strikers pledged to withdraw last. Student leaders agonized over their final decision: whether to withdraw.

The students held hands and together softly sang the "Internationale." During the first marches of the spring, students leading the movement had belted out the revolutionary socialist hymn with beaming, full-throated irony. It became a joyous anthem for the protesters, sung by marching workers, bureaucrats, office workers, schoolchildren, and citizens from many walks of life. Amid the glow of the flames, however, the students painted the bright sarcasm of the workers' hymn in black. As the soldiers closed in on them in the darkness, the students' somber rendition of the "Internationale" promised a new birth with the same dark irony as Blake's ancient bard:

> *Arise ye prisoners of starvation,*
> *Arise ye wretched of the earth,*
> *For justice thunders condemnation,*
> *A better world is in birth.*

Soldiers on the roof of the Great Hall at 4:15 A.M. shone floodlights on troops massing on the steps of the giant edifice on the western side of the square. Gao tightened his grip on the leg of a short wooden stool he had dismantled with three other students. Fifteen minutes later the military turned on the lamppost lights across the square. Soldiers had surrounded much of the monument. Armored personnel carriers had moved into the square and faced the students. Some thirty special troops wearing camouflage uniforms grouped to the north of the monument. Tanks entered the square and, with the armored personnel carriers, crushed the tents. Gao saw no indication that the soldiers looked to see whether students were inside the tents.

A short and fat officer, wearing an emblem designating him as a "Guardian of the Republic," walked with ten heavily armed soldiers from the northeast of the square toward the monument. His name was Zhao Xilai. "*Xia kai!* [Disperse!]" he yelled.

As some students began to leave at just after 5 A.M., the soldiers in camouflage fired over the heads of those remaining behind. Some of the soldiers raced up the base of the monument and shot out the loudspeakers used by student leaders. The hunger strikers implored the students to withdraw.

"Should we leave?" the activists still yelled to one another. More troops moved in, kicking the students and workers or beating them with iron truncheons. They clubbed, shoved, and hurled Gao and other activists away from the monument. The students limped and staggered to the southeast and out of Tiananmen Square.

Gao has made a slow, lingering departure from Tiananmen Square. The massacre destroyed Gao's confidence that students could shape the future for themselves, the party, and democracy in China. It showed that the dominant party faction and the ancient authoritarian tradition were still supreme, at least at that time. Party leaders heeding the old rhythm of repression had unleashed on Gao and other students a chaotic, raw terror worthy of the most tyrannical emperor of old. "It's naive just to say, 'Overthrow the Communist Party!' although it sounds exciting," Gao said. Then comes a hard-won sense of realism. "Young people must realize that history progresses incrementally. When people have enough food to eat and clothes to wear, then we can make significant progress toward democracy."

Although Gao remains committed to liberal ideals, he sometimes fears that in day-to-day life he has submitted to China's autocratic tradition. Outwardly, he seems to have sold out. He has apparently become concerned with fashion, wearing silk shirts and other stylish clothes, and he has grown plump. He works as an editor at an official newspaper and shies from organized dissent. A few months after the massacre, he declined a request to help edit an underground political journal. Like most Chinese, he is wary of angering his employer, the only sure source of his housing, health care, and other vital benefits. To an extent, Gao's wife is also a hostage to his employer. Since being married in 1991, Gao has appealed to his newspaper to transfer the legal residence of his wife from a distant city to Beijing. Separation from his wife also means he is missing the upbringing of his firstborn child, a son born in 1992. Until Gao's employer deigns to unite him with his young family, he will remain alone in Beijing, politically prudent.

Still, when it comes to activism, Gao is dormant, not defeated. Since the party used terror and truncheons to drive Gao and other liberal firebrands from Tiananmen Square, the erstwhile protesters have grown more canny and pragmatic. They have not betrayed the victims of the massacre and sold out to the party; they have just become more realistic. Unlike in his university days, Gao believes that Chinese cannot create democracy in a sudden blossomtime burst of youthful zeal. Rather, they must build democracy from the bottom up over several years by encouraging Chinese to organize and demand their rights. Rapid economic development and increasing prosperity will help China steadily outgrow its tyrannical political tradition, Gao believes.

Gao and other student activists have arrived at these ideas after enduring a wrenching journey in political thought: from wide-eyed romanticism, through harsh experience, to a worldly-wise idealism. Their feelings and thoughts have unfolded in the universal way that William Blake traced through his life and poetry. He was also dazzled by a vision of the apocalypse. Like many British intellectuals in 1789, Blake was captivated by the French Revolution and what he exalted as the "image of truth new born." Like the Beijing Spring two centuries later, the upheaval in Paris began with an exhilarating fervor and a grand promise of liberation and perfect order. But as in Beijing, it descended into bloody tyranny.

Today, Gao often quietly meets with friends and discusses the prospects for political change. Many of his friends have lost all hope of reforming the party and instead seek to work indirectly to build up moderate forces outside party control. Some have gone to work for local governments, helping low-level officials administer burgeoning enterprises. Others have parlayed their political connections into their own businesses, trading in sportswear in Russia or managing fledgling computer companies in Beijing. These former Beijing Spring activists are skirting the traditional party apparatus to build a network of financial support that extends beyond direct party control. "The opinion is that things will evolve in a zig-zag way toward democracy. But until then, it's best to keep your head down politically, build up the economy, and make the government at lower levels more responsive to the needs of people and less controlled by the party," Gao said.

In the aftermath of the Beijing Spring, Gao recognized that common prosperity is a powerful ally for freeing Chinese from the ancient wheel of despotism. Moreover, he learned that he and other liberals can only break China's oppressive historical cycle and bring lasting democracy with a movement that is both broadly based and democratic. Although the students and intellectuals at Tiananmen upheld a banner of popular democracy, they made only tenuous contacts with workers. Their ties with peasants—three out of every four Chinese—were spotty at best. The youthful elite championed government by the people, but they could not claim to represent the people. Ultimately, they proved only a little more responsive to the masses than the scholar-officials of traditional China.

At the same time, the internal politics of the student leadership was a burlesque of democratic procedure. They engaged in a drama of backstabbing and arbitrary decisionmaking. They observed rigid hierarchies, emphasized personality rather than clear procedure, and yielded to mob rule. In short, they gave in to many of the practices of China's tyrannical political cycle.

The story of Gao illustrates how rising prosperity and eased regimentation have energized common Chinese. Ambitious Chinese pursuing big dreams have steadily gained power over many aspects of their lives that were once monopolized by the party and state. They have clambered beyond mere subsistence and are acquiring a sharp sense of political self-interest. Such vibrant individuals show a stronger yen to prosper and express themselves than at any other time in modern China. Chinese are not guaranteed success in future efforts to claim their human rights. But, like Gao, they are increasingly acquiring the wherewithal to make a successful claim.

Senior leader Deng Xiaoping has also enlisted rapid economic growth as an ally but for party dictatorship rather than for democracy. Deng has promoted fast growth in an effort to make China powerful and prosperous and thereby distract Chinese from the harsh denial of their rights and the party's past folly. Although Deng has found wealth from double-digit growth a short-term friend, it is likely to prove a long-term foe. Rapid economic growth will probably fuel political activism and the decline of totalitarian rule.

Since the mid-1970s, fast growth has helped build a foundation for democracy in dozens of developing countries like China. Economic expansion has helped common citizens outgrow autocratic traditions broadly similar to the one bedeviling the Chinese. In countries ranging from South Korea to Spain, a flourishing economy has nurtured a middle class of civil servants, teachers, shopkeepers, executives, and other professionals. Middle-class citizens yearning for a political voice commensurate with their new prosperity have broken a winding path toward democracy by successfully challenging authoritarian regimes during economic crises or after a period of rapid economic growth. The global phenomenon suggests that despite the many forces thwarting democracy, Chinese will someday rise in a bottom-up movement for progressive change.

Indeed, the gripes and injustices that compelled Chinese to take to the streets for the 1989 Beijing Spring have steadily intensified into the mid-1990s. Double-digit inflation has persisted, often flaring at more than 20 percent. Resentment over eroding incomes is growing among the millions of Chinese on fixed wages. Corruption has spread unchecked as officials become more brazen in exploiting the new riches of the market economy.

Meanwhile, the power of the party leadership continues to wane as individuals and local governments amass greater economic power and expand their autonomy. As its ideology steadily decays, the party fails to offer a new vision for ordering China's dynamic society and alleviating conflict, corruption, and crime. Most important, as popular support for the party dwindles, the leadership continues to rely on force to deny basic human freedoms and crush dissent. The longer the party persists with its folly and abuse, the greater the chance that the pell-mell, grassroots force of newly awakened Chinese will rise again.

If Gao and other latent activists hope to lead lasting democratic reform, they must ride this popular seismic groundswell. By heeding the multitude of newly assertive common Chinese, they will sooner pull their country out of the cycle of tyranny. But they will not easily adopt the populist sensitivity crucial to a successful democracy movement. They must resist the long-standing penchant among educated Chinese for elitism. Haughty scholar-officials have long snubbed common Chinese, dividing ruler from ruled and helping to perpetuate the cycle of popular rebellion and autocratic repression. Gao and his peers also must not dwell on a grand, abstract, and remote political illusion—an "image of truth new born." With the support of educated Chinese, leaders from ancient emperors to Mao have promoted magnificent political delusions like divine sanction for a dynastic order or Communist utopia. The rulers have sought to legitimize their power by these exalted false beliefs rather than by the popular will. As a result, rulers have wantonly ignored the needs and wishes of common Chinese.

The image of newborn truth that Gao and other democracy activists should respect is revealed by the faces of common people: the constant squint of migrant seamstress Jin Xiulin as she bends over scissors and cloth; the silent, methodical kowtowing of clan elder Wang Bao as he worships his ancestors; the irrepressible, million-dollar smile of Shanghai cosmopolite Harold Xu; the serenity of Tibetan nomad Sonam as he slowly shuts his eyes and chants an ancient mantra. Activists-in-waiting like Gao will sooner break China from its cycle of tyranny by advancing a democracy movement that, by being democratic itself, pursues the new dreams of awakening Chinese.

About the Book and Authors

This evocative and fascinating book shows how, from muddy village crossroads to raucous city streets, Chinese exhilarated by new dreams are shaping the future of their nation. Over the course of five years spent as China correspondents for the *Christian Science Monitor*, James and Ann Tyson dodged government surveillance and sought out the life stories of Chinese throughout the country: in the yak-hair tents of Tibetan nomads, the cramped Shanghai garret of China's most courageous dissident, the seaside mansion of a multimillionaire, and the tiny sheet-metal workshop of a peasant migrant. Allowing the Chinese to speak for themselves, the Tysons have written a book unique among Western studies of China for painting in vivid detail a firsthand portrait of a broad spectrum of Chinese.

Through these diverse voices, the Tysons reveal how, with economic reform weakening the grip of the state over everyday life, the people of China are taking the future into their own hands. The initiative for change is coming increasingly from below, as millions of Chinese pursuing their own dreams propel reform far beyond the Communist Party's original intent. *Chinese Awakenings* provides an intimate understanding of the feelings, aspirations, and workaday lives of ordinary Chinese. It offers the crucial insight into grassroots society that is essential for discerning what lies ahead for China's 1.2 billion people.

James and Ann Tyson, correspondents for the *Christian Science Monitor*, covered China for the newspaper from 1987 until 1992. Before setting out to report on China and other parts of Asia in 1982, they graduated cum laude from Harvard College with degrees in government and East Asian studies. They now cover the Midwestern United States for the *Monitor*. The Tysons have three children: James, born during the declaration of martial law in Beijing in May 1989; Sarah; and Scott Ezra.